JEREMY BENTHAM'S
ECONOMIC WRITINGS

JEREMY BENTHAM'S ECONOMIC WRITINGS

CRITICAL EDITION
BASED ON HIS PRINTED WORKS AND
UNPRINTED MANUSCRIPTS

BY

W. STARK

VOLUME ONE

Published for
THE ROYAL ECONOMIC SOCIETY
by GEORGE ALLEN & UNWIN LTD
LONDON

PRINTED IN GREAT BRITAIN
in 11 on 12-point Georgian Type
BY THE BLACKFRIARS PRESS LIMITED
SMITH-DORRIEN ROAD LEICESTER

CONTENTS

PREFACE

I N the spring of 1941, the Council of the Royal Economic Society commissioned me to prepare a comprehensive and critical edition of Jeremy Bentham's economic writings, and the present publication is the fruit of this request. The suggestion came originally from J. M. Keynes, the promoter and protector of so many worthy causes, who was personally interested in all that concerned Bentham and Benthamism, but the need for an up-to-date and reliable edition of this interesting material was much more widely, not to say, generally felt. Already, before the war, Dr. P. N. Rosenstein-Rodan had intended to add a textually sound version of the *Manual of Political Economy* to Allen and Unwin's Library of Economics: it might have come out long ago had Dr. Rosenstein-Rodan not heard of our more ambitious project and generously decided to abandon his own plans. I should like to express to him my sincere appreciation and gratitude for this kind and understanding action.

Of Jeremy Bentham's economic writings, only a minor part has so far been available in print. By far the greater part was still in manuscript, and the manuscripts themselves were virtually unexamined and unknown. The material is comprised in three collections: the biggest of them is the one in the Library of University College, London. This contains the bulk of the extant manuscripts, but there are two smaller "caches" which should not be overlooked, one in the Bibliothèque Publique et Universitaire at Geneva, and the other in the British Museum where the Vansittart papers have been deposited not very long ago. All three collections were freely put at my disposal, and I have used them to the full.

The work itself involved immense difficulties. Bentham's handwriting is so bad that it is quite impossible to make anything of his scripts without first copying them out. I saw myself confronted with the necessity of copying no less than nine big boxes of papers comprising nearly 3,000 pages and a number of words that cannot be far from the seven-figure mark. But that was only the first step. The papers are in no kind of order: in fact, it is hard to imagine how they ever became so utterly disordered. They resemble a pack of cards after it has been thoroughly shuffled. I found part of an interesting pamphlet in box 3 of the University College collection, but I was unable to trace the rest of it until I discovered it after much searching in box 166; there I hit upon fragments of another treatise but the bulk of it was hidden away in box 9, and so on. In all this, the catalogue published in 1937 was not of much use: it is by no means detailed enough and can give no more than a first vague orientation in this shapeless and uncharted maze. The pages of some manuscripts, it is true, were numbered, but then they often carried a double and treble numeration so that confusion was worse confounded, and sometimes I wished there had been no pagination at all. In other manuscript collections the fact that sentences run uninterruptedly from one sheet onto another, is of material help in creating order out of chaos. I was denied even this assistance. It was one of Bentham's idiosyncrasies never to begin a new page without beginning at the same time a new paragraph. But I cannot hope to give the reader an adequate idea of the problems which had to be overcome. In so far as I have succeeded in presenting Bentham's works in an orderly and understandable fashion, I count myself royally rewarded.

From the editorial point of view, the available texts fall into three categories: (1) material already known; (2) material known but only partially and/or in a garbled form; and (3) material completely unknown. In this first volume, the *Defence of Usury* (without the postscript) and *Supply without Burthen* (shorter version) belong to the first category; the *Manual of Political Economy* and *Colonies and Navy* to the second; all the rest to the third. Of the projected second volume, nothing at all can be said to be known in a reliable text; the pamphlet shortly entitled *Circulating Annuities* is printed under a different name in John Bowring's *Works of Jeremy Bentham* (vol. III, pp. 105-153), but there is a vast difference between what Bentham wrote and what Bowring made of it; again, all the rest is completely new. In the projected third volume of the present edition, only the comparatively dull pamphlet *On the Spanish Anti-Commercial Decree* has so far been available in the shape in which it came from the author's hands; the *Institute of Political Economy* appears in Bowring's compilation as *Manual of Political Economy*, but large parts are omitted and the whole is riddled with misprints; the great treatise called *The True Alarm* and the valuable shorter essay *Defence of a Maximum* are fresh discoveries. In the case of *The True Alarm* we have no English manuscript at all, and must be glad to be able to fall back on Etienne Dumont's (unpublished)

French translation. I have put this work back into its original language and hope that it has not suffered too much in the process.

It goes without saying that this edition contains the various works of our author in the most final form which he has left; preliminary material had to be largely excluded. That students may have some indication of the nature of this material I propose, however, to include in volume III a "Systematic Survey" of *all* the available manuscripts which will indicate, in a concise form, the contents of every one of the extant sheets. I consider that it is impossible to do more. Volume III will further contain a "Technical Note" setting out the principles of textual criticism and editorial technique which I have followed. I have taken as my general guide the *Report on Editing Historical Documents* published in 1925 by the Anglo-American Historical Committee; but Bentham is a special case, and I have had to elaborate a much more detailed set of rules which, I trust, will be of value to others if any can be found brave enough to dip into the Bentham manuscripts in search of further treasures. Finally, the last volume will also provide the references for the sixty or seventy quotations from Bentham's non-economic writings which are contained in volumes I and III.

The introductory essays at the beginning of each volume do not attempt to analyse Bentham's theories and to assess their value: they are entirely unambitious and only try to provide the historical background necessary for a full understanding of the works that follow, and to draw the reader's attention to a few points of particular interest. They have all the same swollen to considerable size, but I could not possibly further reduce them without suppressing valuable information that ought to be at the disposal of the public.

I could never have hoped to fulfil my obligations to the Royal Economic Society if I had not been able to count on the full-time assistance of one whom I may perhaps refer to here as Dr. Katherine Stark. Her inexhaustible patience and skill in palæography have sensibly reduced the burden on my shoulders. She has helped to copy the manuscripts and typed them, a task which, in view of the strange antiquated spelling, could not have been entrusted to a commercial agency. Words cannot express what this work owes to her. The necessity to re-translate *The True Alarm* into English raised grave linguistic problems which called for more expert attention than I was able to provide. It was my good fortune to enlist the help of Mr. Ian Robertson, M.A., who has gone over my texts and made sure that they are in conformity with early 19th-century usage. He has also made himself responsible for the punctuation of the manuscript material, again in conformity with contemporary habit, a point on which Bentham himself has given no guidance whatsoever. Finally, I should like to thank Mr. C. K. Ogden, the Nestor of Benthamic studies, for the great encouragement he has given me all through the years. I hope these three volumes will please him.

Less personal, but no less sincere acknowledgments are due to the Bentham Committee of University College, London, and especially to the Provost, Dr. D. R. Pye, and the Librarian, Mr. John Wilks. They have made their treasure-house my own. For the same reason I am indebted to the Bibliothèque Publique et Universitaire de Genève and to the British Museum. Among the libraries I have used I should like to mention more particularly the University Library at Cambridge and the National Library of Wales at Aberystwyth. At Cambridge Mr. Harold Pink has much obliged me by his untiring willingness to help in the solution of bibliographical puzzles. The proof-reading was done in the National Library of Scotland, where every conceivable facility was put at my disposal.

I cannot lay down the pen without expressing the hope that now one whole aspect of Bentham's work has been thoroughly investigated, and the high value of the unpublished material proved, other masses of manuscripts will be rescued from oblivion and made available to the public. What we need most is a critical edition of his "ontological" and "deontological" writings, including the treatises on logic and language, and a collection of, or at least a selection from, his invaluable correspondence. It should not be necessary to emphasise that Jeremy Bentham, for all his limitations and scurrilities, was yet one of Britain's greatest sons.

W. STARK

Bonnyfield Lodge
    Barnton
        Midlothian
January 1949

INTRODUCTION

THE *Dictionary of National Biography*, always anxious to do justice to its heroes, pays willing tribute to Jeremy Bentham's universal genius. "He sought to compass the whole field of ethics, jurisprudence, logic, and political economy," we read (ed. 1908, II, 277), " and to deal with points of detail as well as principles." But, the author goes on to say, "to the last science his contributions are of small account." The present publication does not claim to controvert this statement: it only suggests that it should be reconsidered, and it provides the materials on which this reconsideration must be based. When Sir John Macdonell wrote his short biographical sketch and appreciation, he had nothing to go by but the *Defence of Usury* and the few ill-edited pages of the third volume of Sir John Bowring's *Works*, which contain garbled versions of the *Manual of Political Economy* and of the great treatise on *Circulating Annuities*. No wonder that he came to the conclusion that Bentham was not much of an economist! Nevertheless, a more careful assessment even of the printed material proves that he had considerable influence both on contemporary and on later economic thought, and that there was no school in political economy which did not take over at least some of his ideas.[1] But what has so far been available in print is at best the tenth part of his economic writing, and by no means the most interesting and stimulating part of it. Bentham did not write in order to publish: he wrote primarily in order to clear his mind, and he left it willingly to others to make books out of his materials. Without Dumont, without John Stuart Mill, without George Grote and a few others we would know very little of Bentham's thought. It was unfortunate that none of his intimate friends, especially of those who were around him after the end of the century, were interested in, and capable of, editing his economic manuscripts. As it happened, they were all preoccupied with different problems, and so it was that nearly a hundred and fifty years had to elapse before an editor for the bulky and somewhat forbidding collection of Bentham's *economica* could be found. Naturally, the interest in the material is today historical rather than topical, not to say exclusively historical. But who knows? Bentham is not dead yet, nor ever will be, and he is great enough to command attention and offer

---

[1] Cf. my paper in *The Economic Journal*, 1946, pp. 583-608.

stimulation even in our own generation which, after all, cannot pretend to have yet discovered the philosopher's stone.

BENTHAM'S EARLY INTEREST IN ECONOMIC PROBLEMS

Bentham took up the study of political economy in 1786, when he was thirty-eight years of age: he abandoned it in 1804, when he had just turned fifty-six. Thus it can be seen that he devoted eighteen years, perhaps the best years of his life, to the cultivation of a field with which his name has never so far been seriously associated.

It is quite impossible to say how much sustained thought Bentham had given to economic matters before the middle of the 'eighties: the books printed before that date are psychological and juris-prudential rather than sociological and economic. Still, economics must always have been of potential interest to him: could any science have been more important for a reformer who was out to maximise the material welfare of human society? Bentham must have felt on firm and familiar ground, when, on the threshold of middle age, he began to concentrate all his energy on the science of wellbeing and wealth.

However that may be, it is certain that Bentham, during his forma-tive period, met both with men and with books which were apt to turn his mind towards political economy, and that the seeds of many of the ideas which occupied him in later years had been present in him ever since he was very young.

One of the outstanding economists of the age with whom Bentham got early into personal contact was Nathaniel Forster of Balliol College. He met him while still at Oxford "in the year 1762, or there-abouts", but nothing much came of this first contact; Bentham was at that time still a boy. The acquaintance was, however, renewed about ten years later when both men frequented John Lind's com-pany. "I had not many times seen him at Mr. Lind's," Bentham reports, "when, in compliance with an invitation from him, I visited Colchester [where Forster was rector of All Saints] and passed a week or two at his house" (*Works* X, 61 seq.). In his old age Bentham could not recollect how the days were spent, but it is more than likely that political economy was one of the subjects under discussion. Forster was the author of an essay on the rise of prices[1] which McCulloch calls "perhaps the ablest of the many treatises published

---

[1] *An Enquiry into the Causes of the present High Price of Provisions*, 1767.

about this period".[1] The subject occupied Bentham a good deal in later years, and it is not impossible that his interest in this set of problems was first awakened in his stimulating intercourse with Nathaniel Forster.

The early interest of Bentham in economic matters, its humanitarian implication, its practical nature, and, above all, its progressive, not to say revolutionary character, are all alike characterized by an entry into his *Commonplace Book of* 1776. It carries the heading: "Employment for Pauper Manufacturers", i.e. for the unemployed:

"The great evil manufacturers are liable to, is that of a temporary stagnation of trade, which leaves vast numbers at a time without employment, and without subsistence. For a remedy, I propose public works to be set on foot in the neighbourhood of manufacturing towns: to be carried on by none but manufacturers out of employment. For example, digging of canals, deepening of harbours, making of roads, building of fortifications.

"The kind of work must be such as requires no skill, because the workmen will be set to it without preparation.

"The pay must be less than what they can earn by their manufacture, or else they would quit their manufacture. None should be employed about it, but manufacturers out of employment; because it is for their relief that it is designed. When applying to be employed in it, they should therefore be required to produce a certificate of their being manufacturers of such a manufacture, having been so for such a time. When thus confined to them, their pay may be something higher than that of common labourers, as their earnings at their manufactures are generally much greater than those of common labourers. The national or the county fund might make good the difference.

"The parishes where the manufactures are, might well contribute a certain proportion of the charge, as such an establishment would be a great relief to the Poor-rates" (*Works* X, 85).

Written a hundred and fifty years later, these words would still have been to the point. Indeed, they would still have been bold and constructive, and a guide to the future rather than a token of the past!

Needless to say, the perusal of Adam Smith's *Wealth of Nations* was of decisive importance for the later development of Bentham's economic thought. We do not know exactly when he read it, but it

---

[1] *The Literature of Political Economy*, 1845, p 193.

is amply clear that he read it and re-read it until he was thoroughly familiar with the work. It is easy to feel underneath and behind many a classical book the vital familiarity of its author with the Bible: it is perhaps difficult to give chapter and verse for any particular passage, but the language, the diction, the wording, the implication of Holy Writ is unmistakably there. Well, the *Wealth of Nations* was Bentham's economic bible and he assimilated it until he thought in its terms and spoke in its tongue.[1]

Smith was definitely one of Bentham's few heroes. He who was so sparing of praise, was always ready to eulogise the great Scotsman. He calls him "the father of political economy" (*Works* II, 213); "a writer of consummate genius'" (I, 400); an author who has "displayed extraordinary sagacity in all his researches" (II, 208); a "great master" who is characterized by "force and precision" (II, 244); in short, "an authority" (II, 576)—a word which, like the others just mentioned, meant more in Bentham's mouth than it would have done in anybody else's. But he goes even further. Smith is not only a great thinker and a great writer: he is for Bentham a great man. He counts him among "the noblest minds" (III, 185), and describes the *Wealth of Nations* as "a treatise upon universal benevolence" (*The Theory of Legislation*, ed. Ogden, 432). There can be no doubt, then, that a most thorough study of Smith's illustrious treatise was the mainspring of all Bentham's economic knowledge, and he freely acknowledges this fact when, in the *Defence of Usury*, he owns that he is indebted to Smith for "every thing" (Letter XIII).

In spite of this genuine appreciation of Smith's achievement, Bentham was not, however, an uncritical admirer. The *Defence of Usury* is full of eulogies for the great prophet from the north: but its thirteenth letter "to Dr. Smith, on projects in arts, &c." proves Bentham's perfect independence of mind and judgment, because the author of the *Wealth of Nations* is firmly—if politely—taken to task there for his inconsistencies and for his failure to escape "the fascination of sounds". Among Bentham's papers we find not only a neat summary of Smith's work, but also a sheet of "Observations" (U.C. XCIX,[2] 182) on a few problematic points contained therein,

---

[1]Cf. esp. "Panopticon," *Works* IV, pp. 208 and 216. Other interesting references to Smith occur in VI, 184; V, 201; V, 301; III, 442 and 474; *Church of Englandism*, 1818, 262 seq., 298, 302; and *The Theory of Legislation* ed. Ogden, 182.

[2]Box 99 of the collection of Bentham manuscripts in the Library of University College, London.

and a rather more elaborate criticism of a metaphor which he uses in speaking of the circulation of money: the latter piece is more closely scrutinised below[1]: the former is all too scrappy to find a place in this edition, but it deserves to be mentioned, if only to show that Bentham was no respecter of persons, and that he was as unwilling to accept an economic ipsedixitism as any other.

In view of the immediate success of Smith's classical treatise it is perhaps not over-bold to assume that Bentham worked through and assimilated it some time before 1780. Once in possession of all Smith's epoch-making ideas, Bentham could take part, and defend his position, in any discussion on economic affairs. To his admiring friends he was soon not only a great luminary of legal reform but also a coming light of economic science.

It is, none the less, surprising to find him acknowledged as an authority on economic matters long before he had published his first contribution to economic theory. James Anderson, now deservedly famous as the first to enunciate the principle of differential rent, and then universally known as the author of *Observations on the Means of Exciting a Spirit of National Industry*,[2] printed in 1783 a pamphlet for private circulation[3] in which he drew attention to the value and potentialities of the Western Isles for the fishing industry and suggested that this branch of primary production be afforded public protection. Under the influence of George Wilson, Bentham's Scottish friend, he sent a copy to Bentham and asked him what he thought about the proposal he had put forward. Bentham's answer (dated May 28, 1783) is enlightening. He calls himself "a mere novice in political economy" but he is so firm in his convictions that he subjects Anderson's ideas to a devastating critique. The letter with its mock humility and real insolence is not further remarkable but it shows the direction in which Bentham's economic thought was developing. "Supposing," he says, "a greater profit might be made by a given capital employed in this way, than by the same capital employed in any other (a point necessary to be made out, with at least some general show of probability), why am I, who am carrying

[1] Cf. vol. III, Introduction.
[2] Published 1777.
[3] Published in 1785 under the title *An Account of the Present State of the Hebrides and Western Coasts of Scotland; in which an attempt is made to explain the circumstances that have hitherto repressed the industry of the natives; and some hints are suggested for encouraging the fisheries, and promoting other improvements in those countries.*

on a flourishing manufacture at Manchester, to be taxed, to have money taken out of my pocket, to be given to you to catch fish with in the isles of Scotland?" And he answers this question as he would have answered it ten or twenty years later when he had given more and maturer thought to economic problems. "Certainly, I ought not [to be taxed for this purpose], unless with that money you could bring to market a great many more pounds' worth of fish than I could of cloth" (*Works* X, 128).

Although this letter does not in any way prove that Bentham was at that time already an expert economist, it is yet interesting as an indication that he meant to take the subject up. In fact, only three and a half years lie between the day when it was written and the day when he began to draft the *Defence of Usury*, his only well-known essay on an economic problem, and one of his main titles to literary fame. But before we undertake to study the origin, contents and importance of this deservedly famous little book, we shall do well to cast a short glance at the intellectual substructure of general ideas on which all Bentham's economic thinking was based. The reader will find at the beginning of this volume a series of passages culled from all the works Bentham ever published which give us a good insight into his philosophy of economic science. The various items brought together there were written at different times and in different connections, but they nevertheless form a mosaic-like whole, because on these points Bentham's ideas did not undergo any decisive change.

THE PHILOSOPHICAL FOUNDATIONS OF BENTHAM'S ECONOMIC THOUGHT

The key to Bentham's philosophy of economics is, of course, the fact that he was a confirmed materialist. Now, the first and foremost consequence of a materialistic world-view is the conscious or unconscious desire to subordinate the social sciences to, and model them upon, the physical sciences. But at the next step the materialists are already divided against themselves. Some will insist on a severely "disinterested" approach to social and economic life: to them, "science" means "objectivity". But others will wander in the opposite direction. They will emphasise, not the disinterestedness of scientific research, but its practical results, its pragmatical nature, the fact that it serves and benefits the human race: to them, "science" means "power"—power to do good. It is this second type to which Jeremy

Bentham belonged. The pursuit of knowledge for its own sake seemed to him not much more than a waste of time.

Social science, then, like biochemistry and bridge-building, must be useful (cf. I, p. 81); and there is no point in contrasting science and art, or theory and application, which are, as it were, implied in each other; nor yet is it justifiable to distinguish disciplines of immediate applicability, such as medicine, from others which are more remote from it, for instance, logic: the difference is at best relative, and very nearly a *deceptio visus* (cf. II).

As all science is thus for Bentham essentially a guide to action, he is only consistent when he regards political economy as part and parcel of politics (the word here taken in its widest connotation); but politics itself is a subdivision of ethics which, in so far as it is not simply expository, is "knowledge concerning what is proper to be done"; now ethics, in its turn, belongs to the sensitive-faculty-regarding group of disciplines, as contrasted to the intellectual-faculty-regarding group of logic, grammar, and rhetoric; and, finally, the whole sensitive-faculty-regarding group is a sub-group of the wider category which Bentham calls the mind-regarding sciences, in opposition to the body-regarding ones such as botany, zoology, mineralogy, and the like. This, in its barest outline, is Bentham's conception of the place of economics in the system of human knowledge: the conception which is set out with wearisome detail and a somewhat whimsical use of a special terminology in Bentham's *Chrestomathia* (cf. III). A shortened version of his *Encyclopedical* or *Art and Science Table,* and of his running commentary on it, is printed below, at some risk of frightening the reader who does not as yet know the difficulties of the older Bentham's style and mode of expression: if he finds this passage too repulsive, let him disregard it: if he prefers to work through it, he will probably emerge with a heightened respect for Bentham the thinker, because, for all its oddity, this systematic survey of the field of human knowledge shows the extreme tidiness of his mind and the austere discipline of his mental processes.

The totality of human knowledge Bentham calls ontology or eudæmonics: the term ontology is meant to characterize the scientific, the term eudæmonics the pragmatical aspect of it. Corresponding to the totality of human knowledge Bentham envisaged, as the principal *desideratum* and *faciendum,* a Pannomion, or all-comprehensive body of law. The underlying idea of it was, of course, to be the greatest-

B

happiness principle, and the greatest happiness of the race was, in his opinion, to be achieved by establishing universal security, guaranteeing subsistence, maximizing abundance, and reducing, as far as possible, inequality (cf. IV). This fourfold aim of security, subsistence, abundance, and equality was formulated and reformulated by Bentham a hundred times: it will recur in this publication as in all his printed works. The function of thought is simply to discuss the possible methods and means whereby these subordinate ends, and with them the overriding aim of universal felicity, can be furthered— to expose what is detrimental, and to justify what is conducive, to the welfare of society. It is obvious that economics as such is primarily concerned with subsistence and abundance (cf. V), but legislation can do little to promote these directly and must leave it to the acquisitiveness of the individual to produce and provide wealth. Thus it is that, from the legislative point of view, security and equalization of property are of paramount importance to the economist (cf. VI).

When the economist sets out to develop his ideas, or rather to fulfil his duty to the community, he is confronted with peculiar difficulties against which Bentham tries to put him on his guard: it is much more difficult to see the truth in the social sciences than it is in the physical, because there cannot be the same degree of cool detachment and objectivity (cf. VII-IX). In particular, Bentham warns against the free and easy use of metaphors: he points out that it is only in a very restricted sense that a society can sensibly be called a body (cf. X), and that only mischief can result if it is conceived either as a mechanism or as an organism (cf. XI). Had this warning been properly heeded, a good deal of modern sociology would have remained unwritten, and neither Spencer nor Pareto would have developed his system of ideas!

But not only error, even truth itself is sometimes dangerous. It must not only be tested by experience but, what is still more important, it must be kept within its proper bounds: just because it is confirmed by observation in one sector of reality, it is liable to be extended to others where it may not hold good, and lead to disappointments which have often engendered an unjustifiable distrust of all generalization (XII-XIII).

All these pitfalls will be happily avoided, if the search for truth is conducted methodically. Bentham gave much serious thought to, and developed firm convictions on, matters of method. If methodology is essentially a means to an end, or a tool for a job, it

is a means and a tool which will materially influence the final result
of all endeavour, the end achieved and the job performed (cf. XIV).
Now, which is the correct method which the economist should
follow? Should he proceed from the abstract to the concrete, from
the general to the particular, or should he move in the opposite
direction? In other words, should he apply deduction or induction?
Bentham's decided answer is: induction. By deduction it is easier to
teach the truth, but only by induction can it be *found* (cf. XV).
Induction seemed to Bentham the modern method *par excellence*,
the scientific method in the narrower sense of the word, the method
which had led Bacon and Newton to their triumphs (cf. XVI):
deduction he was inclined to condemn as the outmoded scholastic
procedure, the dismal heritage of the metaphysician Aristotle.
Logically and historically, he claims, mankind has progressed from
more concrete observations to more abstract propositions (cf. XVII):
the results once gained, it is true, may be imparted with more ease
and dispatch by abstract propositions than by concrete observations,
but the use of generalities will only be unproblematic and safe when
the instruction given in general terms is accompanied by illustrations
taken from the sphere of particulars (cf. XVIII). It was from the
application of these methodological principles that Bentham
expected striking success in his scientific pursuits, and which inspired
him with the hope that he would become the Newton of the moral
world (cf. XIX).

Induction, then, is the correct method. But, naturally, it has its
problems. Its starting point is the vast expanse of practical life: how
can the limitless mass of possible observations be pressed into some
kind of order? Where is scientific reasoning to begin? If all knowledge is, in the last analysis, part and parcel of the pursuit of
happiness, the starting point of any science will have to be the
potential *utility* of the objects or actions which it sets out to
investigate: and this will also be the best approach from the
psychological point of view as well as the most satisfactory one,
because no aspect of a thing will engage and hold a man's attention
more readily than its tendency to affect his happiness (cf. XX).
Bentham is much concerned to define the term utility which,
incidentally, refers to the individual rather than to society, so that
Bentham is, from the very outset, driven to an atomistic conception
of social life (cf. XXI). Utility may be either direct or indirect
(cf. XXII), just as an action may be either productive or unproductive

(cf. XXIII)—the criterion being in both cases the same, namely, subservience to human use.

In all these passages Bentham treats the promotion of happiness and the prevention of unhappiness as equivalents—consistently enough, because both have the same tendency, to augment the sumtotal of enjoyment. The prevention of unhappiness, or its diminution, is, as it were, the negative counterpart to the promotion of happiness, or its positive increase: the two stand to each other in the relation of + a and − a (cf. XXIV). For Bentham, this is more than just figurative language. We see him here at the brink of one of his boldest ideas—the idea of a calculus of pleasure and pain. It is most fully and clearly set out in his *Axioms of Mental Pathology* (cf. XXV), one of the central pieces and prime achievements of his mind. In these pages Bentham courageously attempts a quantification of mental experiences, to make possible exact comparisons between pleasures and pains: the relevance of these ideas to the theory of value is plain, and as nobody who endeavours to understand Bentham, and to appreciate his position in the history of economic doctrine, will be able to do without a thorough study of these speculations, no attempt is made here to compress them into a short summary survey. They are, moreover, so pregnant with meaning, that it is hardly possible to reduce their content to a still smaller compass. Indeed, the reader who wishes to gain a thorough knowledge of this sector of the field, must not be satisfied with the study of the "axioms" as they are printed below: he must also consult *The Theory of Legislation* (preferably in C. K. Ogden's edition) where many relevant and indeed indispensable passages on the "measure of pleasures and pains" are to be found.

It is obvious that Bentham firmly believed in the quantitative character of mental experiences: to him, pleasures and pains are simply magnitudes. But quantification is not yet measurement: the *Axioms of Mental Pathology* operate with the comparatively vague notions of "greater" and "less": they do not undertake to express their quantities in figures. Did Bentham believe in the possibility of *measuring* pleasures and pains? Professor Everett has unearthed a passage in which a clear answer to this question is given. It is a positive answer. "Money is the instrument of measuring the quantity of pain or pleasure" (cf. XXVI). It cannot be said, however, that Bentham seriously considered the implications and difficulties of this position.[1] A direction in which his mind did travel more successfully is, on the other hand, the realization of the importance of the marginal principle. In point 5, case III, para. 5 of the *Axioms of Mental Pathology* the reader will find a surprisingly clear exposition of the idea of a *minimum sensibile* of wealth, and a short statement written many years later and in a very different connection proves that Bentham always bore the importance of the marginal principle in his mind, even if he did not fully elaborate it anywhere (cf. XXVII).

From all this it can be seen that Bentham's method was not only inductive but also (in its tendency at any rate) exact. In fact, he goes so far as to say that the sphere of ethics is no less amenable to mathematical treatment than the sphere of physics, even though the one has to do with the outer world whose extension lies before our eyes in the clear daylight, while the other deals with the deepest recesses of our inner world in whose darkness we do not easily find anything that is tangible in the true sense of the word (cf. XXVIII).

Still, Bentham was no blind admirer of the mathematical method. Like Marshall after him, he was inclined to regard it as essentially a clear and convenient mode of expression and notation and no more, though he did emphasize that it was of material help in the management of complex chains of reasoning (cf. XXIX). He would have ridiculed an "economic science" juggling with symbols that stand for no concrete and countable quantities, and he knew full well that it was an abuse of mathematics to borrow its prestige for propositions which are not fully borne out by direct observation (cf. XXX, XXXI).

THE "DEFENCE OF USURY" AND ITS "POSTSCRIPT"

Such were the general ideas (whether explicitly thought out, or as yet only implicitly present in his mind) with which Bentham approached the study of political economy. By the middle of the 'eighties, his interest in the subject was thoroughly roused; we see a clear proof of his growing preoccupation with this "branch of eudæmonics" in his desire to read about the "civil and political economy" of Italy before he passed through that country on his way to Russia where he was to spend twenty months or so at Crichoff with his brother Samuel, who was then in Prince Potemkin's service. We find him writing about the matter to Dr. John Symonds,

---

[1] On its mortal weakness, cf. W. Stark, *Diminishing Utility Reconsidered*, Kyklos, 1947, pp. 321-344.

Professor of Modern History at Cambridge, who had resided some time in Italy and was known to Bentham as a contributor to Young's *Annals*. Symonds recommended Genovesi's *Lezioni*[1] as the best book available (*Works* X, 139) and it is highly probable that Bentham had a good look at it. However, there is no reference to Genovesi in any of Bentham's printed works, and we cannot take the correspondence with the Cambridge don for more than a proof of his eagerness to go beyond Scottish literature and English experience.

This keen interest in economic problems seems to have still further increased in Crichoff where comparative social isolation left Bentham's mind free for serious study and intensive work. We hear about it in a curiously roundabout way through a letter which Wilson sent to Bentham on Sept. 24, 1786. "Trail," he writes, "received, on going to town last Friday, a scrap of paper from you, desiring an account of the new taxes; and before he returns, will do what he can to supply you." Several books on political subjects, including information on the sinking fund, had already been dispatched before (*Works* X, 163). Probably Bentham had given a standing order to Trail before he left to provide him, without delay, with all the newest literature in the field of finance and government in general.

It seems, then, that Bentham had already devoted much serious attention and a considerable amount of time to the study of political economy before he first set pen to paper to write upon the subject. How that happened can best be followed in his correspondence with George Wilson. Towards the end of December 1786, Bentham reported that he had heard a rumour according to which Pitt was planning to reduce the legal rate of interest from 5 per cent. to 4. That was an intention of which Bentham would have disapproved even if he had known nothing about its economic implications. The lower the legally admitted rate of interest, the more people were sure to be prosecuted for usury: but usury, according to Bentham's legal theory, was no crime. "A natural classification of offences," he taught, is a "test for distinguishing genuine from spurious ones" — those that should be punished, from those that should not. Now, such a classification had been attempted in the *Introduction to the Principles of Morals and Legislation*, and Bentham had been unable to find a *locus proprius* for usury in the system of mis-

---

[1] *Lezioni di Commercia o sia d'Economia Civile*, Naples 1766/67.

demeanours developed there. "Usury," he says, "which, if it must be an offence, is an offence committed with consent, that is, with the consent of the party supposed to be injured, cannot merit a place in the catalogue of offences, unless the consent were either unfairly obtained or unfreely: in the first case, it coincides with defraudment; in the other, with extortion." In this way, the very concept of usury seemed to him to dissolve in smoke. Few people would perhaps have concluded with Bentham that this "difficulty experienced in the attempt to find a place" for it in a theoretical "system" made usury an "imaginary" offence: but that was definitely Bentham's conviction, and so he became a declared enemy of all who wished to keep penalties for breaches of the maximum rate of interest on the statute-book (cf. *Works* I, pp. III and 118).

But this was in 1780, and we are now in 1786. In the meantime, as has been pointed out, Bentham's thought had become somewhat less formalistic and somewhat more economical. It is an indication of his enhanced understanding of economic affairs that Pitt's reported or rumoured intention should have raised his ire, not so much *qua* lawyer, as *qua* economist. "Tell me what you hear about it," Bentham writes; and he makes it clear that he is up in arms against the proposal and its reputed author. "Were it true," he goes on to say, "I should like to give him a piece of my mind first. I have arguments against it *ready cut* and *dry*: the former epithet you may have some doubt about; the latter you will not dispute. You know it is an old maxim of mine, that interest, as love and religion, and so many other pretty things, should be free" (X, 167). As always happened when Bentham was really interested in a subject, he did not wait for the intelligence which he requested, but set to work at once. In February 1787 the *Defence of Usury* in its first form was well under way. "I am writing letters to *you* abusing Pitt for being about to reduce the rate of interest," he tells Wilson, "and abusing the world for limiting the rate of interest at all" (X, 170). Wilson was meanwhile making the necessary inquiries, but their result was negative. "As to the rate of interest," he writes in April, "no proposal has been made in Parliament to reduce it, nor have we been able to learn that any such intention has been entertained by Mr. Pitt, or any other great man; so that whatever applies to the alteration, as to this time particularly, you will have to alter" (X, 172 seq.). Wilson knew Bentham well; he sensed that this problem of finance and economy had taken a strong hold on the imagination of his friend and aroused his fighting instincts; perhaps Bentham's interest and indignation was strong enough to induce him to finish for once what he had begun and to publish a pamphlet on the question. Always anxious that Bentham should cease day-dreaming and devote his energies to the practical task of building up a great literary reputation, he tried to persuade him not to drop the matter, but to press on with his work. True, he argued, the subject of interest is not topical; but is it not always of importance? Surely, Bentham could say a great deal about it which had never been said before? Perhaps new ideas would carry more weight with the public if they were presented as purely theoretical propositions without connection with a passing quarrel of the day. They would at any rate escape the imputation of having been put together "on the spur of the occasion" (X, 172 seq.).

This time Wilson's hopes were not to be disappointed. In the first days of May Bentham dispatched to him a small parcel which contained the precious manuscript. "My Dear Wilson," he writes in the covering letter, "I send for your edification, a Defence of Usury and some other enormities. Abuse it and keep it, or abuse it and print it, as to your wisdom may seem meet. Don't let Trail see it or hear it (the blasphemous 14th letter I mean[1]) till he has submitted to have his hands tied behind him, for fear of mischief. Douglas's phlegm might be trusted, but he is Attorney-General by this time, and has not time" (X, 174[2]).

From the dates of the relevant letters it appears that the *Defence of Usury* must have been written between the beginning of January and the end of April 1787[3]. It was quick work but that was all to the good because it gave the pamphlet something of the briskness and ease which had gone into its making. Once it was off his hands, Bentham was genuinely anxious to see it launched. "If you do print it," he says, "don't let it linger; but send it to the press quickly, that it may begin the sooner to lay in a little stock of reputation for me against I get home" (ib.). In fact, he was rather concerned to reap the full reward of his originality, which is somewhat surprising as he had not been jealous of Paley when the Archdeacon had invaded his province of utilitarian philosophy and penal reform. His envy is

---

[1] This "blasphemous 14th letter" was not published and its text has not survived.
[2] Cf. Bowring's Memoir for the full text of the letter.
[3] "The letters were begun, I think, in February or January, finished in April" (X, 175). Letters XII and XIII are dated "March, 1787".

directed against a man of much smaller stature: "The intimation given that these ideas of mine about usury are of old standing, as I dare say you and I recollect they are, was a piece of selfish prudence, which you will think vain. There is one Playfair [William Playfair] who published, just before I left England, a trumpery book in quarto, called *The Interest of Money Considered*.[1] Nine-tenths of it is bad writation about the origins of society, and so forth: the other tenth is a perfectly vague and shapeless proposal for relaxing the rigour of the anti-usurious laws in favour of projectors; yet without any argument in it, or any other idea, but that vague one thrown out in almost as general and vague a way as I have stated it in. I understand it has been well enough spoken of by several people."

The next letter to Wilson betrays very great impatience on Bentham's part to see the pamphlet published: "Last post-day, Friday 12, I received yours of July 3/14. You have received, then, my *Defence of Usury*. You think you shall approve of it. You inform me of the imminent danger it is in of losing the appearance of whatever merit it may possess by delay. And *yet*—spite had almost said *therefore*—you delay it—delay it till *I* don't know when, still less *you*. No, you have *not* delayed it: I accuse myself of injustice in attempting to believe you. Yet my anxiety not to see week thus flung away after week, makes me force my mind for a few minutes to this improbable supposition. Send it, then, if you have any desire to acquit yourself of breach of confidence, or I, any power over my own—send it somehow, anyhow, to the press. I wish it were possible for me to devise the least coercive form of words that would be sufficient to produce this very simple effect: no others would I use— but those indeed I would use at any rate" (X, 175). If corrections are needed—it seems that Wilson was concerned about some legal technicalities—let some "publishing lawyer" append them in the form of notes for a fee. "The being seen to be ignorant or mistaken in points of law at 1500 miles distance from all sources of information, gives me not the least concern. I have no opinion-trade to spoil."

It is impossible to say whether Wilson would have sent the manuscript to the press, or whether his scruples would have prevailed. But at this juncture a *deus ex machina* appeared on the scene. Bentham *père* heard of the matter and saw to it that the

---

[1] *The Gentleman's Magazine* (vol. XCIII, 1823, part I, p. 565) mentions, ir Playfair's obituary, a book entitled "Regulations for the Interest of Money" as published in 1785. Bentham left for Russia in August of that year.

pamphlet was printed without further loss of time. He had been astounded, eleven years before, by the success of the *Fragment on Government*. He felt that here was another means of indulging his paternal pride, and the opportunity was too good to be missed. As always, he got things done quickly and efficiently. Thus it happened that Bentham was shown a copy of the little book early in 1788 when he passed through The Hague on his homeward journey, the British ambassador there, Sir James Harris, being something of a friend.

If Bentham was afraid that his pamphlet would not receive the cordial welcome which he was convinced it deserved, he was mistaken. The *Monthly Review* for May 1788 (LXXVIII, p. 361 seq.) calls Bentham an "ingenious author" and his book "a political gem of the finest water." "Among the many valuable works . . . that have claimed our attention," the reviewer remarks, "none demands a higher rank, on account of the perspicuity of its arguments, and perhaps the national importance of its conclusions, than the little volume which forms the subject of the present article." It "requires only to be examined with attention, in order to be admired." The critic did not like Bentham's style; he well discerned in the long sentences and embarrassing parenthetical clauses "an excessive attention to accuracy"; nor did he think Bentham's humour always natural. But for all that the discussion works up to a most impressive climax which would warm the heart of any literary man: "We sincerely thank the author for the pleasure his work has afforded us. In journeying through the dreary fields of criticism, such performances as this yield a grateful refreshment, like the discovery of a spring to an exhausted caravan in the parched desarts of Arabia."

Such was the voice of the anonymous public. The acknowledgments of some outstanding men were perhaps still more acceptable and gratifying. In a letter of May 2, 1788, to his brother Sam, Bentham reports some notable successes in making proselytes for a liberal attitude towards money dealings, but the names he mentions mean little to us today (cf. X, 182). More illustrious converts were, however, soon to follow. No conversion could have given Bentham more pleasure than that of the great Adam Smith. It is reported in a letter of George Wilson dated Dec. 4, 1789. "Did we ever tell you," he writes, "what Dr. Adam Smith said to Mr. William Adam, the Council M.P., last summer[1] in Scotland? The Doctor's expressions

---

[1] i.e. the summer of the same year, 1789.

were that 'the *Defence of Usury* was the work of a very superior man, and that tho' he had given him some hard knocks, it was done in so handsome a way that he could not complain,' and seemed to admit that you were right" (cit. John Rae, *Life of Adam Smith*, 1895, p. 423 seq.). Wilson's words are very cautious. It must remain an open question whether Rae is on firm ground when he says of the *Defence of Usury* "that the book had the very unusual controversial effect of converting the antagonist against whom it was written", and that "it is reasonable to think that if Smith had lived to publish another edition of his work, he would have modified his position on the rate of interest" (ib.). Bentham tried to wring from him an open admission of his change of opinion. He sent him a letter to this effect of which the draft is printed below (vol. I, p. 188 ff.), and hoped for a straightforward answer. Smith seems to have received it in the very last days of his life (his death occurred on July 17, 1790), and all he did by way of acknowledgment was to forward to Bentham a dedication copy of the *Wealth of Nations*. Bentham tells us about it in a different connection[1]: "A present," he says, "I had the melancholy consolation of receiving from Adam Smith at the same time with the news of the loss which, as a citizen of the world, I had sustained by his death, will ever be preserved by me among the choicest of those treasures on which imagination or sentiment stamp a value, and as a token of that magnanimity which, it were to be wished, were always the accompaniment of the inevitable war of opinions, as carried on by writing and thinking men" (U.C. I, 621). There seems to have been no covering letter to the gift. Ailing as he was, Smith cannot have had much relish for a theoretical correspondence in those days when his life and vigour were finally ebbing away. His gesture was certainly charming. But whether it can be construed as a plain acceptance of Bentham's view on usury, is another, and a very doubtful matter. Smith was no doctrinaire. He would not necessarily have approved of the removal of the maximum rate of interest, just because he thought in general freedom preferable to regulation. But we may well believe that he admitted the force of Bentham's arguments, for he was one of the most open-minded men who ever lived.

Another very welcome addition to the list of Bentham's admirers —though not exactly a convert—was Dr. Thomas Reid, the well-known Scottish philosopher and successor of Adam Smith in the

---

[1] In the draft preface to *The True Alarm*, written on March 16, 1801.

Glasgow chair of moral philosophy. He cannot have been over-sympathetic to Bentham's general way of thinking because he opposed the application of mathematical formulæ to ethics[1]; but we find him on Sept. 5, 1788, writing to Professor Gregory of Edinburgh: "I am much pleased with the tract you sent me on Usury. I think the reasoning unanswerable, and have long been of the author's opinion, though I suspect that the general principle, that bargains ought to be left to the judgment of the parties, may admit of some exceptions." The weak stand sometimes in need of protection. "But with regard to the loan of money in a commercial state, the exception can have no place" because "the borrowers and lenders are upon an equal footing" (*Works* X, 176 seq.). Reid was unwilling to accept Bentham's explanation of the origin of the prejudice against usury—a subject on which he had his own ideas, and on which he had written an historical essay.[2] Bentham was much gratified by the acknowledgment received from this quarter and suggested that Reid's treatise should be published together with the second edition of the *Defence of Usury*, but nothing came of the idea.

But the *Defence of Usury* was not only read and appreciated in the British Isles; it carried Bentham's name and fame to the other side of the Channel. On October 3, 1789, the National Assembly of France debated some economic problems connected with the fixation of the rate of interest, and the *Courier de Provence*, Mirabeau's organ, reporting the discussion, added a footnote which must have been music in Bentham's ear. "This question," it reads, "has just been profoundly analysed in an English work of which the translation is being printed at the present moment, and which we intend

---

[1]Cf. his "Essay on Quantity; occasioned by reading a treatise in which simple and compound ratios are applied to virtue and merit," originally published in the *Transactions of the Royal Society* (of London) vol. XLV, 1748. Cf. Sir William Hamilton's *Works of Thomas Reid, D.D.*, Edinburgh 1846 and after.

[2]It seems that neither Dr. Reid himself nor his friends took this investigation very serious. It is not mentioned in Dugald Stewart's *Account of the Life and Writings of Thomas Reid, D.D.* reprinted in every edition of Sir William Hamilton's *Works of Thomas Reid, D.D.* All that Dugald Stewart says is that "the example of his illustrious predecessor, and the prevailing topics of conversation around him, occasionally turned his thoughts to commercial politics, and produced some ingenious essays on different questions connected with trade, which were communicated to a private society of his academical friends" (*l.c.* Section 1). No manuscript of Dr. Reid which discusses the origin of the usury laws has been preserved in the university libraries of Edinburgh and Glasgow.

to make known."[1] Bentham was delighted. He at once resolved to write a series of letters to Mirabeau which would comment on some economic measures which the revolutionary government was taking or was planning to take, such as the confiscation of church lands, the suppression of places and pensions, and the like.[2] These letters were never sent. It was just one more of the many schemes which Bentham planned but never executed. The opening lines of the first epistle are, however, interesting in our connection. "I am proud, as becomes me, of your intention in my favour," Bentham writes. "Meantime, in addition to the honour of calling the Comte de Mirabeau my Translator and Reviewer, permit me that of stiling myself his correspondent." As these words indicate, Bentham was convinced that the great Mirabeau himself was busy translating the *Defence of Usury*. But this was almost certainly a misconception— a misconception based not only on the footnote in the *Courier de Provence* but also, as it seems, on a misunderstood report of a conversation between Mirabeau and Bentham's friend Romilly.[3] Mirabeau certainly had no leisure for such-like pastimes; but it is clear that the translation was made by somebody within his circle as it was brought out by LeJay, the publisher of the *Courier de*

[1]Cf. *Courier de Provence, Pour servir de suite aux Lettres du Comte de Mirabeau à ses Commettans*. No. XLIX. Du 2 au 3 Octobre, [1789] p. 6.

[2]Cf. University College Collection, IX, 37-49, and CLXVI, 6-11, 20. The letters are not interesting enough to be reprinted here. A sketch of the main topics is contained in CLXVI, 1 (University College Collection). It follows here in its original form:—

"Letter I. Supplies: New species proposed — Appropriation of collateral successions.

"II. Retrenchment—Savings: Pensions of retreat, Donations to exalted indigence. Court pageantry, Commercial bounties.

"III. Retrenchments continued: Colonies and colonial defence.

"IV. Discharge of debt: Belief preferable to readiness for war.

"V: Retrenchments: Limits.

"VI. Retrenchments continued: Few judges better than many.

"VII. Supply: Taxes on justice, the worst possible."

Only the first two letters were actually worked out. The material is in boxes IX and CLXVI and should be taken in the following order: Letter I: IX, 37-38; CLXVI, 11; IX, 39-42, 43-44; CLXVI, 7-8, 10, 6, 9; Letter II: CLXVI, 20; IX, 49, 45-48. Cf. also CLXVI, 21-26, in the Summary of unpublished material below: this plan seems to have been substituted for the proposed *Letters to Mirabeau* when the Count died.

[3]I owe this information to Mr. Charles Blount, who has done most valuable research on Bentham's relation to Mirabeau and his group. Mr. Blount is inclined to believe that the *Defence of Usury* was translated by Clavière.

Provence. As it happened, a second French version appeared in the same year (1790) under the title *Lettres sur la Liberté du Taux de l'Intérêt de l'Argent;* its translator was E. Delessert, the publisher Grégoire.[1] And it seems that the French public remained as attached to the little book as the British: as late as 1828 Saint-Amand Bazard republished it in a new form which was based on the fourth English edition.

Another country in which the *Defence of Usury* made a considerable impression was America. To the *Codification Proposal, addressed by Jeremy Bentham to all nations professing liberal opinions,* which was originally printed in 1822, are appended several "testimonials" which are intended to show how favourable an impression our author had created among the modern minded all over the world. A letter from the United States contains the following passage:—

"The influence of your writings has already been extensively felt in the United States. Your work on usury has passed through several editions in this country; and its principles begin to be pretty generally adopted by men of enlarged views and liberal minds amongst us. In the constitution of the new State of Mississippi, which was formed in 1817, it is provided that the legislature of that state shall 'pass no law impairing the obligation of contracts, prior to 1821, on account of the rate of interest, fairly agreed on in writing, between the contracting parties, for a *bona fide* loan of money; but they shall have power to regulate the rate of interest, where no special contract exists in relation thereto'. This provision of the constitution of Mississippi, being limited to four years, was no doubt intended as an experiment; but, having once felt the advantages of unrestrained liberty, and a free competition in this branch of trade, there is little danger of a return to the absurd restrictions which prevail in other States of the Union.

"In the Alabama territory, an act has this year been passed repealing all the laws against usury, and allowing the parties in all cases to fix their own rate of interest.

"A similar law, introduced by Mr. Hayes in the Virginia house of delegates, was rejected by a majority of six or eight votes only, out of two or three hundred.

---

[1] As both translations appeared in the same year it is impossible to say who was "the intelligent Frenchman" to whom Bentham refers in the proposed preface to the second English edition—Delessert or the other; cf. below, p. 191.

"In New Hampshire, the same subject was agitated in the House of Representatives, at their last session; but they are not yet prepared to renounce their old prejudices" (*Works* IV, 579-580).

How much of this actual or intended liberal legislation may be credited to the circulation of the *Defence of Usury* cannot, of course, be decided, but that Bentham's pamphlet won over many a wavering mind in the United States, as it did elsewhere, is virtually certain.

However, the success of an author is not only measured by the number of converts he makes or followers he collects; it is also measured by the number of adversaries he calls forth. No less than five pamphlets were written to controvert Bentham's ideas and break his influence: James Grahame's *Defence of Usury Laws against the Arguments of Mr. Bentham* (1817); Robert Maugham's *Treatise on the Principles of the Usury Laws; with Disquisitions on the Arguments against them by Mr. Bentham* (1824); anonymous *Reasons against the Repeal of the Usury Laws* (1825);[1] Francis Neale's *Essay on Money Lending . . . and . . . Answer to the Objections of Mr. Bentham* (1826); and John Whipple's *Free Trade in Money* (1855) which had as sub-title "Stringent Usury Laws, the best Defence of the People against Hard Times". It is characteristic that the first of these publications appeared thirty years after the original date of Bentham's attack: a fact which shows how long it takes before the public can be roused; but a fact which proves at the same time that Bentham's little work had really left its mark. If Bentham's name was, by the middle of the nineteenth century, an abomination to the sterner moralists, this was in some degree due to the *Defence of Usury* and its advocacy of complete freedom in money matters.

But if Bentham was thus the target for the attacks of those who wished to preserve the governmental fixation of a maximum rate of interest, all the liberal-minded gathered around him and repeated and retailed his arguments. When Edward Sugden (Lord St. Leonards) published his own pamphlet,[2] he presented a copy to Bentham as "the father of the subject". "Truth," he says, "requires sometimes to be repeated; and this is all that I have done," the matter having been, in the *Defence of Usury,* "so entirely and happily exhausted as to leave nothing for future writers to attempt" (X, 473).

---

[1] Not identified by the *Dictionary of Anonymous and Pseudonymous English Literature.*

[2] *A Cursory Inquiry into the Expediency of repealing the Annuity Act and raising the Legal Rate of Interest,* 1812.

This sounds a little like cheap flattery, but the sentiment expressed was genuine enough.

The immediate success of the *Defence of Usury* was greatly enhanced by the fact that the Irish administration of the time contemplated a reduction in the rate of interest (from 6 to 5 per cent.) and sought the approval of Parliament for such a measure. On February 7, 1788, the Commons gave leave to bring in a Bill of this kind; it was brought in accordingly and read for the first time on February 15. The second reading took place after a short delay on February 20, and on that day some opposition to the proposed enactment became obvious. It was suggested that May 1 would be soon enough for the committee stage; but the Chancellor of the Exchequer was unwilling to brook delay. The motion "for going into Committee on a very distant Day," as the Journals have it, was defeated in a division by 75 votes to 27; a further motion substituting April 4 for May 1 was also thrown out, and the very next Saturday fixed for the committee stage. The Bill was duly considered by a committee of the whole House on February 23 "and . . . some Time spent therein". Two days later the matter was again before the Commons and certain minor amendments were agreed to. The third reading was almost at once, on February 26, and so the Bill was ready to be sent to the Lords. Up to this stage the administration could be well pleased: it had defeated the delaying tactics of the opposition and brought the measure safely through the House in a comparatively short time.

In the Lords, however, the opposition was more successful than in the Commons. In fact, the Upper House made short work of the Bill. Several witnesses were called, sworn, and examined, and on March 4 enough had been heard to justify a final condemnation of the proposed enactment. "A Motion was made, that the said Bill be committed to a Committee of the whole House. A Debate arising thereupon, and the Question being put; the House divided; and the Earl of Bellamont reported, that the Contents below the Bar were fourteen, and the Not-Contents in the House were twenty-three. Proxies being called for, and read over by the Clerk, the Lord Chancellor declared, that the Contents with the Proxies were seventeen, and the Not-Contents were twenty-seven." Consequently, the motion "passed in the Negative" and, logically, a further "Motion was made and the Question put, that the said Bill be rejected. It was resolved in the Affirmative" and that was the end of the Chancellor's endeavour.[1]

Bentham was inclined to claim some of the credit for this defeat of an illiberal monetary policy. And it is certain that the *Defence of Usury* had strengthened the hand of the opposition and played its part in the public debate of this interesting problem. A pirated edition had appeared at Dublin in 1788, the year of the parliamentary tussle between the friends and the foes of a governmental limitation of the rate of interest; but even the authorized London edition was widely bought and keenly read in the Irish capital. "It had some little sale in Ireland," Bentham wrote to his brother in May 1788, "and I hope may do something towards preventing the [ultimate] success of the measure of reducing the rate of interest there —a measure which, after having been thrown out of the House of Lords there this winter, is to be brought on by administration the next it is said" (X, 182). In point of fact, the matter was not reopened in 1789. A year and a half later, in December 1790, Bentham reports —rather triumphantly, it would seem—to the same correspondent: "I am known by the name of Usury B[entham] in Ireland. The bookseller is plaguing me about reprinting [my pamphlet], being continually asked for it" (ib. 246).

In a way, it must be admitted, this success of the *Defence of Usury* was due more to stylistic brilliance than to depth of thought. Some of the most impressive rhetorical questions put forward by Bentham are in fact hollow. Why is only a maximum rate of interest prescribed, and why not also a minimum rate? Why is only the price of borrowed money regulated, and why not all other prices as well? Why not forbid a man to sell his goods and chattels at disadvantageous terms, if he is forbidden to enter into disadvantageous monetary bargains? Arguments like these are not ineffective at the bar, and Bentham shows that he would have been an impressive pleader if he could have brought himself to practise his profession. But the charge of inconsistency is not convincing. There may be a good reason for regulating one particular price and leaving all others free, and Bentham was all too quick in assuming that a legal institution could not be justified if he was not aware of its deeper meaning and justification.

To the modern economist, the most outstanding shortcoming of the

---

[1] Cf. *The Journals of the House of Commons of the Kingdom of Ireland*, vol. XII, Dublin 1797, 335, 381, *Journals of the House of Lords*, vol. VI, Dublin, 1792, 155, 164 seq.

C

Defence of Usury is, of course, the complete absence of a theory of interest. Bentham's idea is that the legal rate is simply the prevailing market rate in a legalized form, and in this assumption he is obviously justified; but his next step is somewhat more problematic. There is no reason, he argues, why the prevailing rate should be regarded as particularly expedient, let alone why it should be sanctioned as exclusively right and just (Letter II). It did not occur to him that the "justice" of the market rate could be economic rather than moral: that it might be more expedient than any other because it is in agreement with the given economic realities. The fact that there is an equilibrium price of borrowed money—a "natural" price, as it would have been expressed at the time—is not, of course, in itself a sufficient reason to outlaw usury: but there is no doubt that Bentham here missed a most essential point.

The weakness of Bentham's position is particularly obvious in his discussion with Adam Smith in Letter VII. He takes exception to the assertion contained in the *Wealth of Nations* that no law can reduce the common rate of interest below the lowest ordinary market rate at the time when that law was made.[1] Smith's idea is, of course, that the price must be high enough to exclude all the demand that cannot be satisfied in the given supply situation, and that it "cannot" be brought down below this mark because otherwise not enough capital would be available to satisfy all bidders and chaos must ensue that would only give place to order again when the price has risen sufficiently to fulfil its proper function in the market. But this is a point Bentham does not grasp. If the law does not succeed in reducing the rate of interest, he argues, this failure can only be due to a technical defect of the law—to a defect either in its penning or in its execution.

Nevertheless, some ideas which have played a considerable part in the later history of the theory of interest and capital, are contained in the pages of the *Defence of Usury*.[2] The definition of lending, namely that it is "exchanging present money for future", is in itself significant and pregnant with possibilities; so is the definition of the saver as one who has "the resolution to sacrifice the present to [the]

---

[1] Cf. below p. 147; *Wealth of Nations*, ed. Cannan, 1904, I, p. 339.

[2] No emphasis is laid here on the criticism of Aristotle in Letter X, because it is all too playful to be taken seriously. Of course, Bentham refused to accept the thesis that money is barren; but it would be going too far to conclude from the story of the daric and the lambs introduced in this connection that he inclined towards a "physical productivity" theory, such as it was put forward at the time by Turgot.

future" (Letters II and X respectively). The most interesting passage
in this connection occurs at the beginning of Letter III where
Bentham relates the willingness of a man to save, and the degree of
his saving, to the salient question, "which of two pains may be of
greater force and value to him, the present pain of restraining his
present desires, or the future contingent pain he may be exposed to
suffer from the want to which the expence of gratifying these desires
may hereafter have reduced him?" Does he not hold here one loose
end of the modern theory of interest in his hands?

Bentham also realized, however dimly, that what is commonly
called "interest", is not interest pure and simple, but a compound
which contains, as one ingredient, a risk premium, an insurance
premium as it were, and an indemnification for the hazards a man
takes on himself in the interest of the economic community. Passages
which imply this idea occur in Letters VI and XIII. And if they are
not as clear as one would wish, they can be compared with similar
pronouncements of perfect clarity in the *Theory of Legislation*
which will help to bring out their essential meaning and their
correct interpretation (ed. Ogden, pp. 137/138, 320, 355).[1]

Still, these are openings through which Bentham did not care to
enter, pathways which he did not wish to follow. It is the philosopher
as much as the economist that speaks to us through the *Defence of
Usury*. His major line of attack is a splendid example of his critique
of language which, as C. K. Ogden has so amply and so ably shown,
is the cornerstone of Bentham's philosophic system, and his main
contribution to modern thought. "In the sound of the word usury,"
he says in the opening sentence of Letter II, "lies . . . the main
strength of the argument," the pernicious argument of the enemies
of freedom in money bargains. He fights an abuse of language as
much as an abuse of legislation, and the contention that the odious-
ness of the word is largely responsible for the outlawry of the thing,
is ever present in the pamphlet and sustains a good deal of its train
of thought[2] (cf. esp. Letter XIII).

---

[1]"The risk of loss makes a part of the price of merchandise and of the interest of
money" (*l.c.* 320).

[2]No attempt is made here to summarize this train of thought as a perfectly clear
summary is provided in the work itself (cf. below pp. 124-128). The text printed in
this edition is based on the second edition of 1790 which Bentham himself arranged
after his return from Russia, but deviations from the first edition of 1787 are indicated
in footnotes. The later edition of 1816 is not taken into account because, though
brought out in Bentham's lifetime, it was not produced under his personal care.

The *Defence of Usury* as it stands, has all the slickness and the roundedness of a finished work. But for Bentham himself it was no more than a short halt on a long road. From some papers that have come down to us and are contained in the University College collection (XVII, 1) we can see how his thought was widening out and, starting from the problem of usury, tended to take in the whole field of economics. He planned to add to the second edition for which the publisher soon began to press, a number of postscripts which he sums up as follows: "1. Short observations on the injustice and impolicy of forced reductions of the rate of interest. 2. Development of the principle *No more trade than capital*. 3. Practical consequences of the principle *No more trade than capital*, with respect to colonial government, economy and peace." The first point was of topical interest and inspired by the debates in the Irish Parliament to which reference has already been made (cf. above, p. 33 and the proposed preface to the second edition, below p. 192). The two latter points were not quite so topical but proved all the more fruitful: the idea that trade is limited by the amount of capital available, and that nothing can be done by government to remove this barrier—a real progress in economic insight, compared to the *Defence of Usury*—became the foundation of Bentham's *Manual of Political Economy*, and its application to the problems presented by overseas possessions can be seen in the fragment—the very important fragment—*Colonies and Navy* printed below. Both lines of thought embody convictions which Bentham never abandoned: they are first indicated here, in the postscript to the *Defence of Usury* which Bentham envisaged but did not print. As conclusion to the second edition Bentham wanted to use a rhetorical question "to the partizans of the mercantile system, and the watchers over the ballance of trade", namely: "Which is worth most, a guinea's worth of gold and silver, or a guinea's worth of corn, leather, cotton, silk, or any other thing else?" He must have realized, however, that with these considerations he was already miles and miles from his starting point, the justification of freedom in money dealings, and that he had entered the sphere of general economic theory. That was perhaps the reason why the *Defence of Usury* was in the end reprinted as it stood, with some verbal corrections only, and why the supplementary matter appears here for the first time.

The main problem which Bentham takes up in the postscript is the question of the causal connection between a limitation or reduction of the rate of interest on the one hand, and an increase of national wealth on the other. It is said that there *is* such a connection, and that a lowering of the rate of interest leads to a direct increase in national wealth, as well as to an indirect increase in that it enables the government to borrow more cheaply, and hence to keep taxation at a comparatively low level. Bentham denies both contentions. His discussion does not go into all the details, nor does it cover the whole field systematically, but it is fresh and clear and shows the younger Bentham at his best. To increase wealth, he argues, you must increase capital: usury laws favour the borrower at the expense of the lender: hence they can only increase wealth if borrowers contribute more towards the formation of new capital than lenders— a nonsensical suggestion in view of the fact that a typical lender is a typical saver. There is, of course, a type that can be called an "accumulating borrower"—a borrower who puts what he has borrowed to good use, and thus leaves the nation richer than it was before. But usury laws keep down the overall quantity of capital lent and borrowed, and they keep away foreign money, and both these effects are detrimental to the increase of wealth, even in so far as the activities of the "accumulating borrower", that is, the successful entrepreneur who works with borrowed capital are concerned. To this discussion Bentham appends a few more abstract and apodictic observations on the principle already explained or, at any rate, implied, that "capital limits trade"; in points 4 and 5 he finally and decisively disposes of the argument against which he is fighting all along, that a legal limitation of the interest-rate is "good for trade", by showing how it runs counter to general truth and natural necessity.

So far, he has steadily kept to his subject, the subject of the *Defence of Usury*. But from here onwards he deviates more and more and gets deeper and deeper into generalities: and when he comes to "colonial government, economy and peace", he is at long last quite at sea. Nevertheless, this last section of the intended postscript is of interest because it concerns a topic to which Bentham attributed great importance: colonial policy, or rather colony-holding, of which he was a sworn enemy. The matter, as has been indicated, is more fully expounded in *Colonies and Navy*, a fragment which we shall have to consider in a moment; and it is the sole subject of two pamphlets which he drafted, one addressed to his friends in France— *Emancipate your Colonies* (*Works*, vol. IV)—and the other to his friends in Spain—*Rid yourselves of Ultramaria* (as yet unpublished; U.C. VIII). Bentham's contention—which does not seem to be borne out by the history of the British Empire—is that both mother-country and colony are benefited if the link of dependency is dissolved. His arguments are here conveniently summed up. They are in good part political rather than economic; but there is one economic point which deserves a short glance and scrutiny.

Bentham claims that if the trade with a colony were given up, the capital formerly invested in it and now freed could be used to greater advantage in Britain, "in the improvement of land". He seems to assume that the profit of the colonial trader and the profit of the farmer at home are about equal, but that commerce produces no more than that profit, while agriculture will yield a net rent to boot. Here he momentarily moves towards the physiocratic point of view: and that *rapprochement* with the French school is still more clearly manifest in a passage taken from his preliminary notes and printed below which is—most characteristically—headed "Agriculture not dependent on manufactures". The first sentence sounds almost like the confession of faith of the *secte*: it could have been penned by the great Quesnay himself; so, indeed, could the last. The whole fragment is really remarkable, not only because of this strange bias in favour of agriculture, but also because of the ideas it contains concerning the natural distribution of the national capital through the various branches of the national economy. These ideas, however, point forward rather than back: and the last passage included in this selection from the materials prepared for the second edition of the *Defence of Usury*, concerned as it is with the relation of capital-formation and population-growth, or interest and wages, has altogether a Malthusian and Ricardian flavour.

THE FRAGMENT "COLONIES AND NAVY"

We have seen above (p. 23) that the first intention to write the *Defence of Usury* had sprung from a desire on Bentham's part "to give Pitt a piece of his mind". This desire persisted; it indicates a deep-seated tension between these two great personalities. The papers shortly entitled *Colonies and Navy* are also materials for a projected pamphlet against Pitt. We can only see it in the right perspective if we study a little more closely the relation between the statesman and the philosopher.

Pitt and Bentham met at Bowood, Lord Shelburne's country seat, and it seemed at first as if they would get on together without difficulty. Bentham wrote on Sept. 15, 1781, to his bosom friend Wilson: "Will. Pitt you know for certain; in his conversation there is nothing of the orator—nothing of that hauteur and suffisance one would expect; on the contrary, he seems very good-natured, and a little raw. I was monstrously frightened at him, but, when I came to talk with him, he seemed frightened at me; so that, if anything should happen to jumble us together, we may, perhaps, be good pax; which, however, is not very likely: for I don't know very well what ideas we are likely to have in common" (*Works* X, 100).

This is, as far as it goes, a friendly enough report. But a few days later there are already signs of a certain incompatibility of temperament. On Sept. 24 Bentham speaks about a game of chess in which Pitt was vanquished, and which seems to have left him somewhat peeved and out of spirit. "Finding he had no chance with me, he complained of its hurting his head, and gave it up immediately" (ib. 105). A small matter, an unimportant incident? Certainly. But many a personal hostility has grown out of a stupid cause and a passing ill-humour where the personalities involved were all ready to conflict.

Thus the first foundations of the later animosities were laid in the merry drawing-room of Bowood Castle: but more serious developments were to follow and to foster ill-will between the two antagonists. Lord Shelburne had given Pitt high office when he was Prime Minister: Pitt had no place for Shelburne when the parts were reversed. This act of ingratitude was never forgiven by Bentham, and he bitterly resented it, almost as a personal affront. Nor is this attitude difficult to understand: his fate was linked with Shelburne's star: his success in life depended on Shelburne's influence: Shelburne at the Treasury could have given Bentham the woolsack; Shelburne at the Home Office could have built the Panopticon; Shelburne at the Board of Trade could have realized Bentham's free-trade ideals. But Shelburne in retirement, Shelburne in disgrace, could do nothing for his *protégé*—and who else would do anything for him?

Thus friendship for Lansdowne and enmity towards Pitt merged into one sentiment in Bentham's breast. Keen as he was about that time to enter politics, he was waiting for an opportunity to make his voice heard, and it was not long before a suitable occasion offered itself. The British ministry pursued at this juncture an active anti-

Russian policy. It was feared that the balance of power in Europe would be upset if the expansionist drive of the great Tsarina remained unchecked. A "defensive alliance" was formed which brought London, Berlin and Stockholm into line against Saint Petersburg: in July 1788 war broke out between Sweden and Russia, and the general tension mounted from week to week. One of the first and most obvious moves of the new allies was an attempt to win Denmark over to their coalition, and representations were made in this sense at the court of Copenhagen by the British envoy. The matter was somewhat delicate as Denmark was leagued with Russia and embroiled with Sweden. Yet, in spite of all precautions, inadvertently or purposely, something of the negotiations then carrying on transpired, and was made the subject of public discussion in Great Britain. The opposition was dead against the treaty with Prussia and all it meant and stood for, and Bentham for once abandoned all reserve and plunged head first into the debate. Under the pseudonym "Anti-Machiavel" he wrote three letters to the *Public Advertiser* which he later bitterly regretted. His first two attacks drew an apology from an anonymous individual who signed himself "Partizan," and Bentham took "Partizan" severely to task in a third epistle on June 15, 1789. But "Partizan" was a powerful man— Bentham was even convinced that he was none other than George III —and he attributed the unwillingness of the King to set his sign manual under the Panopticon Bill after it had passed both Lords and Commons, to an enmity engendered in this unfortunate brush.[1]

Even if full allowance is made for the habitual rudeness of political journalism in general and of contemporary pamphleteering in particular,[2] Bentham's attack on the ministry and counter-attack on "Partizan" must be regarded as rather hot-headed and unnecessarily pungent. He accuses the cabinet of a desire to plunge Great Britain into an unjust and useless war without object or pretence; to abet unprovoked aggression with a high hand; to bully Denmark into a breach of faith; and to pursue a cunning plan of knavery. And he calls upon the public to repudiate the government's policy. "Fond as the people of this country are of war and insolence, prone as they have shown themselves, of late years, to make sudden starts from well-grounded and deep-rooted jealousy, to implicit confidence and foolish fondness towards George the Third," he says, "it is too much

---

[1] Cf. X, 211 seq.

[2] "Junius had set the writings of the day to the tune of asperity" (X, 212).

to suppose them capable of being wrought up to such a pitch of infatuation" as to approve of this political venture. He expresses the hope that Parliament will hesitate "to throw away t'other fifty or hundred millions of the nation's money for their amusement, and to saddle it with two or three millions a year more, in taxes, for the pleasure of cutting the throats of a people who never offered them the smallest injury" (X, 204).

These passages from the first letter prove that Bentham meant to speak as a party man; but in the second letter, the philosopher comes again to the fore. The incident obviously meant more to him than just an occasion to make a clever and effective political move. It set him thinking on the problem of international peace. "Justice and humanity have no place in cabinets," he says with bitterness. "It is for weak states to suffer injuries: it is for strong ones to inflict them. Do as you would be done by, a rule of gold for individuals, is a rule of glass for nations" (ib. 206). Out of these mournful reflections arose the pamphlet which is printed below, and which Bowring partially used, when he prepared vol. II of the *Works* for the press, in order to show what Bentham thought about the law of nations and world peace.

"Partizan's" defence of the government introduced economic considerations into the discussion. Why, he asks, should the British cabinet prefer a Russian alliance, the pet idea of the opposition, to the Prussian alliance? "The commercial advantages which this country might derive from a treaty with Russia, the other powers in the Baltic, together with Poland, will be able in a great measure to afford; whilst, from the wisdom of the present administration, we may expect that such encouragement will be given to the cultivation, in the British dominions, of the important articles of hemp and timber, that the immense sums which are paid for them to foreign nations, will, in time, be considerably lessened. The system adopted by the present administration tends likewise manifestly to lessen, if not entirely to annihilate, the influence of France in Turkey and Sweden, which may very probably be attended with such commercial advantages to England, with regard to the former power, that the British trade to the Levant, at present almost entirely superseded by the French, may regain its pristine importance" (X, 206 seq.).

This economic argument incensed Bentham as much as, or more than, any other. He took it as a "specimen of the vulgar common-place mode of arguing on these subjects" and as a striking proof of

"Partizan's" "ignorance, absurdity, false statement, and cool wickedness" (X, 208). His counter-argument is an early pronouncement of pure liberalism: "The political economy of this ministerial advocate is of a piece with his foreign politics. For the credit of office, I hope here at least he is not speaking from his *brief*. Sure I am he has not got his instructions from Dr. Smith. To prevent us from raising the important articles in question there are no legal obstacles, nor ever have been. The obstacle is, that the quantity of them that can be produced upon a given spot of ground, at a given expense, is of not so much value as the production on the same spot, at the same expense, of some other commodity. The good management, we are bid to expect from the *'wisdom of Administration'* consists in the taxing the one part of the community, in order to make a purse to pay another part, for raising a less profitable crop, instead of a more profitable one. The amount of the bounty thus bestowed, of the tax thus wisely imposed and applied, constitutes pretty nearly what, according to my calculation, would be the *loss* by this wise measure. 'No,' says this harbinger of wisdom, 'it is only the deduction from the gain: for the saving of the immense sums which we now pay for hemp, and so forth, would be so much *clear gain*.' And true he says, if the corn, and other productions which, by the supposition, would otherwise have been raised on the same *land* to a *greater* value, would sell for *nothing*" (X, 211).

These are economic considerations. But Bentham did not think that the problems of foreign trade could be adequately discussed without reference to the still more essential and fateful problems of war and peace. It shocked him to see international commerce callously treated as a cause of strife between the nations, while he regarded it as a signal proof of the underlying harmony of interests among them. "Why attempt to 'annihilate', or by violence even to 'lessen', the influence of France in Sweden, in Turkey, or anywhere else? With what hope? with what justice? with what reason? to what use? In what instance, and in what country, has France been attempting to abuse it? Do we feel, have we lately felt, in the Levant or elsewhere, any want of influence? Have we met with any hinderance there, from selling what we had to sell, from buying what we wanted to buy, except in the way of fair and peaceable competition? Are the French never to be permitted to buy anything but of us? How are they to buy anything of us, without being allowed to get anything to pay for it with? Is it so sure a thing that the French will never have hereafter any troops in their armies, any money in their treasures, any resentment of injuries in their bosoms, and that they will always lie still to be trampled upon by the present Administration, and the present Administration's Trumpeter? If to keep them from starving, we can prevail upon our generosity to indulge them in a small pittance of trade anywhere, can we find a more proper field for indulgence than one to which they are twice as near as we are? Is not that superior vicinity sufficient to account for whatever superiority their trade has over ours, without recurring to the unsupported supposition of superiority of influence? Can the sum total of our own trade, at any period, be extended beyond the limits which the quantity of our capital at that period has set to it? Can the sum total of the trade of France be prevented from assuming the extension which the quantity of her capital allows of? Is it to be taken for granted without proof, and against manifest probability, that a trade for which we have farther to go than the French have, must be more profitable than others for which we have not so far to go as they have? Can the wisdom of grasping at any particular branch of trade be shown any otherwise, than by showing that in that trade the gains are greater, or the expense less, than in any other branch?—and is there not in the breasts, and in the heads of merchants, a principle that will lead them to find out the most lucrative, without their being whipped to it, or whistled to it, by the 'wisdom of the present administration'? If the principles I have been reviewing were to be pursued by all who have as good a right to pursue them as we have, a war of all against all would be the consequence, and the race of man would be swept from off the earth" (X, 211).

The political implications of this strong-worded attack on the government become abundantly clear when we read it in conjunction with a letter to Lord Lansdowne dated June 17, 1789—two days after the appearance of the third epistle to the *Public Advertiser*. It runs as follows:[1] "Come, my dear Lord, your pioneer has broke ground, and now is the time for you to bring up your battering cannon. The inclosed will shew you *de quoi il s'agit* now. To heap coals of fire upon Pitt's head, I have written him a letter (bullying because, being a minister, it would not have been decent to write to

---

[1] Quoted here according to a draft preserved in the University College collection (CLXIX, 153). There is no reason to believe that the letter was changed or was not sent.

him otherwise) inclosing duplicates of the inclosed, but offering a quiet memorial if he will read it, and giving him a day to answer on pain of war. He will let the day pass: and then—the Lord hath delivered him into your hands: and the milk of my memorial turns into the *aqua fortis* of a party pamphlet. Tactics[1] have accordingly been suspended, spite of Mirabeau's *'vive impatience'*.—I am ashamed to confess, even to you, how much the wish to see you employed at a time that employment is so necessary, has contributed to this digression of mine" (U.C. CLXIX, 153).

The letter to Pitt was couched in the following terms: "Sir—I fear, or rather hope, the subject of continental connections and commercial preferences has not yet had the benefit of your maturest thoughts. The enclosed papers,[2] if they fail of inducing on your part a similar suspicion, will serve at least to shew that I am in earnest. If you will read a *quiet* memorial from me on the subject, I will write one. If you will then tell me what, if any impression, it has made upon your mind, we shall be quits. There are enough who think with me in this matter, and who, had I then been at leisure, would have brought it on before now, in places where you would have attended to it. I say to them, that of two improbable things, persuading you out of this system and forcing you from it, the former is the quickest and the least improbable. Silence will after . . .[3] be deemed an answer. My recourse must then be to the good people of the country" (U.C. CLXIX, 154).

As it seems, Pitt "let the day pass". Did Bentham have "recourse . . . to the good people of the country"? He almost did. As so often, he began the threatened party pamphlet but had not the stamina to finish it. That it was meant to be *aqua fortis* can be seen from the following passage: "If malevolence and maleficence are proofs of wisdom, Mr. Pitt's title to that attribute will appear unquestionable. If the wisdom be the more sublime, the more gratuitous the mischief,

---

[1] Cf. "Essay on Political Tactics," Bowring II, pp. 299-373—a work written for the French to help them develop a sound technique of parliamentary discussion. The French translation is entitled "Tactique des Assemblées Législatives", the German "Taktik oder Theorie des Geschaeftsganges in deliberierenden Volksstaendeversamm-lungen". These titles suggest more clearly than the English one what problems are discussed in the book.

[2] That the papers sent to Pitt were copies of the *Public Advertiser* is clear not only from the dates as given in the text, but is also proved—and more directly still—by a remark Bentham made to Bowring when he related the story: "I sent the two Anti-Machiavels to Pitt the second. The war was given up" (X, 212).

[3] The draft contains no concrete date.

his glory will appear so much the more splendid. Wickedness is but too apt to be mistaken for greatness, and Mr. Pitt seems to have fallen into that mistake. Part of this mischief appears to have been [committed] in pursuit of an object: an object though chosen erroneously, yet chosen upon a principle of error too general not to be deemed venial. But the greater part appears to have been done without any object whatsoever, good or bad, reasonable or unreasonable, and for the pure love of mischief, if there be such a principle in human nature, or at least from the glory, whatever it be, that is to be had from the being seen to have done mischief, when the mischief is upon a large scale" (U.C. XVII, 50).

Apart from Pitt, Lord Sheffield was also to be publicly attacked. In Pitt, Bentham meant to hit the ruling political clique; in Lord Sheffield, the prevalent economic ideology. Sheffield's *Observations on the Commerce of the American States* had had phenomenal success. First published in 1783, a sixth edition had been reached by 1784. It was a proposal to modify the Navigation Laws for the benefit of the United States which had drawn this writer out: he would not hear of such a measure. He managed to discredit it and to bring it to fall. "The Navigation Act, the palladium of Britain, was defended and perhaps saved by his pen."[1] "That a Lord should think well, or reason well, is too much to expect," Bentham says; and he adds, in a malicious allusion to the recent date of Sheffield's peerage:[2] "Too much not only of a hereditary Lord, but of a new made one." Still, the tune of this part of the fragment is comparatively quiet. Bentham allows that his adversary is "a writer to whom Great Britain, Ireland, America, the world in general are under very eminent obligations". The three sheets of text preserved in the University College collection (XVII, 51-53) contain too little to show Bentham's line of attack; but it is clear what he had to say against an author who had defended "the palladium of Britain", the Navigation Act.

It is characteristic of Bentham that he meant to pour his *aqua fortis* not only over Pitt's head, but destined also a few drops for Lord Sheffield: characteristic because party pamphleteering was not really his *métier*, however much polemic writing was his *force*. He

---

[1]Gibbon in his "Memoirs". Cf. *Memoirs of the Life and Writings of Edward Gibbon, Esq., composed by himself,* London, 1827, I, 242.

[2]Jan. 9, 1781. Cf. *Complete Peerage of England, Scotland, Ireland, Great Britain and the United Kingdom,* 1896, vol. VII, p. 124.

felt irresistibly drawn to those purer regions of fruitful discussion where argument is pitted against argument, and not pun against pun. However, even the task of turning Lord Sheffield's position did not really attract him: to controvert somebody else's opinions is useful after you have stated your own: before, it is pointless, even dangerous. Bentham felt this very clearly, and this is the reason why he concentrated on the more positive parts of his intended pamphlet, the passages printed here below. They belong to the best that has ever come from his pen: the style is simple and lucid, the argument close and cogent, and there is an idealism in it all which is irresistible and convincing.

In the University College collection the papers designated *Colonies and Navy* are divided into two bundles: XVII, 50-57, and XXV, 36-49: the impression of the cataloguer was that the former set dealt with political economy, the latter with international law. Yet these are two aspects which, for Bentham, always formed one: and the simple fact of the matter is that we have to do with one manuscript. To date the one part 1786, the other 1790, is sheer nonsense: all was written at the same time, perhaps in one week, perhaps even on one day. The sequence in which the papers must be arranged in order to yield a coherent argument—and arranging them was like solving a jig-saw puzzle—clearly proves it. Here it is: XXV, 36-38 (39 is a footnote to 36); 44; XVII, 54; XXV, 45, 46; XVII, 55, 56; XXV, 41, 40, 47, 48; XVII, 57; XXV, 49, 42, 43. A partial numeration of the sheets in Bentham's own hand has helped to establish this correct arrangement. XVII, 50 (on Pitt) and 51-53 (on Lord Sheffield) are obviously outwith the *ordo definitivus*. The reason why the papers got so divided and disordered is not far to seek: the second volume of Bowring's *Works* gives the clue to the correct answer. Bowring arbitrarily selected some sheets for inclusion in his edition and as arbitrarily rejected others: the selected pages were XXV, 36-48 and formed the bulk of part IV of the *Principles of International Law* entitled: "A plan for an universal and perpetual peace," not, however, without having been "corrected" and "improved". They are, of course, reprinted here as they came from their author's pen, in their original connection with those passages which did not find John Bowring's favour.

Anyone who has read the postscript to the *Defence of Usury* (cf. below pp. 195—204) and then turns to *Colonies and Navy* will feel at once that he is in exactly the same climate of thought. In fact, the latter pamphlet is essentially an elaboration of the guiding ideas first developed in the former materials. The reasoning is the same, only more confident, more blunt, as it were: the conclusion is also the same, though it is perhaps more guardedly stated. Colonies are economically useless and politically dangerous, Bentham shouts: do away with them and you can dismantle your navies: dismantle your navies and you give Europe peace, especially if you create at the same time an international tribunal and drop secret diplomacy—slogans which must have sounded well in 1790, though they do not sound quite so convincing in our somewhat sobered age. The centre-piece of the economic argument—enunciated in sub-point 1 of point 10— is again the thesis that trade is limited by capital—a "self-evident proposition" acknowledged by such authorities as Adam Smith and Lord Sheffield, but not consistently applied either by them or any- body else. Properly understood, it proves the inanity and mischievous- ness of all governmental attempts to "encourage trade": encourage any particular trade, and you discourage, necessarily and *pro tanto*, some other, because all you do is to redistribute the available capital; encourage colonial trade, and you discourage trade at home. True it is that one branch of trade may be more lucrative than another: but nobody has ever proved that the colonial trade is the most lucrative of all. Nor is it a good argument to say that the closing of this outlet for investment would induce a glut of capital at home: agriculture which creates its own market, and as wide a market as it needs, will always absorb any surplus that is available. And it is agriculture which is, comparatively speaking, the most beneficial of all branches of the national economy, if any can be pronounced more profitable than the rest. Thus the loss of colonial trade would be a gain to agricultural production and, consequently, *per saldo*, a gain to the nation as a whole. With this statement—still reminiscent of physio- cratic ideas, though no longer insisting on the reality of a *produit net*—closes the fragment which is in our hands.

An odd sheet of notes contained in the University College collection (XVII, 77) gives us some indication of the trend of the argument Bentham intended to put forward in the later parts of the pamphlet, the parts which apparently have remained unwritten. Britain, he seems to urge, need not be afraid to follow a bold and decided peace policy, a policy of unilateral disarmament, as the phrase would go today. "Our superiority of strength [is] not tem- porary. It is founded partly on superiority of ports &c. [and] partly on superiority of wealth. But this superiority must go on in an encreasing ratio" while all the time our "insular situation [is] guarding us against the ravages of war." "The anxiety about [our military] strength was formed at a time when it was not groundless"—when Britain was weak. But "at present", Bentham insists, "we keep that anxiety [only] through habit and prejudice". It is an outmoded sentiment and should disappear—the sooner the better.

Another problem Bentham intended to take up in this connection was the question why the export trade is looked upon with greater approval than other branches of economic activity. He thought he could discern three causes of this somewhat irrational preference: 1. "That branch is most conspicuous." It appeals to ministers because its favourable results are tangible, while its unfavourable consequences are much less so. Does an aggressive commercial policy lead to war? Even war does not unduly affect a statesman because he remains far from the battlefield. "A minister who would not kill one man with his own hand, does not mind the being the death of myriads by the hands of others, and at a distance." 2. Export, unlike home industry, is something in which politicians can glory. "It appears more their own work. What they have only drawn off, they fancy, or pretend to fancy, they create." 3. Exporters are more expert at wire-pulling than other social groups: "Merchants collecting in a body, have more influence than dispersed landholders." All these reasons (if reasons they can be called) explain why governments are so anxious to boost exports and to gain markets—but the substance of their arguments cannot stand critical examination.

Lastly, Bentham wished to pitch the opinion of two highly respected authors against the authority of Lord Sheffield. "Two original writers," he notes, "have gone before me in this line: Dean Tucker and Dr. Anderson. The object of the first was to persuade the world of the inutility of war[1] . . . of the second to shew the inutility of the colonies."[2] With both Bentham is most heartily agreed: but we hear no more about the way in which he planned to wind up his argument. The pamphlet is and remains a fragment, and however much we may regret it, we can wring no further information about it from the records of the past.

---

[1] Cf. especially *The Case of going to War for the sake of . . . Trade*, 1763, and *Cui Bono? Or, an Inquiry what Benefits can arise either to the English or the Americans . . . from the greatest Victories . . . in the present War*, 1781.

[2] Cf. especially *The Interest of Great Britain with regard to her American Colonies considered*, 1782.

THE "MANUAL OF POLITICAL ECONOMY"

In the conviction that trade is limited by capital, and that it cannot be artificially increased because capital does not admit of artificial augmentation, Bentham had gained a favourable vantage point from which he could survey the whole field of economic policy. His guiding principle admitted of general application and led with necessity to a consistent liberal theory. It was worked out in the year 1793, as it seems (though there is evidence that Bentham thought about the final form of his *opus* as late as Jan. 29, 1795), and is contained in the *Manual of Political Economy*—a *catalogue raisonné* as it were of the measures at the disposal of government for the support of trade.

The third volume of John Bowring's *Works of Jeremy Bentham* contains an item of this very title, but it has little to do with the book which Bentham intended to publish around the year 1795. The bulk of its material comes from a later manuscript on which Bentham was engaged after the turn of the century and with which he continued to play up to 1804, a manuscript for which he envisaged the title *Institute* rather than the designation *Manual* (cf. below, vol. III). Both writings were intended to be short surveys of the field of political economy and frankly didactic in intention—instruments for the education of the general public to clear thinking in economic matters. Yet there is a decided difference between the two treatises: in the *Manual* of 1795, Bentham discussed contemporary economic problems without bothering much about the difficulties raised by the operation of money: in 1804, in the *Institute,* it was these very difficulties, the deep question of the influence of the circulating medium on the increase of wealth, which preoccupied him above all others. For this reason it is quite inadmissible to jumble the two sets of papers together: it is like trying to build a power-station, partly on the basis of coal, partly on the basis of water-power: but that is precisely what Bowring did. It would be hard to find another editor so supremely unconcerned with the elementary principles of all editing. What he did was simply to insert into the text of the *Institute* a few pages of the original *Manual*—they are paragraphs 10-21 of chapter III in his numeration (*Works* III, pp. 57-65)—and to re-christen the whole *Manual* in the assumption that this title would go down better with the public. By divorcing the two manuscripts and reprinting them both in their entirety we have secured two fine works of great individuality, instead of one obscure medley of

D

disparate ideas which were originally separated from each other by ten years of intensive brain-work and mental development.

We are wont today, when we hear the word "manual", to think of a bulky tome in which all manner of detailed information can be conveniently found, a comprehensive encyclopædia of a special subject. In Bentham's mouth, the term has a somewhat different connotation. For him, a "manual" is less a "hand-book" than a *handy* book, a handy slender volume in which the gist of a scientific discipline can be found in a nutshell. Had this treatise come out, it would most probably have appeared in the guise of a *duodecimo*. The *Wealth of Nations*, on the other hand, had been planned and produced as a typical *quarto*, a *quarto* being the form habitually given to a work heavy with learning and carrying a considerable volume of detail and discussion.

In this difference Bentham saw part of the justification, of the *raison d'être*, of his intended *Manual*, as he explains in chapter, or paragraph, 1. In spite of the ten criticisms of Adam Smith which he puts forward there, he acknowledges that his own doctrine and that of the famous Scot very largely coincide. But he wants to be *concise* as well as systematically *comprehensive*, and that is a virtue of which the *Wealth of Nations* can hardly boast. Apart from this formal point, he strongly stresses his more utilitarian approach. The *Manual* is to be a guide to action, where the *Wealth of Nations* was pre-eminently a description of reality.

The next two chapters introduce the general thesis of the work: chapter 2 speaks of the reasons which make it unwise for the statesman to interfere with economic life; chapter 3 enumerates the ways in which such interference can be effected, and in particular establishes the distinction between "direct" and "indirect" encouragements which underlies Bentham's system and survey. Both chapters contain various definitions of which some seem no more than verbal, while others are really important and prove the acuteness and originality of Bentham's economic thought. To the former group belongs what he says on the term "income" or the term "trade"; to the latter count his definitions of wealth, capital and power.

Chapter 4, on the dependence of trade on capital, was undoubtedly meant to carry the burden of argument in this general part of the *Manual*. Unfortunately it does not seem to have been elaborated, or rather perfected, in the same way as the three foregoing chapters. There were, however, among these manuscripts various notes and pages which would have ultimately formed part of this important section, and they are presented here in what appears to be a reasonable order. Needless to say, the drift and gist of the argument is the same as that in the "Postscript" to the *Defence of Usury* and in *Colonies and Navy*, only that the exposition is more forceful, and also more primitive—the latter fact explicable by the purpose of the *Manual*, namely to be an introduction for all and sundry to the *arcana* of economic science.

The fifth and last chapter of this general part has an interest of its own. Keen as he was to cast away all outmoded economic enactments, Bentham realized that to excise anything from the body social into which it had grown, is bound to be a serious operation. We see here how right Halévy was when, in his *Growth of Philosophic Radicalism*, he emphasized the Tory sympathies of the young Bentham, who was, at this period, not so far from Burke as his later writings might suggest. Unfortunately, the chapter does no more than give a vague and general warning against over-hasty reforms. It is also noteworthy because it contains the first passage to discuss the possibility of an artificial formation of capital under governmental auspices, through enforced saving.

The next chapters, 6-18, form the bulk as well as the core of this little hand-book. They contain variations on a theme—the theme that government cannot favour one branch of trade unless it hampers another, because capital applied here must be withheld or withdrawn there—together with such other incidental arguments as may be brought to bear individually against the various measures discussed. The repetition of the main idea makes the whole somewhat dull reading: but this effect is unavoidable, not to say intended. Bentham had one point, and one point only, which he wanted to ram home: the *Manual* was to be an insistent sermon on this *unum necessarium*: and so repetitiveness lies in the very nature of the book.

Of special points worthy of closer attention, Bentham's attitude to the rate of interest in paragraph 6 should perhaps be noted. He speaks frankly as a *rentier*: forced saving increases the national stock of capital; an increased stock of capital is expressed in a lowered return for it; this lowered return reduces the incomes of the monied classes; and to that extent it is bad. Here again we hear the voice of a conservative policy concerned to preserve those strata who carry the traditions of the community, especially the landed gentry. Paragraph 8, on the other hand, discusses the possibility of a bounty on the production of staple foods—of a premium for the provision of "the most necessary of all necessaries"—food subsidies as we call them today, and here the merits of the measure "in the character of a measure of equalization" are conceded. Bentham may have been a Tory: but he loved the people all the same. Still, he does not really recommend food subsidies because he fears that, *via* the reduction of the capital stock nationally available, they will only tend to reduce wages and thus undo the good they are capable of doing. Behind his words we feel the wages-fund theory present as the decisive concept that determines his attitude.

It is clear from a study of Bentham's notes that the list of "improper measures" discussed would have been very much longer than the thirteen cases actually treated, if he had had the patience to elaborate the *Manual*. U.C. XVII, 62 contains a series of jottings which very briefly sketch the appropriate arguments, not only against "non-importation agreements" and "forbearance to tax exports", but also against several other stock recommendations of the mercantilistic programme: the prohibition of export of raw materials; the prohibition of export of tools; the prohibition of emigration of artificers; the general prohibition of export of capital; the prohibition of export of gold, silver, bullion, and coin; and, lastly, a less frequently discussed and advocated measure of governmental inter-ference, the prohibition of immigration of artificers. A further series of jottings reminiscent of this one, and partly covering the same ground, is found in XVII, 72. It adds to the above list: taxes on the export of capital, including absentee-taxes; bounties for the import of capital; fixation and reduction of the rate of interest; and, finally, a topic that was destined to loom large in Bentham's later thought, bounties for the production of capital, i.e., for saving, or, as he calls it, for "frugality". Here is an instance of Bentham's mode of reasoning which shows that it is essentially always the same:

"Prohib[ition] of Export of Raw Materials. 1. Adds nothing to wealth for the general reason. 2. Throws away the tax that might have been levied on foreigners. 3. In the case of wooll makes mutton dearer? 4. Either adds nothing to wealth or takes from it : Takes from it if the foreign nation, by dint of natural advantages, gets the thing cheaper."

It is perhaps worthy of note that in his discussion of the often advocated prohibition of the emigration of skilled workmen, Bentham uses social arguments alongside the economic ones on which he mainly relies: it would not only turn the country into a prison, but it would also be unjust because "it [would fa]vour the rich to the prejudice of the j[ourne]yman".

More interesting, of course, than the list of *non-agenda*—an ever-open and ever-lengthening series in every liberal mind—is Bentham's list of *agenda* of which only two items are treated more explicitly in the surviving manuscripts: In chapter 19, he advocates the granting of patents for new inventions even though, formally, a patent is a sort of monopoly. An inventor himself, he speaks on the subject with considerable warmth and in a way certain to carry conviction. From the point of view of economic theory, the most interesting passage in this context is the one in which labour is distinguished into mere physical exertion and "the skill or mental power displayed in the exercise of the bodily act". This division of the concept has far-reaching implications: it is bound to affect the definition of capital. Capital can either be thought of as akin to land, a kind of *thing* that is held in private property: or it can be conceived as a refinement of labour, a kind of *knowledge* that gives heightened command over the forces of nature. The former definition was the classical one: but the latter had its attractions for the left-wingers among the economists, such as Hodgskin and Thompson, and it was Bentham to whom they owed this very welcome conception.[1] In favouring patents, copyrights, and the like, Bentham showed that he was a liberal with a difference, and not a blind doctrinaire: extremists like Francesco Ferrara would have disapproved of this section of the *Manual*. The same applies to chapter 20 where the building up, by the public hand, of corn magazines is defended, and even by implication demanded, as a measure of public security and governmental prudence. This *faciendum* was very near to Bentham's heart. It is further elaborated in some preliminary notes which show the general drift of his mind even better than this chapter 20. The following three sentences, though they are short and bare, certainly express his deliberate and well-considered *desiderata*: "1. Prohibition of export of the materials of bread when the price is above what is necessary to indemnify the growers against gluts. 2. Establishment of magazines not to be opened except in time of dearth greater than what the speculations of merchants provide against (except to change the corn). 3. Fixation of the prices of ordinary sorts of bread" (64). These are rather incisive

---

[1]Cf. W. Stark, *The Ideal Foundations of Economic Thought*, ch. II.

steps, but they belong to Bentham's best-thought-out pieces of social
and economic policy, and they come to the fore again later in his
pamphlet of 1801, *Defence of a Maximum.*

Still, although Bentham recommended corn magazines, he was, as
a true liberal, anxious to minimize the role to be played by government even in this business. If he had worked out this chapter he
would have appended some proviso of this kind to his recommendation. This can be seen from a note on XVII, 66: "In case of
magazin[ing], the more was [ma]gazined by [gov]ernment, the [less]
would be by individuals. The only advantage, then, would be the
confining it to the providing for a degree of scarcity higher than any
to which the speculations of individuals extend".

Important as these deviations from the narrow path of liberal
theory are, they are by no means the only ones that occupied
Bentham's mind. The preliminary notes contain many further
measures which he intended to advocate. XVII, 64 and 65 allow us
to discern more fully what he thought the government *could* do
and *should* do for general welfare and opulence.

There are first of all certain measures of general legislation familiar
from Bentham's jurisprudential writings which he wanted to press
for here in the *Manual*: "1. Laws providing security for the fruits of
industry. 2. Laws gently tending to equalisation (general). 3. Laws
for securing the persons and properties of men against damage
through delinquency or through calamity. [4.] Treaties ensuring
against the sudden application of new discouragements, or sudden
removal of old encouragements" (64). All these suggestions belong, as
has been indicated, to Bentham's usual stock-in-trade. But the next
set of suggestions is more specifically economic and not treated
expressly anywhere else, though it is, of course, quite in line with
Bentham's general tenor of thought. "Facienda: 1. Permission of
Commandite. 2. Incorporations for new projects. NB. This is only
repealing a Common Law restriction. 3. Instruction didactic: Courses
of lectures. 4. Courses of experiments. 5. Instruction divulgative:
Publication of prices current. History of success of experiments in
manufactures or in agriculture. 6. Patents for inventions. History of
Patents. 7. Conversion of ecclesiastical and manorial burthens into
redeemable rent-charges. 8. Abolition of institutions tending to withdraw capitals from production to consumption" (64[1]). The last sug-

---

[1]Some of these points are also mentioned on XVII, 60.

gestion sounds somewhat indefinite and elastic: Bentham would, no doubt, have interpreted it in a rather restrictive sense.

There are, furthermore, two *"addenda"* to these "eligible modes of encouragement", which are both technical in character. The one deals with technological problems in the narrower sense of the word, the other rather with questions of export technique and financial steering. Here is the former list of ideas: "[1.] Inventing methods of applying the natural *primum mobiles* with encreased advantage: *1.* Men's force. 2. Animal. 3. Water. 4. Air. 5. Artificial vision. 2. Diminishing the unhealthiness or disgustfulness of certain trades" (64). Bentham probably thought that the government should foster research along these lines. He did not expect the individual always to play the part of the forlorn hope of technical advancement. The second set of suggestions is still less in line with the free-trade point of view. It reads as follows: "1. Securing of existing markets for manufactory— with or without competition—foreign or colonial. 2. Acquisition of new markets—with or without competition—foreign or colonial" (65). How far could Bentham have gone in this respect without abandoning the definite position he had taken up in *Colonies and Navy*?

An expedient which Bentham could advocate with less danger of self-contradiction concerns the mobilization of capital. He notes under "modes of encouragement", along with the above, an "encrease of transportable capital by converting an untransportable into [a] transportable by making a transportable security for, or representation of, untransportable" (65). In a way a very characteristic aim— characteristic both of the man and the period, always ready to favour commerce and industry at the expense of landed property. The subject touched here occupied Bentham again later on, when he wrote his two *Letters on the Stock Note Plan* (cf. vol. II, Introduction), and also, to a certain extent, when he drafted his great work on *Circulating Annuities*.

It is a matter of vain regret that Bentham did not further elaborate some of these points which would have enabled us to discern more clearly the place he occupied in the history of liberalistic thought. But what we possess is enough to produce a shortened version at any rate of the *Manual* as it was thought out and planned by its author.

For the proper arrangement of the given material, XVII, 64 and 65 were again of great assistance. Sheet 65—entitled *Manual. Books and Chapters* and dated 29 Jan. 1795—contains an indication of how Bentham wanted to draw up the general part of his work. Sheet 64—

Tabular View — gives a list of "encouragements direct" and "encouragements indirect" which could also be utilized, especially as it tallied more or less with 65: *Encouragement : Ineligible Modes*. The arrangement here adopted is a combination of both these tentative summaries. But the passage on 65 which has helped to elaborate a table of contents that would have been acceptable to Bentham, has a much wider interest. It shows the whole field he meant to cover and would have covered if he had had the stamina to see his project through. The reader who is interested in the detail will find it below, in the Summary of the manuscripts which were not *in toto* included in this edition.[1]

We have seen above that the *Defence of Usury*, for all its finished form, was no more than a stop on a road leading to deeper and deeper economic insight, and to wider and wider economic knowledge. Exactly the same is true of the *Manual*. Hardly had Bentham half elaborated it when his interest overflowed the borders he had measured out for himself, and took hold of further problems in the fields beyond. Two sheets of rough notes make it possible for us to follow from afar this mental development: the one deals with paper money, the other with population—both topics which can hardly have had a place in the earlier plans for the drafting of the *Manual*.

The notes on paper money, as notes which Bentham jotted down for his own use, are not as clear as one could wish. Yet a few decisive ideas stand out quite clearly. To the salient question whether money in general, and paper money in particular, can be made an instrument for the increase of capital, and hence of wealth, Bentham gives, within limits, a positive answer. Hume had argued that a doubling of everybody's £.s.d. would leave all as it was before. Bentham, on the other hand, sees at least two possible consequences: one, that some of the added coin would be melted down and thus augment the national stock of wealth in the shape of knives, forks, spoons, silver, and the like; the other that, where there is some unemployment, the unemployed would be drawn into the process of production and increase output, because of the "extra pay which the money-holders would be enabled to give"—certainly an interesting suggestion. At the same time Bentham recognizes that the issue of additional paper money has the effects of a tax, or rather of two taxes, one on capital, through the devaluation of it, the other on consumption, through the

---

[1] Cf. vol. III, end.

rise of prices. These facets of economic theory were destined to become Bentham's main preoccupation after September 1800 and loom large in such works as *Paper Mischief [Exposed]* and *The True Alarm*.

If this series of notes points to regions as yet uncharted and unexplored, the passage on population is more or less of a piece with the bulk of the *Manual*. The growth of population ought not to be artificially fostered by governmental interference: nature will do what is needed by her own devices: nor could a governmental measure reasonably hope for lasting success as the numbers of a nation are in the long run determined by its capital (that is, its wages-fund) which cannot be increased at will. All this is only a special version of the general thesis underlying the *Manual*. Connected with these few lines is a defence of the legitimacy of sexual intercourse as a pleasurable experience, even if it does not serve for procreation, even if it is positively unnatural. It is amusing to see that Bentham's delicacy induced him to express these ideas in Latin. The economist need not give them more than a passing glance[1]: Bentham speaks here, not as a social theorist, but as a teacher of morals (or, as some would say with equal justification, as a teacher of immorality).

That the *Manual* did not appear as an independent work during Bentham's life-time is only partially his fault. Always looking out towards the wider world as his proper field of operation, Bentham soon conceived the idea of publishing in French before publishing in English, and one sheet (U.C. XVII, 16), unfortunately so faded that it cannot now be deciphered, is headed *Manuel d'Economie Politique —Avant propos—Préface*. The work of translating and editing was entrusted to Etienne Dumont who, in 1802, brought out Bentham's *Traités de Législation* and thus became the co-author of his fame on

---

[1]The subject is more fully explored elsewhere. Cf. Ogden's edition of the *Theory of Legislation*, pp. 473-497, esp. 486-87. In sharp opposition to the traditional attitude of mercantilism, Bentham claims that infanticide is no crime. Cf. ib. pp. 479 and 487. Cf. also, in *Supply without Burthen* below, paragraph 3, and esp. p. 295, footnote (*). Cf. however, *Works* I, 167, where a different opinion on this subject is expressed. Ogden tells us (l.c. 474 and 519) that Bentham was definitely converted by Malthus in 1802. This seems to be correct. It is true that, in *Scotch Reform*, a work published in 1808, Bentham speaks somewhat disparagingly of Malthus's "inflexibility" and "bitter remedy" (cf. *Works* V, p. 21), but the opinions discernible in the *Constitutional Code*, one of the maturest works, are clearly malthusian (cf. *Works* IX, pp. 372 and 443).

the European continent. He translated a number of the manuscripts[1] and published some detached fragments in the *Bibliothèque Britannique,* but postponed the actual editing from year to year until the matter had become altogether stale. It was only in 1811 that he included a more substantial part of the *Manual* material in his *Théorie des Peines et des Récompenses* (book IV — *Des encouragemens par rapport à l'industrie et au commerce*). When Richard Smith rendered this work into English in 1825, the economic section of it was translated along with the rest and so emerged again in its native guise after having undergone a double transformation. It is still, of course, Bentham according to the spirit, but it is certainly no longer Bentham according to the letter and so must needs remain outside a critical edition such as this. The loss is slight: it would be difficult to find in the *Rationale of Reward* a single idea which is not contained in any of the writings which we have collected here.[2]

"ESCHEAT VICE TAXATION"

The definite position taken up in the *Manual of Political Economy* on matters of economic policy, implied necessarily a no less definite attitude to the problems of taxation. If governmental interference with economic life is detrimental to the nation concerned, it ought to be minimized; and if it is minimized, a correspondent reduction of the burden of taxation follows of course, as a postulate of sheer common sense. The thesis that taxation is an evil in itself was fundamental to Bentham's thought—as fundamental as it is to the conviction of every tax-payer, or even more so. "Exercised at a man's own expence, liberality may be, or may not be, according to circumstances, a virtue," he writes in one connection (*Works* II, 437). "Exercised at the expence of the public, it never can be anything better than vice." In another passage he elaborates an idea which is also contained in the *Manual,* that there is a good "mode of estimating the justness of any public expenditure" which should be done in the following way:

"Compare the amount of the proposed expenditure with an equal

---

[1] For detail see the description of the Dumont papers at the end of vol. III.

[2] Of the sixteen chapters in Dumont's and Smith's book IV, nine (II-X) run roughly parallel to our text; the remaining seven (I and XI-XVI) do not, but they contain some passages which our text also contains, some other passages which are extracts of later works from Bentham's pen (cf. esp. the footnote on p. 312), and sentences which look very much like interpolations by Dumont, so that the omission of genuine Bentham material cannot possibly amount to much.

portion of the produce of the most vexatious and burthensome tax. In this country, for example, let the comparison be made with the produce of the tax on law proceedings, whose effect is the placing of the great majority of the people in a state of outlawry. The option lies between the abolition of this tax and the proposed employment of its produce. They thus become two rival services. It is a severe test for frivolous expences, but it is strictly just. How disgraceful does wasteful luxury appear in the budget, when thus put in competition with the good whose place it occupies, or the evil of which it prevents the cure!

"From these observations the practical conclusion is, that the matter of reward being all of it costly, none of it ought to be thrown away. This precious matter is like the dew: not a drop of it falls upon the earth which has not previously been drawn up from it. An upright sovereign therefore gives nothing. He buys or he sells. His benevolence consists in economy. Would you praise him for generosity? Praise also the guardian who lavishes among his servants the property of his pupils" (*Works* II, 202).

Such, not unnaturally, is Bentham's fundamental attitude. But the dry principle contained in passages like these was to him a point of departure rather than a point of arrival. He had more to teach than just economy. A work, or even works, on taxation must have been on his programme very early on—indeed, for a man of his kidney, this field of endeavour must have had a more or less irresistible attraction. Already in 1783, he is collecting various materials. We find him hunting for a copy of the *Mémoires concernant les Droits et Impositions en Europe,* mentioned in Adam Smith's *Wealth of Nations* (book V, chapter 1) as having been compiled by order of the French Court for the use of a commission that had been appointed to consider the reform of the public finances of France (*Works* X, 126). There is no saying how many tomes of a similar import he may have devoured. His aim was, first of all, to get a comprehensive idea of the public burdens actually in force in the civilized world, and to compile, for his own benefit and satisfaction, a tabular list of them that would allow him to survey the whole field at one glance. The *Analytical View or Summary Sketch of Financial Resources employed and employable* which is printed below, is the fruit of these labours. It plainly speaks for itself and is an eloquent witness to Bentham's mental discipline which never rested until it had reduced chaos to system and confusion to clarity.

The "order of preference" which he wanted to work out is nowhere to be found among the existing papers[1] although we are surely justified in surmising that point II of the *Analytical View* ranges the impositions on ability according to their relative undesirability. Then, there are one or two further passages which allow us, to a certain degree, to fill this unfortunate gap. In *Supply without Burthen* we find, towards the end of paragraph 6, a list of the impositions which Bentham thought most execrable. In chapter 7 of the *Proposal for a Mode of Taxation* we get a few further hints (cf. below, p. 401). In *A Protest against Law-taxes*, he says: "The best of all are taxes on consumption, because not only do they fall nowhere without finding some ability to pay them; but where necessaries are out of the question, they fall on nobody who has not the option of not paying them if he does not choose it. Taxes on property, and those on transfer of property, such as those on contracts relative to property, are the next best: because though they are not optional like the former, they may be so selected as never to call for money but where there is ability, nay even ample ability, to pay them" (*Works* II, 580). This is, at any rate, one definite indication of comparative merits and demerits in the various modes of taxation. The important proviso against taxing necessaries is also expressed in another fragment we possess. "Taxes on the necessaries of life are improper: being payable in the first instance, ability or no ability: and it may be many years before they can be thrown off upon classes endowed [?] with ability, by a rise in the wages of labour" (U.C. CLXVI, 39). The only commodities of universal consumption and in use among the poorer classes which Bentham would have taxed, for very obvious reasons, were "articles unfavourable to cleanliness", such as "tobacco smoked" (ib.).

These few scraps are, of course, quite insufficient to show a well-reasoned-out "order of preference" among the "financial resources employed and employable". But we must not be surprised if Bentham's manuscripts yield no more information on this point. To establish such an order of preference he would have considered effort wasted and labour lost. What is there to pick and choose where the two alternatives open to a man are the Devil and Beelzebub? If all taxes are evil, it is necessary to avoid them all, or rather to abolish them all, and to substitute for taxation an entirely different source of

---

[1] A short passage in the Genevan collection (LI, 284) does no more than touch the outer fringe of this great subject. Cf. the text at the end of vol. III, in the description of the material excluded from the present edition.

public revenue. It was this intriguing problem—which he was very far from regarding as insoluble—to which our author devoted all his ingeniousness in 1794, after he had sketched out, and laid aside, the *Manual of Political Economy*.

By this time Bentham had not yet given up all faith in the decency and reasonableness of the men in power: he still hoped to win them over to his schemes of political reconstruction and reform. He decided to put his financial plans before them, and so we find him, on Oct. 1st, 1794, writing to Charles Long, Pitt's co-Secretary to the Treasury, in his habitual half-serious, half-playful vein: "You are now a holiday-making . . . To vary your pastime, which, perhaps, may be found not unsuitable to the place, permit me to present you with a riddle. What is that pecuniary resource, of which the tenth part would be a tax, and that a heavy one, while the whole is no tax, and would not be felt by anybody?" The solution, Bentham says, lies with the copyist, and will be sent in due course—certainly a very clever way of announcing an essay on so dry a subject. Twelve days later the "solution"—the pamphlet *Supply without Burthen, or Escheat vice Taxation*—seems to have been forwarded to Long. "On the former occasion," Bentham writes (Oct. 13), "I trespassed on the gravity of your situation by the present of a riddle. Permit me now to reconduct you to the style of the subject by a grave apophthegm — *Supply without burthen is victory without blood*. The application of it is what I have been pushing as far as time and faculties would carry me" (*Works* X, 303).

"Supply without burthen is victory without blood." Bentham would have been clearer if, instead of this totally un-Benthamic flourish, he had varied the title of his little book and written: "Substitute escheat for taxation, and you will achieve financial supply without burden to the community." For this is the essential idea in which he wished to interest Charles Long, and, through him, the Cabinet. The feudal law of escheat, he argues, is nearly dead, but not quite: it could be revived and made a copious source of public revenue. Nobody would wish to interfere with a child's right to inherit from his parents and *vice versa*; or with a widowed wife's right to inherit from her husband and *vice versa*; or even with the right of brothers and sisters to inherit from each other. But what about seventh cousins, or uncles six times removed? Here the link of relationship and affection is so tenuous that the law can easily and properly dissolve it, at any rate in part. This is Bentham's guiding idea. Here is his proposal in a nutshell, summed up in his own words: "All estates to be escheatable alike, real as well as personal: immoveable as well as moveable: all that do not consist of ready money or money in the funds to be sold, as in cases of bankruptcy. The deceased leaving neither husband nor lineal relation, brother nor sister, the estate to be divided into two equal portions: the one to fall to the public, the other to remain subject to the power of bequest, as to the produce in ready money. In case of intestacy, the whole property to devolve on the public, where there is no nearer relative than first cousin. The administration to devolve on the public officer, in all cases, where the public has any share. No executor nor ordinary administrator to be allowed. This, that the interest of the public may be in sure hands" (U.C. XX, 58). Paragraph 1 of the pamphlet expounds these principles more fully and gives the reasons—mostly of a psychological nature—why this particular extension and limitation of the law of escheat is advocated.

In paragraph 2 we get a good idea of the book which Bentham originally wanted to write on the subject. It would have been a comprehensive treatment of the project, its possibilities and its problems, from every conceivable angle, practical, psychological, jurisprudential, political, historical, administrative, and economic alike. As usual, this *magnum opus* was never completed; what we possess in print is only a sort of preview laid before the Secretary of the Treasury, and published the year after, when the plan to write a larger work was already virtually given up.[1] It would have been completed, perhaps, if Charles Long had shown more interest in the idea: but he did not, and Bentham's enthusiasm died down as quickly as it had flared up, like a fire which is well kindled but badly fed. Some materials for the "body of the work" were, however, completed, and are printed below, so far as they deserve to be printed for their intrinsic interest.

Paragraph 3 is a vivid account of the supposed advantages of the measure. Bentham was convinced that he had suggested the best conceivable mode of supplying the Exchequer, and here he tells us why. Give a man his great-uncle's heritage and take from him, by way of taxation, a tenth, or a hundredth, or a thousandth of it, and you cause a sensation of loss, of deprivation, and of pain, because he

---

[1] Incidentally, even the pamphlet does not fulfil what it promises: there are no "strictures on the taxes on collateral succession, comprised in the budget of 7th Dec. 1795", even though one additional footnote is dated Dec. 9, 1795.

has to give up what he has come to regard as his own: direct the whole of that inheritance to the Treasury, by reviving the law of escheat, and you can keep the whole without causing any sensation of loss, of deprivation, or of pain, as soon as the law is promulgated and universally understood. The pain in question is essentially expectation thwarted: where escheat is established, expectation cannot be thwarted because it cannot be aroused in the first place, it cannot exist, since "expectation, as far as the law can be kept present to men's minds, follows with undeviating obsequiousness the finger of the law"; it is led by the law, as Bentham says in paragraph 8, as by a "silken string".

This paragraph 3 is the climax of this little work; what follows is definitely anti-climax. Paragraph 4 compares the proposed measure more particularly with death duties, especially the contemporary ones; paragraph 5 tries to assess the probable yield; paragraph 6 suggests that the extra money flowing in should be used, partly to reduce the national debt, and partly to abolish obnoxious taxes. Paragraph 7 is a list of objections, written in what we should call today telegraphic style. (More about this aspect anon.) The remaining three paragraphs are devoted to the legal side of the proposal: paragraph 8 claims that it would bring about a state of affairs that would be more satisfactory than the existing law; paragraph 9 points to the feudal precedent but is anxious to convince the reader that the new version of escheat would be materially sounder than the old; and in paragraph 10 Blackstone's opinion—"this muddy source of argument"—is explored. Amusingly enough, Blackstone is at the same time quoted as an authority and derided: it was impossible, it seems, for Bentham to do the one without doing the other.

Bentham himself has explained how he came to conceive this curious proposal. "It presented itself," he says in a stray sheet, probably prepared for the intended preface, "about ten or twelve years ago in the course of an enquiry which had for its subject the business of legislation in matters of civil law, and for its object the ascertaining by what means [and] how far the comparatively inferior ends of extra-security for subsistence, opulence, and equality might be attained in the utmost degree of perfection without prejudice to the superior interests of security, in comparison of which every other blessing is but a feather in the political scale. Traversing in the course of this enquiry the ground of post-obituary succession and inheritance, weighing the claims of relatives of different degrees and investigating the reasons by which, on the ground of utility, those claims appeared respectively to be supported, I found the force of those reasons, grounded as they were on the wants of individuals, growing weaker and weaker at every step of distance from the source, till by degrees they appeared so faint as to be capable of yielding without repugnance to any regulation that might be suggested by the necessity of providing for the common exigencies of the whole state. First to children, for all sorts of reasons: then to grandchildren [or] other descendants, for the whole or a part of those reasons, but acting with diminished force: then to parents with less force of reason, then to their descendants, and so on: till at last coming to grandparents and their descendants below the uncle, the force of the final causes seemed so weak as to be capable of yielding to the slightest call of utility from any extrinsic quarter. What to do with the inheritance when even uncles and aunts are wanting?—as well give it to any body almost as to cousins. Here then a fund seemed to present itself without a claimant in point of serious exigency, applicable consequently without particular inconvenience to the general exigencies of the state" (U.C. XX, 180-181).

But the inspiration of the proposal was by no means purely fiscal. This is clear from the very reference to the *Principles of the Civil Code,* a book which C. K. Ogden has rightly described as "a treatise on sociology" no less than "a treatise on jurisprudence" (*The Theory of Legislation,* ed. 1931, p. IX). Bentham was painfully aware of the incompatibility of his two main ideals: security—i.e. liberty—and equality. Liberty means liberty to rise in the world, to accumulate wealth: it means liberty to destroy equality. How, then, can equality be preserved without unduly restraining liberty? Bentham saw only one way out: to dam in, as far as feasible, the right to inherit, the main cause of the growing inequalities in every society.[1] As far as feasible: the proviso is essential, because there can be no freedom without the right of bequest, and no family life without parental provision for the children. But the partial disinheritance of *distant* relations *is* feasible without undue hardship and that is the very measure which, in a fiscal guise, Bentham is suggesting here. Seen in this light, the proposal put forward in *Escheat vice Taxation* is a measure of social reform as much as a measure of public finance. But

---

[1]The point, it is hoped, is clearly brought out in the author's contribution to *The Economic Journal,* 1941, pp. 56-79, entitled "Liberty and Equality, or Jeremy Bentham as an Economist." Cf. esp. p. 78.

this is a point which, understandably, Bentham did not care to emphasize.

The chapter which caused Bentham by far the greatest difficulties, is the one numbered 5 in the published pamphlet, and entitled *Produce*. Like so many others in similar circumstances since, he found it impossible to form a clear idea of the magnitudes involved in his financial plan, and even Arthur Young, to whom he turned for help in his quandary, after he had ransacked all his books for the precious—alas! so elusive—data, could not give him much satisfaction. "I have," Bentham writes, "a sort of floating recollection of a calculation, so circumstanced, either in point of authority or argument as to carry weight with it, in which the total value of the landed property in this country (Scotland, I believe, included) was reckoned at a thousand millions, and that of the moveable property at either a thousand millions or twelve hundred millions." Bentham was under the misapprehension that he had taken these figures from Young's work on France;[1] but on referring to it, he found no explicit estimates in it, and what he found was apt to unsettle his mind rather than to put it at ease. "The Land-Tax at 4 s I find, you suppose, were it to be equal all over the country, (it is of England only, I believe, that you speak), would be equivalent to as much as 3 s: on which supposition the rental (the tax at 4 s producing no more than 2,000,000) would amount to no more than £ 13,000,000, nor, consequently, the value at so many years purchase, say 28, to more than 364,000,000; or at 30 to 390,000,000; to which, in order to complete the calculation of the landed property of Great Britain, that of Scotland would have to be added" (X, 302). What is the truth of the matter? Bentham asked Young's guidance on three particular points: he wanted "1. A calculation . . . of the value of the landed property of Great Britain . . . 2. Do. of the value of the personal, i.e. moveable property of Great Britain. 3. The amount of the population of Great Britain". It is clear that he needed these data if he wanted to form an idea, however vague, of what his plan to revive the law of escheat would yield to the Treasury in hard cash. Young's answer (dated Oct. 5) did not give him exactly what he was out to get. "I take the rental of England to be twenty-four millions, exclusive of houses, and the annual product of timber, mines, &c." Young writes. "Houses

---

[1] *Travels during the years 1787, 1788, 1789 and 1790 undertaken more particularly with a view of ascertaining the Cultivation, Wealth, Resources, and National Property of the Kingdom of France.* 2 vols., vol. I 1792, and vol. II 1794.

E

—twelve years' purchase. No data strike me at present to discover the rental, but these are questions I have not of late given my mind to" (*Works* X, 302 seq.).

How was Bentham ever to succeed in this calculation, if even the great Young found it beyond his powers? He could not succeed, of course, but he had a good try. It is reflected in the pages entitled *Calculation of the Produce* which are printed below from the materials contained in box XX of the University College collection. They show, at any rate, how and why he arrived at an estimate between £2,000,000 and £3,000,000 p.a., the figures ultimately published. Measured by up-to-date standards, this attempt to compute the value and the movement of the national wealth of Great Britain must appear primitive and fumbling. But it should not be forgotten that Bentham had neither reliable statistical figures nor elaborate statistical methods at his disposal, and if this is fully taken into account, his effort will have to be acknowledged as a piece of brave and clever pioneering.

A chapter which occurs in nearly all Bentham's writings, and which he was always anxious to think out and to write down, is the chapter on objections. However much he was convinced of their reasonableness and utility, Bentham never expected that his proposals would be accepted without demur, and he wanted to be ready for the discussion which he apprehended would have to come before their final adoption. To this apprehension we owe a comparatively well-worked-out chapter here. It is interesting on several accounts.

Among the thirteen objections taken up and refuted, three major groups can be distinguished. II-IV may be characterized as historical, VI-IX as politico-administrative, and X-XIII as economic. The remaining two, I and V, are jurisprudential. The antiquarian or historical group throws light on an aspect of Bentham's world-view which is little in evidence and may have escaped the attention even of his closer students. What was Bentham's attitude to history? He was inclined, of course, as so many of his stamp, to think in terms of progress: but his psychological theory, namely, that man, by dint of his physical constitution, is always and everywhere out to maximize his happiness, acted as a check on this opinion. Even in the past, he felt, men must have been reasonable and made the best of their possibilities. Thus an element of relativism came in which is displayed here,[1] in the discussion of the mediæval institution of escheat and its gradual extinction. Here again, Bentham moves near to Burke, and this is particularly obvious under head IV where the usefulness of a noble class based on landed property is freely and fully taken for granted. Under English conditions it makes no difference that Bentham wished to allow the major country gentleman of (technically) non-noble status to enter (more formally) the ranks of the nobility proper.

Objections VI-IX try to obviate the apprehension that the proposed resurrection of the feudal law of escheat would upset the constitutional liberties of the subject, or, at any rate, lead to a waste of his money. These headings are self-explanatory and require no comment here. X-XIII are much more attractive for the economist. X argues that the measure would not cause dissaving and diminution of the national stock of capital, while XII and XIII endeavour to show that no serious fall in value of government bonds need be feared. But the most interesting piece of work in this context is XI, on the price of land. Landed estates will come more frequently on the market than before, once escheat in the proposed form is substituted for taxation. Will this not lead to a general slump on the estate market? Bentham is anxious to prove this apprehension unfounded. Land, he argues, will always fetch more than government paper, because of the great social advantages its possession conveys. Yet it has a common market with government paper because these two types of property constitute together the secure sources of permanent income available in the country. Granted that escheat would increase the offer of landed estates in the market, it would at the same time decrease the national debt, and thereby progressively drive capital which had been invested in government bonds before to seek reinvestment in land, so that in the end no material reduction of their price could possibly occur.

Compared to this heading which quite obviously contains some hard economic thinking, the remaining two, I and V, appear somewhat dull. I—strongly reminiscent of paragraph 8 of the pamphlet—claims that the new law of succession which the measure would substitute for the existing law, would be much preferable to the order of inheritance which it would supplant. V is a passionate denunciation of the theory and practice of the "law of nature". What gave these pages their punch and their sting was the fact that they were written

---

[1]Cf. Bentham's "Essay on the Influence of Time and Place in Matters of Legislation", *Works* I, pp. 169-194. Cf. also *Economic Journal*, 1946, pp. 584-594.

under the shadow of the French Terror which dismayed and disgusted Bentham as much as it did those other "honorary citizens of France", Wilberforce and Klopstock. The guillotine, Bentham felt, was the necessary outcome of a legal theory run riot: and he was most anxious to show his English contemporaries that, in his hands, legal reform had no such dangerous tendencies as it had displayed in the hands of a Danton or a "Robertspierre".

It will be noticed that the order in which the various objections are presented here is not the same as that adopted in paragraph 7 of the published pamphlet. This deviation from what would *prima facie* appear to be the authoritative arrangement is easily explained by the fact that the objections themselves are not identical. Bentham seems to have changed the prospective order several times while he was working away at his counter-arguments. U.C. CXLVI, 48 and XX, 12 suggest yet another sequence. In the circumstances, the best thing seemed to be to rely mainly on inner evidence, and the demands of logic and convenience. Thus it was clear that—after giving the general preamble of sheet 128—it would be most expedient to start with sheet 122—i.e. objection X of the pamphlet—because the first sentence of that page was obviously meant to be the first sentence of the whole chapter. The arrangement here adopted would appear to be the most satisfactory that could be employed without doing violence to the text —the sacredness of the text being always the first and foremost consideration of the conscientious editor.

The interesting "objection XI" discussed a moment ago should be read together with certain materials entitled *Indirect and Remote Effects to be expected from the Proposed Measure*. Here Bentham intended to investigate the influence of a revival of escheat on the price system. Unfortunately what we have is very little, and that little rather clumsy and laboured. Still, such as they are, these pages show us Bentham's mind grappling with a really difficult problem of economics and, without them, this edition could not claim to be representative of his effort to further economic thought.

As far as his argument was concerned, Bentham felt that he was on very firm ground. The national stock of capital is once again the centre of his interest. Would its growth be impeded by the measure? If not, there is nothing to worry about. If so, the result would be to slow down the spontaneous fall of the rate of interest which results from, and runs parallel to, economic and technical progress, and in this way to preserve the income and standard of living of the monied man which would otherwise sag. This, too, Bentham felt, was an advantage, if not a national, at least a sectional one. Hence, he seems to argue, no evil can befall in any case. But, be it said in Bentham's honour, this vague mode of argumentation did not satisfy him. He wanted to know how far the one contingency would extend, and how far the other. His investigation, as far as we possess it, is printed below. The gist of it is difficult to grasp. It may be of help to the reader, however, to know the preliminary notes which Bentham jotted down, before he drafted and formulated these passages. Here are what appear to be the decisive sentences: "Taxes take from consumption (principally) to give to consumption (principally). Escheat, if used instead of taxes, will take from *production* in good measure, to give to *consumption*. When it brings land and farming stock, and [also] manufacturing stock, under the hammer, this fixed capital must either perish or be sold, i.e. given in exchange for circulating capital which, by acquiring this productive distinction, is withholden from some other [productive employment], unless where the fall and thence cheapness of the price of the thing sold is an inducement to a purchaser to lay up in this way what he would otherwise have spent. In as far as it is confined to moveable articles destined for immediate consumption, the escheat system, though employed in lieu of taxes, contributes nothing towards lessening thesaurization [and] production. Those articles are *produced* already. All it does is, by causing them to be bought at the auctions, to prevent the buying of articles of the same nature and equal amount at the shops. In as far as it applies to ready money, so far as the money it attaches upon is what was in a course of being employed in farming, in manufacture, or in shop-keeping trade, it takes from production to give to consumption. So with respect to money lent out at interest to a man of the productive class" (U.C. XX, 8).

Hence Bentham seems to admit that, as far at least as monetary capital *in statu nascendi* is concerned, escheat would lead to its dispersal, to dissaving, because it would transfer the sums in question to a typical spender, the Treasury, while, on the other hand, it would hardly have a tendency to stimulate the formation of such, or any other type of capital. But he argues at once that this would be a good thing for the monied, and presumably saving, classes. "The escheat system", he says, "by making saleable property of every kind instead of going into the hands of those who would have had it without giving ready money for it, pass into the hands of those who can not have it without ready money, encreases *pro tanto* the demand for ready money, and raises therefore the value of ready money: i.e. lowers [for the possessors of monetary capital, relatively speaking] the prices of other things" (U.C. XX, 8). Candidly he admits that, by this effect, by keeping up the rate of interest, the escheat system "also retards the rise of the wages of labour" (ib.).

Bentham obviously felt that the proposed measure—and, indeed, the spontaneous development of the economic forces—confronts the economist with two equally disagreeable alternatives: either the capital stock of society is increased, or rises spontaneously; then a meritorious race, the men of property, are damaged because their income falls: or the capital stock of society is not increased, or is even positively reduced by the operation of escheat; then the rate of economic progress is slowed down and, with it, the natural rise of the wages of labour. In the nature of things, there can be only one satisfactory way out of this quandary: to keep the rate of interest steady. The proposed measure, Bentham seems to urge, could—rightly managed—help to steady it. Perhaps this is the note on which the book would have closed, if it had ever been written in full: "The produce of the escheat-fund will be applied either 1. in lieu of taxes: or 2. in aid of taxes towards extinction of the debt. Employing it in lieu [of taxes] (in time of peace) promotes steadiness in the value of ready money by retarding its depreciation. In time of war, the value of ready money has received a sudden encrease. Employing this supply in lieu of taxes, by taking so much ready money out of the market, adds to that encrease. To avoid this it ought to go in aid of taxes, and be applied towards diminishing the debt" (U.C. XX, 8). In this way, an undue rise in the yield of monetary capital would be prevented in times of war, just as an undue reduction of it would be prevented in times of peace by the alternative employment of the "escheat-fund" at the disposal of the Exchequer.[1]

The chapters which Bentham gave comparatively little attention and which are consequently somewhat disjointed and rather unsatisfactory concern the administrative side of the proposal (points 5-9 enumerated in paragraph 2 of the pamphlet). Naturally he saw no

---

[1] Two further passages which confirm that the above summary is a correct sketch of Bentham's ideas on this all-important subject-matter occur in box XX, pp. 178 and 196, of the University College collection. They are printed at the end of volume III, in the survey of the manuscript material that has otherwise been excluded from this edition.

reason to work them out without prospect of practical application. But we have, all the same, a number of notes which allow us to discern the outline of the proposed "official establishment", and they follow here, to assuage the curiosity of the Bentham student, without further comment.

"In each county, a public officer under the name of Escheator, or rather under the name of Administrator General, with powers and duties analogous to those of Assignee in matters of Bankruptcy, or Administrator in the succession of individuals.[1]

"His pay, poundage—so much in the pound upon the money as it is got in. His interest will thus be connected with his duty: his reward proportioned to his diligence. His hands[2] to be emptied every week by remittances to the Bank. All[3] pretence of difficulty or insecurity is obviated by the mail conveyance.

"His accounts published weekly in the county newspaper: all parties concerned will then be enabled to detect errors and to bear witness against mismanagement.

"His account for each person's estate to be made up and made public at the end of the first year, reckoning from the day of his death when he dies within the realm: and so for every subsequent year, so long as there remains any thing to distribute or to pay.

"The Escheator to be examinable *viva voce* on oath by any person interested, and even by leave of the court on the application of any person in the character of an *amicus curiae*.

"Provided that where the complaint against him is deemed not only groundless and vexatious, but either rash or malitious, the party may be punished in a summary way, by imprisonment or by fine applicable either to the use of the public, or in the way of indemnification to the use of the Escheator, as being the party vexed.

"Printed forms to be provided by the law for the transaction of every part of the Escheator's business as far as it can be foreseen, and

---

[1]Bentham explains his preference for the term Administrator General as follows: "The common people to whom the name and the office are equally unknown would be apt instead of *Escheator* to say *Cheater*. Every thing that exposes the law to ridicule ought of course to be avoided, especially in relation to an office which, by the power it would conferr would afford a proportionable provocation to the spirit of opposition, and interest men in giving currency to any mode of speech that could contribute to bring the system into disrepute. Add to this that the term Administrator General, consisting of a familiar addition to a name of office almost equally familiar, would be more significant and expressive."

[2] and [3]This passage is partly covered by a large blot, but the text can hardly differ from the version here given.

as far as a general form is capable of serving for each particular case" (U.C. XX, 77-78).

"In each County again a Judge of Escheat, with powers analogous to those of Commissioners of Bankruptcy. Salary fixed: attendance uninterrupted: his assiduity ensured by residence free of rent, and by payment made at short intervals on the spot. One judge, not more: every judge beyond one is either a cypher or a nuisance. The more judges, the tardier justice. A second, doubling the expence, would but prejudice the service.

"To check the Judge, to add solemnity to oaths, to supply with advantage the place of a second judge, a clergyman as Assessor, the ministers of the 13 circumjacent parishes, serving each a month by rotation, or better still by lot, a week at a time. Were such attendance gratuitous, the hardship would not be great. A small retribution would remove it. Say two guineas a week. Eight guineas a year would make no inconsiderable addition to the provision of a curate" (U.C. XX, 79).

"The Escheator nominated either by the Crown, or *more antiquo*, as the Coroner is, by the freeholders. Better perhaps by the freeholders: to obviate the apprehension of encrease of influence, to conform to precedent where no clear utility indicates departure, and to separate the power of appointment from that of removal; that neither pride, affection, nor connection may be interested in the support of a bad choice. The power of removal at all events in the Crown, and that instantaneous and at discretion, for the mischief that might ensue from the negligence, incapacity or improbity of an Escheator is incalculable.

"The Judge appointed by the Crown.

"Power to the County Escheator of each county to appoint a Sub-Escheator in any or every town within the county, such deputy to be paid by fees to come out of the commission received by the principal.

"Businesses for such Deputy:—

"1. Immediately upon the decease of any person in any house within his district, to repair to such house, there to take an inventory of the effects, if the deceased were the owner of the house, together with the examinations of all persons therein relative to the particulars of such effects and all other assets: if the deceased were not the owner, then not to take the inventory, but only to examine the owner and others with the like view.

"2. To take the examinations of any persons indebted or supposed to be indebted to the deceased, at their respective abodes, in proof of their debts, and to prove the debts due from the deceased by the examination of creditors, as is done before Commissioners of Bankrupts by affidavit" (U.C. XX, 80-84).

"TAX WITH MONOPOLY"

The idea incorporated in the pamphlet *Supply without Burthen, or Escheat vice Taxation* was not the only contribution Bentham thought he could make to the solution of the thorny problem how to finance the state. "Sir," he wrote to Charles Long, after he had laid before him the proposal to tax—or rather to take—away successions, "if the pecuniary resource I ventured t' other day to submit to you, should be deemed ineligible or impracticable, perhaps in some other instance I may be more fortunate. I have two other such resources upon the anvil—the one involving a burthen indeed, but that burthen coupled with an indemnity capable of balancing it, and sooner or later even of outweighing it: the other absolutely pure from all burthen from the very beginning" (*Works* X, 303).[1] The latter suggestion did not mature into a definite pamphlet: at any rate there is no trace of any such manuscript in the University College collection.[2] Bentham summed it up in the following terms:

"Proposal for an unburthensome augmentation of the revenue, as well as for the removal of divers impediments to industry, more especially inventive industry, and superior workmanship, by licences conferring the several faculties undermentioned, viz:—

1. On the part of the moneyed man, faculty of investing a *limited* sum in trade or manufacture, in consideration of a share of the profits —hence, on the part of the manufacturer or trader, a capacity of obtaining capital on such terms.

"At present, by a construction of common law, a man cannot lend a penny upon such terms, without risking his whole fortune. In Ireland,

[1] It is somewhat surprising not to find in this connection a short mention at least of the subject of lotteries. The institution of a state lottery was one of the ideas which passed through Bentham's mind about this time. Little is said about it in the University College collection (cf. CLXVI, 40 and 168), but the Genevan papers contain a coherent passage of some fourteen pages on this topic (LI, 54-67) which Dumont must have translated into French from some English original lost to us. As might be expected, Bentham argued that a state lottery would yield the same benefit as a tax of equal produce without having any of its inconveniences. "*Peut-on souhaiter davantage?*" (For the detail, cf. the summary of the Genevan material at the end of vol. III.)

[2] Cf. however U.C. CLXVI, 13-15.

relief is given to a certain degree against this inconvenience, by a statute of about ten years' standing.

"2. Faculty of lending and borrowing capital at a rate exceeding 5 per Cent, the present legal rate of interest.

"3. Faculty of obtaining Patents for inventions without the present expence, on security given for allowing government an annual consideration in the way of annuity or share of profits.

"This would operate as a saving of so much capital. N.B. Full indemnification to the several offices concerned. The three legal restraints against which these three faculties afford relief, form together an almost total prohibition of *inventive* industry on the part of at least 19 individuals out of 20.

"4. Faculty of exercising a trade without having served an apprenticeship.

"In the instance of all four faculties, the licence to be registered" (*Works* X, 304).

It is impossible to read this summary without regretting that the suggestions contained in it were not further developed and propagated. Nowhere was Bentham nearer to the real needs of economic life than here: nowhere has posterity so faithfully carried out his programme as in these five points. But Bentham was an utopian rather than a realist, and the very soberness of the ideas here put forward may have induced him to lay them quietly aside again.

While this short *aperçu* is all we possess of the one proposal Bentham had "upon the anvil", we are somewhat more fortunate with regard to the other. Its fate in the world was similar to that of *Escheat vice Taxation*: Long was not interested and consequently Bentham lost his interest too. Once again he locked his manuscript away and contented himself with printing—or even with preparing for print[1]— a short excerpt. It was only a very short excerpt this time, a mere broadsheet of two pages. Bowring reprinted it in the *Works* (vol. II, pp. 599-600). In the present edition it serves mainly as an introduction and a summary of what Bentham would have called "the body of the work". In and for itself, it is hardly an impressive presentation of the case.

The broadsheet was called *Tax with Monopoly*, and a *junctim* between the burden of a tax and the benefit of a monopoly is indeed

---

[1] It is impossible to be more definite on this point. Bowring seems to have reprinted from a printed copy, perhaps from an uncorrected proof-sheet. The version published below is—*faute de mieux*, and for no other reason!—based on his text.

the master-idea of the whole proposal. In itself, Bentham knew, a tax on trade is as much of an evil for the producer as a monopoly of trade is for the consumer. But, he thought, there may be cases in which the two evils may conceivably balance and blot each other out. This is the inspiration from which he started in his renewed search for "modes of supply" which would, and yet would not, be burdens on the community.

Bentham's point of departure in the investigation under review is the principle of equity in taxation. Equity, he says, demands that where there is equality in the ability to pay, there should also be equality in the burden imposed. This is particularly desirable in the department of direct taxes, of taxes on income—of "forced" taxes as he calls them, in contradistinction to indirect taxes on expenditure which, apart from the case of absolute necessaries, are "voluntary" in so far as the taxpayer can easily and legitimately avoid them by shunning the articles taxed. Now, precisely in the field of "forced" taxation, the principle of equity and equality is completely disregarded. Landowners pay the Land Tax: but other opulent strata —Bentham gives a whole list of them—pay nothing out of their respective incomes. This injustice could, within limits, be remedied. Within limits: it would not be advisable to impose a tax on people who could shift the burden on to shoulders which economic wisdom and higher considerations alike would counsel to leave free: it would not be advisable, for instance, to tax public creditors who would get their own back from the government at the occasion of later loans, or private lenders who would simply add the tax to the borrowers' charges. In this whole argument, Bentham shows considerable understanding of the problem of the incidence of taxation, and that is perhaps the outstanding quality and the value of this chapter 1.

But if a tax on interest would not be eligible, the "profits of lucrative occupations", i.e. the incomes of manufacturers or traders or professional men, could and should be taxed. There is no reason why they should go free, if land-owners are so grievously burdened. True, professional earnings are "earned income" as we say today, while rents and feu duties are "unearned". Bentham appreciates the difference. But he thinks that a certain abatement in the rate of taxation is all that can reasonably be demanded for earned incomes, and he suggests that they should bear half the percentage imposed on unearned incomes, i.e. 10 per cent, or a tithe. Further "indulgencies" could be granted to sweeten the pill, and—here comes the essential idea at the bottom of the proposal—it could in suitable cases be connected with an indemnity which would cost the government nothing and hurt nobody, while it would greatly benefit the new victims of taxation. This proposed indemnity is discussed in chapter 3. It would consist in closing the occupation, i.e. in the grant of a monopoly *pro futuro*, in a limitation of numbers to their present state. Monopolies are, in general, obnoxious, especially one-man monopolies such as were instituted by the Tudor mercantilists. But, here as everywhere, public prejudice has gone far beyond the bounds of reason. Monopolies are bad if and in so far as they have certain effects—throttling supply, raising the price, and affecting the quality of the goods sold or services rendered—but if and in so far as these tangible effects do not obtain, they are perfectly innocent.

The question then is in what concrete occupations such "innocent privileges" can be established. This crucial problem is investigated in chapter 4. Bentham develops three sets of rules which it is impossible further to compress. Their gist is well brought out in the broadsheet. The upshot of it all is the assertion that there are certain occupations, such as banking and stockbroking, in which neither the quantity nor the quality of the essential services offered can conceivably be impaired, nor the price of them sensibly increased, so that these "branches of industry" can safely be subjected to the proposed "tax with monopoly".

As it happens, bankers and stockbrokers are also particularly fit objects for a measure of this kind from a different point of view: they are, *inter alia,* eligible taxpayers because they keep books, so that their profits can be easily ascertained. Chapter 5 sets out the "apposite mode of collection" and provides further "rules" for the selection of suitable victims or beneficiaries of the proposed new legislation (it is difficult to say what they really are—according to Bentham, both at the same time). The right choice can only be made if the requirements of fiscal and administrative technique are fully considered, alongside the more material economic and political considerations.

With chapter 5 the essay comes virtually to a close. Chapter 6—on precedent—is empty. Chapter 7 ought to be read together with the *Summary Sketch of Financial Resources Employed and Employable* mentioned above and published below. It does not really fit in here because it seems to discuss a much wider problem than the taxation of incomes, namely, the relative merits and demerits of the various existing and conceivable modes of taxation. Such as it is, it is interesting but fragmentary and obscure. It is not unlikely that Bentham at one time intended to set this whole essay into a broader frame of which this "conclusion" is the only existing or surviving part.

As we have seen, all the considerations put forward by Bentham point to the banker as the *prima facie* most attractive object of the suggested burden-cum-indemnity. That is the reason why he appended to his more general pamphlet a concrete "Proposal for a Tax on Bankers". He obviously hoped to word it in a way which would be easily taken in by Mr. Long and his ministerial colleagues and would carry conviction. The industrial tithe or double tithe[1] would be collectable without the slightest difficulty in the case of bankers: the government would simply be in, or rather put itself into, the position of a sleeping partner. At the same time the indemnity held out as a counterbalancing boon would be quite tangible here. The number of banks had been showing a continuous increase for decades: supposing a tax on profits of 20 per cent. were imposed and the establishment of new firms prohibited, the promised indemnity would begin to counterbalance the burden at the time when the number of banking houses would, in the natural course of events, have risen by another 20 per cent. Thus the reality of the indemnification of the "parties damnified" would be clearly visible to every eye. The same, Bentham claims, is true of the economic innocence of the exclusive privilege which would constitute the source of that indemnification. There is no qualitative aspect to the essential function performed by a banker's business: either he lends a customer money, or he does not: if he does, he has to hand him the cash, and that is the beginning and the end of the whole transaction: it cannot be done in a "better" or a "worse" way, unlike, for instance, producing a pair of shoes or rendering any other productive service where the concepts "good" and "bad" have a real meaning and importance. Moreover, bankers not only compete against each other: they compete against all monied men in the community who have capital to lend, and so the pressure of competition would at best be diminished, but certainly not removed, by declaring the present number of London banking houses to be the legal maximum for all time to come.

The paper ends with a somewhat inconclusive discussion of the case of country bankers, and the position of the Bank of England,

---

[1]Bentham speaks here of a tax of 20 per cent.

under the proposed dispensation. There is little in the last two pages that would command special interest. But before Bentham laid down his pen he started an idea—quite casually as it should seem—which was destined to develop into his main preoccupation and to hold his attention for many a long day: the idea of a government-sponsored currency which would enter into competition with the private or semi-private notes already current in the country. The greater part of the second volume in the present edition will be devoted to this theme and its manifold aspects and variations.

THE PHILOSOPHY
OF
ECONOMIC SCIENCE

[THE PHILOSOPHY OF ECONOMIC SCIENCE]

[I]

Philosophy is never more worthily occupied, than when affording her assistances to the economy of common life: benefits of which mankind in general are partakers, being thus superadded to whatever gratification is to be reaped from researches purely speculative. It is a vain and false philosophy which conceives its dignity to be debased by use.

[II]

A cloud of perplexity, raised by indistinct and erroneous conceptions, seems at all times to have been hanging over the import of the terms *art* and *science*. The common supposition seems to have been, that in the whole *field of thought* and *action*, a determinate number of existing compartments are assignable, marked out all round, and distinguished from one another by so many sets of natural and determinate boundary lines: that of these compartments some are filled, each by an *art*, without any mixture of science; others by a *science*, without any mixture of art; and others, again, are so constituted that, as it has never happened to them hitherto, so neither can it ever happen to them in future, to contain in them any thing *either* of art *or* science.

This supposition will, it is believed, be found in every part erroneous; as between *art* and *science*, in the whole field of *thought* and *action*, no one spot will be found belonging to either to the exclusion of the other. In whatsoever spot a portion of either is found, a portion of the other may be also seen; whatsoever spot is occupied by either, is occupied by both: is occupied by them in *joint tenancy*. Whatsoever spot is thus occupied, is so much taken out of the *waste;* and there is not any determinate part of the whole waste which is not liable to be thus occupied.

Practice, in proportion as *attention* and *exertion* are regarded as necessary to due *performance*, is termed *art*. *Knowledge*, in proportion as *attention* and *exertion* are regarded as necessary to *attainment*, is termed *science*.

81

F

In the very nature of the case, they will be found so combined as to be inseparable. Man cannot *do* anything well, but in proportion as he *knows* how to *do* it : he cannot, in consequence of *attention* and *exertion, know* anything but in proportion as he has practised the *art* of *learning* it. Correspondent therefore to every *art,* there is at least one branch of *science;* correspondent to every branch of *science,* there is at least one branch of *art.* There is no determinate line of distinction between *art,* on the one hand, and *science* on the other; no determinate line of distinction between *art* and *science,* on the one hand, and *unartificial practice* and *unscientific knowledge,* on the other. In proportion as that which is seen to be *done,* is more conspicuous than that which is seen or supposed to be *known:* that which has place is apt to be considered as the work of *art:* in proportion as that which is seen or supposed to be *known* is more conspicuous than anything else that is seen to be *done,* that which has place is apt to be set down to the account of *science.* Day by day, acting in conjunction, art and science are gaining upon the above-mentioned waste—the field of *unartificial practice* and *unscientific knowledge.*

Whilst, as to the arts and sciences of immediate and those of more remote utility, it would not be necessary, nor perhaps possible, to preserve between these two classes an exact line of demarcation. The distinctions of theory and practice are equally applicable to all. Considered as matter of theory, every art or science, even when its practical utility is most immediate and incontestable, appears to retire into the division of arts and sciences of remote utility. It is thus that medicine and legislation, these arts so practical, considered under a particular aspect, appear equally remote in respect to their utility with the speculative sciences of logic and mathematics.

[III]
Directly or indirectly, *well-being,* in some shape or other, or in several shapes, or all shapes taken together, is the subject of every thought, and object of every action, on the part of every known *Being,* who is, at the same time, a sensitive and thinking Being. Constantly and unpreventably it actually is so : nor can any intelligible reason be given for desiring that it should be otherwise.

This being admitted, *Eudæmonics,* in some one or other of the divisions of which it is susceptible, or in all of them taken together, may be said to be the *object* of every branch of *art,* and the *subject* of every branch of *science*. *Eudæmonics**—the *art*, which has for the object of its endeavours, to contribute in some way or other to the attainment of *well-being*—and the *science* in virtue of which, in so far as it is possessed by him, a man knows in what manner he is to conduct himself in order to exercise that art with effect.

Considered in the character of an *edifice* or *receptacle*, *Eudæmonics* may, therefore, be termed the *Common Hall*, or *central place of meeting*, of all the *arts* and *sciences:*—change the metaphor, every *art*, with its correspondent *science*, is a branch of *Eudæmonics*.

If the above observation be correct, it is only in one or other of two shapes or characters, viz. that of a *source of happiness*, or that of a security against *unhappiness*, that *being* can in any of its modifications, possess any claim to man's regard.†

---

*Eudæmonics. From a Greek word, which signifies happiness, originally, *attended by a good genius*.

The quantity or degree of *well-being*, experienced during any given length of time, is directly as the *magnitude* (i.e. the *intensity* multiplied by the *duration*) of the sum of the pleasures, and inversely as the *magnitude* of the sum of the *pains*, experienced during that same length of time.

In so far as the sum of the *pleasures* of all kinds, experienced by the person in question, during the length of time in question, is regarded, as *considerable*,—the sum of the *pains* of all kinds, experienced by him during that same length of time, being, moreover, laid out of the account,—the state which in that respect he is regarded as being in, is termed a state of *happiness*.

In so far as the sum of the pain of all kinds, experienced by the person in question, during the length of time in question, is regarded as considerable,—the sum of the *pleasures* of all kinds, experienced by him during that same length of time, being, moreover, laid out of the account,—the state which, in this respect, he is regarded as being in, is termed a state of *unhappiness*.

†The *summum bonum* is a fruit of the tree of *pure good*, upon the taking of which into his mouth, a man experiences at one and the same time every pleasure of which in the nature of a sensitive being he is susceptible, each in the highest degree; pains of all sorts at the same time keeping aloof, so long as this precious fruit remains in any part of the *primæ viæ*.

It is the kernel of that fruit, of which the *philosopher's stone* is the shell. It was lately found by Baron *Munchausen*, in the Island of *Medemusia*, after a careful search made, in pursuance of the directions given by *Aristotle*, *Plato*, and *Cicero*, in whose philosophical repasts,—as, in the codes of those universally admired masters of ethical science, any body may see,—it formed a constant article.

By *Cicero*, in his Tusculan Questions, it has been made plain, to the perfect satisfaction of his *Auditor* (a most perfectly well-bred young gentleman, whom he introduces to us by that name) that *pain is no evil*. But the truth is, as the *philosopher* confessed to the *Baron*, that, during the whole of this dialogue, they were both of them chewing the *summum bonum nut*, to which the *areca*, even when wrapped up in the *betel* leaf, forms a very inadequate substitute. The consequence was—that, all that time, to the philosopher and his agreeable young friend, pain was no evil, whatsoever it may have been, and be about to be, to the vulgar of that and other ages.

Eudæmonics being the name for the universally practised *art*—
the *pursuit of happiness,*—*being* in some of its various shapes, will
be allowed to be an indispensable *means,* without which the object
of that art cannot in any instance be pursued and attained. *Sensitive
being* is the only *seat* of happiness: *being,* in that and other shapes,
is the universal *instrument* of happiness. To the attainment of happiness in any shape or degree, an acquaintance, more or less considerable, with the *seat* of happiness, and with such *beings* as, in each
instance, afford a promise of serving in the character of *instruments*
of happiness,—is more or less conducive, or even necessary. For the
designation, of whatsoever portion of science may be regarded as
capable of being attained, concerning *being* taken in its utmost conceivable extent,—the word *Ontology* has, for ages, been in possession
of being employed.

Eudæmonics is the art of *well-being.* Necessary to *well-being* is
being. In every part, therefore, of the common field,—concomitant
and correspondent to *Eudæmonics* considered as an *art,* runs
Ontology,*—considered as a *science.*

For the expressly declared *subject of division,* let us take the
science: art and science running along every where together, every
division performed on the one, may, on any occasion, be considered
as applying to the other.

By means of this joint consideration, as often as, on looking at the
name of a branch of art and science as it stands in the Table, we
come to consider its *nature,* our attention will be pointed to the only
source and measure of its *value.*

Coenoscopic† and *Idioscopic‡*—by successively attaching to the

---

*Ontology. From two Greek words:—one of which signifies *being* in general; the
other, *an account*:—an account of *being* in general. [The word is here, and throughout the *Chrestomathia,* misprinted "Outology". The mistake is corrected in the text.]

†*Coenoscopic.* From two Greek words: one of which signifies *common*—things
belonging to others in common; the other *looking to.* By *Coenoscopic ontology* then
is designated that part of the science, which takes for its subject those properties,
which are considered as possessed in common by all the individuals, belonging to
the class which the name *ontology* is employed to designate: i.e. by *all beings.*
In the word *Coenobite*—less properly spelt *Cenobite*—the first of these words has
already a footing in the language. In the words *microscope, microscopic,*—*telescope,
telescopic,*—and several others designative of philosophical instruments,—the
termination—*scopic* is become perfectly familiar.

‡*Idioscopic.* From two Greek words, the first of which signifies *peculiar.* In
Idioscopic Ontology then we have that branch of art and science, which takes for

subject *Ontology* these two adjuncts, the field of art and science may thus be divided, the whole of it, into two portions; in one of which, viz. the *coenoscopic*, shall be contained the appalling and repulsive branch of science, to which the no less formidable, and to many a man intensely odious, appellation of *metaphysics*, is sometimes also applied: while to the other — viz. the *idioscopic* — all the other branches of art and science, may, without distinction, be consigned.

Division of Ontology into 1, *Coenoscopic*, and 2, *Idioscopic*.

Matter and *mind*—into these two portions, *being* in general, considered as an aggregate, is wont to be considered as divided. Hence arises,

Division of Idioscopic Ontology into *Somatology*,* or *Somatics*, and *Pneumatology*,† or *Pneumatics*, alias *Psychology*, or *Psychics*.

Division of *Pneumatology* into *Alegopathematic*‡ and *Pathematoscopic*.§

Alegopathematic, or say *Alego-æsthetic* Pneumatology has, for its

---

its subject such properties, as are considered as peculiar to different classes of beings: some appertaining to one such class, others to another.

In the words *idiom, idiomatical, idiosyncracy*, and a few others, though none of them in any very common use—this word has already a footing in the language: a footing, better known in some instances than in others.

Coenosyncratocoscopic and *idiosyncratocoscopic* might be somewhat more expressive, but would be too long-winded. *Coenosyncratic* and *idiosyncratic* would scarcely be equally expressive:—*syncratic*, from *syncrasis*, i. e. *commixture, composition, constitution*.

Somatology. From two Greek words, the first of which signifies *body, matter*, or *corporeal substance*.

†*Pneumatology*. From two Greek words: the first of which (πνευμα) signifies *spirit*, i. e. *incorporeal substance*, in the sense in which it is used as synonymous to *mind*: in their original sense, the Latin as well as the Greek word corresponding to the English word *breath*. In the New Testament, αγιον πνευμα is the name, employed in the original, in designating the object, for the designation of which, in the English version, the compound appellative *Holy Spirit* is employed: more frequently (according to a phrase, which, when, on other occasions, applied to other objects, is either obsolete, or expressive of a different class of beings or supposed beings) *Holy Ghost*. In this sense, *pneumatology* and *pneumatics*, as well as *psychology*, are already in use: though more upon the continent than in Britain. If, on this occasion, and in this sense, the word *pneumatics* were employed, it would need to cease being employed in the sense in which it is at present wont to be employed: viz. that in which it designates the branch of art and science, which has for its subject *bodies in general*, considered as being in the state, which, since *Chemistry* has become a science, has been termed the *gaseous* state.

‡*Alegopathematic*. From two Greek words: the first of which, as above, signifies *to pass by unnoticed*; the other, *sensation, feeling*, or *affection*.

§*Pathematoscopic*. From two Greek words, the first of which signifies *sensation or feeling*, as above.

single-worded synonym, the not unexpressive appellation *Noology*.*

It has for its subject *spirit* or *mind*, considered apart from all *feeling*, whether of the pleasurable or painful kind: considered that is to say with reference to the purely intellectual part of the animal frame: including *simple perception, memory, judgment, reasoning, abstraction, imagination*, &c.

Pathematoscopic Pneumatology may have for its synonym *Pneumatic*, or *Psychological*† *Pathology*.

Division of *Pathematoscopic Pneumatology*, or say *Pneumatic* or *Psychological Pathology*,‡ into *Aplopathematic*§ and *Thelematoscopic*.∥

Aplopathematic Pneumatology has for its subject the aggregate of *Pleasures* and *Pains* of all kinds, considered apart from whatsoever influence, in the character of motives, the prospects of them may have upon the *will* or *volitional* faculty,—and the *acts*, as well purely

---

Noology. From two Greek words, the first of which signifies *mind*, and in particular the *intellectual* part. Though the word thus compounded has not yet found its way into the body of the language, yet among literary men, and in particular in the universities, the first of its elements *nous* has for many years been in use, though rather in a jocular and purely colloquial, than a serious and regularly established sense. A man is said to have some *nous*—or to be not altogether devoid of *nous*—i. e. *understanding—intelligence*.

†*Psychological*. From two Greek words: the first of which signifies *the soul of man*: though, probably enough, it began to do so, not till after it had for some time signified a *butterfly*. The word *psychology*, though more in use on the continent than in England, is already in the English dictionaries. *Animula, vagula, blandula*, &c.—"little foolish, fluttering thing"—was the celebrated address, made, on his death-bed, to his own soul, by the Emperor Adrian, to whose mind the original signification of the word *psyche* seems, on that occasion, to have presented itself.

‡*Pathology*. From two Greek words, the first of which signifies *feeling* or *sensation*. It has long been in the English language, though not often employed in any other than a *medical* sense: in which case the import of it is seldom extended beyond that of *bodily sensation* or *feeling*, considered with a view to some *disorder* with which it may be supposed to be connected.

§*Aplo-pathematic*. From two Greek words: the first of which means *simple*,—relating to the thing in question and nothing else;—the other, *sensation* or *feeling*, as above.

∥*Thelematoscopic*. From two Greek words: the first of which denotes the faculty of the *will*—the *volitional* faculty—as contra-distinguished from the *intellectual*. It seems wonderful, that, neither from the Greek, nor from the Latin, a word so continually in demand as the substantive *will* should have any *conjugate* in the shape of an *adjective* belonging to it. The adjective *volitional*, derived by analogy from the substantive *volition*, is not in *Sheridan's* English Dictionary, nor, probably, in any other: instead of it may be found the word *volitive*, a word which is not at all in use, nor is, by a good deal, so nearly allied in sound.

mental and *internal*, as *corporeal* and *external*, of which those prospects may become the *causes*.*

Thelematoscopic Pneumatology, or *Pathology*, has for a synonym the single-worded appellative *Ethics*,† taken in its largest sense.

In the character of synonyms to Ethics are also used, in some circumstances, the words *Morals* and *Morality*.

First Division of *Ethics* (taken in the largest sense of the word) viz. into *Dicastic*,‡ i.e. *Censorial*, and simply *Exegetic*,§ i.e. *Expository*, or *Enunciative*. *Dicastic*, or *Censorial*, i.e. expressive of a judgment or sentiment of approbation or disapprobation, as intended by the author of the discourse, to be attached to the ideas of the several *voluntary actions*, (or say *modifications of human conduct*), which, in the course of it, are brought to view : in other words—his opinion, in relation to each such art, on the question—whether it *ought* to be done, ought to be left undone, or may, without impropriety, be done or left undone.

Simply *Exegetic*, i.e. *Expository* or *Enunciative*, viz. in so far as, without bestowing any such mark of approbation, disapprobation, or indifference, the discourse has for its object the stating what, in the

---

*Aplopathematic Pathology. Either from the genus *Technology*, or from the genus *Aplopathematic Pathology*, the process of ramification might have been carried on further to an indefinite length. But, on the present occasion,—in consideration partly of the quantity of labour, which, in case of any such formal continuation, would, on the part of the author, have been necessary, partly of the largeness of the draughts which it would have been necessary to make on the patience of the reader,—at this point it has been deemed most advisable to stop.

Under *Aplopathematic Pathology*, the *source* of ramification will be the nature of the *end*, to which the several branches of art and science issuing from it, will respectively and successively be directed : under *Technology*, it will be the nature of the *means* employed for the attainment of that end.

Proceeding from the consideration of the nature of the *end*, the first division might be into *Odynothetic* and *Hedonosceuastic*, or say *Hedonistic—pain-repelling* and *pleasure-producing*.

Widely distant as pain and pleasure are from one another in their extreme degrees, not only in their nearest degrees do they run one into another undistinguishably, but, in instances, to an indefinite extent, by one and the same individual operation, by which the one is excluded—the other is produced. But this is a difficulty which, throughout the whole field, the labours of the logical tactician have to encounter at every step : nor does the nature of things admit of its being either avoided or removed.

†*Ethics.* From a Greek word, which signifies *manner* or *manners* : manner of *conducting* one's self in the course of life.

‡*Dicastic.* From a Greek word, which signifies *to determine, in the character of a judge.*

§*Exegetic.* From a Greek word, which signifies *to set forth in the way of discourse.*

ENCYCLOPEDICAL TABLE, or ART and SCIENCE TABLE:

Exhibiting the first lines of a Tabular Diagram of the principal and most extensive branches of ART and SCIENCE, framed in the exhaustively bifurcate mode.

EUDÆMONICS

(From a Greek word, signifying the work of a good Genius, and thence *felicity*) Is an all-comprehensive name, applicable to ART and SCIENCE in general, and thence to each and every branch of Art and Science, considered as conducive to WELL-BEING; wherein BEING is of course included. Having for its *object*, or *end-in-view*, WELL-BEING, as above—i.e. the existence of sensitive creatures—and that in a desirable state,—and for its subject BEINGS—i.e. creatures in general, considered as being—some of them *receptacles or seats*—all of them *sources or instruments*, of WELL-BEING,—it may, in a more particular manner, in so far as it is considered in the character of an *ART*, be termed, as above, *Eudæmonics*: in which case, in so far as it is considered in the character of a *Science*, it may be termed ONTOLOGY.

EUDÆMONICS then, or ONTOLOGY, is

either
1. COENOSCOPIC;
(*regarding properties or adjuncts common to all Beings;*)
viz.
METAPHYSICS or ONTOLOGY in the common acceptation of the word;

or
2. IDIOSCOPIC;
(*regarding properties or adjuncts peculiar to different classes of Beings.*)

IDIOSCOPIC ONTOLOGY is

either
1. SOMATOSCOPIC;
(*body-regarding;*)
viz.
SOMATOLOGY or SOMATICS:

or
2. PNEUMATOSCOPIC;
(*spirit-regarding or mind-regarding;*)
viz.
PNEUMATOLOGY.

PNEUMATOLOGY is

either
1. NOOSCOPIC;
(*intellectual-faculty-regarding;*)

or
2. PATHOSCOPIC;
(*sensitive-faculty-regarding.*)

PATHOSCOPIC PNEUMATOLOGY is

either
2. *ERGASTIC;*
(work-producing;)
or say
2. *THELEMATOSCOPIC*
(volition-regarding;)
viz.
ETHICS;

or
1. *ANERGASTIC;*
(no-work-producing;)
or say
1. *APLOPATHOSCOPIC*
(mere-sensation-regarding;)

ETHICS is

either
1. *EXEGETIC;*
(simply expository;)

or
2. *DICASTIC;*
(censorial;)
viz.
DEONTOLOGY;
Knowledge concerning what is *proper* to be done.

EXEGETIC and DICASTIC ETHICS are

either
2. *POLIOSCOPIC;*
(state-regarding;)

1. *APOLIOSCOPIC;*
(not-state-regarding;)
viz.
PRIVATE ETHICS.

The completion of this Table, as it now stands, having been posterior by about a twelvemonth to the printing of the letter-press to which it belongs,—in the interval some few changes having presented themselves in the character of amendments, they are here inserted. But, of these alterations one consequence has of course been—a correspondent diversity, between the nomenclature employed in the body of the work and the nomenclature employed in this Table. A convenience had in the interval been found in giving to the termination—*scopic* (*regarding*) a more extensive application than in the first instance had been given to it.

opinion of the author, has, on each such occasion, actually come to pass, or is likely to have come to pass, or to have place at present, or to be about to come to pass in future,—i.e. what act is, on the occasion in question, most likely to have been done, to be doing, or to be about to be done.

This division has for its source the nature of the *mental faculty*, to which the discourse is immediately addressed. In so far as the discourse is of the *Censorial* cast, the faculty to which it addresses itself, and which, in so doing, it seeks to influence, is the *volitional*— the *will*, or at any rate the *pathematic*. In so far as it is of the simply *Expository*, or *Enunciative*, cast, the only faculty to which it immediately applies itself, viz. by seeking to afford *information* to it, is the *intellectual* faculty—the understanding.

For a synonym, *Dicastic Ethics* may have the single-worded appellative *Deontology.**

The principle of division, deduced from this source, will be seen to be applicable, and accordingly applying itself, severally to all the following ones.

Division of *Ethics* (whether *Expository* or *Dicastic*) into *Genicoscopic*,† i.e. *general matters-regarding;* and Idioscopic,‡ i.e. particular-matters-regarding.

Synonyms to *Genicoscopic*, as applied to Ethics, are, 1. *Theoretical;* 2. *Speculative.* Synonyms to Idioscopic, as applied to Ethics, is the word *practical.*

In this, as commonly in other cases, the limits between *general* and *particular* not being determinate, so neither are those between what, on the one hand, is *theoretical* or *speculative,*—on the other, *practical.* Of the observations expressed, such part as is allotted to the

*Deontology. From two Greek words, the first of which signifies *fit, fitting, right, becoming, proper.* Deontology—an account or indication of that which, on the occasion in question, whatsoever it be, is—(i. e. by him who speaks or writes, is regarded as being)—*fit, fitting, becoming, proper.* It is in *sound* only, and not in *signification*, that it has any connexion with the word *ontology*, employed above.

Applied to every branch of Ethics, taken in the largest sense of the word *Ethics*, the use of such a word as *Deontology* affords a promise of being attended with considerable convenience. It will accord equally well with every system which ever has been, or ever can be, devised, in relation to the foundation of moral obligation: —in the use of it, no such incongruity and presumption is involved, as that which is called *petitio principii*—i. e. a begging of the question—an assumption of the matter in dispute.

†*Genicoscopic.* From two Greek words, the first signifying *general.*

‡*Idioscopic.* From two Greek words, the first signifying *particular.*

explanation and fixation of the import of *general words,*—words of extensive import, the use of each of which is spread over the whole field, or a large portion of the whole field, of the art and science,— will belong mostly to the *genicoscopic, theoretical,* or *speculative* branch: and, under the name of *principles,* to the above observations will naturally be added any such *rules,* whether of the expository or the censorial cast, as in this respect are most extensive.

The deeper it descends into particulars, the more plainly it will be seen to belong to the *idioscopic.* In so far as, with the incidents exhibited in the fictitious narrative, any rules of a *deontological* nature (as in modern productions is frequently the case) happen to be intermixed, the matter of *novels* and *romances* comes to be included in, and the immense mass of it forms but a part of, the matter of PRACTICAL ETHICS.

Division of Ethics,—whether Exegetic or Dicastic, and whether Genicoscopic or Idioscopic,—into *Apolioscopic,** i.e. *political-state-not-regarding,* viz. PRIVATE ETHICS—*Ethics* in the more usual sense of the word,—and *Polioscopic* i.e. *political-state-regarding,*† viz. GOVERNMENT,‡ alias POLITICS.§

[IV]

By a Pannomion, understand on this occasion an all-comprehensive collection of law,—that is to say, of *rules* expressive of the will or wills of some person or persons belonging to the community, or say society in question, with whose will in so far as known, or guessed at, all other members of that same community in question, whether from habit or otherwise, are regarded as disposed to act in compliance.

In the formation of such a work, the sole proper all-comprehensive end should be the greatest happiness of the whole community, governors and governed together,—the *greatest-happiness principle* should be the fundamental principle.

The next specific principle is the *happiness-numeration principle.*

Rule: In case of collision and contest, happiness of each party

---

Apolioscopic. From three Greek words: the first of which is the sign of negation; the second signifies a political state, and the third *regarding.*

†*Polioscopic.* From two Greek words, as above.

‡*Government.* §*Politics.* By the word *Government,* the *practice,* and thence the *art,* seems to be more especially signified; by the word *Politics,* the corresponding branch of *science.*

being equal, prefer the happiness of the greater to that of the lesser number.

Maximizing universal security;—securing the existence of, and sufficiency of, the matter of subsistence for all the members of the community;—maximizing the quantity of the matter of abundance in all its shapes;—securing the nearest approximation to absolute equality in the distribution of the matter of abundance, and the other modifications of the matter of property; that is to say, the nearest approximation consistent with universal security, as above, for subsistence and maximization of the matter of abundance:—by these denominations, or for shortness, by the several words *security, subsistence, abundance,* and *equality,* may be characterized the several specific ends, which in the character of means stand next in subordination to the all embracing end—the greatest happiness of the greatest number of the individuals belonging to the community in question.

Correspondent to the axioms having reference to security, will be found the principles following:—

1. Principle correspondent to security, and the axioms thereto belonging, is the *security-providing principle.*

A modification of the security-providing principle, applying to security in respect of all modifications of the matter of property, is the disappointment-preventing principle. The use of it is to convey intimation of the reason for whatever arrangements come to be made for affording security in respect of property and the other modifications of the matter of prosperity, considered with a view to the interest of the individual possessor. In the aggregate of these are contained all the security-requiring objects, as above, with the exception of *person.*

II. Subsistence-securing principle: correspondent subordinate end in view—subsistence. The use of it is to convey intimation of the reason for whatever arrangements come to be made for the purpose of securing, for the use of the community in question, a sufficient quantity of the matter of subsistence.

III. Abundance-maximizing principle: the use of it is to convey intimation of the reasons for whatever arrangements may come to be made in contemplation of their conduciveness to the accomplishment of that end.

IV. Equality-maximizing, or say, more properly, inequality-minimizing principle: the use of it is to convey intimation of the reasons for whatever arrangements come to be made, in contemplation of their conduciveness to this end.

[v]

To political economy apply the axioms and principles relating to subsistence and abundance. To political economy—that is to say, to those portions of the penal and civil codes in the rationale of which considerations suggested by the art and science of political economy are applicable and have place: considerations over and above and independent of the sensations produced by loss and gain.*

By axioms of moral and political pathology, understand so many general propositions, by each of which statement is made of the pleasure or pain (chiefly of the pain) produced by the several sorts of evils, which are the result of human agency on the part of the several individuals respectively affected by them; to wit, by means of the influence exercised by them on the quantity or degree in which the benefits expressed by the fore-mentioned all important words, are by the respective parties, agents and patients, enjoyed, or the opposite burthens constituted by the absence of them endured.

Of these propositions, it will be observed that they divide themselves into *groups;*—one group being relative to security, another to subsistence, a third to abundance, the fourth and last to equality: the first bringing to view the enjoyment derived from the undisturbed possession of security at large—security in the most comprehensive application made of the word, contrasted with the enjoyment producible by the breach of it,—the second group bringing to view the subject of subsistence;—the third group bringing to view the subject of abundance,—and the fourth group bringing to view the subject of equality, and stating the evil consequence of any legislative arrangement by which a defalcation from the maximum of practicable equality is effected.

In each of the axioms, the antagonizing, or say competing, interests of two parties are conjointly brought to view:—in those which relate to security, these parties are, the maleficent agent, or say wrongdoer,

---

*By political economy, is endeavoured to be ascertained how far, and for what particular purposes, chiefly for the general purposes of abundance and subsistence (*i.e.* security for subsistence), the use which otherwise under distributive law each man might make of his own, shall, for the more effectual fulfilment of these several ends, be directed and restricted.

and the patient wronged:—in those which relate to subsistence, abundance, and equality, they are the parties whose interests stand in competition, no blame being supposed to have place on either side. By the legislator, preference should be given to that interest by preference to which the happiness of the greatest number will be most augmented.

[VI]

The distinction marked by the word economy is applicable rather to a branch of the science of legislation, than to a division in a code of laws. It is much easier to say what branch of this science should be called political economy, than to say what laws are economical.

The most powerful means of augmenting national wealth are those which maintain the security of properties, and which gently favour their equalization. Such are the objects of civil and penal law. Those arrangements which tend to increase the national wealth by other means than security and equality (if there be any such,) may be considered as belonging to the class of economical laws.

It may be said, there is a science distinct from every other, which is called *political* economy: the mind can abstractly consider everything which concerns the wealth of nations, and form a general theory concerning it: but I do not see that there can exist a code of laws concerning political economy, distinct and separate from all the other codes. The collection of laws upon this subject would only be a mass of imperfect shreds, drawn without distinction from the whole body of laws.

Political economy, for example, has reference to the penal laws, which create the species of offences which have been called *offences against population,* and *offences against the national wealth.*

Political economy would be found connected with the international code by treaties of commerce, and with the financial code by the taxes, and their effects upon the public wealth.

[VII]

Prone as is the human mind to the making of hasty and imperfectly-grounded inductions on the field of physical science, it cannot but be much more so in the fields of psychology and ethics, in which is included the field of politics; commonly not only is the collection made of *influencing* circumstances incomplete, but *uninfluencing* circumstances, and even *obstacles,* are placed in the station of, and held up to view in the character of, principally or even exclusively operating causes.

Thus superior is the density of the clouds which overhang the relation between cause and effect in the field of morals, as compared with the field of physics. Two concurring considerations may help us to account for this difference,—1. The elements of calculation being in so large a proportion of the psychical class—such as intentions, affections, and motives,—are, in a proportional degree, situated out of the reach of direct observation. 2. In the making of the calculation, the judgment is, in a peculiar degree, liable to be disturbed and led astray by the several sources of illusion,—by original intellectual weakness, by sinister interest, by interest-begotten prejudice, and by adopted prejudice.

[VIII]

In chemistry there is no room for passion to step in and to confound the understanding—to lead men into error, and to shut their eyes against knowledge: in legislation, the circumstances are opposite, and vastly different.

[IX]

Every political and moral question ought to be [put] upon the issue of fact; and [thus] mankind are directed into the only true track of investigation which can afford instruction or hope of rational argument, the track of experiment and observation.

[X]

The figurative expression of a body-politic has produced a great number of false and extravagant ideas. An analogy, founded solely on this metaphor, has furnished a foundation for pretended arguments, and poetry has invaded the dominion of reason.

An assembly or collection of individuals, inasmuch as they are found united together, in order to perform a common act, forms what may in certain respects be called a *body*.

That which constitutes a political body, is the concurrence of many members in the same act. It is therefore clear, that the act of an assembly can only be a declarative act—an act announcing an *opinion* or a *will*.

Every act of an assembly must begin by being that of a single individual: but every declarative act, the expression of an opinion or of a will, beginning by being that of an individual, may finish by being that of a body. "This," says Titius, "is what passes in my mind." "This is precisely what has passed in mine," may Sempronius equally say.

It is, therefore, the power of agreeing in the same intellectual act which constitutes the principle of unity in a body.*

[XI]

The imaginations of writers have been stretched to give to political bodies the properties of different kinds of bodies. Sometimes they are mechanical bodies; and then it is a question of levers and springs—of wheelwork—of shocks—of friction—of balancing—of preponderance.

Sometimes they are animated bodies;—and then they have borrowed all the language of physiology:—they speak of health—of sickness—of vigour—of imbecility—of corruption—of dissolution—of sleep—of death and resurrection. I cannot tell how many political works would be annihilated, if this poetical jargon were abstracted from them, with which their authors have thought to create ideas, when they have only combined words.

It is true, that for purposes of abbreviation, it is lawful to borrow certain traits of figurative language, and that one is even obliged so to do; since intellectual ideas can only be expressed by sensible images. But in this case there are two precautions to be observed: the one, never to lose sight of simple and rigorous truth,—that is to say, to be always ready mentally to translate the figurative into simple language; the other, not to found any conclusion upon a figurative expression, so far as it has anything incorrect in it—that is to say, when it does not agree with the real facts.

Figurative language is very useful for facilitating conception, when it follows in the train of simple language: it is mischievous when it

---

*It is in reality only an intellectual act which can be identical among many individuals, and constitute the principle of unity in a body. It cannot be a physical act: such an act, peculiar to the individual who exercises it, does not offer any foundation for this identity. When the Roman senate decided that the consul Opimius should put Tiberius Gracchus to death, this decision was literally, and without figure, the act of each senator who contributed to it by his vote. When Opimius in consequence slew Gracchus with his sword, the blow struck was the act of Opimius alone. Jurists say that this act was no less the act of the senate than the other. *Qui facit per alium, facit per se.* I am not examining whether this mode of expression, which tends to confound one person with another, may have any use; all that I intend to observe here is, that if, for the sake of abbreviation, or for greater emphasis, this stroke of the sword be represented as the act of the senate, it can only be so in a figurative sense.

occupies its place. It accustoms us to reason upon the most false analogies, and gathers round the truth, a mist which the most enlightened minds are scarcely able to penetrate.

[XII]

A theory is, indeed, no farther good than in so far as its indications receive, as occasion serves, the confirmation of *experience*.

[XIII]

The fear of theory has to a certain extent its foundation in reason. There is a general propensity in those who adopt this or that theory, to push it too far; *i.e.* to set up a general proposition which is not true until certain exceptions have been taken out of it—to set it up without any of those exceptions—to pursue it without regard to the exceptions,—and thence, *pro tanto*, in cases in which it is false, fallacious, repugnant to reason and utility.

The propensity thus to push theory too far is acknowledged to be almost universal.

But what is the just inference? Not that theoretical propositions— *i.e.* propositions of considerable extent—should from such their extent be concluded to be false *in toto;* but only, that in the particular case inquiry should be made, whether, supposing the proposition to be in the character of a general rule generally true, there may not be a case in which, to reduce it within the limits of truth, reason, and utility, an exception ought to be taken out of it.

[XIV]

Till objects are distinguished, they cannot be arranged. It is thus that *truth* and *order* go on hand in hand. It is only in proportion as the former is discovered, that the latter can be improved. Before a certain order is established, truth can be but imperfectly announced: but until a certain proportion of truth has been developed and brought to light, that order cannot be established. The discovery of truth leads to the establishment of order: and the establishment of order fixes and propagates the discovery of truth.

[XV]

Principles, it is said, ought to precede consequences; and the first being established, the others will follow of course. What are the principles here meant? General propositions, and those of the widest

G

extent. What by consequences? Particular propositions, included under those general ones.

That this order is favourable to demonstration, if by demonstration be meant personal debate and argumentation, is true enough. Why? Because, if you can once get a man to admit the general proposition, he cannot, without incurring the reproach of inconsistency, reject a particular proposition that is included in it.

But, that this order is not the order of conception, of investigation, of invention, is equally undeniable. In this order, particular propositions always precede general ones. The assent to the latter is preceded by and grounded on the assent to the former.

If we prove the consequences from the principle, it is only from the consequences that we learn the principle.

Apply this to laws. The first business, according to the plan I am combating, is to find and declare the principles: the laws of a fundamental nature: that done, it is by their means that we shall be enabled to find the proper laws of detail. I say, no: it is only in proportion as we have formed and compared with one another the laws of detail, that our fundamental laws will be exact and fit for service. Is a general proposition true? It is because all the particular propositions that are included under it are true. How, then, are we to satisfy ourselves of the truth of the general one? By having under our eye all the included particular ones. What, then, is the order of investigation by which true general propositions are formed? We take a number of less extensive—of particular propositions; find some points in which they agree, and from the observation of these points form a more extensive one, a general one, in which they are all included. In this way, we proceed upon sure grounds, and understand ourselves as we go: in the opposite way, we proceed at random, and danger attends every step.

What follows? That the proper order is—first to digest the laws of detail, and when they are settled and found to be fit for use, then, and not till then, to select and frame *in terminis,* by abstraction, such propositions as may be capable of being given without self-contradiction as fundamental laws.

What is the source of this premature anxiety to establish fundamental laws? It is the old conceit of being wiser than all posterity—wiser than those who will have had more experience,—the old desire of ruling over posterity—the old recipe for enabling the dead to chain down the living. In the case of a specific law, the absurdity of such a notion is pretty well recognised, yet there the absurdity is much less than here. Of a particular law, the nature may be fully comprehended—the consequences foreseen: of a general law, this is the less likely to be the case, the greater the degree in which it possesses the quality of a general one. By a law of which you are fully master, and see clearly to the extent of, you will not attempt to bind succeeding legislators: the law you pitch upon in preference for this purpose, is one which you are unable to see to the end of.

Ought no such general propositions, then, to be ever framed till after the establishment of a complete code? I do not mean to assert this; on the contrary, in morals as in physics, nothing is to be done without them. The more they are framed and tried, the better: only, when framed, they ought to be well tried before they are ushered abroad into the world in the character of laws. In that character they ought not to be exhibited till after they have been confronted with all the particular laws to which the force of them is to apply.

[xvi]

The only form of reasoning by which instruction is to be acquired, by which Bacon, for example, and Locke and Newton learnt what they have taught us, is that which proceeds from 'particulars to generals'. Induction is that form.

[xvii]

The order in which, by the Aristotelians, the component elements of a system of subalternation are exhibited is the reverse of the historical order in which they made their appearance. By these logicians an immense aggregate is held up to view, the most extensive of which they were capable of conveying or framing a conception: that aggregate is represented as divided, or divisible, into other aggregates; these again, each of them, into others, and so on, till at last comes the last link in this sort of chain;—a link consisting of an aggregate which, not having within it any other aggregates, is composed wholly of individuals, which individuals must, if those spiritual substances are excepted, which, on the occasion, are commonly introduced, of course, consist of portions of matter, being natural bodies, or parts or portions of such bodies.

This order, according to which (the principle of methodization being, in this respect, the principle of priority and posteriority) the object of largest dimension, is that which presents itself in the first instance, is called the analytic order, or the order of *analysis;* analysis from a Greek word, which signifies to melt or break down into a number of parts, an object considered in the character of a whole.

The reverse of this is the order of priority, as chalked out by the hand of Nature. *Sense* is the fountain from which all ideas take their rise. To *sense* no objects but individual ones ever present themselves. The names first in use must, accordingly, have, all of them, been of the sort of names called *proper* names,—names invented and employed for the designation of individual objects.

From the invention of proper names to the invention of common names, must have been a very wide and ample step: long may the race have continued before any instance of its being taken actually occurred.

[XVIII]

In the field of Eudæmonics and Pantognosy, the field of abstractions or the field of concretions,—to which of these two compartments shall the surveying eye apply itself?

In the whole human race, considered at all periods of its history, the knowledge of particulars has preceded that of generals. Abstraction, a branch of Logic, is an art that has been learned by slow degrees.

But, when general conceptions have once been attained, the communication of them is performed with much more despatch, even to the most unfurnished and uninformed minds, than that of particulars; *i.e.* in a given time, much more knowledge may be communicated by the use of more general terms in company with less general terms, than by the use of less general terms alone.

True it is, without the use of particular terms, and even according to the nature of the subject, *i.e.* as it belongs to somatics or psychology, no clear knowledge can be conveyed by general ones, but by a single individual or species, exhibited in the character of a specimen or sample, for the explanation and illustration of a generic term, the exhibition of all the other individuals or particulars contained in the genus of which it is the name, may be saved.

With these explanations, from particulars to generals, may be stated as the actual order of learning or acquisition; but from generals to particulars, the most convenient and extensively efficient order of teaching or communicating instruction.

[XIX]

The present work as well as any other work of mine that has been or will be published on the subject of legislation or any other branch of moral science is an attempt to extend the experimental method of reasoning from the physical branch to the moral. What Bacon was to the physical world, Helvetius was to the moral. The moral world has therefore had its Bacon, but its Newton is yet to come.

[xx]

That arrangement of the materials of any science may, I take it, be termed a *natural* one, which takes such properties to characterize them by, as men in general are, by the common constitution of man's *nature,* disposed to attend to: such, in other words, as *naturally,* that is readily, engage, and firmly fix the attention of any one to whom they are pointed out. The materials, or elements here in question, are such actions as are the objects of what we call Laws or Institutions.

Now then, with respect to actions in general, there is no property in them that is calculated so readily to engage, and so firmly to fix the attention of an observer, as the *tendency* they may have *to,* or *divergency* (if one may so say) *from,* that which may be styled the common *end* of all of them. The end I mean is *Happiness**: and this *tendency* in any act is what we style its *utility*: as this *divergency* is that to which we give the name of *mischievousness.* With respect then to such actions in particular as are among the objects of the Law, to point out to a man the *utility* of them or the mischievousness, is the only way to make him see *clearly* that property of them which every man is in search of; the only way, in short, to give him *satisfaction.*

From *utility* then we may denominate a *principle,* that may serve to preside over and govern, as it were, such arrangement as shall be made of the several institutions or combinations of institutions that compose the matter of this science: and it is this principle, that by putting its stamp upon the several names given to those combinations, can alone render *satisfactory* and *clear* any arrangement that can be made of them.

[xxi]

By utility is meant that property in any object, whereby it tends

---

*Let this be taken for a truth upon the authority of *Aristotle*: I mean by those, who like the authority of Aristotle better than that of their own experience. Πασα τεχνη, says that philosopher, και πασα μεθοδος ομοιως δε πραξις τε και προαιρεσις, αγαθου τινος εφιεσθαι δοκει· διο καλως απεφηναντο ταγαθον, οδ παντα εφιεται. Διαφορα δε τις φαινεται των (understand τοιουτων) ΤΕΛΩΝ. —Arist. Eth. ad Nic. L. I. c. i.

to produce benefit, advantage, pleasure, good, or happiness (all this in the present case comes to the same thing), or (what comes again to the same thing) to prevent the happening of mischief, pain, evil, or unhappiness to the party whose interest is considered: if that party be the community in general, then the happiness of the community: if a particular individual, then the happiness of that individual.

The interest of the community is one of the most general expressions that can occur in the phraseology of morals: no wonder that the meaning of it is often lost. When it has a meaning, it is this. The community is a fictitious *body*, composed of the individual persons who are considered as constituting as it were its *members*. The interest of the community then is, what?—the sum of the interests of the several members who compose it.

It is in vain to talk of the interest of the community, without understanding what is the interest of the individual. A thing is said to promote the interest, or to be *for* the interest, of an individual, when it tends to add to the sum total of his pleasures: or, what comes to the same thing, to diminish the sum total of his pains.

[xxii]

In this case, as in every other, in the instance of this art as in regard to any other, a use is either a modification of the universal *end*, i.e. *well-being*, or a subordinate and subservient end, i.e. a *means* capable of being employed in contributing towards that same universal end.

Be the thing, be the object what it may, if it neither perform, nor contribute to the performance of service in either of these shapes, it is of no use,—real use it has none.

If it have anything belonging to it that can, with propriety and intelligibility, be termed use, it must be either by giving increase in a direct way to the aggregate mass of pleasure, or by applying defalcation to the aggregate mass of pain; or else by contributing or tending to contribute, in some way or other, to the production of one or other, or both of those ever desirable and ultimately only desirable effects.

[xxiii]

Productive and *unproductive,*—under one or other of these denominations, as the case may be, may be referred the action in question, in so far as where, being of the *thelematic*, and, moreover, of the *ergastic kind,* it has for its *end in view* the bringing into existence any intended result in the character of *a work*.

A work has reference to human interests and exigencies. When, in consequence of a motion, or set of motions, of the thelematic kind, in the body or among the bodies in which the motion has terminated, or those to which it has in the whole, or in any part, been communicated, any such change of condition has place, by which, for any considerable portion of time, they are or are not regarded as being rendered, in any fresh shape, subservient to human use, *a work* is spoken of as having thereby been produced.

[XXIV]

In the idea of good in all its shapes, is included the idea of evil in all its shapes. How so? Because whatever be the shape in which it is possible for evil to show itself, the exclusion or removal of it, is a correspondent good: and in the same way, under the idea of evil in all its shapes, is included the idea of good in all its shapes.

Good may accordingly be divided and distinguished into positive and negative. Positive good, is good not consisting in the absence or removal of evil: negative good is good consisting in the exclusion or removal of evil.

Good and evil being opposites, what is predicated of each may, by an appropriate change in the context, be with equal truth and propriety predicated of the other: and so with regard to reward and punishment.

[XXV]

AXIOMS

1. *Axioms of Mental Pathology—a necessary ground for all legislative arrangements.*

By an axiom of mental pathology, considered as a ground for a legislative arrangement, understand a proposition expressive of the consequences in respect of pleasure or pain, or both, found by experience to result from certain sorts of occurrences, and in particular from such in which human agency bears a part: in other words, expressive of the connexion between such occurrences as are continually taking place, or liable to take place, and the pleasures and pains which are respectively the results of them.

Practical uses of these observations, two:—1. With regard to pleasures, the learning how to leave them undisturbed, and protected against disturbance—(for as to the giving increase to them by the power of the legislator to anything beyond a very inconsiderable amount, it is neither needful nor possible;) 2. With regard to pains, the learning how on each occasion to minimize the amount of them in respect of magnitude and number—number of the individuals suffering under them—magnitude of the suffering in the case of each individual.

Arithmetic and medicine—these are the branches of art and science to which, in so far as the maximum of happiness is the object of his endeavours, the legislator must look for his means of operation:—the pains or losses of pleasure produced by a maleficent act correspond to the symptoms produced by a disease.

Experience, observation, and experiment—these are the foundations of all well-grounded medical practice: experience, observation, and experiment—such are the foundations of all well-grounded legislative practice.

In the case of both functionaries, the subject-matter of operation and the plan of operation is accordingly the same—the points of difference these:—In the case of the medical curator, the only individual who is the subject-matter of the operations performed by him, is the individual whose sufferings are in question, to whom relief is to be administered. In the case of the legislator, there are no limits to the description of the persons to whom it may happen to be the subject-matter of the operations performed by him.

By the medical curator, no power is possessed other than that which is given either by the patient himself, or in case of his inability, by those to whose management it happens to him to be subject:—by the legislatorial curator, power is possessed applicable to all persons, without exception, within his field of service; each person being considered in his opposite capacities—namely, that of a person *by whom* pleasure or pain, or both, may be experienced, and that of a person *at whose hands* pleasure or pain, or both, may be experienced.

Axioms of *corporal* pathology may be styled those most extensively applicable positions, or say propositions, by which statement is made of the several sorts of occurrences by which pleasure or pain are or have place in the human body:—as also, the results observed to follow from the performance of such operations as have been performed, and the application made of such subject-matters as have been applied for the purpose of giving increase to the aggregate of pleasure, or causing termination, alleviation, or prevention, to have place in regard to pain.

Axioms of *mental* pathology may be styled those most commonly applicable propositions by which statement is made of the several occurrences by which pleasure or pain is made to have place in the human mind:—as also, the results observed to follow from the performance of such operations as have been performed, and the application of such subject-matters as have been applied for the purpose of effecting the augmentation of the aggregate of the pleasures, or the diminution of the aggregate of the pains, by the termination, alleviation, or prevention of them respectively, when individually considered.

Security—subsistence—abundance—equality—*i.e.* minimization of inequality:—by these appellatives, denomination has been given to the particular ends which stand next in order to the universal, and the greatest happiness of the greatest number. This being admitted, these are the objects which will be in view in the formation of the several axioms of pathology which present themselves as suitable to the purpose of serving as guides to the practice of the legislatorial curator.

Unfortunately, on this occasion, the imperfection of language has produced an embarrassment, which it does not seem to be in the power of language altogether to remove: all that can be done, is to lessen and alleviate it. Subsistence—abundance—equality,—these three immediately subordinate ends are conversant about the same matter; to wit, the matter of wealth. But security, besides a matter of its own, is conversant with that same matter, with which, as above, they are conversant; to wit, the matter of wealth: security for the matter of wealth—or say, to each individual, security for that portion of the matter of wealth which at the time in question belongs to him, and is called his. Security is accordingly security against all such maleficent acts by which any portion of the matter of wealth which ought to be at the disposal of the individual in question, is prevented from being at his disposal at the time in question. Now, the not having at his disposal at the time in question a certain portion of the matter of wealth, is indeed one efficient cause of pain to the individual in question, be he who he may, but it is but one out of several. In addition to the matter of wealth, sources of pleasure, and of exemption from pain, are certain others which have been found reducible under the following denominations; to wit, power, reputation, and condition in life:—condition in life, to wit, in so far as, reference had to the individual whose it is, the effect is considered as beneficial — this complex subject-matter including in it the three subject-matters above mentioned — that is to say, the matter of wealth, or in two words, power and reputation.

Correspondent to these several subject-matters of security are so many classes of offences—of maleficent acts, by the performance of which such security is disturbed. Offences affecting property—offences affecting power—offences affecting reputation—offences affecting condition in life.

But all these subject-matters are, with reference to the individual in question, distinct from him, and exterior to him;—and in a more immediate way—and otherwise than through the medium of any of these outworks, he stands exposed to be made to suffer pain, as well of mind as of body, by the agency of every other individual, in whose instance a motive adequate to the purpose of producing an act by which it will be inflicted, has place. Thus, then, in addition to offences affecting property—offences affecting power—offences affecting reputation—offences affecting condition in life,—we have offences affecting person, considered with reference to its two distinguishable parts, body and mind.

So many of these classes of maleficent acts, so many branches of security: in which list, as being the most obviously and highly important, and most simple in the conception presented by it, security *against* maleficent acts affecting *person* — more shortly, security for person, presents itself as claiming to occupy the first place; after which, security for property, and so forth, as above.

2. *Axioms applicable to Security for Person.*

Axioms forming the grounds for such legislative arrangements as have for their object and their justification, the affording security for person against such maleficent acts, to which it stands exposed.

1. The pleasure derivable by any person from the contemplation of pain suffered by another, is in no instance so great as the pain so suffered.

2. Not even when the pain so suffered has been the result of an act done by the person in question, for no other purpose than that of producing it.

Hence, one reason for endeavouring to give security against pain of body or mind, resulting from human agency, whether from design or inattention.

Now, suppose the pain to be the result of purely natural agency,— no human agency having any part in the production of it—no human being deriving any satisfaction from the contemplation of it,—the result is still the same.

Hence one reason for endeavouring to give security against pain of body or mind resulting from casualty, or as the word is, when the evil is considered as having place upon a large scale,—*calamity*.

Axiom indicative of the reasons which form the grounds of the enactments prohibitive of maleficent acts, productive of evil, affecting persons—that is to say, either in body or mind—in any mode not comprised in one or other of the modes of maleficence from which the acts constituted offences in and by the penal code receive their denomination, viz. Offences produced by the irascible appetite:—

When by one person, without gratification sought other than that derived from the contemplation of suffering in this or that shape, as about to be produced on the part of that other gratification in a certain shape, is accordingly produced in the breast of such evil doer, —call the gratification the pleasure of *antipathy satisfied*—or of *ill-will satisfied*.

If this antipathy has had its rise in the conception that by the party in question (say the victim), evil in any shape has been done to the evil doer,—the pleasure of antipathy gratified takes the name of the pleasure of *vengeance*—or say *revenge*.

Axiom. In no case is there any reason for believing that the pleasure of antipathy gratified is so great as the pain suffered by him at whose expense, as above, the pleasure is reaped.

Offences to which the axiom applies are—1. Offences affecting body; 2. Offences affecting the mind other than those belonging to the other classes; 3. Offences affecting reputation—the reputation of the sufferer—other than those by which the reputation of the evil doer is increased; 4. Offences affecting the condition in life of the sufferer, other than those by which the reputation of the evil doer is increased or expected to be increased.

For justification of the legislative arrangements necessary to afford security against maleficent acts affecting the person, what it is necessary to show is, that by them pain will not be produced in such quantity as will cause it to outweigh the pleasure that would have been produced by the maleficent acts so prevented.

For this purpose, in order to complete the demonstration and render it objection-proof, in certain cases, it will be necessary to take into account not only the evil of the first order, but the evil of the second order likewise.

First, then, considering the matter on the footing of the effects of the first order on both sides,—Axioms bearing reference to the effects of the first order on both sides, are the following:—

Axioms serving as grounds and reasons for the provision made by the legislator for general security;—to wit, against the evils respectively produced by the several classes and genera of offences.

Case 1. An offence affecting person, or say corporal vexation, in any one of its several shapes—offender's motive, ill-will or spite—the enjoyment of the offender will not be so great as the evil of the first order, consisting in the suffering experienced by the party vexed.

Case 2. So if the offence be an offence productive of mental vexation —and the motive the same.

Case 3. So if the offence be an offence affecting reputation.

Case 4. So, exceptions excepted, in the case of every other class or genus of offences, the motive being ill-will or spite, as above.

Case 5. Exceptions are among offences affecting person and reputation jointly, the offences having for their motive sexual desire; to wit—1. Sexual seduction, allurative, or say enticitive; 2. Sexual seduction compulsory; 3. Rape; 4. Vexatious lascivious contrectation.

In any of these cases, what may happen is—that the enjoyment of the offender may be equal or more than equal to the suffering of the party wronged; in either of which cases the evil of the first order has no place. But to all other persons, the suffering of the one part will present itself as being to an indefinite degree greater than the enjoyment of the offender and proportioned to the apparent excess will be the actual alarm on the part and on behalf of persons exposed to the like wrong from the same cause: and thence, so far as regards alarm, will be the evil of the second order.

Addendum to security axioms:—

Be the modification of the matter of prosperity what it may, by losing it without an equivalent, a man suffers according to, and in proportion to, the value of it in his estimation—the value by him put upon it.

Value may be distinguished into—1. General, or say value in the way of *exchange*; and 2. Special, or say idiosyncratical—value in the way of *use* in his own individual instance.

Note, that the value of a thing in the way of exchange arises out of, and depends altogether upon, and is proportioned to, its value in the way of use:—for no man would give anything that had a value in the way of use in exchange for anything that had no such value.

But value in the way of use may be distinguished into *general,* which has place so far as, and no further than, the thing is of use to persons in general—and *special* or idiosyncratical, which has place in so far as, in the case of this or that person in particular, the thing has a value in the way of use over and above the value which it has in the case of persons in general: of which use, that of the *pretium affectionis,* the *value of affection,* is an example.

Definition: When from any cause—human agency or any other—a mass of the matter of wealth, or of the matter of prosperity in any other shape, is made to go out of an individual's possession or expectancy without his consent, the pain produced in his breast by contemplation of its non-existence, or say by the loss of it, call *the pain of disappointment*: he being disappointed at the thought of the good which, it having been in his possession or expectancy, he has thus lost.

Among the objects of law in every community, is the affording security against this pain in this shape.

Axiom: The pleasure of antipathy or revenge produced in the breast of the evil-doer by the contemplation of a pain of disappointment produced in the breast of the sufferer, is not in any case so great in magnitude as that same pain.

To this axiom corresponds, as being thereon grounded, a fundamental principle entitled the *disappointment-preventing principle.*

3. Axioms pathological, applicable to Subsistence.

Axiom 1. Though to each individual his own subsistence be, by the nature of man, rendered the chief object of his care, and during his infancy an object of care to the author of his existence, yet a considerable portion of the aggregate number of the members of the community there will always be, in whose instance a subsistence cannot have place without provision made by the legislator to that effect.

2. For the subsistence of all, and accordingly of these, provision will to a certain degree have been made by the provision for security in all its shapes, and for security of property in particular: as also for abundance; for abundance, because of the abundance possessed by some is composed a stock, a fund, out of which matter is capable of being taken applicable to the purpose of affording, whether immediate or through exchange, subsistence to others. But for the subordinate end to the purpose here in question, the utmost of what can be done for

these two other subordinate ends, taken together, will not of itself be sufficient.

Of the nonpossession of the matter of subsistence in such quantity as is necessary to the support of life, death is the consequence: and such natural death is preceded by a course of suffering much greater than what is attendant on the most afflictive violent deaths employed for the purpose of punishment.

Rather than continue to labour under this affliction, individuals who are experiencing it will naturally and necessarily, in proportion as they find opportunity, do what depends upon them towards obtaining, at the charge of others, the means of rescuing themselves from it: and in proportion as endeavours to this purpose are employed, or believed to be intended to be employed, security for property is certainly diminished—security for person probably diminished on the part of all others.

By the coercive authority of the legislator provision cannot be made for the indigent, otherwise than by defalcation from the mass of the matter of abundance possessed by the relatively opulent, nor yet, without a correspondent defalcation more or less considerable, from security for property on their part.

In every habitable part of the earth, people, so soon as they behold themselves and their eventual offspring secured against death for want of the matter of subsistence, which security cannot be afforded otherwise than by correspondent defalcation from the matter of abundance in the hands of the relatively opulent, will continue to effect addition to the number of its inhabitants. But this augmentation thus produced will proceed with much greater rapidity than any addition that can be made to the quantity of the matter of subsistence possessed, as above, by the indigent, by defalcation made at the expense of security for property, as well as from the matter of abundance, by correspondent defalcation from the matter of abundance in the hands of the relatively opulent.

The consequence is, that sooner or later, on every habitable part of the earth's surface, the community will be composed of three classes of inhabitants:—1. Those by whom, with the addition of more or less of the matter of abundance, the matter of subsistence is possessed in a quantity sufficient for the preservation of life and health;—2. Those who, being in a state in which they are perishing for want of the matter of subsistence, are on their way to speedy death;—3. Those who to save themselves from impending death are occupied in waging war upon the rest, providing the means of subsistence for themselves at the expense of the security of all, and the matter of subsistence and abundance in the possession of all.

So long as by arrangements taken for the purpose by government, the thus redundant part of the population can be cleared off by being conveyed from the habitable part of the globe in question to some other part, these two classes of quickly perishing individuals may be prevented from receiving formation, or if formed, from receiving increase. But in no one part of the habitable globe can this be done by government without expense, nor the matter of expense be obtained without defalcation made from security, and suffering from loss, by forced contribution as above; and sooner or later, in proportion as property and security for property establishes itself, the whole surface of the habitable globe cannot but be fully peopled, in such sort, that from no one spot to any other could human creatures be transplanted in a living and about to live state.

Human benevolence can, therefore, hardly be better employed than in a quiet solution of these difficulties, and in the reconciliation of a provision for the otherwise perishing indigent, with this continual tendency to an increase in the demand for such provision.

4. *Axioms applying to Abundance.*

1. Included in the mass of the matter of abundance, is the mass of the matter of subsistence. The matter of wealth is at once the matter of subsistence and the matter of abundance: the sole difference is the quantity;—it is less in the case of subsistence—greater in the case of abundance.

2. If of two persons, one has the minimum of subsistence without addition,—and the other, that same minimum with an addition,—the former has the matter of subsistence, the latter the matter of abundance:—understand, in comparison with him who has nothing beyond the minimum of the matter of subsistence,—the term abundance being a comparative, a relative term.

3. The matter of subsistence being, in the instance of each individual, necessary to existence, and existence necessary to happiness, —suppose a quantity of the matter of wealth sufficient for the subsistence of 10,000 persons, at the disposition of the legislator;—more happiness will be producible, by giving to each one of the 10,000 a particle of the matter of subsistence, than by giving to 5,000 of them a portion of the matter of abundance composed of two particles of the

matter of subsistence, and then giving none to the remaining 5,000: since, on that supposition, the 5,000 thus left destitute would soon die through a lingering death.

4. But suppose that, after giving existence to the 10,000, and to each of them a particle of the matter of subsistence, the legislator have at his disposal a quantity of the matter of wealth sufficient for the subsistence of other 10,000 persons, and that he have the option— of either giving existence to an additional number of persons to that same amount, with a minimum of the matter of subsistence to each, —or instead, without making any addition to the first 10,000, of giving an addition to the quantity of wealth possessed by them,—a greater addition to the aggregate quantity of happiness would be made by dividing among the first 10,000 the whole additional quantity of wealth, than by making any addition to the number of persons brought into existence. For, supposing the whole 10,000 having each of them the minimum of the matter of subsistence on any given day, —the next day, in consequence of some accident, they might cease to have it, and in consequence cease to have existence: whereas, if of this same 10,000, some had, in addition to his minimum of the matter of subsistence, particles one or more of the matter of abundance, here would be a correspondent mass of the matter of wealth, capable of being by the legislator so disposed of as to be made to constitute the matter of subsistence to those who, otherwise being without subsistence, would soon be without existence.

5. Not that, as between the matter of subsistence, and the matter of abundance, the identity is other than virtual—identity with reference to the purpose here in question, to wit, the effect on happiness;—and this virtuality depends upon the facility of obtaining one of the sorts of matter necessary to subsistence, in exchange for matter neither necessary, nor so much as contributing to subsistence—potatoes, for example, in exchange for coin; but so far as is necessary to the guidance of the legislator's practice, this virtual identity always has had. and is likely always to have place.

6. Thus it is that the matter of abundance, as contradistinguished from the matter of subsistence, is contributory to happiness, in three distinguishable ways or capacities:—1. As contributing in a direct way to enjoyment, in a degree over and above what could be contributed by the mere matter of subsistence; 2. As contributing in an indirect way to security, to wit, by its capacity of serving, in the way of exchange, for the obtainment of the efficient instruments of security

in any of these shapes; 3. As eventually contributing, in the same indirect way, to subsistence.

5. *Axioms applying to Equality, in respect of wealth.*

I. Case or state of things the first.—The quantities of wealth in question, considered as being in a quiescent state, actually in the hands of the two parties in question: neither entering into, nor going out of the hands of either.

1. *Cæteris paribus,*—to every particle of the matter of wealth corresponds a particle of the matter of happiness. Accordingly, thence,

2. So far as depends upon wealth,—of two persons having unequal fortunes, he who has most wealth must by a legislator be regarded as having most happiness.

3. But the quantity of happiness will not go on increasing in anything near the same proportion as the quantity of wealth:—ten thousand times the quantity of wealth will not bring with it ten thousand times the quantity of happiness. It will even be matter of doubt, whether ten thousand times the wealth will in general bring with it twice the happiness.* Thus it is, that,

4. The effect of wealth in the production of happiness goes on diminishing, as the quantity by which the wealth of one man exceeds that of another goes on increasing: in other words, the quantity of happiness produced by a particle of wealth (each particle being of the same magnitude) will be less and less at every particle; the second will produce less than the first, the third than the second, and so on.

5. Minimum of wealth, say £10 per year;—greatest excess of happiness produced by excess in the quantity of wealth, as 2 to 1:—magnitude of a particle of wealth, £1 a year. On these data might be grounded a scale or table, exhibiting the quantities of happiness produced, by as many additions made to the quantity of wealth at the bottom of the scale, as there are pounds between £10 and £10,000.

II. Case, or state of things the second,—the particles of wealth about to enter into the hands of the parties in question.

1. Fortunes unequal:—by a particle of wealth, if added to the wealth of him who has least, more happiness will be produced, than if added to the wealth of him who has most.

2. Particles of wealth at the disposition of the legislator, say 10,000; —happiness of the most wealthy to that of the least wealthy, say (as per No. 5,) as 2 to 1:—by giving to each one of 10,000 a particle of

---

*In England a disproportion still greater than this is actually exemplified.

H

wealth, the legislator will produce 5,000 times the happiness he would produce by giving the 10,000 particles to one person.

3. On these data might be grounded a scale, exhibiting the quantities of happiness produced, by so many additions made as above to the minimum of wealth, to the respective happiness of any number of persons, whose respective quantities of wealth exceed one another, by the amount of a particle in each instance.

III. Case, or state of things the third,—the particles of wealth about to go out of the hands of the parties.

1. By the subtraction of a particle of the matter of wealth, a less subtraction from happiness will be produced, if made from the wealth of him who has the matter of abundance, than if from the wealth of him who has the matter of subsistence only.

2. So, if from the wealth of him who has a larger portion of the matter of abundance, than if from the wealth of him who has not so large a portion of the matter of abundance.

3. Fortunes equal, and the aggregate sum subtracted being given, the greater the number of the persons from whose wealth the subtraction is made, the less will be the subtraction thereby made from the aggregate of happiness.

4. Fortunes unequal, still less will be the subtraction of happiness, if it be in the ratio of their fortunes that the subtraction is made, the greatest quantity being subtracted from those whose fortunes are greatest.

5. A quantity of the matter of wealth may be assigned, so small, that if subtracted from the fortune of a person possessed of a certain quantity of the matter of abundance, no sensible subtraction of happiness would be the result.

6. The larger the fortune of the individual in question, the greater the probability that, by the subtraction of a given quantity of the matter of wealth, no subtraction at all will be made from the quantity of his happiness.

7. So likewise, if the ratio of the sum to be subtracted, to the aggregate mass from which it is to be subtracted, be so great, that by the subtraction of it, subtraction of a quantity, more or less considerable, cannot but be made from the aggregate of happiness,—still the larger, in the case of each individual, the aggregate of wealth is from which the subtraction is made, the less will be the quantity of happiness so subtracted, as above.

IV. Case, or state of things the fourth,—the particles of wealth about to go out of the hands of the one party into the hands of the other.

1. Fortunes equal:—take from the one party a portion of the matter of wealth and give it to the other,—the quantity of happiness gained to the gainer of the wealth will not be so great as the quantity of happiness lost to the loser of the wealth.

2. Fortunes unequal:—the poorer the loser, the richer the gainer: greater in this case is the diminution produced in the mass of happiness by the transfer, than in the last mentioned case.

3. Fortunes again unequal:—the richer the loser, the poorer the gainer: the effect produced on happiness by the transfer may in this case be either loss or gain.

Whether it be the one or the other, will depend partly upon the degree of the inequality, partly upon the magnitude of the portion of wealth transferred. If the inequality be very small, and the wealth transferred also small, the effect produced on the sum of happiness may be loss. But if either be—much more if both be other than, very small, the effect on happiness will be gain.

4. Income of the richer, say £100,000 a-year—income of the less rich, say £99,999 a-year: wealth taken from the first, and transferred to the less rich, £1 a-year:—on the sum of happiness the effect will be on the side of loss;—more happiness will be lost by the richer than gained by the less rich.

Hence one cause of the preponderance produced on the side of evil by the practice called gaming.

5. Income of the richer loser, £100,000 a-year:—income of the less rich gainer, £10 a-year;—wealth lost to the richer, gained by the less rich, £1 a-year:—on the sum of happiness the effect will be on the side of gain. More happiness will be gained by the less rich gainer, than lost by the more rich loser.

Thus it is, that if the effects of the first order were alone taken into account, the consequence would be, that, on the supposition of a new constitution coming to be established, with the greatest happiness of the greatest number for its end in view, sufficient reason would have place for taking the matter of wealth from the richest and transferring it to the less rich, till the fortunes of all were reduced to an equality, or a system of inequality so little different from perfect equality, that the difference would not be worth calculating.

But call in now the effects of the second and those of the third order, and the effect is reversed: to maximization of happiness would be substituted universal annihilation in the first place of happiness—in the next place of existence. Evil of the second order,—annihilation of happiness by the universality of the alarm, and the swelling of danger into certainty:—Evil of the third order,—annihilation of existence by the certainty of the non-enjoyment of the fruit of labour, and thence the extinction of all inducement to labour.

Independently of the destruction which would thus be produced by carrying, or even by the known intention of carrying to its utmost possible length the equalization, or say levelling system, as above, diminution would be effected in the aggregate of happiness, by the extinction of the fund afforded by the matter of abundance for keeping undiminished the stock of the matter of wealth necessary for subsistence.

On consideration of what is stated above, it will be found that the plan of distribution applied to the matter of wealth, which is most favourable to universality of subsistence, and thence, in other words, to the maximization of happiness, is that in which, while the fortune of the richest—of him whose situation is at the top of the scale, is greatest, the degrees between the fortune of the least rich and that of the most rich are most numerous,—in other words, the gradation most regular and insensible.

The larger the fortunes of the richest are, the smaller will be the number of those whose fortunes approach near to that high level: the smaller, therefore, the number of those from whose masses of property the largest defalcation could by possibility be made:—and, moreover, the larger those masses, the greater would be the difficulty which the legislator would experience as to the obtaining at their charge such defalcation as the nature of the case would not exclude the possibility of making.

Thus, for example, it would, in case of over population, be easier in England, or even in Ireland, to ward off famine for a time, than it would be in British India.

Equality requires, that though it be at the expense of all the other members of the community, the income of those whose income is composed of the wages of labour be maximized. Reason: Of these are composed the vast majority of the whole number of the members of the community.

Exceptions excepted, equality requires that the profits of stock be minimized. Reason: Because the net profit of stock is composed of the mass, or say portion remaining to the employer of the stock, after deduction made of the wages of the labour applied to it.

Exception will be—if this supposed case be really exemplified—where the possessors of the wages of labour are so many, and the possessors of the profits of stock so few, that by a small addition to the one, no sensible defalcation will be made from the other.

6. *Axioms relating to Power, Rank, and Reputation.*

By axioms relating to power, understand self-serving power, exempt from the obligation by which it is converted into trust.

As between individual and individual, the pleasure to the superior, to the power-holder, from the possession and exercise of the power, is not so great as the pain experienced by the party subjected.

Therefore, only when converted into extra-benefiting by appropriate obligation, can it be conducive to greatest happiness.

The same observations will equally apply to rank, and factitious estimation produced by rank.

So also to extra reputation, or say estimation, unless when acquired by service rendered to others.

The principle corresponding to these axioms, as to equality, is *the inequality-minimizing principle.*

[XXVI]

If I having a crown in my pocket, and not being athirst hesitate whether I should buy a bottle of claret with it for my own drinking, or lay it out in providing for a family I see about to perish for want of any assistance, so much the worse for me at the long run : but it is plain that, so long as I continue hesitating, the two pleasures of sensuality in the one case, of sympathy in the other, were exactly worth to me five shillings, to me they were exactly equal.

I beg a truce here of our man of sentiment and feeling while from necessity, and it is only from necessity, I speak and prompt mankind to speak a mercenary language. The Thermometer is the instrument for measuring the heat of the weather : the Barometer the instrument for measuring the pressure of the Air. Those who are not satisfied with the accuracy of those instruments must find out others that shall be more accurate, or bid adieu to Natural Philosophy. Money is the instrument of measuring the quantity of pain or pleasure. Those who are not satisfied with the accuracy of this instrument must find out some other that shall be more accurate, or bid adieu to politics and morals.

Let no man therefore be either surprized or scandalized if he find me in the course of this work valuing everything in money. 'Tis in this way only can we get aliquot parts to measure by. If we must not say of a pain or a pleasure that it is worth so much money, it is in vain, in point of quantity, to say anything at all about it, there is neither proportion nor disproportion between Punishments and Crimes.

[xxvii]

Between *"real service and its reward"* the exact common measure is the least quantity of the matter of reward that he who is able to render the service consents to take in return for it. This is the measure of all *prices*: this is the measure of the value of all good things that are at once valuable and tangible. This is the measure of the value of all *labour,* by which things tangible are produced; as also of all labour by which, though nothing tangible is produced, valuable service in some other shape is rendered.

[xxviii]

It was from Beccaria's little treatise on crimes and punishments that I drew, as I well remember, the first hint of this principle, by which the precision and clearness and incontestableness of mathematical calculation are introduced for the first time into the field of morals—a field to which in its own nature they are applicable with a propriety no less incontestable, and when once brought to view, manifest, than that of physics, including its most elevated quarter, the field of mathematics.

[xxix]

Note, that *arithmetical* expression is throughout but an abridgement of ordinary ditto: *algebraical,* of arithmetical and ordinary mixed.

Note also, that of whatever matter is expressed by arithmetical and algebraical signs, there is not a particle that could not be expressed by the signs employed in ordinary discourse; and note that in this case it would be intelligible, and without effort, to non-mathematical readers at large.

And yet, of that stock of information which has been obtained by the use of those signs,—more especially that most formidable sort, composed of letters of the alphabet,—it seems clear enough, that not more than a comparatively small part could have been obtained without them.

The reason is—that, but for these modes of compression, to such a bulk would the matter have swollen, that, before the result had been obtained, the minds of writers and readers would have been bewildered and put to a stand: the conceptive faculty not being able to grasp, at once, the whole quantity necessary to the obtainment of the result.

[xxx]

A general proposition which has no individual object to which it is truly applicable, is not a true one. It is no more a true proposition than an army which has no soldier in it is a true army; a fagot which has no stick in it, a true fagot.

A mathematical proposition which has no individual portion of matter or space to which it is truly applicable, is a general proposition which has no individual object to which it is truly applicable.

[xxxi]

I have by me a large quarto of mathematics, written by a mathematician and politician of deserved eminence, in which the utility of numbers, as a security for good judicature, is assumed.[1] The conclusions of mathematicians, though always mathematically just, are not unfrequently physically false: that is, they would be true if things were not as they are. Some necessary element is omitted to be taken into the account: and thus the only effect of the operation is to mislead.

---

[1][A key to the question as to what treatise Bentham actually had in mind is afforded by his pamphlet "Scotch Reform" (*Works* V, 1sq). There he mentions, in a similar connection, Condorcet (19), and it is obvious that he is referring to the latter's "Essai sur l'application de l'analyse à la probabilité de décisions rendues à la pluralité des voix", Paris 1785. Bentham speaks, it is true, of "a quarto volume with 460 well-filled pages in it" while the work has in fact some 490 pages; yet this is probably a misprint or a lapsus calami since the "axiom" against which he argues, is in fact formulated on p. 24 of the preface which he quotes: ". . . plus le nombre des Votans augmentera, plus la probabilité de la verité de la décision sera grande: la limite de cette probabilité sera la certitude; en sorte qu'en multipliant le nombre des Votans, on aura une possibilité aussi grande qu'on voudra d'avoir une décision vraie . . . " Against this opinion Bentham set the view that a single judge is the best, above all because he alone feels the full weight of his responsibility—"it being . . . of the nature of responsibility (in the burthensome sense of the word) to go on diminishing ad infinitum, in proportion as the number of those who are sharers in the burthen is increased" (*Works* V, 116; cf. also 184).]

DEFENCE OF USURY

DEFENCE of USURY;

Shewing the Impolicy of the

PRESENT LEGAL RESTRAINTS

ON THE TERMS OF

PECUNIARY BARGAINS

IN A

SERIES OF LETTERS TO A FRIEND

TO WHICH IS ADDED

A LETTER

TO

ADAM SMITH, Esq; LL.D.

On the Discouragements opposed by the above
Restraints to the Progress of

INVENTIVE INDUSTRY

1787

LETTERS
IN
DEFENCE OF USURY, &c.

CONTENTS

Lett. I. *Introduction.*

to get money at an extraordinary than at the ordinary rate; What they do get, they get at the ordinary rate, of their friends;

3. Preventing their getting what they want at a high rate, in the way of borrowing, prevents not their getting it in the way of taking up goods on credit; Conclusion, that the effect of these laws with regard to prodigality, as far as it has any, is to increase it; The only effectual check to prodigality, an *interdict*, as under the Roman law.

Lett. IV. *Reasons for Restraint.*
3. *Protection of Indigence.*

The advantage it may be of to a man to borrow money, and the need he may have of it, admitting of an undetermined number of degrees, so may the consideration he pays for it; No legislator can judge, so well as each individual for himself, whether money is worth to him any thing, and how much, beyond the ordinary interest; Repression of projectors.—This subject referred to the letter to Dr. Smith.

Lett. V. *Reasons for Restraint.*
4. *Protection of Simplicity.*

No simplicity short of idiotism can render an individual so bad a judge in this case as the legislator; It would be to no purpose to prevent a man from being imposed upon in this way, unless he was prevented from being imposed upon in purchases and sales; A man is not so liable to imposition in this way, as in those; And in this way imprudence admits of a remedy, which it does not in those others; viz. borrowing at a lower rate to pay off the first loan.

Lett. VI. *Mischiefs of the anti-usurious Laws.*

Various ways in which the laws against usury may do mischief;
1. By precluding many from assistance altogether;
2. Forcing men upon more disadvantageous ways of obtaining it; Detriment suffered in this way by many during the war;
3. Or upon more disadvantageous terms in the very way forbidden; In as far as the law appears open to evasion, it is either nugatory, or else mischievous, in any one of those three ways, according to circumstances;
4. Exposing an useful class of men to unmerited suffering and disgrace;
5. Encouraging and protecting treachery and ingratitude; Difference in this respect between the rewards held out to informers in this

case, and those held out to informers at large; — or even to real criminals informing against accomplices; Caution against extending to those cases the censure passed on this occasion.

LETT. VII. *Efficacy of the anti-usurious Laws.*

Position of Dr. Smith's, that a law attempting to reduce interest below a certain rate must be inefficacious; The position not warranted by the fact alledged in support of it; Nothing can destroy the efficacy of such restraint in regard to one rate of interest, that does not in regard to others; Why such destruction would be more apparent with regard to one rate than another; Conjecture concerning the real state of the fact, in the instance alluded to by Dr. Smith; The English laws on this head how far open to evasion; Russian laws[:] their perfect inefficacy on this head.

LETT. VIII. *Virtual Usury allowed.*

Cases where interest above the ordinary rate has been taken by *evasion* of the law;

1. Drawing and re-drawing;
2. Selling bills of exchange at under price;

Cases where it is taken by allowance of the law;

1. Pawnbroking;
2. Bottomry and respondentia;

Other cases more indirectly related to usury, such as insurance, buying annuities, &c.

LETT. IX. *Blackstone considered.*

In Blackstone's opinion, the harm of making too hard a bargain stands on the same footing in the hire of a horse as of money; If so, consistency requires the subjecting both businesses to the same restraints; Popular prejudice has got the length of giving bad names in both cases; Blackstone's reasoning concerning the money-trade applied to the horse-trade; Proposal for fixing by law the same price for all horses; The values of horses differ not more than the value of money on different occasions.

LETT. X. *Grounds of the Prejudices against Usury.*

Causes of the discountenance shewn to the lender of money at interest;

1. The prevalence of the ascetic principle among Christians;
2. The horror of every thing Jewish;
3. Aristotle's aphorism about the natural barrenness of money;
4. The motives, selfish as well as social, which concur in render-

ing the profuse character more amiable than the saving; A proof of
this, the unfavourable light in which money-lenders, and other men
of thrift, are always represented on the stage; Hence, even from legislators, the lender's interest has met with less attention and favour
than the borrower's; Yet by this partiality the parties meant to be
favoured, have been the greatest sufferers.

LETT. XI. *Compound Interest.*

Compound interest, how far discountenanced by the law; No argument against it, but the notion of usury, or that of hardship;
Inconsistency and mischief of such discountenance; The casual
inability of the borrower is a reason, not for such discountenance, but
for a respite, which the law never gives; Effects of such false tenderness in breeding *mala fide* delays.

LETT. XII. *Maintenance and Champerty.*

Inexpediency of restraining men in their bargains for money, in
the instance where the money is wanted for purchasing the assistance
of the laws; Such bargains forbidden, by the laws against maintenance and champerty; Case of a gentleman who lost £3,000 a year by
those laws; Absurdity of continuing laws made to obviate a mischief
of which no traces remain; The above case may serve also to evince
and illustrate the mischief of the laws restraining the rate of interest.

LETT. XIII. *To Dr. Smith, on Projects in Arts, &c.*

Occasion of this address; The object of it, the defence of projectors;
Passage, in which Dr. Smith approves of the law fixing the rate of
interest, on account of its tendency to repress them; Prejudice under
which they labour; The law, and therefore the censure past on them
by the approbation given to that law, admits of no discrimination in
favour of the innocent and meritorious; The projector cannot hope
for money at the highest rate of interest at present legal, because that
may always be had with more safety from old-established trades;
The censure on projectors necessarily involves the authors of all the
arts to which the world owes its prosperity; And the laws, the approbation of which is connected with that censure, must, as far as their
influence has extended, have operated as obstacles to that prosperity;
Another passage, in which the censure passed on projectors is plainly
extended to all improvers; The censure passed on projectors is inconsistent with some fundamental ideas of Dr. Smith; Concerning the
natural prevalence of prudence over imprudence—even that which
manifests itself in prodigality — and the progress of improvement

which has been the consequence; Grounds for not attributing that prosperity to the operation of the laws in restraining projectors; Great advances in prosperity had been made prior to the earliest of those laws; That their tendency can only have been to lessen the total number of projectors, without lessening the proportion of bad to good; The greatest mischief that could have been done by projecting, if totally unrestrained, could not, according to Dr. Smith, warrant the interposition of the law, because, according to him, that done by prodigals does not warrant that interposition; But prodigality is at any rate much more certainly ruinous, and much more common, than projecting; In controuling prodigality the law controuls passion by reason: in controuling projects, it controuls knowledge by ignorance; Dr. Smith condemns this latter interference also, in the censure he passes on the laws which attempt to direct individuals in their private concerns; The argument repeated—that the censure on projects involves all past improvements; But future projects, as such, must be less dangerous than the past ones were; The only case, in which the restraints applied by these laws to projects attaches upon them, is that in which they are best guarded against hazard, viz. by the necessity of their being discussed before a judge whose prepossession is rather on the other side; The ruin of every projector, without exception, would not be sufficient to disprove the utility of projects; Of two towns instanced by Dr. Smith, that which is most of a projecting town is most prosperous; Approbation bestowed by Dr. Smith himself on projects, under another name, as also on other laws that favour them, a warning to guard against the delusion of sounds; Censure passed on projectors hostile to the object of the Society of Arts; Probable grounds of this censure;

1. Popular opinion, as expressed by the bad sense contracted by the word "Projector";

2. Too hasty generalization;

Hopes of his turning against the current of popular prejudice, in this instance, grounded on the others in which he has done so; Expedients proposed for taking away the restraint of the anti-usurious laws from projectors only;

1. Bonds and affidavits to secure the applying the money obtained at extra-interest to this use;

2. Boards to grant licences for that purpose: ex. gr. the Committees of the Society of Arts;

This a bad and unnecessary expedient.

DEFENCE OF USURY

LETTER I

Introduction.

Crichoff, in White Russia, January 1787.

AMONG the various species or modifications of liberty, of which
on different occasions we have heard so much in England, I
do not recollect ever seeing any thing yet offered in behalf of
the *liberty of making one's own terms in money-bargains.* From so
general and universal a neglect, it is an old notion of mine, as you
well know, that this meek and unassuming species of liberty has
been suffering much injustice.

A fancy has taken me, just now, to trouble you with my reasons:
which, if you think them capable of answering any good purpose,
you may forward to the press: or in the other case, what will give you
less trouble, to the fire.

In a word, the proposition I have been accustomed to lay down to
myself on this subject is the following one, viz. that *no man of ripe
years and of sound mind, acting freely, and with his eyes open, ought
to be hindered, with a view to his advantage, from making such
bargain, in the way of obtaining money, as he thinks fit: nor,* (what
is a necessary consequence) *any body hindered from supplying him,
upon any terms he thinks proper to accede to.*

This proposition, were it to be received, would level, you see, at
one stroke, all the barriers which law, either statute or common, have
in their united wisdom set up, either against the crying sin of Usury,
or against the hard-named and little-heard-of practice of Champerty;
to which we must also add a portion of the multifarious, and as little-
heard-of offence, of Maintenance.

On this occasion, were it any individual antagonist I had to deal
with, my part would be a smooth and easy one. "You, who fetter
contracts; you, who lay restraints on the liberty of man, it is for you"
(I should say) "to assign a reason for your doing so." That contracts
in general ought to be observed, is a rule, the propriety of which, no
man was ever yet found wrong-headed enough to deny: if this case is
one of the exceptions (for some doubtless there are) which the safety

and welfare of every society require should be taken out of that general rule, in this case, as in all those others, it lies upon him, who alledges the necessity of the exception, to produce a reason for it.

This, I say, would be a short and very easy method with an individual: but, as the world has no mouth of its own to plead by, no certain attorney by which it can "come and defend this force and injury," I must even find arguments for it at a venture, and ransack my own imagination for such phantoms as I can find to fight with.

In favour of the restraints opposed to the species of liberty I contend for, I can imagine but five arguments.

1. Prevention of usury.
2. Prevention of prodigality.
3. Protection of indigence against extortion.
4. Repression of the temerity of projectors.
5. Protection of simplicity against imposition.

Of all these in their order.

LETTER II
Reasons for Restraint.—Prevention of Usury.

I will begin with the *prevention of usury*: because in the sound of the word *usury* lies, I take it, the main strength of the argument: or, to speak strictly, of what is of more importance than all argument, of the hold which the opinion I am combating has obtained on the imaginations and passions of mankind.

Usury is a bad thing, and as such ought to be prevented: usurers are a bad sort of men, a very bad sort of men, and as such ought to be punished and suppressed. These are among the string of propositions which every man finds handed down to him from his progenitors: which most men are disposed to accede to without examination, and indeed not unnaturally nor even unreasonably disposed, for it is impossible the bulk of mankind should find leisure, had they the ability, to examine[1] into the grounds of an hundredth part of the rules and maxims, which they find themselves obliged to act upon. Very good apology this for John Trot: but a little more inquisitiveness may be required of legislators.

You, my friend, by whom the true force of words is so well understood, have, I am sure, gone before me in perceiving, that to say usury is a thing to be prevented, is neither more nor less than begging the

---

[1][Misprinted in the second edition as "xamine".]

matter in question. I know of but two definitions that can possibly be given of usury: one is, the taking of a greater interest than the law allows of: this may be stiled the *political* or *legal* definition. The other is the taking of a greater interest than it is usual for men to give and take: this may be stiled the *moral* one: and this, where the law has not interfered, is plainly enough the only one. It is plain, that in order for usury to be prohibited by law, a positive description must have been found for it by law, fixing, or rather superseding, the moral one. To say then that usury is a thing that ought to be prevented, is saying neither more nor less, than that the utmost rate of interest which shall be taken ought to be fixed; and that fixation enforced by penalties, or such other means, if any, as may answer the purpose of preventing the breach of it. A law punishing usury supposes, therefore, a law fixing the allowed legal rate of interest: and the propriety of the penal law must depend upon the propriety of the simply-prohibitive, or, if you please, declaratory one.

One thing then is plain; that, antecedently to custom growing from convention, there can be no such thing as usury: for what rate of interest is there that can naturally be more proper than another? what natural fixed price can there be for the use of money more than for the use of any other thing? Were it not then for custom, usury, considered in a moral view, would not then so much as admit of a definition: so far from having existence, it would not so much as be conceivable: nor therefore could the law, in the definition it took upon itself to give of such offence, have so much as a guide to steer by. Custom therefore is the sole basis, which, either the moralist in his rules and precepts, or the legislator in his injunctions, can have to build upon. But what basis can be more weak or unwarrantable, as a ground for coercive measures, than custom resulting from free choice? My neighbours, being at liberty, have happened to concur among themselves in dealing at a certain rate of interest. I, who have money to lend, and Titius, who wants to borrow it of me, would be glad, the one of us to accept, the other to give, an interest somewhat higher than theirs: why is the liberty they exercise to be made a pretence for depriving me and Titius of ours?

Nor has blind custom, thus made the sole and arbitrary guide, any thing of steadiness or uniformity in its decisions: it has varied, from age to age, in the same country: it varies, from country to country, in the same age: and the legal rate has varied along with it: and indeed, with regard to times past, it is from the legal rate, more readily than from any other source, that we collect the customary. Among the Romans, till the time of Justinian, we find it as high as 12 per cent.: in England, so late as the time of Hen. VIII, we find it at 10 per cent.: succeeding statutes reduced it to 8, then to 6, and lastly to 5, where it stands at present. Even at present in Ireland it is at 6 per cent.; and in the West-Indies at 8 per cent.; and in Hindostan, where there is no rate limited by law, the lowest customary rate is 10 or 12. At Constantinople, in certain cases, as I have been well informed, thirty per cent. is a common rate. Now, of all these widely different rates, what one is there, that is intrinsically more proper than another? What is it that evidences this propriety in each instance? what but the mutual convenience of the parties, as manifested by their consent? It is convenience then that has produced whatever there has been of custom in the matter: What can there then be in custom, to make it a better guide than the convenience which gave it birth? and what is there in convenience, that should make it a worse guide in one case than in another? It would be convenient to me to give 6 per cent. for money: I wish to do so. "No," (says the law) "you shan't."—Why so? "Because it is not convenient to your neighbour to give above 5 for it." Can any thing be more absurd than such a reason?

Much has not been done, I think, by legislators as yet in the way of fixing the price of other commodities: and, in what little has been done, the probity of the intention has, I believe, in general, been rather more unquestionable than the rectitude of the principle, or the felicity of the result. Putting money out at interest, is exchanging present money for future: but why a policy, which, as applied to exchanges in general, would be generally deemed absurd and mischievous, should be deemed necessary in the instance of this particular kind of exchange, mankind are as yet to learn. For him who takes as much as he can get for the use of any other sort of thing, an house for instance, there is no particular appellation, nor any mark of disrepute: nobody is ashamed of doing so, nor is it usual so much as to profess to do otherwise. Why a man who takes as much as he can get, be it six, or seven, or eight, or ten per cent. for the use of a sum of money should be called usurer, should be loaded with an opprobrious name, any more than if he had bought an house[1] with it, and made a proportionable profit by the house, is more than I can see.

---

[1] [First edition: "a house".]

Another thing I would also wish to learn, is, why the legislator should be more anxious to limit the rate of interest one way, than the other? why he should set his face against the owners of that species of property more than of any other? why he should make it his business to prevent their getting *more* than a certain price for the use of it, rather than to prevent their getting *less*? why, in short, he should not take means for making it penal to offer less, for example, than 5 per cent. as well as to accept more? Let any one that can, find an answer to these questions; it is more than I can do: I except always the distant and imperceptible advantage, of sinking the price of goods of all kinds; and, in that remote way, multiplying the future enjoyments of individuals. But this was a consideration by far too distant and refined, to have been the original ground for confining the limitation to this side.

LETTER III
Reasons for Restraint.—Prevention of Prodigality.

Having done with sounds, I come gladly to propositions; which, as far as they are true in point of fact, may deserve the name of reasons. And first, as to the efficacy of such restrictive laws with regard to the *prevention of Prodigality*.[1]

That prodigality is a bad thing, and that the prevention of it is a proper object for the legislator to propose to himself, so long as he confines himself to, what I look upon as, proper measures, I have no objection to allow, at least for the purpose of the argument; though, were this the principal question, I should look upon it as incumbent on me to place in a fair light the reasons there may be for doubting, how far, with regard to a person arrived at the age of discretion, third persons may be competent judges, which of two pains may be of greater force and value to him, the present pain of restraining his present desires, or the future contingent pain he may be exposed to suffer from the want to which the expence of gratifying these desires may hereafter have reduced him. To prevent our doing mischief to one another, it is but too necessary to put bridles into all our mouths: it is necessary to the tranquillity and very being of society: but that the tacking of leading-strings upon the backs of grown persons, in order to prevent their doing themselves a mischief, is not necessary either to the being or tranquillity of society, however

---

[1] [First edition: "prodigality".]

conducive to its well-being, I think cannot be disputed. Such paternal, or, if you please, maternal, care, may be a good work, but it certainly is but a work of supererogation.

For my own part, I must confess, that so long as such methods only are employed, as to me appear proper ones, and such there are, I should not feel myself disinclined to see some measures taken for the restraining of prodigality: but this I can not look upon as being of the number. My reasons I will now endeavour to lay before you.

In the first place, I take it, that it is neither natural nor usual for prodigals, as such, to betake themselves to this method, I mean, that of giving a rate of interest above the ordinary one, to supply their wants.

In the first place, no man, I hope you will allow, prodigal or not prodigal, ever thinks of borrowing money to spend, so long as he has *ready money*[1] of his own, or effects which he can turn into ready money without loss. And this deduction strikes off what, I suppose, you will look upon as the greatest proportion of the persons subject, at any given time, to the imputation of prodigality.

In the next place, no man, in such a country as Great Britain at least, has occasion, nor is at all likely, to take up money at an extra-ordinary rate of interest, who has *security*[2] to give, equal to that upon which money is commonly to be had at the highest ordinary rate. While so many advertise, as are to be seen every day advertising, money to be lent at five per cent. what should possess a man, who has any thing to offer that can be called a security, to give, for example, six per cent. is more than I can conceive.

You may say, perhaps, that a man who wishes to lend his money out upon security, wishes to have his interest punctually, and that without the expence, and hazard, and trouble, and odium of going to law; and that, on this account, it is better to have a sober man to deal with than a prodigal. So far I allow you; but were you to add, that on this account it would be necessary for a prodigal to offer more than another man, there I should disagree with you. In the first place, it is not so easy a thing, nor, I take it, a common thing, for the lender upon security to be able to judge, or even to form any attempt to judge, whether the conduct of one who offers to borrow his money is or is not of such a cast, as to bring him under this description. The question, prodigal or not prodigal, depends upon two pieces of information:

---

[1] and [2][No italics in the first edition.]

neither of which, in general, is very easy to come at: on the one hand, the amount of his means and reasonable expectations; on the other hand, the amount of his expenditure. The goodness or badness of the security is a question of a very different nature: upon this head, every man has a known and ready means of obtaining that sort of information, which is the most satisfactory the nature of things affords, by going to his lawyer. It is accordingly, I take it, on their lawyers opinion, that lenders in general found their determination in these cases, and not upon any calculations they may have formed, concerning the receipt and expenditure of the borrower. But even supposing a man's disposition to prodigality to be ever so well known,[1] there are always enough to be found, to whom such a disposition would be rather an inducement than an objection, so long as they were satisfied with the security. Every body knows the advantage to be made in case of mortgage, by foreclosing or forcing a sale: and that this advantage it not uncommonly looked out for, will, I believe, hardly be doubted by any one, who has had any occasion to observe the course of business in the court of Chancery.

In short, so long as a prodigal has any thing to pledge, or to dispose of, whether in possession, or even in reversion, whether of a certain or even of a contingent nature, I see not, how he can receive the smallest benefit, from any laws that are, or can be made to fix the rate of interest. For, suppose the law to be efficacious as far as it goes, and that the prodigal can find none of those monsters called usurers to deal with him, does he lie quiet? No such thing: he goes on and gets the money he wants, by selling his interest instead of borrowing. He goes on, I say: for if he has prudence enough to stop him any where, he is not that sort of man, whom it can be worth while for the law to attempt stopping by such means. It is plain enough then,[2] that to a prodigal thus circumstanced, the law cannot be of any service; on the contrary, it may, and in many cases must, be of disservice to him, by denying him the option of a resource, which, how disadvantageous soever, could not well have proved more so, but would naturally have proved less so, than those which it leaves still open to him. But of this hereafter.

I now come to the only remaining class of prodigals, viz. those who have nothing that can be called a security to offer. These, I should

---

[1] [First edition: ". . . so well known, I take it there are . . ."]
[2] [The first edition here again interpolates "I take it . . ."]

think,[1] are not more likely to get money upon an extraordinary rate of interest, than an ordinary one. Persons who either feel, or find reasons for pretending to feel, a friendship for the borrower, can not take of him more than the ordinary rate of interest: persons, who have no such motive for lending him, will not lend him at all. If they know him for what he is, that will prevent them of course: and even though they should know nothing of him by any other circumstance, the very circumstance of his not being able to find a friend to trust him at the highest ordinary rate, will be sufficient reason to a stranger for looking upon him as a man, who, in the judgment of his friends, is not likely to pay.

The way that prodigals run into debt, after they have spent their substance, is, I take it, by borrowing of their friends and acquaintance, at ordinary interest, or more commonly at no interest, small sums, such as each man may be content to lose, or be ashamed to ask real security for; and as prodigals have generally an extensive acquaintance (extensive acquaintance being at once the cause and effect of prodigality), the sum total of the money a man may thus find means to squander, may be considerable, tho'[2] each sum borrowed may, relatively to the circumstances of the lender, have been inconsiderable. This I take to be the race which prodigals, who have spent their all, run at present, under the present system of restraining laws: and this, and no other, I take it, would be the race they would run, were those laws out of the way.

Another consideration there is, I think, which will compleat your conviction, if it was not compleat before, of the inefficacy of these laws, as to the putting any sort of restraint upon prodigality. This is, that there is another set of people from whom prodigals get what they want, and always will get it, so long as credit lasts, in spite of all laws against high interest; and, should they find it necessary, at an expence more than equal to an excess[3] of interest they might otherwise have to give. I mean the tradesmen who deal in the goods they want. Every body knows it is much easier to get goods than money. People trust goods upon much slenderer security than they do money: it is very natural they should do so: ordinary profit of trade upon the whole capital employed in a man's trade, even after the expence of warehouse-rent, journeymen's wages, and other such general charges,

---

[1] [Instead of "I should think", the first edition reads: "I take it".]
[2] [First edition: "though".]
[3] [First edition: "any excess".]

are taken into the account, and set against it, is at least equal to double interest; say 10 per cent. Ordinary profit upon any particular parcel of goods must therefore be a great deal more, say at least triple interest, 15 per cent.: in the way of trading, then, a man can afford to be at least three times as adventurous, as he can in the way of lending, and with equal prudence. So long, then, as a man is looked upon as one who will pay, he can much easier get the goods he wants, than he could the money to buy them with, though he were content to give for it twice, or even thrice the ordinary rate of interest.

Supposing any body, for the sake of extraordinary gain, to be willing to run the risk of supplying him, although they did not look upon his personal security to be equal to that of another man, and for the sake of the extraordinary profit to run the extraordinary risk; in the trader, in short in every sort of trader whom he was accustomed to deal with in his solvent days, he sees a person who may accept of any rate of profit, without the smallest danger from any laws that are, or can be made against usury. How idle, then, to think of stopping a man from making six, or seven, or eight per cent. interest, when, if he chuses to run a risk proportionable, he may in this way make thirty or forty per cent. or any rate you please. And as to the prodigal, if he cannot get what he wants upon these terms, what chance is there of his getting it upon any terms, supposing the laws against usury to be away? This then is another way, in which, instead of serving, it injures him, by narrowing his option, and driving him from a market which might have proved less disadvantageous, to a more disadvantageous one.

As far as prodigality, then, is concerned, I must confess, I cannot see the use of stopping the current of expenditure in this way at the fosset, when there are so many unpreventable ways of letting it run out of the bung-hole.

Whether any harm is done to society, upon the whole, by letting so much money drop at once out of the pockets of the prodigal, who would have gone on wasting it, into the till of the frugal tradesman, who will lay it up, is not worth the enquiry for the present purpose: what is plain is, that, so far as the saving the prodigal from paying at an extraordinary rate for what he gets to spend, is the object of the law, that object is not at all promoted, by fixing the rate of interest upon money borrowed. On the contrary, if the law has any effect, it runs counter to that object: since, were he to borrow, it would only be, in as far as he could borrow at a rate inferior to that at which otherwise he would be obliged to buy. Preventing his borrowing at an extra-rate,[1] may have the effect of increasing his distress, but cannot have the effect of lessening it: allowing his borrowing at such a rate, might have the effect of lessening his distress, but could not have the effect of increasing it.

To put a stop to prodigality, if indeed it be worth while, I know but of one effectual course that can be taken, in addition to the incompleat and insufficient courses at present practicable, and that is, to put the convicted prodigal under an *interdict*, as was practised formerly among the Romans, and is still practised among the French, and other nations who have taken the Roman law for the ground-work of their own. But to discuss the expediency, or sketch out the details of such an institution, belongs not to the present purpose.

LETTER IV

Reasons for Restraint.—Protection of Indigence.

Besides prodigals, there are three other classes of persons, and but three, for whose security I can conceive these restrictive laws to have been designed. I mean the indigent, the rashly enterprizing, and the simple: those whose pecuniary necessities may dispose them to give an interest above the ordinary rate, rather than not have it, and those who, from rashness, may be disposed to venture upon giving such a rate, or from carelessness combined with ignorance, may be disposed to acquiesce in it.

In speaking of these three different classes of persons, I must beg leave to consider one of them at a time: and accordingly, in speaking of the indigent, I must consider indigence in the first place as untinctured with simplicity. On this occasion, I may suppose, and ought to suppose, no particular defect in a man's judgment, or his temper, that should mislead him, more than the ordinary run of men. He knows what is his interest as well as they do, and is as well disposed and able to pursue it as they are.

I have already intimated, what I think is undeniable, that there are no one or two or other limited number of rates of interest, that can be equally suited to the unlimited number of situations, in respect of the degree of *exigency*, in which a man is liable to find himself: insomuch that to the situation of a man, who by the use of money can make for example 11 per cent, six per cent. is as well adapted,

---

[1] [No hyphen in the first edition.]

as 5 per cent. is to the situation of him who can make but 10; to that of him who can make 12 per cent. seven,[1] and so on. So, in the case of his wanting it to save himself from a loss, (which is that which is most likely to be in view under the name of *exigency*) if that loss would amount to 11 per cent. 6 per cent. is as well adapted to his situation, as 5 per cent. would be to the situation of him, who had but a loss amounting to ten per cent. to save himself from by the like means. And in any case, though, in proportion to the amount of the loss, the rate of interest were even so great, as that the clear saving should not amount to more than one per cent. or any fraction per cent. yet so long as it amounted to any thing, he would be just so much the better for borrowing, even on such comparatively disadvantageous terms. If, instead of gain, we put any other kind of benefit or advantage—if, instead of loss, we put any other kind of mischief or inconvenience, of equal value, the result will be the same.

A man is in one of these situations, suppose, in which it would be for his advantage to borrow. But his circumstances are such, that it would not be worth any body's while to lend him, at the highest rate which it is proposed the law should allow; in short, he cannot get it at that rate. If he thought he *could* get it at that rate, most surely he would not give a higher: he may be trusted for that: for by the supposition he has nothing defective in his understanding. But the fact is, he cannot get it at that lower rate. At a higher rate, however, he could get it: and at that rate, though higher, it would be worth his while to get it: so he judges, who has nothing to hinder him from judging right; who has every motive and every means for forming a right judgment; who has every motive and every means for informing himself of the circumstances, upon which rectitude of judgment, in the case in question, depends. The legislator, who knows nothing, nor can know any thing, of any one of all these circumstances, who knows nothing at all about the matter, comes and says to him—"It signifies nothing; you shall not have the money: for it would be doing you a mischief to let you borrow it[2] upon such terms."—And this out of prudence and loving-kindness!—There may be worse cruelty: but can there be greater folly?

The folly of those who persist, as is supposed, without reason, in not taking advice, has been much expatiated upon. But the folly of those

---

[1][First edition: ". . . 12 per cent., seven . . ."]

[2][First edition: "for it would be a mischief to you to borrow it upon such terms."]

who persist, without reason, in forcing their advice upon others, has been but little dwelt upon, though it is, perhaps, the more frequent, and the more flagrant of the two. It is not often that one man is a better judge for another, than that other is for himself, even in cases where the adviser will take the trouble to make himself master of as many of the materials for judging, as are within the reach of the person to be advised. But the legislator is not, can not be, in the possession of any one of these materials.—What private, can be equal to such public folly?

I should now speak of the *enterprizing*[1] class of borrowers: those, who, when characterized by a single term, are distinguished by the unfavourable appellation of *projectors*: but in what I shall have to say of them, Dr. Smith, I begin to foresee, will bear so material a part, that when I come to enter upon that subject, I think to take my leave of you, and address myself to him.

LETTER V
Reasons for Restraint.—Protection of Simplicity.

I come, lastly, to the case of the simple. Here, in the first place, I think I am by this time entitled to observe, that no simplicity, short of absolute idiotism, can cause the individual to make a more groundless judgment, than the legislator, who, in the circumstances above stated, should pretend to confine him to any given rate of interest, would have made for him.

Another consideration, equally conclusive, is, that were the legislator's judgment ever so much superior to the individual's, how weak soever that may be, the exertion of it on this occasion can never be any otherwise than useless, so long as there are so many similar occasions, as there ever must be, where the simplicity of the individual is equally likely to make him a sufferer, and on which the legislator cannot interpose with effect, nor has ever so much as thought of interposing.

Buying goods with money, or upon credit, is the business of every day: borrowing money is the business, only, of some particular exigency, which, in comparison, can occur but seldom. Regulating the prices of goods in general would be an endless task, and no legislator has ever been weak enough to think of attempting it. And supposing he were to regulate the prices, what would that signify for

---

[1] [No italics in the first edition.]

the protection of simplicity, unless he were to regulate also the quantum of what each man should buy? Such quantum is indeed regulated, or rather means are taken to prevent buying altogether; but in what cases? In those only where the weakness is adjudged to have arrived at such a pitch, as to render a man utterly unqualified for the management of his affairs: in short, when it has arrived at the length of idiocy.

But in what degree soever a man's weakness may expose him to imposition, he stands much more exposed to it, in the way of buying goods, than in the way of borrowing money. To be informed, beforehand, of the ordinary prices of all the sorts of things, a man may have occasion to buy, may be a task of considerable variety and extent. To be informed of the ordinary rate of interest, is to be informed of one single fact, too interesting not to have attracted attention, and too simple to have escaped the memory. A few per cent. enhancement upon the price of goods, is a matter that may easily enough pass unheeded; but a single per cent. beyond the ordinary interest of money, is a stride more conspicuous and startling, than many per cent. upon the price of any kind of goods.

Even in regard to subjects, which, by their importance would, if any, justify a regulation of their price, such as for instance land, I question whether there ever was an instance where, without some such ground as, on the one side fraud, or suppression of facts necessary to form a judgment of the value, or at least ignorance of such facts, on the other, a bargain was rescinded, merely because a man had sold too cheap, or bought too dear. Were I to take a fancy to give a hundred years purchase instead of thirty, for a piece of land, rather than not have it, I don't think there is any court in England, or indeed any where else, that would interpose to hinder me, much less to punish the seller with the loss of three times the purchase money, as in the case of usury. Yet when I had got my piece of land, and paid my money, repentance, were the law ever so well disposed to assist me, might be unavailing: for the seller might have spent the money, or gone off with it. But, in the case of borrowing money, it is the borrower always, who, according to the indefinite, or short term for which money is lent, is on the safe side: any imprudence he may have committed with regard to the rate of interest, may be corrected at any time: if I find I have given too high an interest to one man, I have no more to do than to borrow of another at a lower rate, and pay off the first: if I cannot find any body to lend me at a lower, there cannot be a more certain proof that the first was not in reality too high. But of this hereafter.

LETTER VI

Mischiefs of the anti-usurious Laws.

In the preceding Letters,[1] I have examined all the modes I can think of, in which the restraints, imposed by the laws against usury, can have been fancied to be of service.

I hope it appears by this time, that there are no ways in which those laws can do any good. But there are several, in which they can not but do mischief.

The first, I shall mention, is that of precluding so many people, altogether, from the getting the money they stand in need of, to answer their respective exigencies. Think what a distress it would produce, were the liberty of borrowing denied to every body: denied to those who have such security to offer, as renders the rate of interest, they have to offer, a sufficient inducement, for a man who has money, to trust them with it. Just that same sort of distress is produced, by denying that liberty to so many people, whose security, though, if they were permitted to add something to that rate, it would be sufficient, is rendered insufficient by their being denied that liberty. Why the misfortune, of not being possessed of that arbitrarily exacted degree of security, should be made a ground for subjecting a man to a hardship, which is not imposed on those who are free from that misfortune, is more than I can see. To discriminate the former class from the latter, I can see but this one circumstance, viz. that their necessity is greater. This it is by the very supposition: for were it not, they could not be, what they are supposed to be, willing to give more to be relieved from it. In this point of view then, the sole tendency of the law is, to heap distress upon distress.

A second mischief is, that of rendering the terms so much the worse, to a multitude of those, whose circumstances exempt them from being precluded altogether from getting the money they have occasion for. In this case, the mischief, though necessarily less intense than in the other, is much more palpable and conspicuous. Those who cannot borrow may get what they want, so long as they have any thing to sell. But while, out of loving-kindness, or whatsoever other motive, the law precludes a man from *borrowing*, upon terms which he [sic] deems too disadvantageous, it does not preclude him from

---

[1] [First edition: "letters".]

selling, upon any terms, howsoever disadvantageous. Every body knows that forced sales are attended with a loss: and, to this loss, what would be deemed a most extravagant interest bears in general no proportion. When a man's moveables are taken in execution, they are, I believe, pretty well sold, if, after all expences paid, the produce amounts to two thirds of what it would cost to replace them. In this way the providence and loving-kindness of the law costs him 33 per cent. and no more, supposing, what is seldom the case, that no more of the effects are taken than what is barely necessary to make up the money due. If, in her negligence and weakness, she were to suffer him to offer 11 per cent. per annum for forbearance, it would be three years before be paid what he is charged with, in the first instance, by her wisdom.

Such being the kindness done by the law to the owner of moveables, let us see how it fares with him who has an interest in immoveables. Before the late war, 30 years purchase for land might be reckoned, I think it is pretty well agreed, a medium price. During the distress produced by the war, lands, which it was necessary should be sold, were sold at 20, 18, nay, I believe, in some instances, even so low as 15 years purchase. If I do not misrecollect, I remember instances of lands put up to public auction, for which nobody bid so high as fifteen. In many instances, villas, which had been bought before the war, or at the beginning of it, and, in the interval, had been improved rather than impaired, sold for less than half, or even the quarter, of what they had been bought for. I dare not here for my part pretend to be exact: but on this passage, were it worth their notice, Mr. Skinner, or Mr. Christie, could furnish very instructive notes. Twenty years purchase, instead of thirty, I may be allowed to take, at least for illustration. An estate then of £100 a year, clear of taxes, was devised to a man, charged, suppose, with £1,500 with interest till the money should be paid. Five per cent. interest, the utmost which could be accepted from the owner, did not answer the incumbrancer's purpose: he chose to have the money. But 6 per cent. perhaps, would have answered his purpose, if not, most certainly it would have answered the purpose of somebody else: for multitudes there all along were, whose purposes were answered by five per cent. The war lasted, I think, seven years: the depreciation of the value of land did not take place immediately: but as, on the other hand, neither did it immediately recover its former price upon the peace, if indeed it has even yet recovered it, we may put seven years for the time, during which it would be more advantageous to pay this extraordinary rate of interest than sell the land, and during which, accordingly, this extraordinary rate of interest would have had to run. One per cent. for seven years, is not quite of equal worth to seven per cent. the first year: say, however, that it is. The estate, which before the war was worth thirty years purchase, that is £3,000 and which the devisor had given to the devisee for that value, being put up to sale, fetched but 20 years purchase, £2,000. At the end of that period it would have fetched its original value, £3,000. Compare, then, the situation of the devisee at the 7 years end, under the law, with what it would have been, without the law. In the former case, the land selling for 20 years purchase, i.e. £2,000 what he would have, after paying the £1,500 is £500; which, with the interest of that sum, at 5 per cent. for seven years, viz. £175 makes, at the end of that seven years, £675. In the other case, paying 6 per cent. on the £1,500 that is £90 a year, and receiving all that time the rent of the land, viz. £100 he would have had, at the seven years end, the amount of the remaining ten pound during that period, that is £70 in addition to his £1,000.— £675 substracted from £1,070 leaves £395. This £395 then, is what he loses out of £1,070[,] almost 37 per cent. of his capital, by the loving-kindness of the law. Make the calculations, and you will find, that, by preventing him from borrowing the money at 6 per cent. interest, it makes him nearly as much a sufferer as if he had borrowed it at ten.

What I have said hitherto[1] is confined to the case of those who have present value to give, for the money they stand in need of. If they have no such value, then, if they succeed in purchasing assistance upon any terms, it must be in breach of the law; their lenders exposing themselves to its vengeance: for I speak not here of the accidental case, of its being so constructed as to be liable to evasion. But, even in this case, the mischievous influence of the law still pursues them; aggravating the very mischief it pretends to remedy. Though it be inefficacious in the way in which the legislator wishes to see it efficacious, it is efficacious in the way opposite to that in which he would wish to see it so. The effect of it is, to raise the rate of interest, higher than it would be otherwise, and that in two ways. In the first place, a man must, in common prudence, as Dr. Smith observes,[2] make a point of being

---

[1][Here follows a comma in the first edition.]
[2][Wealth of Nations, bk. II, ch. IV.]

indemnified, not only for whatsoever extraordinary risk it is that he runs, independently of the law, but for the very risk occasioned by the law: he must be *insured*, as it were, against the law. This cause would operate, were there even as many persons ready to lend upon the illegal rate, as upon the legal. But this is not the case: a great number of persons are, of course, driven out of this competition by the danger of the business; and another great number, by the disrepute which, under cover of these prohibitory laws or otherwise, has fastened itself upon the name of usurer. So many persons, therefore, being driven out of the trade, it happens in this branch, as it must necessarily in every other, that those who remain have the less to withhold them from advancing their terms; and without confederating, (for it must be allowed that confederacy in such a case is plainly impossible) each one will find it easier to push his advantage up to any given degree of exorbitancy, than he would, if there were a greater number of persons of the same stamp to resort to.

As to the case, where the law is so worded as to be liable to be evaded, in this case it is partly inefficacious and nugatory, and partly mischievous. It is nugatory, as to all such, whose confidence of its being so is perfect: it is mischievous, as before, in regard to all such who fail of possessing that perfect confidence. If the borrower can find nobody at all who has confidence enough to take advantage of the flaw, he stands precluded from all assistance, as before: and, though he should, yet the lender's terms must necessarily run the higher, in proportion to what his confidence wants of being perfect. It is not likely that it should be perfect: it is still less likely that he should acknowledge it so to be: it is not likely, at least as matters stand in England, that the worst-penned law made for this purpose should be altogether destitute of effect: and while it has any, that effect, we see, must be in one way or other mischievous.

I have already hinted at the disrepute, the ignominy, the reproach, which prejudice, the cause and the effect of these restrictive laws, has heaped upon that perfectly innocent and even meritorious class of men, who, not more for their own advantage than to the relief of the distresses of their neighbour, may have ventured to break through these restraints. It is certainly not a matter of indifference, that a class of persons, who, in every point of view in which their conduct can be placed, whether in relation to their own interest, or in relation to that of the persons whom they have to deal with, as well on the score of prudence, as on that of beneficence, (and of what use is even benevo-

K

lence, but in as far as it is productive of beneficence?) deserve praise rather than censure, should be classed with the abandoned and profligate, and loaded with a degree of infamy, which is due to those only whose conduct is in its tendency the most opposite to their own.

"This suffering," it may be said, "having already been taken account of, is not to be brought to account a second time: they are aware, as you yourself observe, of this inconvenience, and have taken care to get such amends for it, as they themselves look upon as sufficient." True: but is it sure that the compensation, such as it is, will always, in the event, have proved a sufficient one? Is there no room here for miscalculation? May there not be unexpected, unlooked-for incidents, sufficient to turn into bitterness the utmost satisfaction which the difference of pecuniary emolument could afford? For who can see to the end of that inexhaustible train of consequences that are liable to ensue from the loss of reputation? Who can fathom the abyss of infamy? At any rate, this article of mischief, if not an addition in its quantity to the others above-noticed, is at least distinct from them in its nature, and as such ought not to be overlooked.

Nor is the event of the execution of the law by any means an unexampled one: several such, at different times, have fallen within my notice. Then comes absolute perdition: loss of character, and forfeiture, not of three times the extra-interest, which formed the profit of the offence, but of three times the principal, which gave occasion to it.*

The last article I have to mention in the account of mischief, is, the corruptive influence, exercised by these laws, on the morals of the people; by the pains they take, and cannot but take, to give birth to treachery and ingratitude. To purchase a possibility of being enforced, the law neither has found, nor, what is very material, must it ever hope to find, in this case, any other expedient, than that of hiring a man to break his engagement, and to crush the hand that has been reached out to help him. In the case of informers in general, there has been no troth plighted, nor benefit received. In the case of real criminals invited by rewards to inform against accomplices, it is by such *breach* of faith that society is held together, as in other cases by the *observance* of it. In the case of real crimes, in proportion as their mischievousness is apparent, what can not but be manifest even to

---

*See Introduction to the Principles of Morals and Legislation, 4to. 1789. Ch. 14. On the proportion between punishments and offences. [There is no footnote in the first edition.]

the criminal, is, that it is by the adherence to his engagement that he would do an injury to society, and, that by the breach of such engagement, instead of doing mischief he is doing good: in the case of usury this is what no man can know, and what one can scarcely think it possible for any man, who, in the character of the borrower, has been concerned in such a transaction, to imagine. He knew that, even in his own judgment, the engagement was a beneficial one to himself, or he would not have entered into it: and nobody else but the lender is affected by it.

LETTER VII
Efficacy of anti-usurious Laws.

Before I quit altogether the consideration of the case in which a law, made for the purpose of limiting the rate of interest, may be inefficacious with regard to that end, I can not forbear taking some further notice of a passage already alluded to[1] of Dr. Smith's: because, to my apprehension, that passage seems to throw upon the subject a degree of obscurity, which I could wish to see cleared up, in a future edition of that valuable work.

"No law" says he,* "can reduce the common rate of interest below the lowest ordinary market rate, at the time when that law was made. Notwithstanding the edict of 1766, by which the French king attempted to reduce the rate of interest from five to four per cent. money continued to be lent in France at five per cent. the law being evaded in several different ways."

As to the general position, if so it be, so much, according to me, the better: but I must confess I do not see why this should be the case. It is for the purpose of proving the truth of this general position, that the fact of the inefficacy of this attempt seems to be adduced: for no other proof is adduced but this. But, taking the fact for granted, I do not see how it can be sufficient to support the inference. The law, we are told at the same time, was evaded: but we are not told how it came to be open to evasion. It might be owing to a particular defect in the penning of that particular law: or, what comes to the same thing, in the provisions made for carrying it into execution. In either case, it affords no support to the general position: nor can that position be a just one, unless it were so in the

[1][First edition: "alluded of Dr. Smith's".]
*B. ii. c. 10. vol. ii. p. 45. edit. 8vo. 1784.

case where every provision had been made, that could be made, for giving efficacy to the law. For the position to be true, the case must be, that the law would still be broken, even after every means of what can properly be called *evasion* had been removed. True or untrue, the position is certainly not self-evident enough to be received without proof: yet nothing is adduced in proof of it, but the fact above-noticed, which we see amounts to no such thing. What is more, I should not expect to find it capable of proof. I do not see, what it is, that should render the law incapable of "reducing the common rate of interest below the lowest ordinary market rate," but such a state of things, such a combination of circumstances, as should afford obstacles equally powerful, or nearly so, to the efficacy of the law against all higher rates. For destroying the law's efficacy altogether, I know of nothing that could serve, but a resolution on the part of all persons any way privy not to inform: but by such a resolution any higher rate is just as effectually protected as any lower one. Suppose the resolution,[1] strictly speaking, universal, and the law must in all instances be equally inefficacious; all rates of interest equally free;[2] and the state of men's dealings in this way just what it would be, were there no law at all upon the subject. But in this case, the position, in as far as it limits the inefficacy of the law to those rates which are below the "lowest ordinary market rate," is not true. For my part, I cannot conceive how any such universal resolution could have been maintained, or could ever be maintained, without an open concert, and as open a rebellion against government; nothing of which sort appears to have taken place: and, as to any particular confederacies, they are as capable of protecting any higher rates against the prohibition, as any lower ones.

Thus much indeed must be admitted, that the low rate in question, viz. that which was the lowest ordinary market rate immediately before the making of the law, is likely to come in for the protection of the public against the law, more frequently than any other rate. That must be the case on two accounts: first, because by being of the number of the ordinary rates, it was, by the supposition, more frequent than any extraordinary ones: secondly, because the disrepute annexed to the idea of usury, a force which might have more or less efficacy in excluding, from the protection above spoken of, such extraordinary rates, cannot well be supposed to apply itself, or at least not

---

[1][First edition: "Suppose it, strictly speaking . . ."]
[2][First edition: "all rates of interest are equally free".]

in equal degree, to this low and ordinary rate. A lender has certainly less to stop him from taking a rate, which may be taken without disrepute, than from taking one, which a man could not take without subjecting himself to that inconvenience: nor is it likely, that men's imaginations and sentiments should testify so sudden an obsequiousness to the law, as to stamp disrepute to-day, upon a rate of interest, to which no such accompaniment had stood annexed the day before.

Were I to be asked how I imagined the case stood in the particular instance referred to by Dr. Smith; judging from his account of it, assisted by general probabilities, I should answer thus:—The law, I should suppose, was not so penned as to be altogether proof against evasion. In many instances, of which it is impossible any account should have been taken, it was indeed conformed to: in some of those instances, people who would have lent otherwise, abstained from lending altogether; in others of those instances, people lent their money at the reduced legal rate. In other instances again, the law was broken: the lenders trusting, partly to expedients recurred to for evading it, partly to the good faith and honour of those whom they had to deal with: in this class of instances it was natural, for the two reasons above suggested, that those where the old legal rate was adhered to, should have been the most numerous. From the circumstance, not only of their number, but of their more direct repugnancy to the particular recent law in question, they would naturally be the most taken notice of. And this, I should suppose,[1] was the foundation in point of fact for the Doctor's general position above-mentioned, that "no law *can* reduce the common rate of interest below the lowest ordinary market rate, at the time when that law was made."

In England, as far as I can trust my judgment and imperfect general recollection of the purport of the laws relative to this matter, I should not suppose that the above position would prove true. That there is no such thing as any palpable and universally-notorious, as well as universally-practicable receipt for that purpose, is manifest from the examples which, as I have already mentioned, every now and then occur, of convictions upon these statutes. Two such receipts, indeed, I shall have occasion to touch upon presently: but they are either not obvious enough in their nature, or too troublesome or not extensive enough in their application, to have despoiled the law altogether of its terrors or of its preventive efficacy.

---

[1][First edition: "And this, I take it . . ."]

In the country in which I am writing, the whole system of laws on this subject is perfectly, and very happily, inefficacious. The rate fixed by law is 5 per cent.: many people lend money; and nobody at that rate: the lowest ordinary rate, upon the very best real security, is 8 per cent.: 9, and even 10, upon such security, are common. Six or seven may have place, now and then, between relations or other particular friends: because, now and then, a man may choose to make a present of one or two per cent. to a person whom he means to favour. The contract is renewed from year to year: for a thousand roubles, the borrower, in his written contract, obliges himself to pay at the end of the year one thousand and fifty. Before witnesses, he receives his thousand roubles: and, without witnesses, he immediately pays back his 30 roubles, or his 40 roubles, or whatever the sum may be, that is necessary to bring the real rate of interest to the rate verbally agreed on.

This contrivance, I take it, would not do in England: but why it would not, is a question which it would be in vain for me to pretend, at this distance from all authorities, to discuss.

LETTER VIII
Virtual Usury allowed.

Having proved, as I hope, by this time, the utter impropriety of the law's limiting the rate of interest, in every case that can be conceived, it may be rather matter of curiosity, than any thing else, to enquire, how far the law, on this head, is consistent with itself, and with any principles upon which it can have built.

1. *Drawing and re-drawing* is a practice, which it will be sufficient here to hint at. It is perfectly well known to all merchants, and may be so to all who are not merchants, by consulting Dr. Smith.[1] In this way, he has shewn how money may be, and has been, taken up, at so high a rate, as 13 or 14 per cent.[—]a rate nearly three times as high as the utmost which the law professes to allow. The extra interest is in this case masked under the names of *commission,* and price of *exchange.* The commission is but small upon each loan, not more, I think, than ½ per cent.: custom having stretched so far but no farther, it might be thought dangerous, perhaps, to venture upon any higher allowance under that name. The charge, being repeated a number of times in the course of the year, makes up in frequency

---

[1] [Wealth of Nations, bk. II, ch. II.]

what it wants in weight. The transaction is by this shift rendered more troublesome, indeed, but not less practicable, to such parties as are agreed about it. But if usury is good for merchants, I don't very well see what should make it bad for every body else.

2. At this distance from all the fountains of legal knowledge, I will not pretend to say, whether the practice of *selling accepted bills* at an under value, would hold good against all attacks. It strikes my recollection as a pretty common one, and I think it could not be brought under any of the penal statutes against usury. The adequateness of the consideration might, for aught I know, be attacked with success, in a court of equity; or, perhaps, if there were sufficient evidence (which the agreement of the parties might easily prevent) by an action at common law, for money had and received. If the practice be really proof against all attacks, it seems to afford an effectual, and pretty commodious method of evading the restrictive laws. The only restraint is, that it requires the assistance of a third person, a friend of the borrower's; as for instance: B, the real borrower, wants £100 and finds U, a usurer, who is willing to lend it to him, at 10 per cent. B. has F, a friend, who has not the money himself to lend him, but is willing to stand security for him, to that amount. B. therefore draws upon F, and F. accepts, a bill of £100 at 5 per cent. interest, payable at the end of a twelvemonth from the date. F. draws a like bill upon B.: each sells his bill to U. for fifty pound; and it is indorsed[1] to U. accordingly. The £50 that F. receives, he delivers over without any consideration to B. This transaction, if it be a valid one, and if a man can find such a friend, is evidently much less troublesome than the practice of drawing and re-drawing. And this, if it be practicable at all, may be practised by persons of any description, concerned or not in trade. Should the effect of this page be to suggest an expedient, and that a safe and commodious one, for evading the laws against usury, to some, to whom such an expedient might not otherwise have occurred, it will not lie very heavy upon my conscience. The prayers of usurers, whatever efficacy they may have in lightening the burthen, I hope I may lay some claim to. And I think you will not now wonder at my saying, that in the efficacy of such prayers I have not a whit less confidence, than in that of the prayers of any other class of men.

One apology I shall have to plead at any rate, that in pointing out

---

[1][First edition: "endorsed".]

these flaws, to the individual who may be disposed to creep out at them, I point them out at the same time to the legislator, in whose power it is to stop them up, if in his opinion they require it. If, notwithstanding such opinion, he should omit to do so, the blame will lie, not on my industry, but on his negligence.

These, it may be said, should they even be secure and effectual evasions, are still but evasions, and, if chargeable upon the law at all, are chargeable not as inconsistencies but as oversights. Be it so. Setting these aside, then, as expedients practised or practicable, only behind its back, I will beg leave to remind you of two others, practised from the day of its birth,[1] under its protection and before its face.

The first I shall mention is *pawnbroking*. In this case there is the less pretence for more than ordinary interest, inasmuch as the security is, in this case, not only equal to, but better than, what it can be in any other: to wit, the present possession of a moveable thing, of easy sale, on which the creditor has the power, and certainly does not want the inclination, to set such price as is most for his advantage. If there be a case in which the allowing of such extraordinary interest is attended with more danger than another, it must be this: which is so particularly adapted to the situation of the lowest poor, that is, of those who, on the score of indigence or simplicity, or both, are most open to imposition. This trade however the law, by regulating, avowedly protects. What the rate of interest is, which it allows to be taken in this way, I can not take upon me to remember: but I am much deceived, if it amounts to less than 12 per cent. in the year, and I believe it amounts to a good deal more. Whether it were 12 per cent. or 1200, I believe would make in practice but little difference. What *commission* is in the business of drawing and re-drawing, *warehouse-room* is, in that of pawnbroking. Whatever limits then are set to the profits of this trade, are set, I take it, not by the vigilancy of the law, but, as in the case of other trades, by the competition amongst the traders. Of the other regulations contained in the acts relative to this subject,[2] I recollect no reason to doubt the use.

The other instance is that of *bottomry* and *respondentia*: for the two transactions, being so nearly related, may be spoken of together. Bottomry is the usury of pawnbroking: respondentia is usury at

---

[1][First edition: "practised from time to time, . ."]

[2][No comma in the first edition.]

large, but combined in a manner with insurance, and employed in the assistance of a trade carried on by sea. If any species of usury is to be condemned, I see not on what grounds this particular species can be screened from the condemnation. "Oh but" (says sir William Blackstone, or any body else who takes upon himself the task of finding a reason for the law) "this is a maritime country, and the trade, which it carries on by sea, is the great bulwark of its defence." It is not necessary I should here enquire, whether that branch, which, as Dr. Smith has shewn,[1] is, in every view but the mere one of defence, less beneficial to a nation, than two others out of the four branches which comprehend all trade, has any claim to be preferred to them in this or any other way. I admit, that the liberty which this branch of trade enjoys, is no more than what it is perfectly right it should enjoy. What I want to know is, what there is in the class of men, embarked in this trade, that should render beneficial to them, a liberty, which would be ruinous to every body else. Is it that sea adventures have less hazard on them than land adventures? or that the sea teaches those, who have to deal with it, a degree of forecast and reflection which has been denied to landmen?

It were easy enough to give farther and farther extension to this charge of inconsistency, by bringing under it the liberty given to insurance in all its branches, to the purchase and sale of annuities, and of *post-obits*, in a word to all cases where a man is permitted to take upon himself an unlimited degree of risk, receiving for so doing an unlimited compensation. Indeed I know not where the want of instances would stop me: for in what part of the magazine of events, about which human transactions are conversant, is certainty to be found? But to this head of argument, this argument *ad hominem*, as it may be called, the use of which is but subsidiary, and which has more of confutation in it than of persuasion or instruction, I willingly put an end.

LETTER IX

Blackstone considered.

I hope you are, by this time, at least, pretty much of my opinion, that there is just the same sort of harm, and no other, in making the best terms one can for one's self in a money loan, as there is in any other sort of bargain. If you are not, Blackstone however is,

---

[1] [Wealth of Nations, bk. II, ch. V.]

whose opinion I hope you will allow to be worth something. In speaking of the rate of interest,* he starts a parallel between a bargain for the loan of money, and a bargain about a horse, and pronounces, without hesitation, that the harm of making too good a bargain, is just as great in the one case, as in the other. As money-lending, and not horse-dealing, was, what you lawyers call, the *principal case,* he drops the horse-business, as soon as it has answered the purpose of illustration, which it was brought to serve. But as, in my conception, as well the reasoning by which he supports the decision, as that by which any body else could have supported it, is just as applicable to the one sort of bargain as to the other, I will carry on the parallel a little farther, and give the same extent to the reasoning, as to the position which it is made use of to support. This extension will not be without its use; for if the position, when thus extended, should be found just, a practical inference will arise; which is, that the benefits of these restraints ought to be extended from the money-trade to the horse-trade. That my own opinion is not favourable to such restraints in either case, has been sufficiently declared; but if more respectable opinions than mine are still to prevail, they will not be the less respectable for being consistent.

The sort of bargain which the learned commentator has happened to pitch upon for the illustration, is indeed, in the case illustrating, as in the case illustrated, a loan: but as, to my apprehension, loan or sale makes, in point of reasoning, no sort of difference, and as the utility of the conclusion will, in the latter case, be more extensive, I shall adapt the reasoning to the more important business of selling horses, instead of the less important one of lending them.

A circumstance, that would render the extension of these restraints to the horse-trade more smooth and easy, is, that in the one track, as well as in the other, the public has already got the length of calling names. *Jockey-ship,* a term of reproach not less frequently applied to the arts of those who sell horses than to the arts of those who ride them, sounds, I take it, to the ear of many a worthy gentleman, nearly as bad as *usury*: and it is well known to all those who put their trust in proverbs, and not less to those who put their trust in party, that when we have got a dog to hang, who is troublesome and keeps us at bay, whoever can contrive to fasten a bad name to

---

*B. ii. ch. 30.

his tail, has gained more than half the battle. I now proceed with my application. The words in *italics* are my own: all the rest are Sir William Blackstone's: and I restore, at bottom, the words I was obliged to discard, in order to make room for mine.

"To demand an exorbitant price is equally contrary to conscience, for the loan of a horse, or for the loan of a sum of money: but a reasonable equivalent for the temporary inconvenience, which the owner may feel by the want of it, and for the hazard of his losing it entirely, is not more immoral in one case than in the other. . . . .

"*As to selling horses,* a capital distinction must be made, between a moderate and an exorbitant profit: to the former of which we give the name of *horse-dealing,** to the latter the truly odious appellation of *jockey-ship*†: the former is necessary in every civil state, if it were but to exclude the latter. For, as the whole of this matter is well summed up by Grotius, if the compensation allowed by law does not exceed the proportion of the *inconvenience which it is to the seller of the horse to part with it*‡, or the want *which the buyer has of it*§, its allowance is neither repugnant to the revealed law, nor to the natural law: but if it exceeds these bounds, it is then an oppressive *jockey-ship*‖: and though the municipal laws may give it impunity, they never can make it just.

"We see, that the exorbitance or moderation of *the price given for a horse*¶ depends upon two circumstances: upon the inconvenience of parting with *the horse one has***, and the hazard of not *being able to meet with such another*††. The inconvenience to individual *sellers of horses*‡‡[1], can never be estimated by laws; the *general price for horses*§§ must depend therefore upon the usual or general inconvenience. This results entirely from the quantity of *horses*‖‖ in the kingdom: for the more *horses*¶¶ there are *running about*** in any nation, the greater superfluity there will be beyond what is necessary to carry on the business of the mail coaches††† and the common concerns of life. In every nation or public community there is a certain quantity of horses‡‡‡ then necessary, which a person well skilled in political arithmetic might perhaps calculate as exactly as

---

*interest. †usury. ‡hazard run. §felt by the loan. ‖usury. ¶interest for the money lent. **it for the present. ††losing it entirely. ‡‡lenders. §§rate of general interest. ‖‖money. ¶¶specie. ***circulating. †††exchange. ‡‡‡money.

[1][First edition: "individuals, *sellers of horses*".]

a private *horse-dealer** can the demand for running *horses* in his own
stables†: all above this necessary quantity may be spared, or lent,
or sold, without much inconvenience to the respective lenders *or
sellers*: and the greater the national superfluity is, the more numerous
will be the *sellers‡*, and the lower ought *the national price of horse-
flesh§* to be: but where there are not enough, or barely enough *spare
horses‖* to answer the ordinary uses of the public, *horse-flesh¶* will be
proportionably high: for *sellers*** will be but few, as few can submit
to the inconvenience of *selling††*."—So far the learned commentator.

I hope by this time you are worked up to a proper pitch of indignation, at the neglect and inconsistency betrayed by the law, in not
suppressing this species of jockey-ship, which it would be so easy to
do, only by fixing the price of horses. Nobody is less disposed than I
am to be uncharitable: but when one thinks of the £1500 taken for
Eclipse, and £2000 for Rockingham, and so on, who can avoid being
shocked, to think how little regard those who took such enormous
prices must have had for "the law of revelation and the law of
nature?" Whoever it is that is to move for the municipal law, not
long ago talked of, for reducing the rate of interest, whenever that
motion is made, then would be the time for one of the Yorkshire
members to get up, and move, by way of addition, for a clause for
fixing and reducing the price of horses. I need not expatiate on the
usefulness of that valuable species of cattle, which might have been
as cheap as asses before now, if our lawgivers had been as mindful of
their duty in the suppression of *jockey-ship,* as they have been in the
suppression of *usury.*

It may be said, against fixing the price of horse-flesh, that different
horses may be of different values. I answer—and I think I shall shew
you as much, when I come to touch upon the subject of champerty—
not more different than the values which the use of the same sum
of money may be of to different persons, on different occasions.

LETTER X

Grounds of the Prejudices against Usury.

It is one thing, to find reasons why it is *fit* a law *should* have been
made: it is another to find the reasons why it *was* made: in other
words, it is one thing to justify a law: it is another thing to
account for its existence. In the present instance, the former task,

---

*banker. †cash in his own shop. ‡lenders. §the rate of the national interest.
‖circulating cash. ¶interest. **lenders ††lending.

if the observations I have been troubling you with are just, is an impossible one. The other, though not necessary for conviction, may contribute something perhaps in the way of satisfaction. To trace an error to its fountain head, says lord Coke, is to refute it; and many men there are who, till they have received this satisfaction, be the error what it may, cannot prevail upon themselves to part with it. "If our ancestors have been all along under a mistake, how came they to have fallen into it?" is a question that naturally presents itself upon all such occasions. The case is, that in matters of law more especially, such is the dominion of authority over our minds, and such the prejudice it creates in favour of whatever institution it has taken under its wing, that, after all manner of reasons that can be thought of, in favour of the institution, have been shewn to be insufficient, we still cannot forbear looking to some unassignable and latent reason for its efficient cause. But if, instead of any such reason, we can find a cause for it in some notion, of the erroneousness of which we are already satisfied, then at last we are content to give it up without further struggle; and then, and not till then, our satisfaction is compleat.

In the conceptions of the more considerable part of those through whom our religion has been handed down to us, virtue, or rather godliness, which was an improved substitute for virtue, consisted in self-denial: not in self-denial for the sake of society, but of self-denial for its own sake. One pretty general rule served for most occasions: not to do what you had a mind to do; or, in other words, not to do what would be for your advantage. By this of course was meant temporal advantage: to which spiritual advantage was understood to be in constant and diametrical opposition. For, the proof of a resolution, on the part of a being of perfect power and benevolence, to make his few favourites happy in a state in which they *were to be,* was his determined pleasure, that they should keep themselves as much strangers to happiness as possible, in the state in which they *were.* Now to get money is what most men have a mind to do: because he who has money gets, as far as it goes, most other things that he has a mind for. Of course nobody was to get money: indeed why should he, when he was not so much as to keep what he had got already? To lend money at interest, is to get money, or at least to try to get it: of course it was a bad thing to lend money upon such terms. The better the terms, the worse it was to lend upon them: but it was bad to lend upon any terms, by which any thing could be got. What made it much the worse was, that it was acting like a Jew: for though all Christians at first were Jews, and continued to do as Jews did, after they had become Christians, yet, in process of time, it came to be discovered, that the distance between the mother and the daughter church could not be too wide.

By degrees, as old conceits gave place to new, nature so far prevailed, that the objections to getting money in general, were pretty well over-ruled: but still this Jewish way of getting it, was too odious to be endured. Christians were too intent upon plaguing Jews, to listen to the suggestion of doing as Jews did, even though money were to be got by it. Indeed the easier method, and a method pretty much in vogue, was, to let the Jews get the money any how they could, and then squeeze it out of them as it was wanted.

In process of time, as questions of all sorts came under discussion, and this, not the least interesting, among the rest, the anti-jewish side of it found no unopportune support in a passage of Aristotle: that celebrated heathen, who, in all matters wherein heathenism did not destroy his competence, had established a despotic empire over the Christian world. As fate would have it, that great philosopher, with all his industry, and all his penetration, notwithstanding the great number of pieces of money that had passed through his hands (more perhaps than ever passed through the hands of philosopher before or since), and notwithstanding the uncommon pains he had bestowed on the subject of generation, had never been able to discover, in any one piece of money, any organs for generating any other such piece. Emboldened by so strong a body of negative proof, he ventured at last to usher into the world the result of his observations, in the form of an universal proposition, that *all money is in its nature barren.* You, my friend, to whose cast of mind sound reason is much more congenial than ancient philosophy, you have, I dare to say, gone before me in remarking, that the practical inference from this shrewd observation, if it afforded any, should have been, that it would be to no purpose for a man to try to get five per cent. out of money—not, that if he could contrive to get so much, there would be any harm in it. But the sages of those days did not view the matter in that light.

A consideration that did not happen to present itself to that great philosopher, but which had it happened to present itself, might not have been altogether unworthy of his notice, is, that though a *daric* would not beget another daric, any more than it would a ram, or an

ewe, yet for a daric which a man borrowed, he might get a ram and a
couple of ewes, and that the ewes, were the ram left with them a
certain time, would probably not be barren. That then, at the end of
the year, he would find himself master of his three sheep, together
with two, if not three, lambs; and that, if he sold his sheep again to
pay back his daric, and gave one of his lambs for the use of it in the
mean time, he would be two lambs, or at least one lamb, richer[1] than
if he had made no such bargain.

These theological and philosophical conceits, the offspring of the
day, were not ill seconded by principles of a more permanent complexion.

The business of a money-lender, though only among Christians,
and in Christian times, a proscribed profession, has no where, nor at
any time, been a popular one. Those who have the resolution to sacrifice the present to future, are natural objects of envy to those who
have sacrificed the future to the present. The children who have eat
their cake are the natural enemies of the children who have theirs.
While the money is hoped for, and for a short time after it has been
received, he who lends it is a friend and benefactor: by the time the
money is spent, and the evil hour of reckoning is come, the benefactor is found to have changed his nature, and to have put on the
tyrant and the oppressor. It is an oppression for a man to reclaim his
own money: it is none to keep it from him. Among the inconsiderate,
that is among the great mass of mankind, selfish affections conspire
with the social in treasuring up all favour for the man of dissipation,
and in refusing justice to the man of thrift who has supplied him.
In some shape or other that favour attends the chosen object
of it, through every stage of his career. But, in no stage of
his career, can the man of thrift come in for any share of
it. It is the general interest of those with whom a man lives,
that his expence should be at least as great as his circumstances
will bear: because there are few expences which a man can launch
into, but what the benefit of it is shared, in some proportion or other,
by those with whom he lives. In that circle originates a standing law,
forbidding every man, on pain of infamy, to confine his expences
within what is adjudged to be the measure of his means, saving
always the power of exceeding that limit, as much as he thinks
proper: and the means assigned him by that law may be ever so

---

[1] [First edition: "richer, than . . ."]

much beyond his real means, but are sure never to fall short of them. So close is the combination thus formed between the idea of merit and the idea of expenditure, that a disposition to spend finds favour in the eyes even of those who know that a man's circumstances do not entitle him to the means: and an upstart, whose chief recommendation is this disposition, shall find himself to have purchased a permanent fund of respect, to the prejudice of the very persons at whose expence he has been gratifying his appetites and his pride. The lustre, which the display of borrowed wealth has diffused over his character, awes men, during the season of his prosperity, into a submission to his insolence: and when the hand of adversity has overtaken him at last, the recollection of the height, from which he has fallen, throws the veil of compassion over his injustice.

The condition of the man of thrift is the reverse. His lasting opulence procures him a share, at least, of the same envy, that attends the prodigal's transient display: but the use he makes of it procures him no part of the favour which attends the prodigal. In the satisfactions he derives from that use, the pleasure of possession, and the idea of enjoying, at some distant period, which may never arrive, nobody comes in for any share. In the midst of his opulence he is regarded as a kind of insolvent, who refuses to honour the bills, which their rapacity would draw upon him, and who is by so much the more criminal than other insolvents, as not having the plea of inability for an excuse.

Could there be any doubt of the disfavour[1] which attends the cause of the money-lender, in his competition with the borrower, and of the disposition of the public judgment to sacrifice the interest of the former to that of the latter, the stage would afford a compendious,[2] but a pretty conclusive proof of it. It is the business of the dramatist to study, and to conform to, the humours and passions of those, on the pleasing of whom he depends for his success: it is the course which reflection must suggest to every man, and which a man would naturally fall into, though he were not to think about it. He may, and very frequently does, make magnificent pretences, of giving the law to them: but wo be to him that attempts to give them any other law than what they are disposed already to receive. If he would attempt to lead them one inch, it must be with great caution, and not

---

[1][First edition: "disfavour, which . . ."]

[2][No comma in the first edition.]

without suffering himself to be led by them at least a dozen. Now, I question, whether, among all the instances in which a borrower and a lender of money have been brought together upon the stage, from the the days of Thespis to the present, there ever was one, in which the former was not recommended to favour in some shape or other, either to admiration, or to love, or to pity, or to all three; and the other, the man of thrift, consigned to infamy.

Hence it is that, in reviewing and adjusting the interests of these apparently rival parties, the advantage made by the borrower is so apt to slip out of sight, and that made by the lender to appear in so exaggerated a point of view. Hence it is, that though prejudice is so far softened[1] as to acquiesce in the lender's making some advantage, lest the borrower should lose altogether the benefit of his assistance, yet still the borrower is to have all the favour, and the lender's advantage is for ever to be clipped, and pared down, as low as it will bear. First it was to be confined to ten per cent.[,] then to eight, then to six, then to five, and now lately there was a report of its being to be brought down to four; with constant liberty to sink as much lower as it would. The burthen of these restraints, of course, has been intended exclusively for the lender: in reality, as I think you have seen, it presses much more heavily upon the borrower: I mean him who either becomes or in vain wishes to become so. But the presents directed by prejudice, Dr. Smith will tell us, are not always delivered according to their address.[2] It was thus that the mill-stone designed for the necks of those vermin, as they have been called, the dealers in corn, was found to fall upon the heads of the consumers. It is thus— but further examples would lead me further from the purpose.

LETTER XI
Compound Interest.

A word or two I must trouble you with, concerning *compound interest*; for compound interest is discountenanced by the law; I suppose, as a sort of usury. That, without an express stipulation, the law never gives it, I well remember: whether, in case of an express stipulation, the law allows it to be taken, I am not absolutely certain. I should suppose it might: remembering covenants in mortgages that interest should become principal. At any rate, I think the law cannot well punish it under the name of usury.

---

[1][First edition: "softened, as . . ."]
[2][Wealth of Nations, bk. IV, ch. V.]
L

If the discountenance shewn to this arrangement be grounded on the horror of the sin of usury, the impropriety of such discountenance follows of course, from the arguments which shew the un- *"sinfulness of* that *sin."*[1]

Other argument against it, I believe, was never attempted, unless it were the giving to such an arrangement the epithet of a *hard* one: in doing which, something more like a reason is given, than one gets in ordinary from the common law.

If that consistency were to be found in the common law, which has never yet been found in man's conduct, and which perhaps is hardly in man's nature, compound interest never could have been denied.

The views which suggested this denial, were, I dare to say, very good: the effects of it are, I am certain, very pernicious.

If the borrower pays the interest at the day, if he performs his engagement, that very engagement to which the law pretends to oblige him to conform, the lender, who receives that interest, makes compound interest of course, by lending it out again, unless he chooses rather to expend it: he expects to receive it at the day, or what meant the engagement? if he fails of receiving it, he is by so much a loser. The borrower, by paying it at the day, is no loser: if he does not pay it at the day, he is by so much a gainer: a pain of disappointment takes place in the case of the one, while no such pain takes place in the case of the other. The cause of him whose contention is to *catch a gain,* is thus preferred to that of him whose contention is to avoid a loss: contrary to the reasonable and useful maxim of that branch of the common law which has acquired the name of equity. The gain, which the law in its tenderness thus bestows on the defaulter, is an encouragement, a reward, which it holds out for breach of faith, for iniquity, for indolence, for negligence.

The loss, which it thus throws upon the forbearing lender, is a punishment which it inflicts on him for his forbearance: the power which it gives him of avoiding that loss, by prosecuting the borrower upon the instant of failure, is thus converted into a reward which it holds out to him for his hard-heartedness and rigour. Man is not quite so good as it were to be wished he were; but he would be bad indeed, were he bad on all the occasions where the law, as far as depends on her, has made it his interest so to be.

---

[1] [No inverted commas and italics in the first edition.]

It may be impossible, say you, it often is impossible, for the borrower to pay the interest at the day: and you say truly. What is the inference? That the creditor should *not* have it in his power to ruin the debtor for not paying at the day, and that he *should* receive a compensation for the loss occasioned by such *failure*.[1]—He *has*[2] it in his power to ruin him, and he has it *not*[3] in his power to obtain such compensation. The judge, were it possible for an arrested debtor to find his way into a judge's chamber instead of a spunging-house, might award a proper respite, suited to the circumstances of the parties. It is not possible: but a respite is purchased, proper or not proper, perhaps at ten times, perhaps at a hundred times the expence of compound interest, by putting in bail, and fighting the creditor through all the windings of mischievous and unnecessary delay. Of the satisfaction due either for the original failure, or for the subsequent vexation by which it has been aggravated, no part is ever received by the injured creditor: but the instruments of the law receive, perhaps at his expence, perhaps at the debtor's, perhaps ten times, perhaps a hundred times the amount of that satisfaction. Such is the result of this tenderness of the law.

It is in consequence of such tenderness that on so many occasions a man, though ever so able, would find himself a loser by paying his just debts: those very debts of which the law has recognized the justice. The man who obeys the dictates of common honesty, the man who does what the law pretends to bid him, is wanting to himself. Hence your regular and securely profitable writs of error in the house of lords: hence your random and vindictive costs of one hundred pounds, and two hundred pounds, now and then given in that house. It is natural, and it is something, to find, in a company of lords, a zeal for justice: it is not natural, to find, in such a company, a disposition to bend down to the toil of calculation.

LETTER XII
Maintenance and Champerty.

Having in the preceding letters had occasion to lay down, and, as I flatter myself, to make good, the general principle, that *no man of ripe years, and of sound mind, ought, out of loving-kindness to him, to be hindered from making such bargain, in the way of obtaining money, as, acting with his eyes open, he deems conducive to his interest,* I will take your leave for pushing it a little

---

[1] [2] [3][No italics in the first edition.]

farther, and extending the application of it to another class of regulations still less defensible. I mean the antique laws against what are called Maintenance and Champerty.

To the head of *Maintenance,* I think you refer, besides other offences which are not to the present purpose, that of purchasing, upon any terms, any claim, which it requires a suit at law, or in equity, to enforce.

Champerty, which is but a particular modification of this sin of Maintenance, is, I think, the furnishing a man who has such a claim, with regard to a real estate, such money as he may have occasion for, to carry on such claim, upon the terms of receiving a part of the estate in case of success.

What the penalties are for these offences I do not recollect, nor do I think it worth while hunting for them, though I have Blackstone at my elbow. They are, at any rate, sufficiently severe to answer the purpose, the rather as the bargain is made void.

To illustrate the mischievousness of the laws by which they have been created, give me leave to tell you a story, which is but too true an one, and which happened to fall within my own observation.

A gentleman of my acquaintance had succeeded, during his minority, to an estate of about £3,000 a year; I won't say where. His guardian, concealing from him the value of the estate, which circumstances rendered it easy for him to do, got a conveyance of it from him, during his nonage, for a trifle. Immediately upon the ward's coming of age, the guardian, keeping him still in darkness, found means to get the conveyance confirmed. Some years afterwards, the ward discovered the value of the inheritance he had been throwing away. Private representations proving, as it may be imagined, ineffectual, he applied to a court of equity. The suit was in some forwardness: the opinion of the ablest counsel highly encouraging: but money there remained none. We all know but too well, that, in spite of the unimpeachable integrity of the bench, that branch of justice, which is particularly dignified with the name of equity, is only for those who can afford to throw away one fortune for the chance of recovering another. Two persons, however, were found, who, between them, were content to defray the expence of the ticket for this lottery, on condition of receiving half the prize. The prospect now became encouraging: when unfortunately one of the adventurers, in exploring the recesses of the bottomless pit, happened to dig up one of the old statutes against Champerty. This blew up the whole project: however the defendant, understanding that, some how or other, his antagonist had found support, had thought fit in the mean time to propose terms, which the plaintiff, after his support had thus dropped from under him, was very glad to close with. He received, I think it was, £3,000: and for that he gave up the estate, which was worth about as much yearly, together with the arrears, which were worth about as much as the estate.

Whether, in the barbarous age which gave birth to these barbarous precautions, whether, even under the zenith of feudal anarchy, such fettering regulations could have had reason on their side, is a question of curiosity rather than use. My notion is, that there never was a time, that there never could have been, or can be a time, when the pushing of suitors away from court with one hand, while they are beckoned into it with another, would not be a policy equally faithless, inconsistent, and absurd. But, what every body must acknowledge, is, that, to the times which called forth these laws, and in which alone they could have started up, the present are as opposite as light to darkness. A mischief, in those times, it seems, but too common, though a mischief not to be cured by such laws, was, that a man would buy a weak claim, in hopes that power might convert it into a strong one, and that the sword of a baron, stalking into court with a rabble of retainers at his heels, might strike terror into the eyes of a judge upon the bench. At present, what cares an English judge for the swords of an hundred barons?—Neither fearing nor hoping, hating nor loving, the judge of our days is ready with equal phlegm to administer, upon all occasions, that system, whatever it be, of justice, or injustice, which the law has put into his hands. A disposition so consonant to duty could not have then been hoped for: one more consonant is hardly to be wished. Wealth has indeed the monopoly of justice against poverty: and such monopoly it is the direct tendency and necessary effect of regulations like these to strengthen and confirm. But with this monopoly no judge that lives now is at all chargeable. The law created this monopoly: the law, whenever it pleases, may dissolve it.

I will not however so far wander from my subject as to enquire what measure might have been necessary to afford a full relief to the case of that unfortunate gentleman, any more than to the cases of so many other gentlemen who might be found, as unfortunate as he. I will not insist upon so strange and so inconceivable an arrangement, as that of the judge's seeing both parties face to face in the first instance, observing what the facts are in dispute, and declaring, that as the facts should turn out this way or that way, such or such would be his decree. At present, I confine myself to the removal of such part of the mischief, as may arise from the general conceit of keeping men out of difficulties, by cutting them off from such means of relief as each man's situation may afford. A spunge in this, as in so many other cases, is the only needful, and only availing remedy: one stroke of it for the musty laws against maintenance and champerty: another for the more recent ones against usury. Consider, for example, what would have respectively been the effect of two such strokes, in the case of the unfortunate gentleman I have been speaking of. By the first, if what is called equity has any claim to confidence, he would have got, even after paying of[f] his champerty-usurers, £1500 a year in land, and about as much in money: instead of getting, and that only by an accident, £3000 once told. By the other, there is no saying to what a degree he might have been benefited. May I be allowed to stretch so far in favour of the law as to suppose, that so small a sum as £500 would have carried him through his suit, in the course of about three years? I am sensible, that may be thought but a short sum, and this but a short term, for a suit in equity: but, for the purpose of illustration, it may serve as well as a longer. Suppose he had sought this necessary sum in the way of borrowing; and had been so fortunate, or, as the laws against the sin of usury would stile it, so unfortunate, as to get it at 200 per cent. He would then have purchased his £6000 a year at the price of half as much once paid, viz. £3000; instead of selling it at that price. Whether, if no such laws against usury had been in being, he could have got the money, even at that rate, I will not pretend to say: perhaps he might not have got it under ten times that rate, perhaps he might have got it at the tenth part of that rate. Thus far, I think, we may say, that he might, and probably would, have been the better for the repeal of those laws: but thus far we must say, that it is impossible he should have been the worse. The terms, upon which he met with adventurers willing to relieve him, though they come not within that scanty field, which the law, in the narrowness of its views, calls usury, do, in the present case, at twenty years purchase of the £3000 a year he was content to have sacrificed for such assistance, amount, in effect, to 4000 per cent. Whether it was likely that any man, who was disposed to venture his money, at all, upon such a chance, would have thought of insisting upon such a rate of interest, I will leave you to imagine: but thus much may be said with confidence, because the fact demonstrates it, that, at a rate not exceeding this, the sum would actually have been supplied. Whatever becomes then of the laws against maintenance and champerty, the example in question, when applied to the laws against usury, ought, I think, to be sufficient to convince us, that so long as the expence of seeking relief at law stands on its present footing, the purpose of seeking that relief will, of itself, independently of every other, afford a sufficient ground for allowing any man, or every man, to borrow money on any terms on which[1] he can obtain it.

Crichoff,
in White Russia,
   March 1787.

LETTER XIII
To Dr. Smith, on Projects in Arts, &c.

   SIR,

I forget what son of controversy it was, among the Greeks, who having put himself to school to a professor of eminence,[2] to learn what, in those days, went by the name of wisdom, chose an attack upon his master for the first public specimen of his proficiency. This specimen, whatever entertainment it might have afforded to the audience, afforded, it may be supposed, no great satisfaction to the master: for the thesis was, that the pupil owed him nothing for his pains. For my part, being about to shew myself in one respect as ungrateful as the Greek, it may be a matter of prudence for me to look out for something like candour by way of covering to my ingratitude: instead therefore of pretending to owe you nothing, I shall begin with acknowledging, that, as far as your track coincides with mine, I should come much nearer the truth, were I to say I owed you every thing. Should it be my fortune to gain any advantage over you, it must be with weapons which you have taught me to wield, and with which you yourself have furnished me: for, as all the great standards of truth, which can be appealed to in this line, owe, as far as I can understand, their establishment to you, I can see scarce any other way of convicting you of any error or oversight, than by judging you out of your own mouth.

In the series of letters to which this will form a sequel, I had

---

[1][The words "on which" are not in the first edition.]
[2][First edition: ". . . to school, to a professor . . ."]

travelled nearly thus far in my researches into the policy of the laws fixing the rate of interest, combating such arguments as fancy rather than observation had suggested to my view,[1] when, on a sudden, recollection presented me[2] with your formidable image, bestriding the ground over which I was travelling pretty much at my ease, and opposing the shield of your authority to any arguments I could produce.

It was a reflection mentioned by Cicero as affording him some comfort, that the employment his talents till that time had met with, had been chiefly on the defending side. How little soever blest, on any occasion, with any portion of his eloquence, I may, on the present occasion, however, indulge myself with a portion of what constituted his comfort: for, if I presume to contend with you, it is only in defence of what I look upon as, not only an innocent, but a most meritorious race of men, who are so unfortunate as to have fallen under the rod of your displeasure. I mean *projectors*: under which inviduous name I understand you to comprehend, in particular, all such persons as, in the pursuit of wealth, strike out into any new channel, and more especially into any channel of invention.

It is with the professed view of checking, or rather of crushing, these adventurous spirits, whom you rank with "prodigals", that you approve of the laws which limit the rate of interest, grounding yourself on the tendency, they appear to you to have, to keep the capital of the country out of two such different sets of hands.

The passage, I am speaking of, is in the fourth chapter of your second book, volume the second of the 8vo edition of 1784. "The legal rate" (you say) "it is to be observed, though it ought to be somewhat above, ought not to be much above, the lowest market rate. If the legal rate of interest in Great Britain, for example, was fixed so high as eight or ten per cent. the greater part of the money which was to be lent, would be lent to prodigals and projectors, who alone would be willing to give this high interest. Sober people, who will give for the use of money no more than a part of what they are likely to make by the use of it, would not venture into the competition. A great part of the capital of the country would thus be kept out of the hands which were most likely to make a profitable and advantageous use of it, and thrown into those which were most likely to waste and destroy it. Where the legal interest, on the contrary, is fixed

---

[1][First edition: ". . . views, . . ."]
[2][Misprinted "we" in the first edition.]

but a very little above the lowest market rate, sober people are universally preferred as borrowers, to prodigals and projectors. The person who lends money, gets nearly as much interest from the former, as he dares to take from the latter, and his money is much safer in the hands of the one set of people than in those of the other. A great part of the capital of the country is thus thrown into the hands in which it is most likely to be employed with advantage."

It happens fortunately for the side you appear to have taken, and as unfortunately for mine, that the appellative, which the custom of the language has authorized you, and which the poverty and perversity of the language has in a manner forced you, to make use of, is one, which, along with the idea of the sort of persons in question, conveys the idea of reprobation, as indiscriminately and deservedly applied to them. With what justice or consistency, or by the influence of what causes, this stamp of indiscriminate reprobation has been thus affixed, it is not immediately necessary to enquire. But, that it does stand thus affixed, you and every body else, I imagine, will be ready enough to allow. This being the case, the question stands already decided, in the first instance at least, if not irrevocably, in the judgments of all those, who, unable or unwilling to be at the pains of analysing their ideas, suffer their minds to be led captive by the tyranny of sounds;[1] that is, I doubt, of by far the greater proportion of those whom we are likely to have to judge us. In the conceptions of all such persons, to ask whether it be fit to restrain projects and projectors,[2] will be as much as to ask, whether it be fit to restrain rashness, and folly, and absurdity, and knavery, and waste.

Of prodigals I shall say no more at present. I have already stated my reasons for thinking, that it is not among them that we are to look for the natural customers for money at high rates of interest. As far as those reasons are conclusive, it will follow, that, of the two sorts of men you mention as proper objects of the burthen of these restraints, prodigals and projectors, that burthen falls exclusively on the latter. As to these, what your definition is of projectors, and what descriptions of persons you meant to include under the censure conveyed by that name, might be material for the purpose of judging of the propriety of that censure, but makes no difference in judging of the propriety of the law, which that censure is employed to justify. Whether you yourself, were the several classes of persons made to

---

[1] [First edition: ". . . sounds: that is . . ."]
[2] [First edition: " . . projects, and projectors . . ."]

pass before you in review, would be disposed to pick out this or that class, or this and that individual, in order to exempt them from such censure, is what for that purpose we have no need to enquire. The law, it is certain, makes no such distinctions:[1] it falls with equal weight, and with all its weight, upon all those persons, without distinction[2] to whom the term *projectors,* in the most unpartial and extensive signification of which it is capable, can be applied. It falls at any rate (to repeat some of the words of my former definition), upon all such persons, as, in the pursuit of wealth, or even of any other object, endeavour, by the assistance of wealth, to strike into any channel of invention. It falls upon all such persons, as, in the cultivation of any of those arts which have been by way of eminence termed *useful,* direct their endeavours to any of those departments in which their utility shines most conspicuous and indubitable; upon all such persons as, in the line of any of their pursuits, aim at any thing that can be called *improvement;* whether it consist in the production of any new article adapted to man's use, or in the meliorating the quality, or diminishing the expence, of any of those which are already known to us. It falls, in short, upon every application of the human powers, in which ingenuity stands in need of wealth for its assistant.

High and extraordinary rates of interest, how little soever adapted to the situation of the prodigal, are certainly, as you very justly observe, particularly adapted to the situation of the projector: not however to that of the imprudent projector only, nor even to his case more than another's, but to that of the prudent and well-grounded projector, if the existence of such a being were to be supposed. Whatever be the prudence or other qualities of the project, in whatever circumstance the novelty of it may lie, it has this circumstance against it, viz. that it is new. But the rates of interest, the highest rates allowed, are, as you expressly say they are, and as you would have them to be, adjusted to the situation which the sort of trader is in, whose trade runs in the old channels, and to the best security which such channels can afford. But[3] in the nature of things, no new trade, no trade carried on in any new channel, can afford a security equal to that which may be afforded by a trade carried on in any of the old ones: in whatever light the matter might appear to per-

---

[1][First edition: ". . . distinctions, it falls . . ."]
[2][First edition: ". . . distinction, to whom . . ."]
[3][First edition: "But, in . ."]

fect intelligence, in the eye of every prudent person, exerting the best powers of judging which the fallible condition of the human faculties affords, the novelty of any commercial adventure will oppose a chance of ill success, superadded to every one which could attend the same, or any other, adventure, already tried, and proved to be profitable by experience.

The limitation of the profit that is to be made, by lending money to persons embarked in trade, will render the monied man more anxious, you may say, about the goodness of his security, and accordingly more anxious to satisfy himself respecting the prudence of a project[1] in the carrying on of which the money is to be employed, than he would be otherwise: and in this way it may be thought that these laws *have* a tendency to pick out the good projects from the bad, and favour the former at the expence of the latter. The first of these positions I admit: but I can never admit the consequence to follow. A prudent man, (I mean nothing more than a man of ordinary prudence) a prudent man acting under the sole governance of prudential motives, I still say will not, in these circumstances, pick out the good projects from the bad, for he will not meddle with projects at all. He will pick out old-established trades from all sorts of projects, good and bad; for with a new project, be it ever so promising, he never will have any thing to do. By every man that has money, five per cent. or whatever be the highest legal rate, is at all times, and always will be, to be had upon the very best security, that the best and most prosperous old-established trade can afford. Traders in general, I believe, it is commonly understood, are well enough inclined to enlarge their capital, as far as all the money they can borrow at the highest legal rate, while that rate is so low as 5 per cent.[,] will enlarge it. How it is possible therefore for a project, be it ever so promising, to afford, to a lender at any such rate of interest, terms equally advantageous, upon the whole, with those he might be sure of obtaining from an old-established business, is more than I can conceive. Loans of money may certainly chance, now and then, to find their way into the pockets of projectors as well as of other men: but when this happens it must be through incautiousness, or friendship, or the expectation of some collateral benefit, and not through any idea of the advantageousness of the transaction, in the light of a pecuniary bargain.

I should not expect to see it alledged, that there is any thing, that

---

[1][First edition: ". . . project, in . . ."]

should render the number of well-grounded projects, in comparison of the ill-grounded, less in time future, than it has been in time past. I am sure at least that I know of no reasons why it should be so, though I know of some reasons, which I shall beg leave to submit to you by and by, which appear to me pretty good ones, why the advantage should be on the side of futurity. But, unless the stock of well-grounded projects is already spent, and the whole stock of ill-grounded projects that ever were possible, are to be looked for exclusively in the time to come, the censure you have passed on projectors, measuring still the extent of it by that of the operation of the laws in the defence of which it is employed, looks as far backward as forward: it condemns as rash and ill-grounded, all those projects, by which our species have been successively advanced from that state in which acorns were their food, and raw hides their cloathing, to the state in which it stands at present: for think, Sir, let me beg of you, whether whatever is now the *routine* of trade was not, at its commencement, *project*? whether whatever is now *establishment,* was not, at one time, innovation?

How it is that the tribe of well-grounded projects, and of prudent projectors (if by this time I may have your leave for applying this epithet to some at least among the projectors of time past), have managed to struggle through the obstacles which the laws in question have been holding in their way, it is neither easy to know, nor necessary to enquire. Manifest enough, I think, it must be by this time, that difficulties, and those not inconsiderable ones, those laws must have been holding up,[1] in the way of projects of all sorts, of improvement (if I may say so) in every line, so long as they have had existence: reasonable therefore it must be to conclude, that, had it not been for these discouragements, projects of all sorts, well-grounded and successful ones, as well as others, would have been more numerous than they have been: and that accordingly, on the other hand, as soon, if ever, as these discouragements shall be removed, projects of all sorts, and among the rest, well-grounded and successful ones, will be more numerous than they would otherwise have been: in short, that, as, without these discouragements, the progress of mankind[2] in the career of prosperity, would have been greater than it has been under them in time past, so, were they to be removed, it would be at least proportionably greater in time future.

---

[1][First edition: "holding, in . . ."]
[2][First edition: ". . . mankind, in . . ."]

That I have done you no injustice, in assigning to your idea of
projectors so great a latitude, and that the unfavourable opinion you
have professed to entertain of them is not confined to the above
passage, might be made, I think, pretty apparent, if it be material, by
another passage in the tenth chapter of your first book.* "The establishment of any new manufacture, of any new branch of commerce,
or of any new practice in agriculture," all these you comprehend by
name under the list of *"projects"*: of every one of them you observe,
that "it is a speculation from which the *projector* promises himself
extraordinary profits. These profits (you add) are sometimes *very
great*, and sometimes, *more frequently perhaps*, they are *quite otherwise*: but in general they bear no regular proportion to those of other
old trades in the neighbourhood. If the project succeeds, they are
commonly at first very high. When the trade or practice becomes
thoroughly established and well known, the competition reduces them
to the level of other trades." But on this head I forbear to insist: nor
should I have taken this liberty of giving you back your own words,
but in the hope of seeing some alteration made in them in your next
edition, should I be fortunate enough to find my sentiments confirmed
by your's. In other respects, what is essential to the publick, is, what
the error is in the sentiments entertained, not who it is that entertains
them.

I know not whether the observations which I have been troubling
you with, will be thought to need, or whether they will be thought to
receive, any additional support from those comfortable positions, of
which you have made such good and such frequent use, concerning
the constant tendency of mankind to get forward in the career of
prosperity, the prevalence of prudence over imprudence, in the sum
of private conduct at least, and the superior fitness of individuals for
managing their own pecuniary concerns, of which they know the
particulars and the circumstances, in comparison of the legislator,
who can have no such knowledge. I will make the experiment: for,
so long as I have the mortification to see you on the opposite side, I
can never think the ground I have taken strong enough, while any
thing remains that appears capable of rendering it still stronger.

"With regard to misconduct, the number of prudent and successful undertakings" (you observe†) "is every where much greater than
that of injudicious and unsuccessful ones. After all our complaints of

*Edit. 1784, 8vo. p. 177.
†B. II. ch. iii. edit. 8vo. 1784, vol ii. p. 20.

the frequency of bankruptcies, the unhappy men who fall into this misfortune make but a very small part of the whole number engaged in trade, and all other sorts of business; not much more perhaps than one in a thousand."

'Tis in support of this position that you appeal to history for the constant and uninterrupted progress of mankind, in our island[1] at least, in the career of prosperity: calling upon any one who should entertain a doubt of the fact, to divide the history into any number of periods, from the time of Cæsar's visit down to the present: proposing for instance the respective æras of the Restoration, the Accession of Elizabeth, that of Henry VII.[,] the Norman Conquest, and the Heptarchy, and putting it to the sceptic to find out, if he can, among all these periods, any one at which the condition of the country was not more prosperous than at the period immediately preceding it; spite of so many wars, and fires, and plagues, and all other public calamities, with which it has been at different times afflicted, whether by the hand of God, or by the misconduct of the sovereign. No very easy task, I believe: the fact is too manifest for the most jaundiced eye to escape seeing it:—But what and whom are we to thank for it, but projects, and projectors?

"No," I think I hear you saying, "I will not thank projectors for it, I will rather thank the laws, which by fixing the rates of interest have been exercising their vigilance in repressing the temerity of projectors, and preventing their imprudence from making those defalcations from the sum of national prosperity which it would not have failed to make, had it been left free. If, during all these periods, that adventurous race of men had been left at liberty by the laws to give full scope to their rash enterprizes, the increase of national prosperity during these periods might have afforded some ground for regarding them in a more favourable point of view. But the fact is, that their activity has had these laws to check it; without which checks you must give me leave to suppose, that the current of prosperity, if not totally stopt, or turned the other way, would at any rate have been more or less retarded. Here then" (you conclude) "lies the difference between us: what you look upon as the cause of the increase about which we are both agreed, I look upon as an obstacle to it: and what you look upon as the obstacle, I look upon as the cause."

Instead of starting[2] this as a sort of plea that might be urged by

---

[1][First edition: ". . . in one island . . ."]
[2][First edition: ". . . stating . . ."]

you, I ought, perhaps, rather to have mentioned it as what might be urged by some people in your place: for as I do not imagine your penetration would suffer you to rest satisfied with it, still less can I suppose that, if you were not, your candour would allow you to make use of it as if you were.

To prevent your resting satisfied with it, the following considerations would I think be sufficient.

In the first place, of the seven periods which you have pitched upon, as so many stages for the eye to rest at in viewing the progress of prosperity, it is only during the three last, that the country has had the benefit, if such we are to call it, of these laws: for it is to the reign of Henry VIII. that we owe the first of them.

Here a multitude of questions might be started: Whether the curbing of projectors formed any part of the design of that first statute, or whether the views of it were not wholly confined to the reducing the gains of that obnoxious and envied class of men, the moneylenders? Whether projectors have been most abundant before that statute, or since that statute? And whether the nation has suffered, as you might say—benefited, as I should say, most by them, upon the whole, during the former period or the latter? All these discussions, and many more that might be started, I decline engaging in, as more likely to retard, than to forward, our coming to any agreement concerning the main question.

In the next place, I must here take the liberty of referring you to the proof, which I think I have already given, of the proposition, that the restraints in question could never have had the effect, in any degree, of lessening the proportion of bad projects to good ones, but only of diminishing, as far as their influence may have extended, the total number of projects, good and bad together. Whatever therefore was the general tendency of the projecting spirit previously to the first of these laws, such it must have remained ever since, for any effect which they could have had in purifying and correcting it.

But what may appear more satisfactory perhaps than both the above considerations, and may afford us the best help towards extricating ourselves from the perplexity, which the plea I have been combating (and which I thought it necessary to bring to view, as the best that could be urged) seems much better calculated to plunge us into, than bring us out of, is, the consideration of the small effect which the greatest waste that can be conceived to have been made within any compass of time, by injudicious projects, can have had on the sum of prosperity, even in the estimation of those whose opinion is most unfavourable to projectors, in comparison of the effect which within the same compass of time must have been produced by *prodigality*.

Of the two causes, and only two causes, which you mention, as contributing to retard the accumulation of national wealth, as far as the conduct of individuals is concerned, projecting, as I observed before, is the one, and prodigality is the other: but the detriment, which society can receive even from the concurrent efficacy of both these causes, you represent, on several occasions, as inconsiderable; and, if I do not misapprehend you, too inconsiderable, either to need, or to warrant, the interposition of government to oppose it. Be this as it may with regard to projecting and prodigality taken together, with regard to prodigality at least, I am certain I do not misapprehend you. On this subject you ride triumphant, and chastise the "impertinence and presumption of kings and ministers," with a tone of authority, which it required a courage like your's to venture upon, and a genius like your's to warrant a man to assume.* After drawing the parallel between private thrift and public profusion,[1] "It is" (you conclude) "the highest impertinence and presumption therefore in kings and ministers *to pretend to watch over the economy of private people,* and to restrain their expence, either by sumptuary laws, or by prohibiting the importation of foreign luxuries. They are themselves always, and without exception, the greatest spendthrifts in the society. Let them look well after their own expence, and they may safely trust private people with theirs. If their own extravagance does not ruin the state, that of their subjects never will."

That the employing the expedients you mention for restraining prodigality, is indeed generally, perhaps even without exception, improper, and in many cases even ridiculous, I agree with you; nor will I here step aside from my subject to defend from that imputation another mode suggested in a former part of these papers. But however presumptuous and impertinent it may be for the sovereign to attempt in any way to check by legal restraints the *prodigality* of individuals, to attempt to check their *bad management* by such restraints seems abundantly more so. To err in the way of prodigality is the lot, though, as you well observe, not of *many* men, in comparison of the whole mass of mankind, yet at least of *any* man:

---

*B. II. ch. iii. vol. ii. p.27. edit. 8vo 1784.

[1][No comma in the first edition.]

the stuff fit to make a prodigal of is to be found in every alehouse, and under every hedge. But even to *err* in the way of projecting is the lot only of the privileged few. Prodigality, though not so common as to make any very material drain from the general mass of wealth, is however too common to be regarded as a mark of distinction or as a singularity. But the stepping aside from any of the beaten paths of traffic, *is* regarded as a singularity, as serving to distinguish a man from other men. Even where it requires no genius, no peculiarity of talent, as where it consists in nothing more than the finding out a new market to buy or sell in, it requires however at least a degree of courage, which is not to be found in the common herd of men. What shall we say of it, where, in addition to the vulgar quality of courage, it requires the rare endowment of genius, as in the instance of all those successive enterprizes by which arts and manufactures have been brought from their original nothing to their present splendor? Think how small a part of the community these must make, in comparison of the race of prodigals; of that very race, which, were it only on account of the smallness of its number, would appear too inconsiderable to you to deserve attention. Yet prodigality is essentially and necessarily hurtful, as far as it goes, to the opulence of the state: projecting, only by accident. Every prodigal, without exception, impairs, by the very supposition impairs, if he does not annihilate, his fortune. But it certainly is not every projector that impairs his: it is not every projector that would have done so, had there been none of those wise laws to hinder him: for the fabric of national opulence, that fabric of which you proclaim, with so generous an exultation, the continual increase, that fabric, in every apartment of which, innumerable as they are, it required the reprobated hand of a projector to lay the first stone, has required some hands at least to be employed, and successfully employed.[1] When in comparison of the number of prodigals, which is too inconsiderable to deserve notice, the number of projectors of all kinds is so much more inconsiderable—and when from this inconsiderable number, must be deducted, the not inconsiderable proportion of successful projectors —and from this remainder again, all those who can carry on their projects without need of borrowing—think whether it be possible,[2] that this last remainder could afford a multitude, the reducing of which would be an object, deserving the interposition of government

[1] [First edition: ". . . employed, and that successfully employed."]
[2] [First edition: ". . . whether it is possible, . . ."]

M

by its magnitude, even taking for granted that it were an object proper in its nature?

If it be still a question, whether it be worth while for government, by its *reason*, to attempt to controul the conduct of men visibly and undeniably under the dominion of *passion*, and acting, under that dominion, contrary to the dictates of their own reason; in short, to effect what is acknowledged to be their better judgment, against what every body, even themselves, would acknowledge to be their worse; is it endurable that the legislator should by violence substitute his own pretended reason, the result of a momentary and scornful glance, the offspring of wantonness and arrogance, much rather than of social anxiety and study, in the place of the humble reason of individuals, binding itself down[1] with all its force to that very object which he pretends to have in view?—Nor let it be forgotten, that, on the side of the individual in this strange competition, there is the most perfect and minute knowledge and information, which interest, the whole interest of a man's reputation and fortune, can ensure: on the side of the legislator, the most perfect ignorance. All that he knows, all that he can know, is, that the enterprize is a *project*, which, merely because it is susceptible of that obnoxious name, he looks upon as a sort of cock, for him, in childish wantonness, to shie at.— Shall the blind lead the blind? is a question that has been put of old to indicate the height of folly: but what then shall we say of him who, being necessarily blind, insists on leading, in paths he never trod in, those who can see?

It must be by some distinction too fine for my conception, if you clear yourself from the having taken, on another occasion, but on the very point in question, the side, on which it would be my ambition to see you fix.

"What is the species of domestic industry which his capital can employ, and of which the produce is likely to be of the greatest value, every individual" (you say*), "it is evident, can, in his local situation, judge much better than any statesman or lawgiver can do for him. The statesman, who should attempt to direct private people in what manner they ought to employ their capitals, would not only load himself with a most unnecessary attention, but assume an authority which could safely be trusted, not only to no single person, but to no council or senate whatsoever, and which would no where be so

---

[1][First edition: ". . . binding itself with all its force . . ."]
*B. iv. ch. 2. vol. ii. p. 182. edit. 8vo.

dangerous as in the hands of a man who had folly and presumption enough to fancy himself fit to exercise it.

"To give the monopoly of the home market to the produce of domestic industry, in any particular art or manufacture, is in some measure to direct private people in what manner they ought to employ their capitals, and must in almost all cases be either a useless or a hurtful regulation."—Thus far you: and I add, to limit the legal interest to a rate at which the carriers on of the oldest and best-established and least hazardous trades are always glad to borrow, is to give the monopoly of the money-market to those traders, as against the projectors of new-imagined trades, not one of which but, were it only from the circumstance[1] of its novelty, must, as I have already observed, appear more hazardous than the old.

These, in comparison, are but inconclusive topics. I touched upon them merely as affording, what appeared to me the only shadow of a plea, that could be brought, in defence of the policy I am contending against. I come back therefore to my first ground, and beg you once more to consider, whether, of all that host of manufactures, which we both exult in as the causes and ingredients of national prosperity, there be a single one, that could have existed at first but in the shape of a project. But, if a regulation, the tendency and effect of which is merely to check projects, in as far as they are projects, without any sort of tendency, as I have shewn, to weed out the bad ones, is defensible in its present state of imperfect efficacy, it should not only have been defensible, but much more worthy of our approbation, could the efficacy of it have been so far strengthened and compleated as to have opposed, from the beginning, an unsurmountable bar to all sorts of projects whatsoever: that is to say, if, stretching forth its hand[2] over the first rudiments of society, it had confined us, from the beginning, to mud for our habitations, to skins for our cloathing, and to acorns for our food.

I hope you may by this time be disposed to allow me, that we have not been ill served by the projects of time past. I have already intimated, that I could not see any reason why we should apprehend our being worse served by the projects of time future. I will now venture to add, that I think I do see reason, why we should expect to be still better and better served by these projects, than by those. I mean better upon the whole, in virtue of the reduction which experience,

---

[1][First edition: "circumstances".]
[2][First edition: ". . . if stretching forth its hand . . ."]

if experience be worth any thing, should make in the proportion of the number of the ill-grounded and unsuccessful, to that of the well-grounded and successful ones.

The career of art, the great road which receives the footsteps of projectors, may be considered as a vast, and perhaps unbounded, plain, bestrewed with gulphs, such as Curtius was swallowed up in. Each requires an human victim to fall into it ere it can close, but when it once closes, it closes to open no more, and so much of the path is safe to those who follow. If the want of perfect information of former miscarriages renders the reality of human life less happy than this picture, still the similitude must be acknowledged: and we see at once the only plain and effectual method for bringing that similitude still nearer and nearer to perfection; I mean, the framing the history of the projects of time past, and (what may be executed in much greater perfection were but a finger held up by the hand of government) the making provision for recording, and collecting and publishing as they are brought forth, the race of those with which the womb of futurity is still pregnant. But to pursue this idea, the execution of which is not within my competence, would lead me too far from the purpose.

Comfortable it is to reflect, that this state of continually-improving security, is the natural state not only of the road to opulence, but of every other track of human life. In the war which industry and ingenuity maintain with fortune, past ages of ignorance and barbarism form the forlorn hope, which has been detached in advance, and made a sacrifice of for the sake of future. The golden age, it is but too true, is not the lot of the generation in which we live: but, if it is to be found in any part of the track marked out for human existence, it will be found, I trust, not in any part which is past, but in some part which is to come.

But to return to the laws against usury, and their restraining influence on projectors. I have made it, I hope, pretty apparent, that these restraints have no power or tendency to pick out bad projects from the good. Is it worth while to add, which I think I may do with some truth, that the tendency of them is rather to pick the good out from the bad? Thus much at least may be said, and it comes to the same thing, that there is one case in which, be the project what it may, they may have the effect of checking it, and another in which they can have no such effect, and that the first has for its accompaniment, and that a necessary one, a circumstance which has a strong tendency to separate and discard every project of the injudicious stamp, but which is wanting in the other case. I mean, in a word, the *benefit of discussion.*

It is evident enough, that upon all such projects, whatever be their nature, as find funds sufficient to carry them on, in the hands of him whose invention gave them birth, these laws are perfectly, and if by this time you will allow me to say so, very happily, without power. But for these there has not necessarily been any other judge, prior to experience, than the inventor's own partial affection. It is not only not necessary that they should have had, but it is natural enough that they should not have had, any such judge: since in most cases the advantage to be expected from the project depends upon the exclusive property in it, and consequently upon the concealment of the principle. Think, on the other hand, how different is the lot of that enterprize which depends upon the good opinion of another man, that other, a man possessed of the wealth which the projector wants, and before whom necessity forces him to appear in the character of a suppliant at least: happy if, in the imagination of his judge, he adds not to that degrading character, that of a visionary enthusiast or an impostor! At any rate, there are, in this case, two wits, set to sift into the merits of the project, for one, which was employed upon that same task in the other case: and of these two there is one, whose prejudices are certainly not most likely to be on the favourable side. True it is, that in the jumble of occurrences, an over-sanguine projector may stumble upon a patron as over-sanguine as himself; and the wishes may bribe the judgment of the one, as they did of the other. The opposite case, however, you will allow, I think, to be by much the more natural. Whatever a man's wishes may be for the success of an enterprize not yet his own, his fears are likely to be still stronger. That same pretty generally implanted principle of vanity and self-conceit, which disposes most of us to over-value each of us his own conceptions, disposes us, in a proportionable degree, to under-value those of other men.

Is it worth adding, though it be undeniably true, that could it even be proved, by ever so uncontrovertible evidence, that, from the beginning of time to the present day, there never was a project that did not terminate in the ruin of its author, not even from such a fact as this could the legislator derive any sufficient warrant, so much as for wishing to see the spirit of projects in any degree repressed?— The discouraging motto, *Sic vos non vobis,* may be matter of serious consideration to the individual, but what is it to the legislator? What general, let him attack with ever so superior an army, but knows that hundreds, or perhaps thousands, must perish at the first onset? Shall he, for that consideration alone, lie inactive in his lines? "Every man for himself—but God," adds the proverb (and it might have added the general, and the legislator, and all other public servants), "for us all." Those sacrifices of individual to general welfare, which, on so many occasions, are made by third persons against men's wills, shall the parties themselves be restrained from making, when they do it of their own choice? To tie men neck and heels, and throw them into the gulphs I have been speaking of, is altogether out of the question: but if at every gulph a Curtius stands mounted and caparisoned, ready to take the leap, is it for the legislator, in a fit of old-womanish tenderness, to pull him away? Laying even public interest out of the question, and considering nothing but the feelings of the individuals immediately concerned,[1] a legislator would scarcely do so, who knew the value of hope, "the most precious gift of heaven."

Consider, Sir, that it is not with the invention-lottery (that great branch of the project-lottery, for the sake of which I am defending the whole, and must continue so to do until you or somebody else can shew me how to defend it on better terms), it is not I say with the invention-lottery, as with the mine-lottery, the privateering-lottery, and so many other lotteries, which you speak of, and in no instance, I think, very much to their advantage. In these lines, success does not, as in this, arise out of the embers of ill success, and thence propagate itself, by a happy contagion, perhaps to all eternity. Let Titius have found a mine, it is not the more easy, but by so much the less easy, for Sempronius to find one too: let Titius have made a capture, it is not the more easy, but by so much the less easy, for Sempronius to do the like. But let Titius have found out a new dye, more brilliant or more durable than those in use, let him have invented a new and more convenient machine, or a new and more profitable mode of husbandry, a thousand dyers, ten thousand mechanics, a hundred thousand husbandmen, may repeat and mutiply his success: and then, what is it to the public, though the fortune of Titius, or of his usurer, should have sunk under the experiment?

Birmingham and Sheffield are pitched upon by you as examples,

---

[1][First edition: ". . . but the feelings of individuals, a legislator . . ."]

the one of a projecting town, the other of an unprojecting one.* Can you forgive my saying, I rather wonder that this comparison of your own chosing, did not suggest some suspicions of the justice of the conceptions you had taken up, to the disadvantage of projectors. Sheffield is an old oak: Birmingham, but a mushroom. What if we should find the mushroom still vaster and more vigorous than the oak? Not but the one as well as the other, at what time soever planted, must equally have been planted by projectors: for though Tubal Cain himself were to be brought post from Armenia to plant Sheffield,[1] Tubal Cain himself was as arrant a projector in his day, as ever Sir Thomas Lombe was, or bishop Blaise: but Birmingham, it seems, claims in common parlance the title of a projecting town, to the exclusion of the other, because, being but of yesterday, the spirit of project smells fresher and stronger there than elsewhere.

When the odious sound of the word *projector* no longer tingles in your ears, the race of men thus stigmatized do not always find you their enemy. Projects, even under the name of "dangerous and expensive experiments," are represented as not unfit to be encouraged, even though monopoly be the means: and the monopoly is defended in that instance, by its similarity to other instances[2] in which the like means are employed to the like purpose.

"When a company of merchants undertake at their own risk and expence to establish a new trade, with some remote and barbarous nation, it may not be unreasonable" (you observe) "to incorporate them into a joint-stock company, and to grant them, in case of their success, a monopoly of the trade for a certain number of years. It is the easiest and most natural way, in which the state can recompense them, for hazarding a dangerous and expensive experiment, of which the public is afterwards to reap the benefit. A temporary monopoly of this kind may be vindicated, upon the same principles, upon which a like monopoly of a new machine is granted to its inventor, and that of a new book to its author."

Private respect must not stop me from embracing this occasion of giving a warning, which is so much needed by mankind. If so original and independent a spirit has not been always able to save itself from being drawn aside by the fascination of sounds, into the paths of vulgar prejudice, how strict a watch ought not men of common

---

*B. I. ch. x. vol. i. p. 176. edit. 8vo. 1784.
[1] [First edition: ". . . from Armenia to England to plant Sheffield, . . ."]
[2] [First edition: ". . . instances, in which . . ."]

mould to set over their judgments, to save themselves from being led astray by similar delusions?

I have sometimes been tempted to think, that were it in the power of laws to put *words* under proscription, as it is to put *men*, the cause of inventive industry might perhaps derive scarcely less assistance from a bill of attainder against the words *project* and *projectors*, than it has derived from the act authorizing the grant of patents. I should add, however, for a time: for even then the envy, and vanity, and wounded pride, of the uningenious herd, would sooner or later infuse their venom into some other word, and set it up as a new tyrant, to hover, like its predecessor, over the birth of infant genius, and crush it in its cradle.

Will not you accuse me of pushing malice beyond all bounds, if I bring down against you so numerous and respectable a body of men,[1] as the members of the *Society for the Encouragement of Arts*? I do not, must not, care: for you command too much respect to have any claim to mercy. At least you will not accuse me of spiriting up against you barbarian enemies, and devoting you to the vengeance of Cherokees and Chicasaws.

Of that popular institution, the very professed and capital object[2] is the encouragement of projects, and the propagating of that obnoxious breed, the crushing of which you commend as a fit exercise for the arm of power. But if it be right to crush the acting malefactors, it would be downright inconsistency not to crush, at the same time, or rather not to begin with crushing, these their hirers and abettors. Thank then their inadvertence, or their generosity, or their prudence, if their beadle has not yet received orders to burn in ceremony, as a libel on the society, a book that does honour to the age.

After having had the boldness to accuse so great a master of having fallen unawares into an error, may I take the still farther liberty, of setting conjecture to work to account for it? Scarce any man, perhaps no man, can push the work of creation, in any line, to such a pitch of compleatness, as to have gone through the task of examining with his own eyes into the grounds of every position, without exception, which he has had occasion to employ. You heard the public voice, strengthened by that of law, proclaiming all round you, that usury was a sad thing, and usurers a wicked and pernicious set of men: you heard from one at least of those quarters, that projectors were either a fool-

---

[1][First edition: ". . . so useful and public-spirited a body of men, . . ."]
[2][First edition: "objects".]

ish and contemptible race, or a knavish and destructive one: Hurried
away by the throng, and taking very naturally for granted, that what
every body said must have some ground for it, you have joined the
cry, and added your suffrage to the rest. Possibly too, among the
crowd of projectors which the lottery of occurrences happened to
present to your observation, the prejudicial sort may have borne such
a proportion to the beneficial, or shewn themselves in so much
stronger colours, as to have given the popular notion a firmer hold in
your judgment, than it would have had, had the contrary proportion
happened to present itself to your notice. To allow no more weight to
examples that fall close under our eyes, than to those which have
fallen at ever so great a distance—to suffer the judgment on no
occasion to indulge itself in the licence of a too hasty and extensive
generalisation—not to give any proposition footing there, till after all
such defalcations have been made, as are necessary to reduce it
within the limits of rigid truth—these are laws, the compleat
observance whereof forms the ultimate, and hitherto, perhaps for
ever, ideal term of human wisdom.

You have defended against unmerited obloquy two classes of men,
the one innocent at least, the other highly useful; the spreaders of
English arts in foreign climes,* and those whose industry exerts
itself in distributing that necessary commodity[1] which is called by
the way of eminence the staff of life. May I flatter myself with having
succeeded at last in my endeavours, to recommend to the same powerful protection, two other highly useful and equally persecuted sets of
men, usurers and projectors.—Yes—I will, for the moment at least,
indulge so flattering an idea: and, in pursuance of it, leaving usurers,
for whom I have said enough already, I will consider myself as joined
now with you in the same commission, and thinking with you of the
best means of relieving the projector from the load of discouragement
laid on him by these laws, in so far as the pressure of them falls
particularly upon him. In my own view of the matter, indeed, no
temperament, no middle course, is either necessary or proper: the
only perfectly effectual, is the only perfectly proper remedy,—a
spunge. But, as nothing is more common with mankind, than to give
opposite receptions, to conclusions flowing with equal necessity from
the same principle, let us accommodate our views to that contingency.

According to this idea, the object, as far as confined to the present

---

*B. IV. ch. 8. vol. ii. p. 514. *et alibi*, edit. 8vo. 1784.
[1][First edition: ". . . commodity, which . . ."]

case, should be, to provide, in favour of projectors only, a dispensation from the rigour of the anti-usurious laws: such, for instance, as is enjoyed by persons engaged in the carrying trade, in virtue of the indulgence given to loans made on the footing of *respondentia* or bottomry. As to abuse, I see not why the danger of it should be greater in this case than in those. Whether a sum of money be embarked, or not embarked, in such or such a new manufacture on land, should not, in its own nature, be a fact much more difficult to ascertain, than whether it be embarked, or not embarked, in such or such a trading adventure by sea: and, in the one case as in the other, the payment of the interest, as well as the repayment of the principal, might be made to depend upon the success of the adventure. To confine the indulgence to new undertakings, the having obtained a patent for some invention, and the continuance of the term of the patent, might be made conditions of the allowance given to the bargain: to this might be added affidavits, expressive of the intended application, and bonds, with sureties, conditioned for the performance of the intention so declared; to be registered in one of the patent-offices or elsewhere. After this, affidavits once a year, or oftener, during the subsistence of the contract, declaring what has been done in execution of it.

If the leading-string is not yet thought tight enough, boards of controul might be instituted to draw it tighter. Then opens a scene of vexation and intrigue: waste of time consumed in courting the favour of the members of the board: waste of time, in opening their understandings, clenched perhaps by ignorance, at any rate by disdain, and self-sufficiency, and vanity, and pride: the favour (for pride will make it a favour) granted to skill in the arts of self-recommendation and cabal, devoid of inventive merit, and refused to naked merit unadorned by practice in those arts: waste of time on the part of the persons themselves engaged in this impertinent inquiry [*sic*]: waste of somebody's money in paying them for this waste of time. All these may be necessary evils, where the money to be bestowed is public money: how idle where it is the party's own! I will not plague you, nor myself, with enquiring of whom shall be composed this board of nurses to grown gentlemen: were it only to cut the matter short, one might name at once the committees[1] of the Society of Arts. There you have a body of men ready trained in the conduct of enquiries, which resemble that in question, in every circumstance, but that

---

[1][First edition: "Committees".]

which renders it ridiculous: the members or representatives of this democratic body would be as likely, I take it, to discharge such a trust with fidelity and skill, as any aristocracy that could be substituted in their room.

   Crichoff,
in White Russia,
   March 1787.

[LETTER] TO DR. SMITH

A little tract of mine, in the latter part of which I took the liberty of making use of your name, (the *Defence of Usury*), having been some time out of print, I am about publishing a new edition of it. I am now therefore at a period at which, if I have done you or any body any injustice, I shall have the opportunity, and assuredly I do not want the inclination, to repair it: or if in any other respect I have fallen into an error, I could give myself and the public the benefit of its being set right. I have been flattered with the intelligence that, upon the whole, your sentiments with respect to the points of difference are at present the same as mine: but as the intimation did not come directly from you, nor has the communication of it received the sanction of your authority, I shall not without that sanction give any hint, honourable as it would be to me, and great as the service is which it could not but render to my cause.

I have been favoured with the communication from Dr. Reid of Glasgow of an inedited paper of his on the same subject, written a good many years ago. He declares himself now fully of my opinion on the question of expediency, and had gone a considerable length towards it at that time. The only ground on which he differs from me, is that of the origination of the prejudice, of which his paper gives, as might be expected, an account more ecclesiastical than mine. Anxious to do my cause as much service as it is capable of receiving, I write to him now, to endeavour to persuade him to give his paper to the world, or if he looks upon so much of it as concerns the question of utility [as] superseded by mine, that he will either communicate the historical part—that part which he prefers to mine —to some general repository for short publications, or allow me the honour of forwarding it to the world in company with mine. The account that has been given by the Marquis de Condorcet of the sentiments of Turgot on the same subject, is already every body's without leave[1]: I shall accordingly annex, by way of appendix to my new edition, the original as well as a translation of that short passage. I am the more anxious to collect all the force I can muster, in as far as I find from the printed debates, as well as from private intelligence, that the project of reducing the rate of interest in Ireland is not yet given up: though this perseverance is hardly reconciliable

---

[1] [The passage Bentham refers to is to be found in the anonymously published *Vie de M. Turgot* by Condorcet (Londres 1786), pp. 53-56, cf. ib. p. 228.]

with the account I receive from the same quarter, of the impression made in that country by the *Defence of Usury*. Yet the subjecting the rate of interest to a further reduction by a new law, is a much more mischievous and less defensible measure than the continuing of the restraint upon the old footing: and adds to the mischief of the old established regimen others of a new and much more serious nature. It would be a tax upon the owners of money, much heavier than ever was levied upon the proprietors of land: with this circumstance to distinguish it from all other taxes, that, instead of being brought into the treasury for the public service, it is made a present of to the collectors, in expectation of the good they are to do the nation by the spending of it. If this be good thrift, in the name of consistency and equality let them impose a Land Tax to the same amount, and dispose of the produce in the same manner. What makes my anxiety the greater, is the uncertainty whether this project of plunder without profit may not be still hovering over this island. Last year it was roundly and positively asserted in the Irish H[ouse] of Commons, as if upon personal knowledge, to be determined upon in the Cabinet here: and the Administration being appealed to, though they of course would not acknowledge, would no contradict it. Its suspension hitherto may have resulted from nothing more than a doubt whether the nation were yet ripe, according to the Irish phrase, for this mode of enrichment: as if there were a time at which a nation were riper for plunder and waste than at another. I am truly sorry I can not find time to make one effort more for the express purpose of stemming the torrent of delusion in that channel. The straw I have planted has done something: what might not be hoped for, if your oak-stick were linked with it?

As the world judges, one upon examination and nine hundred and ninety-nine upon trust, the declaration of your opinion upon any point of legislation would be worth, I won't pretend to say how many votes: but the declaration of your opinion in favour of a side to which conviction and candour had brought you over from the opposite one, would be worth at least twice or thrice as many: under such circumstances, the authority of the converter would tell for little in comparison of that of the proselyte, especially such a proselyte. We should have the Irish Chancellor of the Exchequer abjuring his annual motion in the face of the House, and L[or]d Hawkesbury who, it has been said, is Mr. Pitt's tutor in this wise business, quietly and silently putting his papers and calculations into the fire.

If, then, you agree with me in looking upon this as a most pernicious measure, you would, like me, be glad to see it put an end to, and for that purpose the acknowledgement of your opinion on a subject which you have made so much and so honourably your own, is an expedient to the use of which, I should hope, you would not see any objection: the less as you would hardly, I suppose, let another edition of your great work go abroad with opinions in it that were yours no longer. If, then, you think proper to honour me with your allowance for that purpose, then and not otherwise I will make it known to the public, in such words as you give me, that you no longer look upon the rate of interest as fit subject for restraint: and then, thanks to you and Turgot and Dr. Reid, the *Defence of Usury* may be pronounced, in its outworks at least, a strong-hold.

[PROPOSED] PREFACE [TO THE SECOND EDITION]

When the first edition of these letters was published, I was still in the distant country from which they were written. It is about two years, since that impression was exhausted: it is about a year and a half since this reimpression was compleated, the publication having been retarded till now by causes not worth mentioning. The alterations made in this second edition are few, and those merely verbal and of no importance. In this interval, had I heard of any objection, total or partial, I would have either admitted the force of it, or answered it: but I have not been able to meet with any. I have scarce heard of a reader who has not acknowledged himself convinced. The practical conclusion is the repealing of the laws against usury, together with those others that are here pointed out as depending on the same principle. That matters are at all the nearer to such a measure since the publication of this work than they were before, is more than I can pretend to have any ground for supposing: for in great political questions, wide indeed is the distance between conviction and practice. An intelligent Frenchman, of whom I have not been able to learn enough to distinguish him more particularly, published a few months since a translation he had made for his own amusement, a considerable time before the commencement of the Revolution, he says, not long after the work found its way to France. He kept back the translation, thinking the country not ripe for it. The general slaughter that has been made of all sorts of prejudices in that country may now, he thinks, have opened the way for it. But if its turning to any account in practice depends upon the overthrow of prejudice, who shall calculate [the] period, at which any good can be expected from it here?

It is to the attempt made in Ireland to effect a fresh forced reduction of the legal rate of interest in that country, that the reimpression there published must naturally have been indebted for a circulation proportionably more extensive than here. Between that measure and the laws condemned by this investigation, the connection is close and evident. Had the reduction so proposed been naturally productive of the advantage expected from it, and at the same time not attended with any additional hardship or other inconvenience superior to that advantage, such a reduction would then have had no other objections to combat than the objections, [1]decisive as they are represented in this work,[1] which apply to the original fixation. According to my conception of the matter, [however,] that advantage is altogether illusory; the measure is attended with hardships much more than sufficient to outweigh the advantage, were it real, and of these, several are distinct from, and superadded to, those which result from the impropriety of ever having fixed any rate at all. Had I divined the politico-economical advantage proposed from this ulterior and fresh reduction, I should have set it down among the reasons capable of being alledged in support of the original fixation: for the advantage, if it were one, of the proposed future reduction, must proportionably have resulted from the precedent ones. The fact is, I must confess, that in the situation I was then in, sequestered not less from political converse than from books, this supposed advantage had equally escaped my recollection and my imagination as applicable to the original fixation, though recollection had represented it as capable of having been supposed to result from successive reductions. From newspapers I had learnt thus much, that in England a fresh reduction had lately been proposed, as tending some how or other to the benefit of trade: but the sound of the word *trade* being all I was able to collect, what that benefit was, or how it was to be brought about, was more than I could conceive. To apply it to the immediate subject I was treating of, it was necessary I should have some conception of the force of it: and unfortunately I was unable to perceive any force or meaning in it at all. It had equally escaped Dr. Smith: for his reasons in support of the limitation of the rate of interest are confined to the discouragement of prodigals and projectors: of any supposed benefit to trade that was to follow from it in any other way, he betrays not the smallest suspicion: and blindness may be confessed without much shame, where eyes like Dr. Smith's have failed to see. I little suspected, I must confess, that so many intelligent and ingenious men would so compleatly have mistaken a consequence for a cause. Instructed by the debates of the Irish Parliament, I now understand clearly what benefit was expected from it, but how that benefit was to flow from it is as much a mystery to me as ever. I will however avail myself now of that intelligence. By way of postscript, I have accordingly given a very short, but what appeared to me compleat, answer to the argument afforded by that supposed benefit to my system: and being thereby engaged to touch upon the measure

---

[1][Later brackets.]

of an ulterior reduction by which this supposed advantage was brought to view, I have stated such other considerations as appear to combat the propriety of that ulterior reduction, though not all of them applicable to the continuing of the rate at its present level.

As little can I pretend to say, whether a project of the same nature has received any check from it in England. Infallibility is among the appendages of power: and if it be a dream, it is one of those which do not own themselves as such, and from which men are seldom thankful for being awaked. Several circumstances render probable that a project of this sort was not very long ago entertained: a positive assertion to that effect made in the Irish Parliament received no contradiction. Of late, nothing has been heard of it. The notion perhaps may be, that the country is not yet ripe for it. My notion is that no country ever was, or ever can be.

I do not pretend here to exhaust the subject, or to urge all that can be urged against the measure: nor to trace out to the last link the whole chain of its consequences. Such an undertaking would require more paper perhaps than it is worth, at any rate more time than at present I can spare. All I pretend to is to give what shall be sufficient to demonstrate its impolicy and injustice.

The propositions here given as conclusions from the [decisive][1] principle arc, most of them, maintained by Dr. Smith. The proposition here given as a principle itself is also laid down in the same admirable work[2]: but without emphasis, and for any direct use that has been made of it, it might as well have not been there. Wide is the difference between a full view of a principle and a side glance. The principle which forms the basis of Locke's Essay is to be found, in so many words, in Aristotle: yet what was the world the better for it while it was in the hands of Aristotle, till Locke put it out to use? This same principle is also to be found, stated still more pointedly, in L[or]d Sheffield's elaborate and useful work.[3] Yet what came of it? The whole work is full of advice as repugnant to that principle as it is to the doctrines of Dr. Smith's book: that very book which his Lordship quotes in those terms of respect which is its due, for the sake of stating almost the only doctrine in which the authority is in

---

[1] [The MS speaks of "the above principle", but in fact it has not been mentioned yet. The principle in question is the proposition that "trade is limited by capital."]
[2] [Wealth of Nations, bk. IV, ch. II.]
[3] [On Lord Sheffield cf. the introduction to *Colonies and Navy*, above p. 45f. and especially below p. 213, where the exact reference to the passage in question is given.]

N

his favour, passing by the whole of what is against him, that is almost the whole contents of the book, as if they had not been there.

Colonies. Dr. Smith observes[1] that, by the expence they have produced instead of revenue, they have been always hitherto worth so much less than nothing, and by the expence of wars waged for them, a hundred and so many millions less than nothing. What is his practical inference? that they should be given up? no: but that either they should be given up, or made to yield a revenue, which is impossible. The idea of giving them up is started—but how? as the extremity of misfortune, the horrors of which should drive us into schemes for making [them yield] a revenue, as the only alternative common sense admitts of. We are to give them up: how? with the same emotions of regret, with which a man who found a necessity of retrenching, would lay down his equipage. The separation would be a misfortune not to us only, but to them. Why to them? because nothing but our superior wisdom and virtue could prevent their falling together by the ears. The event has not been favourable to this prophecy. Among these rebels, every thing breathes content and unanimity. Ill will there never has been: and the last spark of so much as a difference of opinion, patience has now finally extinguished. In the principal of our still loyal colonies, whose petitions for these six years we have not been able to find time to listen [to], the discontent is as notorious as it is just. May it be effectual!

---

[1] [Wealth of Nations, bk. IV, ch. VII, pt. III.]

Postscript
SHORT OBSERVATIONS ON THE INJUSTICE AND IMPOLICY OF FORCED REDUCTIONS OF THE RATE OF INTEREST

Since the writing of the preceding letters, I have heard of some other advantages supposed to result from the limitation of the rate of interest which, I must confess, had not then occurred to me as resulting from the restraints thus [laid][1] on the liberty of contracting.

These are

1. Encreasing the sum of national wealth.

2. Enabling the state to take and to keep money at interest upon more advantageous [terms] than it could otherwise, and thus diminishing the sum of the public burthens which are the deductions from national wealth, encreasing therefore in this negative way the clear sum of national wealth upon the whole.

Examine into these supposed advantages, you will find them both altogether illusory, and that, did they not only exist, but exist in the utmost degree that was ever attributed to them, they could not be obtained but at the expence of inconveniences much more considerable.

The first of them does not exist in point of fact: such a limitation has scarce any perceptible tendency in any way whatever to add to the mass of national wealth, and it tends in a variety of ways to diminish it.

As to the second, neither does that exist in the shape of an advantage. The public may or may not hold money of individuals at interest upon more advantageous terms, but from this circumstance the mass of national [wealth] is not rendered a jot more considerable than it would be otherwise.

At no time, therefore, does the nation, collectively considered, derive any advantage from this limitation: and as often as any fresh limitation is applied whereby the restraint is drawn tighter, the nation suffers the inconvenience of an unequal and very heavy tax, without reaping the advantages that it does from other taxes.

First supposed advantage—Encreasing in a direct way the mass of national wealth in the hands of individuals.

This advantage, I say, will not be found to result in any degree from this measure.

---

[1][The MS reads "late".]

Every accession made to the national stock of wealth, is the result of labour employed by the help of capital, the result of preceding labour.

No accession to wealth in any hands, public or private, can take place but in one or other of two ways: 1. By the augmentation of the mass of capital employed in giving motion to industry: 2. By a more advantageous application of the existing stock of capital, [its application] in a more advantageous manner.

That the measure in question can contribute in the latter of these two modes to the encrease of wealth, has never been, nor ever will be supposed.

On the other hand I have already shewn that it has a contrary effect. Every more advantageous mode than was before known of applying a part of the quantity of capital in hand is, previously to trial and success, a *project*: and the effect of this limitation in discouraging projects has already been displayed.

2. It has no particular tendency to encrease the quantity of capital.

It has, it is true, a tendency to modify in a certain manner the distribution of wealth among the different sharers: it is only in proportion as it has this tendency, that this or any other regulation relative to property can have any effect at all.

It must also be admitted that, if in any degree it tends to augment the quantity of wealth employed in the shape of capital, with reference to, and at the expence of, that part which is employed in the shape of unproductive consumption and expenditure, it must in proportion operate in augmentation of the mass of capital employed as capital in the production of wealth, and thence of the growing stock of national wealth.

Whoever saves money, as the phrase is, adds proportionably to the general mass of capital.

There is scarce any description of people that does not include some individuals that save money: but some descriptions are likely to include more such frugal individuals than others. If the tendency of the measure in question be to throw or to keep money in the hands of persons of particular descriptions in preference to others, and those descriptions are more likely to be of a frugal cast upon the whole than the descriptions of people at whose expence it is thus disposed of, the measure possesses in so far a tendency to produce the intended effect. But no such particular tendency is discoverable in it.

The persons on whom it operates, belong to one or other of two

classes, borrowers and lenders: its property is to favour the former at
the expence of the latter. If of borrowers in general it could be said
that they were more frugal than lenders, a favour shewn to borrowers
as such would be a help given to frugality.

But no such proposition thus taken in the lump can be received as
true. Neither reason nor so much as prejudice plead in favour of it.
Ask prejudice, the answer will be that, in comparison of borrowers,
lenders are not only frugal, but frugal to such a degree as to be
avaricious. The supposition of their proneness to avarice is the very
thing that excites prejudice against them, and disposes the bulk of
mankind to favour all regulations, the tendency of which is to lay
them under a disadvantage. It is because they are hoarders that they
are to be discouraged—to what end?—in order to encourage hoarding.
Such is the consistency of blind and vulgar prejudice, hitherto in so
many important points the arbiter of the destiny of nations.

Setting prejudice aside, and taking reason for our guide, it is
impossible to [say] whether the cause of frugality be prejudiced or
served by the favour thus shewn to borrowers, untill it be specified
for what purpose a man means to borrow.

When a man borrows, it is either to spend or to accumulate.

So far as it favours the dissipating class of borrowers, the measure
directly counteracts this its proposed object: it adds, as far as it
operates, to the amount of what they are enabled to employ in
dissipation.

It is not incumbent on those who take the side I take, to go about to
prove a negative, viz. that in the class of borrowers there is *not*
likely to be more frugality than in the class of lenders. It is incumbent
on [those][1] who take the side I combat, to establish the opposite affirmative proposition. Every restraint on liberty is so far an evil: and it
lies on him who proposes any such restraint, to shew the greater good
by which this evil is counterbalanced. This has never been attempted:
nor, howsoever it may have been tacitly taken for granted, has it in
any instance been directly and explicitly affirmed. Propositions
diametrically opposite are both received with open arms, to justify the
propensity to injure and oppress the class of lenders. At one time
lenders are to be pinched, because borrowers are more likely to be
spendthrifts than hoarders: at another time, because they are more
likely to be hoarders than spendthrifts.

Persons concerned in bargains of this kind may be distinguished

[1][The MS reads "whom".]

into three classes: possessors of capital who risk to lend it, [i.e.] money lenders; dissipating borrowers; and accumulating borrowers. The restraint in question favours the two latter classes at the expence of the former. That in as far as it favours dissipating borrowers, it counteracts its avowed purpose, is manifest at any rate: does it promote that purpose in as far as it favours accumulating borrowers? This can not so clearly be averred. It does so only in as far as the accumulating borrowers are greater accumulators than the persons of whom they borrow.

Take an instance. The money that is borrowed by accumulators engaged in trade, of whom is it borrowed principally? of persons who spend all their income? No, but of other accumulators—of other persons as great accumulators as themselves: of shopkeepers or wholesale dealers in the way of goods ordered on credit: or of bankers or merchants in the way of discount. And thus far, therefore, it is evident that accumulation is not more favoured by the restraint in one way, than it is checked in the other.

In another way the restraint in question counteracts this part of its object in a more manifest and conspicuous manner: viz. by lessening the quantity of borrowed capital employed in accumulation.

The world can augment its capital only in one way: viz. by parsimony. A nation may augment its capital, as an individual may augment his capital, in either of two ways: by saving, or by borrowing. By borrowing capital for the purpose of accumulation, is it likely to add to the stock of national wealth? Yes: if the value of what is thereby produced is greater than the value of what is paid for interest: in that case the clear amount of the accumulation, the clear gain to the nation, is to the amount of the difference. But this it may always be reckoned, and that on two different accounts which concurr in encreasing the advantage: 1. In the first place, the general rate of mercantile profit is greater every where than the rate of interest: it is in general at least double: 2. In the next place, in *manufactures**the rate of profit encreases with the encrease of capital by the advantages derivable from the division of labour, and the making the same quantity of machinery and warehouse room and even labour in some cases serve for a larger quantity of work than[1] would have been necessary for a smaller.

---

*I say in manufactures: for it is otherwise in buying and selling. See Smith['s Wealth of Nations, *passim*].

[1][The MS reads "that".]

It has already been shewn in the body of the work that the quantity of good success in all branches of industry taken together is much superior to the quantity of ill success: and this it is not less likely to be in the instances where a man aids his original by borrowed capital than in others. If a man engaged in industry did not expect to get more by the money he borrows than he pays for it, he would not borrow it: and it has been shewn that such expectations are much more frequently realised than frustrated. To seek to restrain industrious men from borrowing money under the apprehension of its not answering to them would be an additional instance, but an instance not more flagrant than those which are perpetually exhibited, of the ignorance and folly, and blindness, and vanity, and presumption, and despotism that hitherto have been endemial among legislators.

Look into pamphlets and debates, you will find people disposed to quarrel with outlandish money, because it is outlandish, at least for the purpose of the argument. The popular notion that *illgotten* money does not thrive, howsoever hacknied by superstition, has not only a much better effect, but even a more rational ground.

Two ill effects are attributed to outlandish money:

1st. That the interest paid for it is so much money sent out of the country. But were not the interest sent out of the country, the profit would not come into it. And profit, we have seen, ought to be estimated at more than double the value of the interest. The force of this argument depends upon the forgetting altogether the chapter of profit: and supposing that the money thus sent out of the country, is sent out for nothing. It is an argument that applies against selling any thing to foreigners: or indeed to any body on any terms.

What are the particular courses taken by such imported money, whether for example it being laid out in the public funds or lent out to individuals, makes no sort of difference. If the money laid out by the Dutch in the English funds, that is, lent to the English government, had not been so disposed of, English money to the same amount must have lain there: there would therefore have been so much less English money to be applied in the support of English industry, in the encrease of the sum of the national wealth of England.*

*The quantity of money belonging to the Dutch and other foreigners in the English funds, has been reckoned at ¹thirty¹ millions: if this be just, the annual clear gain to Great Britain from this importation of foreign capital (reckoning interest in the funds at 4 per Cent, and profit upon stock at 8 per Cent) is £2,400,000.

¹[Later brackets.]

2dly. That money borrowed of foreigners will be perpetually liable to be recalled.

To render this an objection, two circumstances must concur.

1. The foreign money must be more liable to be recalled than home money.

2. When recalled, the prejudice resulting from the recall must be likely to be greater than all the advantage reaped before the recall.

Neither of these propositions has ever been attempted to be proved: nor does either seem likely to be true.

1. It may happen to any lender to recall his money: but this is not more likely to happen to a man of one country than of another. You may put cases where an Englishman who has lend [sic] his money in Ireland* may be disposed to recall that money: but it is just as easy to put cases in which an Irishman who has lent his money in Ireland may be disposed to do the same thing. An Irishman who is upon the spot is more likely to look for, to spy out, and to improve such opportunities, than an Englishman who is at a distance, and who, if he lends his money in such a way, is more likely to have lent it with views of permanence, and as a means of providing himself for life, without farther sollicitude, a settled income.

2. If there were any reason to apprehend that the time when the foreign lender may call in his money would be more inconvenient to the lender than the time when a home lender might call in his, the danger of recall might sooner afford an objection to the importation of foreign capital. But no such reason can be assigned. The disposition of the foreign lender to call in his money will not be governed by the consideration of the inconvenience to the borrower, but by the consideration of his own convenience. But that convenience is not the more likely to clash with the convenience of the borrower on account of the lender's being a foreigner: not more likely to do so than that of a lender at home. We have seen that on one account it is less likely: because a foreign lender is less likely to be tempted by opportunities of occasional profit to clasp and change his security than a native. It is also on another account: a lender at home is more in the way of being acquainted with the circumstances and exigencies of his borrower: more in the way of having quarrels with him: of watching opportunities of distressing him in a time of need, either

---

*What Holland is to England in this respect, England is to Ireland: except that the uneasiness with regard to the supposed profit to the lender and loss to the borrower, are still more unreasonable.

for the sake of hurting him, or for the sake of making a profit of his distress.

Whatever may, by accident, be the disadvantage resulting to A or B in this way from a recall [of] a foreign capital, a capital thus imported will, so long as it continues unrecalled, be productive to the nation that has imported it, of a clear revenue to the amount just stated. If the use of a million for ten years would have been worth £600,000, the use of the same million for one year will have been £60,000. Recall it when you will, it will have had its value from the time of its importation to the time of its recall. To furnish an argument against the import, the inconvenience likely to result from the recall must be not only very considerable, but superior to the whole amount of the benefit reaped previously to the recall.

DEVELOPMENT OF THE PRINCIPLE "NO MORE TRADE THAN CAPITAL", OR "CAPITAL LIMITS TRADE".

1. No branch of productive industry can be carried on without the help of a certain quantity of capital previously accumulated.

2. The whole quantity of productive industry each individual can carry on, is limited by the quantity he has of his own, or is able to borrow of other individuals. The whole quantity of productive industry a nation can carry on, is limited by the quantity of capital it has of its own, or can borrow from other nations. The whole quantity of productive industry the world can carry on, is limited by the capital it has of its own, till it can find another world to borrow of.

3. Credit need not be taken separately into the account: since credit is but capital borrowed, and the quantity that can be borrowed is limited by the quantity possessed.

4. The quantity of capital limiting the quantity of productive industry, limits in the same proportion the possible quantity, and amount in value, of the produce of that industry, and thence of whatever part of it is capable of becoming the subject of trade. The quantity of capital sets the limit to the quantity of wealth: [it likewise sets the limit] to the quantity of trade.

5. Therefore no regulations nor any efforts whatsoever, either on the part of subjects or governors, can raise the quantity of wealth produced during a given period to an amount beyond what [the] productive powers of the quantity of capital in hand at the commencement of that period are capable of producing.

6. [1]A given quantity of capital may enable the employer to produce a greater quantity of wealth when employed in one way than when employed in another. Let the number of possible ways of employing capital be any number whatever, suppose a thousand: if a minister could make out that one certain mode would be more productive than any one of the remaining 999, he would have reason for wishing that a certain portion of the national capital should be applied to that branch, in preference to all others.* But he would have no sufficient reason for so much as wishing it, till he had made out that superiority with respect to all the 999.† And though he had made it out ever so clear, he could have no warrantable ground for employing coercive measures to induce any one to engage in this most advantageous of all branches. For the more evident its superiority, the more certain it is that, as soon as that superiority was made evident to them, men would betake themselves to that superior branch of their own accord, without being either hired or forced to do so.

7. Vanity and weakness can alone give him a plea which would be sufficient to his own conscience, to warrant his employing force‡ to such a purpose. And whichever plea such a persuasion might afford to his own conscience, it is a plea that could never be valid in the eyes of any other men. To every bystander the refusal of the persons concerned to engage in the business without being thus compelled or hired, would be a stronger reason for looking upon it as not being an advantageous one, than any it could ever be possible for him to give on the other side.[1]

PRACTICAL CONSEQUENCES OF THE PRINCIPLE "NO MORE TRADE THAN CAPITAL" WITH RESPECT TO COLONIAL GOVERNMENT, ECONOMY AND PEACE

What is it that would be the loss, suppose it to amount to any thing, that a nation would sustain by the giving up of any colony? The difference between the profit to be made by the employing in

---

*To wit more and more, the addition of capital not ceasing till the superiority of profit ceased.

†Opportunity of collecting the particular information, necessary time for reflecting on it, interest in forming a right judgment, in all these particulars he falls infinitely short of the persons themselves whom he would wish to see thus employed.

‡Bounties and prohibitions, it is to be observed, are equally coercive. The only difference is, that the coercion is applied in the one case to one set of people, in the other to another. No bounty that does not necessitate a proportionable tax. and to tax is to coerce. Monopolies and other prohibitions are even the milder and least bad expedient of the two if nobody in particular suffers by them, as is the case, for instance, where the trade prohibited is as yet untried.

[1][A question mark is written over this passage.]

that trade so much capital as would be employed in it were the
colony kept, and the profit that would be made by the employment
of the same capital in any other way, suppose in the improvement
of land. The loss is nothing, if the same capital employed in the
improvement of land would be more productive: and it would be
more productive by the amount of so much as would go to form
the annual rent: for deducting that rent, capital employed in the
improvement of land produces as much as if employed in any other
way. If the loss were any thing, would it then amount to the whole
difference between the profit upon that trade, and the profit upon the
next most profitable one? no: but only [to][1] the difference between
so much of that difference as would be produced if the colony were
retained in subjection, and so much as would be produced if the
colony were declared free.

The value of a colony to the mother country, according to the
common mode of computation, is equal to the sum total of imports
from that colony and exports to it put together.

From this statement, if the foregoing observation be just, the
following deductions will come to be made:

1. The whole value of the exports to the colony.

2. So much of the imports as is balanced by the exports.

3. Such a portion of the above remainder as answers to so much of
the trade as would be equally carried on, were the colony independent.

4. So much of that reduced profit as would be made, were the same
capital employed in any other trade or branch of industry lost by the
independence of the colony.

5. But the same capital, if employed in agriculture, would have produced a rent over and above the ordinary profits of capital: which
rent, according to a general and undisputed computation, may be
stated at a sum equal to the amount of those profits. Thence [arises a
further deduction, viz. the] loss to the nation [caused] by employing
the capital in the trade to the colony, in preference to the improvement of land, and thence upon the supposition that the continuance
of the trade depended upon the keeping the colony in subjection.

The other mischiefs resulting from the keeping of a colony in
subjection, are:

1. The expence of its establishment, civil and military.

---

[1] [The MS reads "if".]

2. The contingent expence of wars and other coercive measures for keeping it in subjection.

3. The contingent expence of wars for the defence of it against foreign powers.

4. The force, military and naval, constantly kept on foot under the apprehension of such wars.

5. The occasional danger to political liberty from the force thus kept up.

6. The contingent expence of wars produced by alliances contracted for the purpose of supporting wars that may be brought on by the defence of it.

7. The corruptive effects of the influence resulting from the patronage of the establishment, civil and military.

8. The damage that must be done to the national stock of intelligence by the false views of the national interest, which must be kept up in order to prevent the nation from opening their eyes and insisting upon the enfranchisement [of the colony].

9. The sacrifice that must be made of the real interest of the colony to this imaginary interest of the mother-country. It is for the purpose of governing it badly, and for no other, that you wish to get or keep a colony. Govern it well, it is of no use to you.

To govern its inhabitants as well as they would govern themselves, you must choose to govern them those only whom [they] would [themselves][1] choose, you must sacrifice none of [their][2] interests to your own, you must bestow as much time and attention to their interests as they would themselves, in a word, you must take those very measures and no others, which they themselves would take. But would this be governing? And what would it be worth to you, if it were?

After all, it would be impossible for you to govern them so well as they would themselves, on account of the distance.

10. The bad government resulting to the mother-country from the complication, the indistinct views of things, and the consumption of time occasioned by this load of distant dependencies.

---

[1][The MS reads "it" and "itself" respectively.]
[2][The MS reads "its".]

Agriculture Not Dependent On Manufactures

The most advantageous employment for the community that can be made of capital is agriculture, because there the idle landlord shares in equal proportion with the labouring farmer.

This can not be extended *ad infinitum*, to the exclusion of other employments of capital. It can be extended no farther than so far as the farmer finds his profit equal to the profit of stock in other employments of capital, which he would cease to do if this business were to be overstocked.

What follows?—that as soon as this branch of business became so far stocked as to be less productive than others, capital would cease to be applied to it; capital, instead of being applied to this business, would be applied to some other, i.e. manufactures.

There would therefore be no occasion for employing artificial means to draw it to manufactures: it would go there of its own accord.

It is therefore not true to say that manufactures are necessary to agriculture, and that manufactures must first be encreased before agriculture can be encreased.

On the contrary, it is true to say that agriculture is necessary to manufactures, and that agriculture must first be encreased before manufactures can be encreased.

Men must exist, before they can begin to work: raw materials of manufacture must exist before they can be worked.

What makes the mistake is this. It is true that, when manufactures have encreased within the reach of an intercourse with cultivators, agriculture can be carried on in various respects to more advantage.

Manufactures as well as agriculture afford by parsimony and storing a capital: and when a capital is laid up from manufactures, any part of it may as well be applied to agriculture as to any thing else. When applied to agriculture, the improvement of land enables a given quantity of land and labour to produce a greater quantity of produce.

Each profits by the overflowings of the capital saved out of the other. But this does not make it necessary, but unnecessary, to take capital by force from either, in order to bestow it upon the other.

Could capital be drawn from the clouds, like manna, by praying, there would be no use in bestowing it upon one branch of industry in preference to another: for so much of this miraculous capital as was thrown into any channel, so much natural would be kept from flowing into it.

Agriculture without manufactures, contributes most to population: agriculture with manufactures to wealth.

Agriculture without manufactures makes men more numerous, and less wealthy: agriculture with manufactures makes men more wealthy, and consequently less numerous.

The relative quantity of capital will encrease, and consequently the rate of interest fall, where thesaurisation goes on faster than population: and vice versa.

When men have got more food than they want, they will be able and willing to give part of it for finer cloaths and finer furniture. But this does not make it necessary to set men to work to make finer cloaths and furniture, in order to induce others to produce food.

The consumption of some sorts of corn in particular ways is limited, while the number of consumers is limited. When a man has as much bread as he can eat, he will not give any thing for any more. But this is not the case with other sorts of corn, or with the same sort of corn employed in another way.

In England, the lowest wages of labour will always find a man more bread than he can eat: therefore considerably more wheat than is produced at present, would, if not exported, not find purchasers. But the lowest wages of labour, nor wages much above the lowest, will not find a man as much strong beer as he can drink, nor even as he can drink without hurting himself. Therefore, even independently of exportation, there is no danger of the nation's being overstocked with such of the productions of agriculture as are fit for [making]¹ beer.

Apply this to oats for horses, hay for horses and cows.

There is no fear of there being at the same time more cream produced than every body who has any thing to give for it is able to eat, more fruit of all sorts, more poultry, more saddle horses, more coach-horses.

With bread-corn it is possible that a market may be overstocked: but with such luxuries, and with all these luxuries put together, it is impossible that the market should be overstocked. And agriculture is just as capable of producing these articles as bread-corn.

Agriculture then will always find a sufficient market for itself: it is impossible it should ever fail to do so.

Therefore, for the purpose of a market, it can never stand in need of

¹[The MS reads "mankind".]

manufactures. And it has been shewn that it can not [stand in need of manufactures] for the purpose of laying up capital. Therefore it can not [stand in need of manufactures] for any purpose.

Quere: when capital is plenty, what is the correlative that is comparatively scarce?

Hands[1] adult and in actual readiness to work.

When capital is plenty, interest will be low, and real price of labour high.

When capital is scarce, interest will be high, and the price (real) of labour low, unless kept up by an unnatural occasional demand such as that by war.

What keeps down the quantity, and thence the value of capital is procreation, which multiplies little children who occasion expence before they can produce profit.

These children as they grow up, encrease the number of labourers —thence they 1. keep down the price of labour, and 2. lessen the *ratio* of capital to *hands*.

The same causes that promote accumulation, promote procreation.

If accumulation goes on faster than procreation, capital will proportionably encrease, and the rate of interest proportionably sink.

---

[1] [The MS reads "1. Hands . . ." but there is no "2.".]

COLONIES AND NAVY

o

COLONIES AND NAVY

[A FRAGMENT]

Circa 1790

THE ensuing sheets are dedicated to the common welfare of all civilised nations: but more particularly of Great Britain and France.

The design in view is to recommend three grand objects: simplicity of government, national frugality, and peace.

Reflection has satisfied me of the truth of the following propositions:—

1. That it is not the interest of Great Britain to have any foreign dependencies whatsover.*

2. That it is not the interest of Great Britain to keep up any naval force, beyond what may be sufficient to defend its commerce against pirates.

3. That it is not the interest of Great Britain to have any treaty of alliance, offensive or defensive, with any other power whatsoever.

4. That it is not the interest of Great Britain to have any treaty with any power whatsoever, for the purpose of possessing any advantage whatsoever in point of trade, to the exclusion of any other nation whatsoever.

5. That it is not the interest of Great Britain to keep on foot any regulations whatsoever of distant preparation for the augmentation or maintenance of its force: such as the Navigation Act, bounties on the Greenland trade, and other trades regarded as nurseries for seamen. This proposition is a necessary consequence of the second.

6, 7, 8, 9 & 10. That all these several propositions are also true of France.

---

*Distant dependencies encrease the chances of war

1. By encreasing the number of possible subjects of dispute.

2. By the natural obscurity of title in case of new settlements or discoveries.

3. By the particular obscurity of the evidence, resulting from the distance. Instances: 1. Spanish war of 1742 or thereabouts—Violence by their *guarda-costas*. 2. French war of 1754. Hostilities in N[orth] America. Hostilities in the E[ast] Indies.

4. By men's caring less about wars when the scene is remote, than where it is nearer home.

As far as Great Britain is concerned, I rest the proof of these several propositions principally upon two very simple principles.

1. That the encrease of growing wealth of every nation [in] a given period, is necessarily limited by the quantity of capital it possesses at that period.

. 2. That Great Britain, with or without Ireland, and without any other dependency, can have no reasonable ground to apprehend injury from any one nation upon earth.

Turning to France, I substitute to the last of the two just-mentioned propositions the following:—

3. That France, standing singly, has at present nothing to fear from any other nation than Great Britain: nor, if standing clear of her foreign dependencies, would she have[1] any thing to fear from Great Britain.

11. That supposing Great Britain and France thoroughly agreed, the principal difficulty would be removed to the establishment of a plan of general and permanent pacification for all Europe.

12. That the maintenance of such a pacification might be considerably facilitated by the establishment of a common court of judicature for the decision of differences between the several nations, although such court were not to be armed with any coercive powers.

13. That secresy in the operations of the foreign department ought not to be endured in England; being altogether useless, and equally repugnant to the interests of liberty and to those of peace.

The first of these principles, viz. that [the] trade of every nation is limited by the quantity of capital, is so plainly and obviously true as to challenge a place among self-evident propositions. But self-evident propositions must not expect to be easily admitted, if [they are admitted] at all, if the consequences of them clash with prevalent passions and confirmed prejudices.

Nations are composed of individuals. The trade of a nation must be limited by the same causes that limit the trade of the individual. Each individual merchant, when he has as much trade as his whole capital, and all the credit he can get by means of his capital, can suffice for carrying on, can have no more. This being true of each merchant, is not less true of the whole number of merchants put together.

This truth you find frequently recognized. I question whether it ever was disputed. I know of no instance of its being so. Dr. Adam

---

[1][The MS reads "having".]

Smith begins his book with it, or something very like it* : but though he has fallen upon many of the conclusions deducible from it, he seems scarcely to build them upon it directly, nor does he seem to be fully aware of half the use that may be made of it. L[ord] Sheffield stumbles upon it *en passant,* as if by accident, almost at the end of his book on the American trade. Had he seen the value of the consequences of it, the world would have been deprived of a work on other accounts very valuable, for there needs little more than this simple truth, added to that of the self-sufficiency of the British power, to prove the impropriety of every measure he recommends. *"No country* (says he, p. 284, 6th edition) can carry its trade beyond its *capital"* : and again three pages after: "We have only a certain capital to employ; industry will find out the best means of employing it". So far the noble Lord's direct assertions and expressions: but his book, from beginning to end, is founded on the opposite doctrine tacitly taken for granted.

Many books, then, directly recognise that the quantity of trade a nation can carry on, is limited: limited by the quantity of its capital. None dispute the proposition: but almost all, somewhere or other, proceed upon the opposite supposition. They suppose the quantity of trade to have no limitation whatsoever.

It is folly to buy manufactured good[s]; wise to buy raw materials. Why? because you sell them to yourselves, or, what is still better, to foreigners, manufactured: and the manufacturer's profit is all clear gain to you. What they forget is, that the manufacturer, to carry on his business, must have a capital: and that just so much capital as is employed in that way, is prevented from being employed in any other.

Hence the perfect inutility and mischievousness of all laws and public measures whatsoever, for the pretended encouragement of trade: all prohibitions of rival foreign trade: bounties in every shape whatsoever: all non-importation agreements and engagements to

---

*Introd[uction] p. 3. "Whatever be the actual state of the skill, dexterity, and judgment with which labour is applied in any nation, the abundance or scantiness of its annual supply must depend, during the continuance of that state, upon the proportion between the number of those who are annually employed[1] in useful [labour], and that of those who are not so employed. The number of useful and productive labourers, it will hereafter appear, is every where [in proportion][2] to the quantity of capital stock which is employed in setting them to work, and to the particular way in which it is so employed. The second book, therefore, treats of the nature of capital stock" &c.
    [1][Bentham incorrectly spells "employ'd".]
    [2][Bentham incorrectly quotes "proportioned".]

consume home manufacture in preference to foreign in any other view than to afford temporary relief to temporary distress.

But of the two—prohibitions and bounties, penal encouragements and remuneratory—the latter are beyond comparison the most mischievous. Prohibitions, except while they are fresh, and drive men at a great expence out of the employments they are embarked in, are only nugatory: bounties are wasteful and oppressive. They force money from one man, in order to pay another man for carrying on a trade which, if it were not a losing one, there would be no need of paying him for.

Productive industry may be divided into five main branches: 1. production of raw materials including agriculture, mining, and fisheries: 2. manufacture: 3. home trade: 4. foreign trade: 5. carrying trade. The National Assembly has already a committee for the improvement of waste lands: it has, or will have, committees for the encouragement of all those other branches of productive industry. Each of these committees are or will be so many rival powers fighting the war of encouragement against one another, and against all the world beside: all at the national expence. The committee of waste lands gives money to people that they may employ their capital in the bringing into the general poor and bad cultivation the waste lands, instead of employing it in fisheries or mining, or manufacture or home trade or foreign trade or carrying trade: or bringing the land already in bad cultivation into better. The committee of fisheries will in like manner be for paying mankind [a premium] for laying out their capital upon fishing, and not upon improving waste lands or in any of the other ways just mentioned: and thus the policy goes round.

Suppose ten of these committees (there might as well be that number as a smaller or larger) and that each has credit enough with the Assembly to get £100,000 to be employed for their respective purposes—What is the consequence? that not one of all those objects is promoted in the smallest degree. The whole nation is taxed to the amount of a million to pay a part of the nation for doing in the same manner exactly as they, or somebody else, would have done, had there been no such taxes.

For maintaining colonies there are several avowed reasons, besides others which are not avowed: but of the avowed reasons, by far the principal one is, the benefit of trade. If your colonies were not subject to you, they would not trade with you; they would not buy any of your goods: nor let you buy any of theirs; at least you could not be sure of their doing so: if they were subject to any body else, they would not do so: for the colonies of other nations are, you see, not suffered to trade with you. Give up your colonies, you give up so much of your trade as is carried on with your colonies. No, we do not give up any such thing: we do not give up any thing whatsoever. Trade to colonies can not, any more than any where else, be carried on without capital: just so much of our capital as is employed in our trade with the colonies, just so much of it is not employed elsewhere: just so much is either kept or taken from other trades.

When the colonies are to be made out to be beneficial to the mother country, and the quantum of the benefit [is] to be estimated, the mode in which the estimate is conducted is curious enough. An account is taken of what they export, which is almost the whole of what they produce. All this, they say, while you have colonies, is yours: this is exactly what you lose if you lose the colonies. How much of all this is really yours? Not one single halfpenny. When they let you take it from them, do they give it you for nothing? Not they indeed: they make you pay for it just as any body else would do. How much? Just as much as you would pay them if they belonged to themselves or to any body else.

What then? are all modes of productive industry alike—may not one be more profitable than another? certainly. But the favourite one, is it, in fact, more profitable than any other? That is the question, and the only question, that ought to be put: and that is the very question which nobody ever thinks of putting.

Were it even put and answered, and answered ever so clearly, it never could be of any use as a ground for any permanent plan of policy. Why? because no sooner hardly is one branch known to be more profitable than the rest, than it ceases so to be. Men flock to it from all other branches: and the old equilibrium is presently restored. Your merchants have the monopoly as against foreigners? true: but they have [no monopoly][1] as against one another. Men can not in every instance quit the less productive branch their capitals are already employed in, to throw them into this more productive one: true: but there are young beginners as well as old stagers: and the first concern of a beginner, who has a capital to employ in a branch of industry, is to look out for the most profitable.

Objection: Oh! but it is manufacture that creates the demand for the productions of agriculture. You can not therefore encrease the

---

[1][The MS reads "not".]

productions of agriculture but by encreasing manufacture. No such thing. I admitt the antecedent: I deny the consequence. Encrease of manufactures certainly does create an encrease in the demand for the productions of agriculture. Equally certain is it that the encrease of manufactures is not necessary to produce an encrease in that demand. Farmers can subsist without ribbons, gauzes, or fine cambrics [sic]. Weavers of ribbons, gauzes, or fine cambricks [sic] can not subsist without the productions of agriculture. Necessary subsistence never can lose its value. Those who produce it, are themselves a market for the produce. Is it possible that provisions should be too cheap? Is there any present danger of it? Suppose (in spite of the extreme absurdity of the supposition) that provisions were growing gradually too cheap, from the encrease of the quantity produced, and the want of manufacturers to consume them. What would be the consequence? The encreasing cheapness would encrease the facility and disposition to marry: it would thence encrease the population of the country: and the children thus produced, eating as they grew up, would keep down this terrible evil of a superabundance of provisions.

It is possible for farmers, not only to live and go on farming without the particular branch of manufacture employed in the production of ribbons and gauzes, but without any branch of manufacture whatsoever. His food may be potatoes: his cloathing the skins of wild-cats or foxes: his habitation a hole in the ground: his fewel such sticks as he can pick up in the woods. The supposition is almost realised [?] in Ireland.

But without running into exaggeration, a farmer in the common course of husbandry can not carry on his business without the help of a great variety of manufacturers: smiths, carpenters, leather-sellers, sacking-weavers and others out of number. But these must eat as well as he: and these must come to him for what they eat, as he goes to them for what he uses. By promoting an encrease of the productions of agriculture, therefore, you create a demand for the industry of those who afford a demand for the productions of agriculture. Do not smiths and carpenters eat as well as ribbon-weavers? And the demand they create for the productions of agriculture, is it not as effectual and encouraging an one as that created by ribbon-weavers? What they supply in return, is it not as useful and as necessary as gauzes or ribbons?

Provisions, the produce of agriculture, constantly and necessarily

produce a market for themselves. The more provisions a man raises
over and above what is necessary for his own consumption, the more
he has to give to others to induce them to provide him with whatever
besides provisions he chooses to have. In a word, the more he has to
spare, the more he has to give to manufacturers, who, by taking it
from him and paying him with the produce of their labour, afford the
encouragement requisite to the production of the fruits of agriculture.

It is impossible therefore you can ever have too much agriculture.
It is impossible that, while there is ground untilled, or ground that
might be better tilled than it is, any detriment should ensue to the
community from the withholding or withdrawing capital from any
other branch of industry and employing it in agriculture. It is
impossible, therefore, that the loss of any branch of trade can be
productive of any detriment to the community, excepting always the
temporary distress experienced by the individuals concerned in it for
the time being, where the decline is a sudden one.

Profitable industry [as has been observed above] has five branches.
The quantity of it that can be carried on in a country being limited
by that of the capital which the country can command, it follows
that no part of that quantity can be bestowed upon any one branch,
but it must be either withdrawn from, or withholden from, all the
others. No encouragement, therefore, can be given to any one, but it
must be a proportionable discouragement to all the others. Nothing
can be done by government to induce a man to begin or continue to
employ his capital in any one of those branches, but it must induce
him in the same degree to withdraw or withhold that capital from all
the rest. Of these five branches, no one is to such a degree more
beneficial to the public than the rest, as that it should be worth its
while to call forth the powers of law to give it an advantage. But if
there were any, it would unquestionably be the improvement and
cultivation of land. Every factitious encouragement to any one of
these rival branches being a proportionable discouragement to all the
rest, every encouragement to any branch but agriculture is a proportionable discouragement to agriculture. Every encouragement to any
branch of manufacture [consequently] is a proportionable discouragement to agriculture. Every encouragement to any of those branches
of manufacture which produce articles that are at present sold to the
colonies, is a proportionable discouragement to agriculture.

Suppose any branch of trade or manufacture to decline. Suppose
it lost altogether: is this any permanent loss to the nation, to the

whole nation taken together? Not the smallest. We know the worst that can happen from any such loss: the capital that would otherwise have been employed in the lost branch will be employed in agriculture. The loss of the colonies, if the loss of the colony-trade were the consequence of the loss of the colonies, would at the worst be so much gain to agriculture.

MANUAL OF
POLITICAL ECONOMY

MANUAL OF POLITICAL ECONOMY

1793-95

[TABLE OF CONTENTS]

[PART ONE: GENERAL OBSERVATIONS]

1. *Introduction*

THIS little treatise is meant to serve as a manual of political economy. Political economy may be considered as a science or as an art. But in this instance, as in others, it is only as a guide to the art that the science is of use.

Political economy, considered as an art exercisible by those who have the government of a nation in their hands, is the art of directing the national industry to the purposes to which it may be directed with the greatest advantage.

The object of this little treatise is to shew in a general way, what ought to be done in the way of political economy, and what ought not to be done.

The general result is that of the much that has been done in this way and with these views scarce any thing ought to have been done: and that of what ought to be done, as matters stand, almost the whole consists in undoing what has been done, and in obviating the inconveniences that would result from the carrying on this process of undoing in an abrupt and inconsiderate manner.

It will naturally occur to some as an objection to this work, in short to any work on this subject, that it has already been treated of by Dr. Adam Smith; that Dr. Smith is a writer of great and distinguished merit, and that this subject has been treated of by him very copiously. The objection will naturally appear the stronger in proportion as it is observed that the principles here laid down concurr with those laid down by that illustrious writer.*

---

*Be the doctrine true or false, this concise sketch will serve at any rate to give a view of the state of the question upon all the topics of political economy that can come under the consideration of the legislature. To this doctrine, the habitual practice of the legislature is in many, I may say in most points, in diametrical opposition. If the doctrine be erroneous, exhibited as it is here, it will not be difficult to correct the error: if it be just, those who may be disposed to make use of it for the correction of the errors that guide the present practice, may now do so with little trouble.

Concise as it is, it will be found not more concise than comprehensive. It was designed to embrace the whole of the subject, [and] as far as I can trust my conceptions, it does so. It certainly embraces all the topics and all the arguments touched upon by Dr. Smith: and it as certainly embraces several topics, as well as several arguments, which he has not touched upon.

In answer to this objection I offer the following observations:

1. The design of this work is different from that of his. His had two objects, the το ον and the το πρεπον. But the το ον is evidently the principal: the other comes in incidentally as it were. In this, the sole object is the το πρεπον. His object was the science: my object is the art. By him the art is touched upon incidentally only and piecemeal, and as it were without intending it, in treating of the science: by me it is treated of directly and professedly. His views seem scarcely to have carried him beyond the science: by me the science is considered only as a means to an end: and as no otherwise worth occupying one's self about than in proportion to its subserviency to that end. This work is to Dr. Smith's, what a book on the art of medicine is to a book of anatomy or physiology.

2. He has not made the utmost of his argument.

3. He has not embraced the whole of the subject.

4. He has not compressed his argument within the smallest compass.

5. He has not given it the most advantageous method.

6. With matters belonging to political economy, he has mixed matters foreign to that subject.

7. He has not taken for the sole or for the principal, or even for any part of the professed object of his enquiry, the question how, with regard to all these matters, the law ought to be: he has considered principally the science: what he has said of the art has come in rather incidentally than professedly.

8. Along with the matter employed in the enquiry what the law ought to be, [is] intermixed matter employed in the description of the course that human industry takes abstractedly from the consideration of law. This matter, instead of being *censorial* [i.e.] critical with regard to the state of the law, [is] *expository* or descriptive with regard to the actual course of nature. And of this expository matter by far the greatest part of his book is composed.

The great object, the great *desideratum,* is to know what ought and what ought not to be done by government. It is in this view, and in this view only, that the knowledge of what is done and takes place without the interference of government can be of any practical use. Otherwise than in this view the knowledge of what spontaneously takes place is matter of curiosity rather than use. The only use of the science is the serving as a foundation to the art. For what purpose does it concern us to know how ¹things are? Only in order that we may know how to deal with them, and to dispose of ourselves in respect of them.

9. He has not employed in argument the position which I make use of as the groundwork of the whole: viz. the limitation of industry by the limitation of capital. If he had, it might have spared him some inconsistencies and mistakes: a position which, [if] I am not very much mistaken, draws the argument into a very small compass, and places the whole subject, at the very outset, in a very clear point of view.

10. In combating error, or what has appeared to him in that light, instead of taking opinions one by one, he has taken them in the lump and made them up into systems: a mode of proceeding which is never favourable to perspicuity, and scarce ever perfectly reconciliable to truth.*

At any rate, this treatise, whether better upon the whole than Dr. Smith's or not so good, is in point of method very different. If some there are, who find it easier to gain instruction from that book, others there may be who find it easier to gain it from this. Although not better, yet if not much worse, it will therefore at any rate in virtue of that difference have its use, as giving two chances for the easiest mode of instruction instead of one.

---

¹[Three words not readable.]

*By making propositions into systems and representing such systems as being adopted not only by individuals, but by whole parties, a man virtually asserts and renders it incumbent on him to prove that there are large assemblages of known individuals by every one of whom the propositions in question are every one of them embraced: that every man of the party maintains every one of the propositions: a position which is seldom true, which is never worth proving, which is very apt to be disputed, and which, if disputed, is scarcely capable of being proved. Taking this course, a man can scarcely avoid giving into the error which Aristotle in his catalogue of fallacies characterizes by the name of the fallacy *secundum plures ut unum.*

While he reasons feebly, the proposition, erroneous or not erroneous, stands its ground, and he fails that way: if he attacks the proposition forcibly, and so forcibly that nobody can find any thing to say in its defence, nobody owns it: if he finds no owner for it, he is charged with beating the air: if he finds one, he is charged with calumny and injustice.

In exposing errors, or what are taken for such, the best way therefore both for reader and writer is to take them separately, and exhibit them one by one. Both the nature of the proposition, and its erroneous quality, if it be erroneous, are thus distinctly brought to view: and if it be embraced generally, there can scarcely be any difficulty of finding some one writer who has fathered it, and in whose words it may be exhibited.

P

2. *Fundamental principles*

Under the general name of *wealth* is comprised every object which, being within the reach of human desires, is within the grasp of human possession, and as such either actually subservient, or capable of being made subservient, to human use.

The wealth of any community is the sum of the portions of wealth belonging to the several individuals of which that community is composed.

All wealth is the joint result or product of land and labour: of human labour operating either immediately upon land, or upon something issuing more or less immediately from land.

The ends or uses of wealth may be all comprized under the four following terms: 1. subsistence: 2. enjoyment: 3. security: 4. encrease.*

As wealth can not be put to any of its uses without consumption, the stock subsisting at any given period, far from being augmented, can not so much as be kept up without continual encrease.

Wealth considered as flowing in at successive periods is stiled *income* or *revenue*.

All wealth issuing either immediately or mediately from land, the produce of which renews itself for the most part periodically, in virtue of the influence of the seasons,† income or revenue is accordingly for the most part *periodical*, i.e. flowing in at stated periods, owing to the vicissitude or successive recurrence of the same seasons.

A portion of wealth considered as employed for the purpose of encrease is stiled *capital*.‡

A man, while he is employed in any way in giving encrease to wealth, must have 1. *materials* to work upon: 2. *instruments* to work with: 3. a *place* to work in: 4. a place to be in, when not at work: 5. food, and other consumable means of subsistence, to maintain him.

---

*Equality is a [further]¹ end which law ought to propose to itself, as far as [it] is consist[ent] with the others: but what has been done, or may be done, with this view, will hardly be thought to come within the pale of political economy. As far as it concerns wealth, it will hardly be reckoned an object distinct from opulence: since the end in view, in whatever may be done in the design of favouring equality, is nothing but the making those who would otherwise be poorer richer, [or] rather that the poorer should be less poor rather than that the richer should be less rich.

†Vegetables immediately—Animals, through vegetables—Minerals, not.

‡Land, in as far as it is necessary, may be considered as coming under the head of capital, especially as far as concerns any improvement it has received from industry. The original unimproved land is a portion of capital furnished by nature.

¹[The MS in fact reads "fourth."]

All these, considered as directed to the end in question, viz. the giving encrease to wealth, come under the denomination of capital.

Capital may be distinguished into *fixed*, and *outgoing*. Under the denomination of *outgoing* may be comprehended: 1. the consumable means of subsistence: 2. the materials above mentioned, before they have received the portion of labour destined to be applied to them by the individual in question, [i.e. before] they have been prepared for use: 3. of the instruments in question, such, if any, as have been compleatly consumed before the article in question has been prepared for use. All the other modifications of capital may be referred to the denomination of *fixed*.

The article, whatever it be, in the production of which the encrease given to wealth consists, may be distinguished by the general appellation of *finished work*.

An article of finished work, if instead of being consumed or kept for use by him by whom or for whom it is made, or by or for some one else to whom he gives it *gratis*, is given in exchange for something else, becomes an article of *sale*, an article or object of *trade*, *commerce*, *traffic*, or *merchandize*.

In all communities that have made any sort of progress in the career of civilisation, a class of men has formed itself, who derive a livelyhood from buying goods of the maker, in order to sell [them] again to the consumer who wants them for use.

The makers of goods for sale may be termed, in contradistinction to those who sell them without making them, *manufacturers*: and the latter, in contradistinction to the former, *venders*.

Among venders there is a distinction which, on several accounts, comes often to be noticed. The most numerous are those who sell goods retail as well as wholesale, in small quantities as well as in large, therefore more frequently to him who wants them for use, than to him who buys them only to sell again, exposing them accordingly in most instances to the indiscriminate view of the public passengers in a *shop*. A few there are in comparison who can find their account in selling goods in large quantities only, accordingly to those chiefly or exclusively who buy them to sell again, and thence without the necessity of exposing them purposely to the indiscriminate view of the public in a shop or otherwise. Such persons are termed in contradistinction to the former, [the shopkeepers] *merchants*.

As it is necessary for some purposes that these different classes of men should in the way of speaking of them be kept distinct, so is it for other purposes that they should be comprehended under one denomination which, without confining itself to any one of the classes, shall include them all.—*traders,* and *commercial men* are terms which may be exclusively appropriated to this purpose.*

The business of selling and making for sale may accordingly be comprehended under the common denominations of *trade* and *commerce.*

As labour can in no instance be bestowed upon any object in any considerable quantity without capital, the quantity of labour that can be bestowed upon any object will be limited by the quantity of capital that can be bestowed upon it.

The quantity of capital employed in a community being given, the quantity of encrease given to the stock of wealth within a given period will be in proportion to the degree of advantage with which that capital is applied, in other words, in proportion to the advantageousness of the direction given to it.

The degree of advantage with which a quantity of capital is applied being given, the quantity of encrease given to the stock of wealth within a given period will be in proportion to the quantity of capital which the community has had at command and employed within that period.

The encrease of wealth made in any community within a given period, depends then upon two things: 1. upon [the] quantity of capital: 2. upon the advantageousness of the direction given to it.

The possible ways then, in which any extraordinary degree of encrease can be given to the quantity of wealth in any community within a given period, are all reducible to these two: [1.] adding to the quantity of capital employed in it: 2. adding to the degree of advantageousness with which the capital, whatever there be of it, is employed.

Except in as far as a more advantageous direction is given to the capital of the community than would have been given to it otherwise, it is therefore impossible by any means or efforts whatsoever to add any thing to the encrease that would otherwise have been given to the stock of wealth in a community, without making an addition to the quantity of capital employed in it: and all measures taken by

---

*In law, *trader* does this, *tradesman* includes manufacturers without including merchants.

government or individuals in any such view must necessarily be unavailing.

The advantageousness of the direction given to a quantity of capital in any instance depends upon two things: 1. the choice of the trade itself: 2. the choice of the mode of carrying it on.

In both cases the chance which there is of the best choice relative to both points will be [1.] in proportion to the degree of interest which he, by whom the choice is made, has in making the best possible: 2. in proportion to the chance he has of possessing the faculties of knowledge and judgment in relation to the business in the highest degree possible.

The chance there is of a man's possessing in this superior degree the faculties of knowledge and judgment depends itself in great measure on the degree of interest he has in the concern: since the degree in which those faculties are possessed depends, as far as temperament and opportunity are given, in great measure upon the measure of attention bestowed on the business, which [in its turn] depends on the degree of interest he takes, and is likely to take in it.

The interest which a man takes in the affairs of another, a member of the sovereignty for example in those of a subject, is not likely to be so great as the interest which either of them takes in his own: still less where that other is a perfect stranger to him.

Judgment depends partly upon *natural faculties,* partly upon *acquired faculties,* partly upon *acquired knowledge*: knowledge depends partly upon *opportunity,* partly upon measure of *attention*: measure of attention depends partly upon *intensity* of attention, partly upon the quantity of *time* bestowed in it. Opportunity depends partly upon causes *within the power* of the man in question, partly upon causes *out of his power.*

In not one of these particulars is the statesman likely to be more than upon a par with the individual whose choice relative to the subjects in question he is so ready to controul: in almost all of them he is constantly and necessarily inferior beyond all measure.

A first Lord of the Treasury for instance, or other Member of Parliament, or a first Lord of Trade, is not likely to have had so many opportunities of acquiring knowledge relative to farming as a farmer, relative to distilling as a distiller, relative to manufacturing of stuffs as a manufacturer of stuffs, relative to the selling of the produce of any of those trades at home or abroad as one who has made the selling of them the business of his life.

A first Lord [of the Treasury, or other Member of Parliament, or a first Lord of Trade] is not likely to have bestowed attention for so great a length of time on the business of farming as a farmer, on that of distilling as a distiller, on that of manufacturing stuffs in all its branches as a manufacturer of stuffs.

A first Lord of the Treasury, or of Trade, or any other Member of the Legislature, is not likely, during the time he is bestowing attention, to bestow it with equal energy on the business of farming as a farmer, on that of distilling as a distiller [and so on].

A first Lord of the Treasury, or of Trade, or any other Member of the Legislature, is therefore not likely to possess either so much knowledge or so much judgment relative to the business of farming as a farmer [or relative to the business of distilling as a distiller, and so on].

A first Lord of the Treasury therefore, or of Trade, or any other Member of the Legislature, is not likely in the instance of any one of the many thousand trades that exist in the world, to form relative to the best mode of carrying on that trade a choice so good as that which would be formed by a person embarked, or intending to be embarked, on the trade in question : still less in the instance of every one of those trades.

But the choice of the most advantageous among a number of trades depends among other things on the knowledge of the most advantageous mode in which each of those trades respectively can be carried on : it is only by knowing the utmost degree of advantage that can be reaped from each, each being carried on in the most advantageous mode, that it can be known which of them, and in what degree, is more advantageous than another.

A first Lord of the Treasury therefore, or of Trade, or any other Member of the Legislature is still less likely to make a better choice in regard to the option to be made of one out of the many thousand trades existing or capable of existence, and in that sense in regard to the most advantageous direction to be given to capital, than in regard to the mode of carrying on any one in particular of those trades, and in that other sense in regard to the advantageousness of the direction to be given to capital.

Though a first Lord of the Treasury or of Trade or any other Member of Parliament happened by any accident or industry to be apprised of a circumstance demonstrating that this or that particular sort of trade, or this or that mode of carrying on a particular sort of trade, would be particularly advantageous, and though it were sure that in that particular, and by that accident, the statesman were better acquainted with the interest of the trader than the trader himself, yet even this would not afford them any sufficient warrant for endeavouring to employ the power of government in inducing any individual or individuals to embark in such branch of trade, unless the statesman had also a stronger regard for the interest of the trader than the trader himself, in other words, loved every man better than any man loves himself: for in that case simple information would be sufficient to produce the effect without any exercise of power: and so sure it is[1] that the information is true, so sure is it that the exercise of power would be unnecessary, and to no use.

The quantity of capital existing in the world at the end of a certain period, depends not upon the quantity of wealth produced down to that period, but upon the difference between the whole quantity that has been produced, and that part which has been consumed.

The quantity of capital in the world can therefore receive an encrease by the care of man in one way only which is by *frugality*.

The quantity of capital in any particular community may receive encrease in either of two ways: 1. by frugality: or 2. by importation from some other community.

Capital imported into a community may be imported either with the proprietors, or without the proprietors: if without the proprietors, either with or without an equivalent: if without an equivalent, either with or without consent: if with consent, that consent may have been forced or free: if with an equivalent, with an equivalent preceeding, or one to come: that is, either in the way of plunder, tribute, gift, payment, or loan.

3. *Modes of operating in the power of government in the pursuit of the ends of political economy*

In the track of political economy as in any other, whatever is done towards the attainment of the object, must be by creating inclination or by bestowing power:

Inclination can only be operated upon by inducements—as

1. by applications of a coercive or obligatory nature: which are either injunctions or prohibition[s]: or
2. by applications of an invitative nature or encouragements [2]which again are either direct or indirect.[3]

---

[1][The MS reads "is it".]
[2] [3][Put into brackets at a later date.]

Power may to this purpose be distinguished into 1. legal: 2. physical: 3. intellectual, or knowledge.

[1.] Legal power may be conferred *1.* by forbearing to impose on the party proposed to be assisted, coercion of any kind: 2. by coercing others in such manner as to prevent them from obstructing his making use of the power of the preceding kind: 3. by compelling them to afford him assistance. In the two first of these cases, *power* is no more than *liberty*.

2. Physical power is conferred by giving him the physical instruments requisite to the attainment of the end proposed: viz. money or something that is to be had for money. This can only be done by legal power of one or other of the three kinds above-mentioned.

3. Intellectual power is either *1.* active power, or 2. knowledge. If active power be given by law, it can only be in some indirect way. through physical, and thence through legal power.

Knowledge is either 1. of the modes of operating towards the end proposed, viz. which are good, which bad: which worst, which best: or 2. of matter of fact: which may be conducive to this end either *1.* by pointing out *inducement.* 2. by pointing out legal power. *3.* by conducing to physical power: or by conducing to intellectual power, either as leading to knowledge of the modes of operating, or to other matters of fact more immediately leading to such knowledge.

Encouragements may be distinguished into 1. direct, and 2. indirect. Direct consist of rewards commonly called in this instance *bounties,* given to him who shall exercise his industry in such or such a way. Indirect consist in discouragements opposed in the way of others, in the view of restraining them from exercising their industry in such or such a way, i.e. in such a way as shall prevent his exercising his [industry] in the way desired. If discouragements thrown in the way of A answer the purpose of encouragement to B. it is because A's acting in the track he is thus discouraged from, would have tended to discourage B from acting in the track he is meant to be encouraged to act in, by diminishing the reward, natural or factitious, he would have got in some way or other by acting in it.

To the head of encouragements may also be added operations, the tendency of which is to confer power, and in particular physical power: such as the giving or lending money or money's worth to be employed in the shape of capital towards the carrying on a branch of industry meant to be encouraged.

In whichever of the above ways aid is applied, it must be either 1.

with a view of encreasing the quantity of industry in general: or 2. with a view of encreasing the relative quantity of a particular branch of industry.

[4. *Of the limit set to the operation of government by the dependence of trade on capital*]

[1]In a state of civilized society, no branch of industry can be carried on at all, much less in an augmented degree, without a certain quantity of capital. The quantity of wealth has [therefore] for its necessary limit the quantity of capital.[2]

The course taken with relation to this maxim by the two most celebrated of our writers on this branch of science (Dr. Smith, and L[ord] Sheffield) is curious enough.

The former, without ever saying a syllable about it, conforms to it in every recommendation he gives [and] writes almost throughout as if it were constantly uppermost in his thoughts: the other, after expressly bringing it into view, and recognizing its supremacy, scarce recommends a measure that does not fly in the face of it;[3] [the one] without taking any notice of it [as][4] a principle, conforms to it in practice: the other, after ushering it in, and paying homage to it, tramples upon [it] in practice [and] rebels against it on every page.[5]

What a difference between apprehending a truth, and embracing it with all its consequences! How easy may a truth be embraced, without embracing a consequence which, when once recognized to be its genuine offspring, is seen to be an immediate one!

One circumstance there is, which affords a plain proof of men's insensibility to this seemingly obvious truth. When they recommend the encouraging this and that and t'other branch of trade, it is not because they are so much as pretended to bring more profit than other branches of trade, but because they are so many branches of trade. In short, trade in general is mentioned as [a thing][6] that ought to be, and requires to be, encouraged, as if all trade would [?] not bring with [it] its own encouragement: as if an unprofitable trade could be worth encouragement, or a profitable one stand in need of it.

Eating is as indubitably beneficial as trade, and more immediately

---

[1] [2][Crossed out in the MS.]
[3][Semi-colon interpolated.]
[4][MS reads "in".]
[5][On Lord Sheffield, cf. above, p. 213.]
[6][The word of the MS looks like "think".]

so: it is a wonder that no politician in his wisdom ever thought of giving bounties [?] upon eating.

The only reason given, the only reason thought necessary to be given, for the encouragement of such or such a branch of trade is that it may be carried on with advantage, i.e. that it may be made to yield some profit; without thinking of enquiring whether it will yield more profit than any other.

[Yet] before you give any encouragement to any particular branch of industry in the view to opulence, one point is indispensably incumbent on you to ascertain: that is, that of all other known and possible branches of industry there is no other as yet unencouraged, which is not less advantageous than that you are going to encourage: in a word, you ought to have a list of all the branches of industry, actual and possible, ranged in the order of their advantageousness, and to have ascertained by calculation and proof that this promises to be in the foremost rank of them. But this list is what no one ever thought of making. Why? because it has never occurred to him, that whatever is given to any one branch, is so much taken from the rest. The industry [and] wealth they had only brought to view, they supposed they had brought into existence: what they had transferred, they thought they had created.

To justify the vulgar and hitherto almost universal practice, one or other of two positions must be assumed: that the agent of the public is more likely to understand and do what is most for the interest of the individual than the individual himself is, and that, the quantity of capital in every nation being infinite, or new branches of industry requiring no capital, no new capital, capital not being necessary to trade, whatever wealth is produced by a new or newly favoured trade is so much clear over and above that which, had it not been for such new or newly favoured trade, would have been brought into existence.

Both of these positions being contrary to truth, vulgar practice and vulgar opinion is consequently erroneous. It is wrong because those positions are, both of them, contrary to truth: but if either of them were [true],[1] the practice might not be erroneous. If the statesman were more likely to pursue in this particular the true interest of the individual than the individual himself is, the necessary limitation of the quantity of capital in the nation would afford no sufficient argument against his interference: more capital than there is he could not

---

[1] [For no apparent reason crossed out in the MS.]

make, but to the capital there was he could give a direction more advantageous than it would have taken otherwise. If a new or newly favoured trade could be carried on without new capital, or if the legislator, like God Almighty, could create out of nothing the capital he bestowed upon that trade, his not being likely to make so much of that capital as the individual would have done, had he the same capital with the liberty of choice as to the sort of trade and the mode of carrying it on, would neither in this case afford a sufficient argument against his interference: the profit made, though not so great as it might have been, had these particulars been left to individuals, would however be a perfectly real profit: in short, whatever it was, it would be just so much more than would have been made, had he left them to themselves.

This truth, it may be said, is too obvious to be disputed. Be it so: but is the other less so? The fact is, that if there be any truth too plain to have been disputed, and I must confess I know of none, there are at least none so plain as never [?] to have been overlooked.

What is certain, is that either one, or other, or both, have been either disputed or overlooked: and that this, in short, is hitherto very generally, if not universally, the case. Of one of them at least it is true, that when standing by itself without the other, so far from its not being capable of being overlooked, it has a thousand and a thousand times, even when produced in form, been produced without effect, at least without any other effect than that which is the ordinary one that adverse and consequently [?] unwelcome [?] truths produce upon minds closed by prejudice, that is upon the bulk of minds, that of a warning [to] turn the deaf ear [and] look another way.

If I have a capital (ready money and credit together) to the amount of a thousand pound and no more, with which capital I mean to embark in trade, and two trades are proposed to me, each of which may be carried on with a profit to the amount of twenty per Cent with a thousand pound, and neither with any thing less, it is plain that one of those trades it is in my power to carry on with that profit, so long as I confine myself to that one: and that carrying on that one, it is not in my power to carry on the other with a profit to the same amount, if to any amount.

Were I to take part of my capital from one of these trades and bestow it upon the other, what could I gain more than my 20 per Cent?—By the supposition nothing: how much less, there is no saying: it will be according to acci[?]dent and the nature of the trade: perhaps 15 per Cent, perhaps 10 per Cent, perhaps nothing: perhaps loss instead of gain.

Had I a thousand such trades all of a sudden laid open to me, what should I be the better?—nothing. Were all the thousand all of a sudden forbidden me, what should I be the worse?—as little. The tyranny of the [one] measure might draw shame on its author, but me it would do no harm [because it would] leave [me] where it found me. The generosity of the [other] measure might throw lustre on the character of its author: but I should be but where I was.

Nature gives a premium for the application of industry to the most advantageous branch, a premium which is sure to be disposed of to the best advantage: if the artificial premium takes the same course with the natural one, it is needless: if a different one, it is misapplied.*

[5. Of the] regard due to subsisting interests, or dangers to be guarded against in a change

[1]The quantity of wealth [then] produced in a given society within a given time, will depend [upon its capital:] partly upon the value of the capital employed, partly upon the more or less advantageous direction given to that capital.

---

*Truths seemingly mysterious accounted for by the principle of the dependence of trade on capital.

1. Trade greatest where labour is dearest.

Solution: Abundance of capital in proportion to general wealth makes abundance of employment, which, requiring abundance of hands, makes labour dearer by the competition.

In the cheap-labour country, there are the hands, but there is not the capital to set them to work. It is owing to the want of capitals coming into competition with each other for the purchase of it, that the price of labour, the pay given to labouring hands, is so low. The dearness of labour is certainly not a cause of the magnitude of the trade, viz. of the production: it is, as far as it goes, an obstacle: but it is a *co-effect* of the cause to which the magnitude of the trade is owing, viz. the abundance of that capital without which no trade can exist, and in proportion to which is the magnitude of trade in every instance.

2. Innocence of bad laws for the regulation of trade.

Solution: By checking this and that and t'other branch of trade, they do not necessarily diminish the sum of trade, since what is lost by one branch of trade, is got by others. They do not, in general, destroy the product of labour to any very considerable amount: they only transfer labour from trade to trade.

All the mischief they can do is reducible to two heads: 1. to traders, [loss by the] difference in point of profit between the most profitable trade that could have been chosen, where that happens to be the trade against which the discouragement is levelled, and the next most profitable: 2. to consumers, loss by the difference in price, where a cheaper article is prohibited in favour of a dearer one.

[1][See footnote on page 237.]

Unless in an indirect way, by furnishing information, government can do nothing in the way of improving the direction.

Towards encreasing the quantity, there is but one sort of operation [by][3] which government can do any thing considerable, and that is an oppressive one, inconsistent with what is, or at least ought to be, the end of civil society, viz. the forcing accumulation by imposing taxes, and adding the produce to the capital employed in industry.[2]

[4]Much however has been done by government with both these views: the whole of it always perfectly useless, and always more or less pernicious. Conceit or inadvertence, or both, have been the causes of these errors: the conceit of understanding each man's interest better than he does himself: inadvertence in not considering that, while nothing is added to the quantity of capital, whatever labour and consequently capital is given to any one branch of industry is so much taken from all the rest.[5]

With respect to any one of these measures, incompetent as it may be with regard to the end here in question, we are not to conclude immediately for its correction;[6] especially for its immediate correction, two cautions are necessary: 1. not to pass a conclusive sentence of condemnation on it till we have seen whether it be not conducive in some shape or other to some other of the four ends of political economy: 2. not to pronounce for the abolition of it till we have attended to the effects of the correction.

Ill-judged and pernicious as these measures were, all of them, more or less, at the time of their first institution, there are few instances in which their abolition, if instantaneous and unconditional, would not be attended with temporary ill effects which, for the time they lasted, would more than outweigh the benefits of the abolition, or in other words the inconveniences of the measure thus abolished. Hence [arises] a topic of enquiry with respect to every one of these measures, viz. the regard due to the subsisting interests of the individuals concerned, [that is to say] affected by reform.

---

[1] [2][Crossed out in the MS.—See page 236.]
[3][MS reads "in".]
[4] [5][A question mark is written over this passage.]
[6][This semi-colon is interpolated.]

[PART TWO: OPERATIONS OF GOVERNMENT WITH A VIEW TO
POLITICAL ECONOMY]

[I (a) IMPROPER MEASURES: DIRECT ENCOURAGEMENTS]

[6.] *Loans of capital*

Of all measures capable of being taken on the part of the sovereign with a view to encrease the mass of wealth in the nation by giving direction in particular instances to the current of industry, that of issuing money or money's worth in the way of loan to individuals on condition of its being employed in the shape of capital towards the carrying on a particular branch of industry stands the clearest from objection.

This mode of encouragement is defensible or indefensible according to the relation which is supposed to subsist between the sovereign and the people which he governs. Consider them as his property, nothing can be wiser or more unexceptionable: consider him as their trustee, it is a breach of trust, make the best of it, which can not be vindicated from the imputation of injustice.

All money thus employed by the sovereign is the produce of taxation*: whatever therefore is lent in this way to B must first have been taken from A, and that by force: for whatever is yielded in payment of a tax, is taken by force: and it is that which distinguishes a tax from a free-gift.

In a mass [of] money thus raised and applied, two portions may in idea always be distinguished: one part is taken from expenditure: the other part from capital: one part, if not thus taken, would have been spent: the other part would have been laid up in store. The first part is so much taken from the present enjoyments of the contributor: the other part from his means of bettering his condition in future. It is the first part only that by being thus applied, goes, or at least is designed to go, in addition to the general mass of capital in the nation: the other part is only so much shifted from hand to hand. The first part, it must be owned, will always be the most considerable: in the most frugal nation, what is hoarded in any given year, will always bear but a small proportion to what is spent.

---

*This at least will hold good untill an instance can be shewn in which the revenue of the sovereign is derived from no other source than the rent of land, or the interest of a capital saved out of a fund of that nature. Even the curious instance of the Commonwealth of Bern will not come up to this mark: for succeeding to the antient patrimony of the Church, tithes form part of its demesne, and tithes are taxes.

Were the money thus levied and issued, faithfully repaid in every instance and that for ever, the hardship and injustice attendant on such policy would be confined to the period at which the capital thus made use of was collected. Call it a hundred thousand pound, and suppose it levied, the whole of it, in a particular year: in that year the injustice will have begun and ended.

But money thus destined and disposed of has a natural tendency to be misapplied and purloined or dissipated: this we shall see more particularly farther on.

Money thus disposed of may be applied either to the encouragement of some old established trade, or to the establishment of a new one. The last mode of application is that which is most natural: in this case the most natural object is the giving to industry a direction supposed to be peculiarly advantageous. Where it turns out to be so, there results a proportionable advantage to [be] set against the bad effects inseparable from, or incident to, this policy.

But here again it is evident that the sovereign and his agents are full as much exposed to be deceived in regard to the productiveness of the trade, as in regard to the trustworthiness of the person.

In which soever of the two ways the money is disposed of, this sort of forced frugality is attended with one bad effect which is inseparable from it, viz. the accelerating in this forced and artificial way the reduction of the market rate of interest: which is a tax upon those whose fortune consists in money, a tax of which the whole produce, instead of being gathered in for the use of the state, is granted away to those who have occasion to borrow money. Sum for sum, and man for man, the suffering of him who incurrs a loss is always greater than the enjoyment of him who makes a gain: and the difference between this suffering and this enjoyment gives in this point of view the mischief of the measure. According to common estimation the gain, instead of being regarded as inferior to the loss, has hitherto been regarded as if it were clear: because in political arithmetic, blinded by passions or prejudices, men count but on one side. Reckoning the man whose fortune lies in the air or in some thing else besides money as every body, and his feelings as the only feelings worth attending to, and him whose fortune consists in ready money as nobody or as [a being] without feeling, or as one whose feelings are not worth regarding, what is gained by the one is carried to the side of national profit, while what is lost to the other is sunk in the account of national loss: and it is thus that bills given on to the nation by ministers for pretended services done to the nation are made out.

This gradual diminution of the incomes of moneyed men, or to avoid the notion of opulence attached to the appellation, of men whose million or whose mite happens to have taken the shape of ready money, is an evil as it must be confessed to be, an evil to a certain degree unavoidable, and the inseparable attendant on an effect which is good, though not a greater good. This consideration, whatever reason it affords for submitting to the evil with patience when it does happen, affords none to the legislator for going out of his way to accelerate and encrease it. Losses which grow out of the known and ordinary course of nature are not only born[e] with patience when they occur, but by being expected and provided for before hand are prevented from being felt. Losses which have the caprices and ignorances of man for their cause, confound by their suddenness, while they provoke by their injustice.

Upon the whole, the following then appear to be the inconveniences attached to this least exceptionable of all modes of applying public encouragement with a view to the encrease of opulence:

1. the hardship and injustice attendant on the tax necessary to provide the capital in question;
2. the danger of the necessity of fresh taxes for the same purpose in consequence of the probability of embezzlement or dissipation;
3. the danger of the misapplication of the money to the promotion of a branch of industry not so productive as those to which it would have found its way of its own accord;
4. the tendency which a forced accumulation thus effected of the quantity of capital has to accelerate the deperition in value of a particular species of property, viz. that which consists in ready money.

We have now seen the instance in which the mischief of the interference of government in this view appears in its slightest and most questionable shape. [1]Happy the nations if it had never been felt in any other![2] Accordingly it is that in which it has shewn itself the most seldom. In Great Britain, scarce in any instance: in Ireland it is not without example in particular instances. In the Prussian Monarchy it has been much more frequent. In the Belgic provinces we shall find it grown up into an establishment.

Should the money by chance take the most advantageous direction

---

[1] [2][Put into brackets, apparently at a later date.]

possible, the measure has no title to the merit of the advantage. In order to give his capital in every instance this most advantageous of all directions, a man needs only to know what that is: information, not money, is the thing wanted. If the government can not tell what that direction is, it can not give its money that direction: if it can tell, telling is all it need do. If the government money had not taken that direction, private money would, if the government would have given it leave: the addition made by government to the stock of wealth ought never therefore to be reckoned as any more than would have been made, had the trade thus encouraged been of the number of the most ordinary, and least productive, trades.

[7. *Gifts of money and in kind: gratuitous loans*]

Gifts of money to be employed in the shape of capital is the next mode of encouragement that presents itself to our consideration. The impropriety is in this case the same *in specie* as in the former one: it differs only in magnitude. There the mischief confined itself to the period of levying the money which, on that supposition, was to be lent. Indeed, without the view of getting it back again, principal and interest, it never ought to be given: for a trade which does not in the event of its success afford a reasonable expectation of reimbursing, not only the interest, but, within a moderate time, the principal, never can be worth attempting to set on foot. When repayment took place, if ever it did take place, the same sum might do the same office a second time. Here the money being thrown away in the first instance, as often as the same sort of encouragement comes to be given to the same amount, the same process of unjust taxation comes to be repeated, and as often as it is repeated, so often may the produce of it be said to be thrown away, with reference to the use that might have been made of it in alleviation of the public burthens.

Sometimes capital has been lent in this view without interest: sometimes at an under interest. In the first case, if repayment is honestly made, it is not the capital that is thrown away, but only the interest: in the second case, not the whole interest, but only the difference between this inferior rate of interest, and the ordinary one. It is in all these cases the same false policy in kind, differing only in magnitude.

Grants of capital have sometimes been made not in money but in kind: by giving or advancing, to a manufacturer for instance, such or such articles in the list of the implements of the manufacture. This

Q

does something towards ensuring the application of the value in question to the purposes to which it is destined: though it can seldom be applied with so much advantage as it might be if the man had money to equal value in his pocket, with free liberty to go to market in his own way. As it is not the best course to take with the most trust-worthy, so neither is it with the least trust-worthy: since these, when they have got the articles, may convert them at any loss to money and dissipate it or run away with it. This danger, it is true, may be obviated by taking security, in cases which admitt of it. Much will depend upon particular circumstances: in some instances the one course may be the least ineligible, in others another: but as the whole measure is radically bad under any mode, it would be lost labour to engage in discussions relative to the mode.

[8.] *Of bounties on production*

At this next step we make a great stride in the career of absurdity. In the former cases it was an expence [or] a risk for the sake of an object which, if sure to be attained, would not warrant it, and without any sufficient grounds for depending on the attainment of that object. Here it is an expence incurred under the certainty of the non-attainment of the object, and for the very reason that the object is unattainable.

In the case of grants or loans of capital, there is thus much to be said for the measure, that its natural tendency is to give encrease or perhaps existence to a branch of industry which might not have received such encrease or existence otherwise: whatever become of the question whether the gain to that particular branch of national wealth would be a gain to the whole mass.

In the case of a bounty on produce, not only the end is a wrong one, but the means employed are such of which the distinctive property is to contribute nothing to the end.*

---

*The most signal instance known of this species of profusion was that exhibited by the government of the late King of Prussia [Frederick II]. Great elogiums have been bestowed on him on this account.

He who robbs and restores is certainly better than he who takes without restoring. But a better than either of them is he who abstains from robbery, and leaves every man his own.

A great part, however, of what that monarch gave was given in the way of indemnification for losses sustained by war or natural calamity. This was strictly just and unexceptionable. The principle of insurance is founded on utility, and cannot be extended too far so [long] as the danger of abuse does not exceed the benefit.

It is because the trade is a disadvantageous trade, and for that reason only, that money is to be given to support it: for if it were an advantageous trade, it would support itself. It is because what the tradesman can get for the commodity by one who wants it, does not amount to ordinary profit, that he is to have money given to him by government in order to make up the difference.

Be the trade good or bad, the money thus given under the notion of encouragement does nothing towards putting it in the *power* of the trader to carry it on: the power he must have derived already from some other source. When the thing is made, then, and not before, he gets the price [and] the reward for making it: but how is he to contrive to make it? It is evident, it must be from some other resources than any which this encouragement can give him. The faculty it acts upon is his inclination, and his inclination only: his power, his ability, it leaves where it was.

Bounties have been given to a trade because it is an old and because it is a young one: because it is flourishing and because it is weak: because it is a gainful and because it is a losing one: because there are hopes of its being better and because there is danger of its being worse: and as for all these opposite reasons bounties and other encouragements have been applied for and given, and still continue to be given, there is no trade under the sun which has not upon the ground of some part of this reasoning a claim to a bounty, and that at every period, actual and possible, of its existence.

It is in the case of the old established trade that the mischief of the measure is most weighty: [1]it is in the case of the new trade that its inefficacy is most glaring.[2] Such old trade is generally very extensive: and it is the great extent of it that affords the great plea for its support. Its actual extent, whatever that be, is to be kept up at any price. The trade must in this case for the purpose of the argument be deemed at once a profitable and a losing one: a profitable one, to dispose the public to set a value on it, [that is to say] to fear to lose it, and a losing one, to dispose them to take the requisite measures for preserving it.*

---

[1] [2][Put into brackets, apparently at a later date.]

*True it is that though it may not be worth while for a nation to give artificial support to a trade with a view to wealth, it does not follow but that it may nevertheless [be advisable to grant such support] with a view to subsistence and defence. True it also is, that though it may not be worth while to support a trade for the sake of the established utility of the trade in any of those points of view, it may nevertheless for the sake of preventing the mischief that might ensue by the distress

In the instance of the new trade, the futility of the measure is its ruling feature. No plea here with the mask of necessity on its face: no pompous elogiums on the vast extent and magnitude of the trade. The plea here is that, were it but established, it would be lucrative and extensive: but what it wants is to be established. To establish it then, what is it men do?—they take measures which, ere they can operate, require it to have been established. Could the thing be but once made, it would sell so well that 50 per Cent. might be got by selling it: but to make it requires a good deal of money: so much money that there is a doubt whether people will be found to advance it under the risk which is looked upon as attending a new trade. What is to be done—Give the capital?—no: that would be extravagance. Lend it?—no: that would be hazardous. We will give a bounty upon the thing when it is once made: and then, unless our object is gained, and untill it is gained, we do not part with our money: therefore in addition to the 50 per Cent. which we think a man may make by it in the way of sale, we will give 10 per Cent. more. Very well: and with the help of this reasoning, when is it that the encouragement is not given?—so long as there is occasion for it. When is it that it is given?—as soon as the event has proved that there was no occasion for it. It is given for the purpose of causing a thing to be done: and it never can be given but in the event of the things being done already: done without it, and by other means.

Jealousy and short-sightedness, a suspicious temper and a confused head, are not uncommonly allied. The great cause of the preference given in some countries to bounties over grants or loans of capital is the apprehension of being cheated in the latter case. If we give £10,000 at once, before the thing is made, we may never get it back again: for fear of this they give, after the thing is made, £10,000 a year, no part of which ever can come, or is so much as expected to come, back again.

Instead of being a benefit, the burthen grows with the growth of the trade: the encouragement, after having been instituted for one

of the persons, masters or workmen, actually embarked in that trade: but these are separate matters.

[In any case, however] measures of relief taken for the support of branches of industry labouring under distress, ¹whether the cause be of a temporary or of a permanent kind, ought never to be any other than temporary.

The period at which the support in question shall cease [or rather] be withdrawn, ought to be precisely fixed, fully notified, and inflexibly adhered to.

¹[Two words illegible.]

reason, must be continued for the opposite one. At first, in order to gain it: now, for fear of losing it. What was requisite for gaining it, if it was to be so gained, was a small matter: but to what must be paid for keeping it, there is no end.

What is advanced in the way of capital used for the encouragement of a new trade is done in the way of experiment, and need never be given but on a comparatively small scale: and this little may be got back again. What is given in the shape [of a bounty] is always given, at least is always meant and hoped to be given, upon the largest scale: for unless a great deal of the commodity is made and sold, and consequently a great deal paid for making and selling it, the project is not looked upon as having succeeded, the object is not looked upon as being gained.

Where the article on which the bounty is given is one which, without the bounty, it would not have been worth men's while to produce, the amount of the bounty is so much thrown away. Where the article would have been produced, though the bounty had not been given, a part only of that amount is thrown away. Making an addition, and that a very conspicuous, to the ordinary rate of mercantile [?] profit, it attracts adventure[r]s, and by their competition proportionably hales [?] down the price: it makes the article come cheaper to market and, in the long run, cheaper to the exact amount of the bounty.* In this state of things it may appear that it will do neither good nor harm: the subject saving as much by the reduction of the price, as he loses by the tax, by the produce of which the reduction is effected.

This would accordingly be the case, were the persons who contribute in the one case the same persons precisely as those who get the relief in the other, were the amount of each man's contribution exactly the same as that of his relief, were the relief received as soon as the contribution were paid, and were all the lost labour necessary to the management of all this to be had for nothing. But the reverse of all this is unfortunately the case. There are scarce any two taxes that bear, each of them, upon [all] the citizens of a state: there are none that bear equally, one neither more nor less than the other, upon those on whom they respectively bear: a tax must always be paid a considerable time before the produce of it is given back in the

*That is to the clear value of it deducting the expences of claiming and receiving it, which always eat up a part, and may sometimes eat up even the whole, of it.

shape of a bounty: and the expence of all this useless circulation is always very great.

From what has been said it is evident that a bounty on production can never in the long run encrease in the smallest degree the plenty of the article, whatever diminution it may produce in the price of it. The reward which the producer gets for producing it is no greater than before: it only comes from different hands. Without the bounty those only pay the price for the article who enjoy the benefit: with the bounty they pay a part only in a direct way, the remainder being paid by the public in general of which they form a part, that is [1]in a greater or less degree[2] by a great many who have no benefit from it.[*]

But though a bounty on production adds nothing to the merchant's profit upon an article of universal consumption [or] to the plenty of the article in proportion to the demand, it takes from the price which he who makes use of it, has to pay for it. Suppose a bounty in Scotland upon the production of oats: and the bounty paid by a tax upon liquors brewed from oats. Oats will not [be produced in] more plenty than before: but oats, and whatever is made from oats, without brewing, will come cheaper to market, [1]the merchant making the same profit all the while,[2] while whatever is brewed from oats will come proportionably dearer. The wages of the consumer of oats will not go farther upon the whole than they did before: but he will find more oats to be had for his money or for his labour in the shape in which they are fit to be eaten, and fewer in the shape in which they are fit to drink and to get drunk with.

I speak of the relative plenty in proportion to the ordinary consumption and thence to the ordinary demand: in short, superfluity in comparison of the ordinary demand. The cheaper it is made in comparison of other things, the more of it may be in demand among those who have it in their choice to buy that or other things. More of it may on that account be made: but as it is the demand that preceded it, more will not be made over and above the quantity demanded than before. If superfluity be wanted, as for certain purposes—superfluity, i.e. a quantity always at command over and above the usual quantity produced—other measures must be taken for that purpose.

If a bounty on production were to be justified in any shape, it

---

[1] [2][Put into brackets, apparently at a later date.]

[*]Hence [Adam] Smith has made a mistake, in putting [a] bounty on production as a means of [producing] plenty above [a] bounty on exportation. [cf. bk. IV., ch. V.]

would be in the instance where the article thus favoured were an article of the most universal consumption. Such is wheat for example in England: oatmeal in Scotland: potatoes in Ireland: rice in Hindostan. In what character? in the character of a measure of equalization: in that and in no other. It tends not, as we have seen, in the smallest degree to encrease the plenty of the article: what it does do is to take money out of the pockets of the richer classes* and put it into those of the poorer. The article of the most universal consumption in a country is always the most necessary of all necessaries. It is the article most in use among the poor. The richer a man is, the greater proportion his consumption of other articles, which are not articles of universal consumption, bears to his consumption of the article of the greatest consumption. Suppose a bounty upon the production of oats in Scotland. If nothing else but oats were produced in Scotland, or of those things which are produced in Scotland nothing were taxed but oats, the same persons, it is evident, who receive the relief would be the same persons who sustained the burthen, and that in the same proportion, and the expence of management would be the only result of the measure. But things of all sorts are consumed in Scotland: and things of a great many sorts are taxed there as elsewhere. Oats therefore, the article of most universal consumption, the article most in use among the poor, being the object not of a tax but of a bounty, and other articles of less general consumption, articles more in use among all other classes than among the poorest being the objects of the taxes out of which this bounty is collected, a bounty upon the production of oats would cause the poor to have the article most in use amongst them at a price really less than that at which they would have it otherwise.

Thus much is true. At the same time, would the condition of the poor be at all made the better by this favour? No such thing. Oats would be sold to the poor for less money to the amount of the bounty, but they would get less money to buy oats with. What the poorest class of the poor has to live upon, is the wages of labour: that is the quantity of *wealth* given them in exchange for their labour. But the rate of wages depends upon, and is necessarily governed solely and exclusively by, the degree of opulence in the country at the time: that is by the proportion of the quantity of wealth in readiness to be employed in the shape of capital in the

---

*This supposes a multitude of other taxes imposed upon luxuries or articles of less necessity than the one on which the bounty is given.

purchase of labour to the number of persons for whose labour there is a demand: and this degree of opulence is supposed in both instances to be the same. The cheapness thus effected by the bounty will therefore afford no relief to the class of persons in question: since the cheaper it is made to them, the measure of opulence of the country remaining the same, the less they will have to buy it with. Let the relative measure of wealth of the country encrease, their condition will be bettered proportionabl[y] although no reduction in the price of oats, real or nominal, be effected: let the degree of general opulence [remain][1] stationary all the time, their condition will not be bettered, whatever reduction in the price of oats be made: let the degree of general opulence diminish, their condition will be impaired though the reduction in the price of oats be ever so great, since the reduction in the price offered for their labour will go on at a still greater rate—since the lower the price of the oats is, the less will they be able to get by a given quantity [of] labour of that, whatever it be, with which oats are purchased: or what comes to the same thing, if it is for an allowance of oats they labour, the more of their labour will they be obliged to give for the same allowance of oats.

[9.] *Bounties on exportation*

In the case of bounties on exportation the absurdity is not quite so palpable as in that of bounties on production: but the mischief is still greater. In both cases the money is all of it thrown away: the difference lies in the hands into which it is given: in the first case it is given to our own people: in the other case it is given to foreigners*. It is a contrivance for getting foreigners slily to receive tribute of you without their knowing any thing of the matter: as the Irishman put off a light guinea by slipping it in between two half pence.

In the case of a bounty on production, though the bounty may serve to keep up a losing trade which could not be kept up without it, and constitute the whole of the gain that is made on that trade,

---

[1][The MS reads "may".]

*A bounty on production given on an article of which there is an export, is to the amount of what is exported, a bounty upon export: so far as this is the case, it is either money's worth totally sunk and flung away, or a present made to foreigners. So long as it does no more than just cover the expence of carriage, it is money thrown into the sea: what it does more than this, is money given to foreigners. Where the encouragement of the export trade is the final cause in view, [a] bounty on production, however, is not likely to be given: foreigners, and foreigners alone, being the persons for whom the douceur is intended, it would be so much thrown away were our own people to share in it.

it may, for a time at least, add to the gains of a trade which would have been gainful, and gainful enough, without it. In the first case, it is just so much money thrown away without making any more trade than there would have been without it: by annexing a merchantable profit to a trade which otherwise would not have been attended with such a profit, and which would therefore sooner or later have been abandoned for some better one, it deprives the community of so much as would have been obtained if the capital had been employed, as otherwise it could not have failed to have been employed, in some other trade that would have produced such a profit of itself. In the other case, it has ultimately the same sort of effect, and is likely to do more mischief since by the magnitude of the gain it is likely to draw more and more concurrents till their competition reduces the price in such a degree that the bounty, as far as it goes, constitutes the whole of the profit. But in the mean time, untill the extra rate of profit is reduced by the competition, it goes in the shape of gain into the pockets of the first adventurers. And those who consume it, being our own people, part of the waste becomes gain to them in proportion to the extra-cheapness.

In the instance of the bounty given on exportation, no advantage can be reaped by any body in the nation in any case: in any case, whatever is given is either so much sunk and wasted as if it had been thrown into the sea, or else given to foreigners.

Had [there]¹ been no such bounty, either the article would have been exported, or it would not: it would, if it could be produced at such an expence as, compared with the price that foreigners were willing to give for it, would yield an ordinary profit: it would not have been exported, if it could not have been manufactured for such a price. In the latter case, foreigners get the article which they would not otherwise have got for the money they give for it, and the amount of the bounty, as before, is so much sunk outright and lost to every body: in the other case, foreigners, after getting the article as before for their money, get paid for buying it: no more of the article is produced or exported than would have been produced without the bounty, and all the effect of the bounty is to get foreigners to accept of so much of our money. The more our government gives to him who exports the article, the less the foreigner to whom it is exported has need to give. He of course, as every man in his situation would do, gives no more than the least price which the exporter will

¹[The MS reads "their".]

accept of. He has no need to give more: since if one man would not supply it at that price, some other man always would, since, by the supposition, it would always be worth somebody's while: the reduction of price being effected by the encrease of competition, which would be the result of the extra profit. Here then at any rate our own nation sustains a certain loss to the amount of the bounty: which loss is either loss to the whole world, or gain to the foreign nation at the expence of our own, as it may happen—either lost to every body or picked up by some body, viz. the foreign nation, as it may happen.

If an article of our own manufacture is already bought by a foreign nation before any bounty on the export of it is given, what will be the effect of the giving such a bounty? Plainly the sinking of the price of it in that foreign nation. A bounty of 1d a lb is given for a thing that sold for 5d a lb: before, it was not worth the exporter's while to sell it for less than 5d: now it is: it is as much well worth his while to sell it for 4d as before it was to sell it for 5d: his own government making up to him the difference. He will therefore sell it for the 4d, knowing that if he did not, some body else would, in which case, instead of selling it for 5d, he would not be able perhaps to sell it at all. Just then what our government gives, just so much do the foreign importers save: the effect of the encouragement given is just nothing at all: what is exported with the bounty is neither more nor less than what would have been exported without it.

Though a bounty on export thus circumstanced should fail of making a branch of trade more flourishing than it would have been otherwise, it will at any rate not make it the less flourishing: but the more flourishing it is, the greater the loss which the nation sustains by it.

A great deal has been said about disadvantageous trades and great apprehensions shewn lest trade, if left to itself, should come under this predicament. Under this predicament it is impossible for any trade, when left to itself, to come: it requires contrivance on the part of government to bring about such an effect, and by this contrivance it has been brought about. To the individual trader as such, disadvantageous it certainly is not, nor for any continuance ever can be: for so sure as it were, so sure would he be to have nothing more to do with it: the disadvantage is to the public at large, to the public in its taxable capacity, and the bounty, which is the sole cause, is the exact measure of that disadvantage.

The Irishman who got rid of his light guinea in the manner above mentioned was very cunning, but there have been Frenchmen, not to mention Englishmen, who are still more cunning than he, too cunning to be taken in by him in that manner. Let a cunning man find out that you have a point to gain in your dealings with him, his wits set themselves to work mechanically to prevent you, without staying to enquire what harm it would be to him, if you had your way. From your appearing to look upon it as an advantage to you, he takes for granted that it must be a proportionable disadvantage to himself, and he finds it shorter and, as he thinks, safer to be guided by your opinion than his own. Aware of this disposition in mankind, a wag for a wager stood at one of the most public thoroughfares in Paris with a bag of the best crown pieces that were to be had, offering five of them for a louis which was worth but four, and in five hours he did not put off more than 5 louis worth.

When individuals at large have to such a degree been the dupes of suspicion, it would be strange indeed if governments, managing affairs which in general they understand as little about as they care, should escape the snare. One government out of its cunning has given a bounty upon its own export to force the vent of it in another nation. What has the other nation done in consequence? Alarmed at the danger, it has taken every measure that could be taken to repel it. Where it durst, it has prohibit[ed] the article, [1]and thrown the money into the kennel[2], where it durst not it has given a counterbounty on some article of its own [1]export or at least of its own produce[2]. Not daring to refuse accepting ten new crowns for two louis, it has slipt in a small diamond slily between the louis, and thus the biter has been bit.

Absurdity like this, when painted in its genuine colours and stripped of the veil which the magnitude of the object and the elevation of the agents throw upon it, appears too flagrant to be believed: it requires an example of the fact to prove the possibility.

[Yet examples of such mad policy abound on every side.] In the dealings as between nation and nation, men are content to make goods [1]though it be[2] at a loss, [1]so as they make them themselves,[2] in order to avoid rather than buy them cheaper of other men. Such folly is not seen in the dealings between individual and individual. Were we to see any individual merchant doing so, and doing so with

---

[1][2][Put into brackets, apparently at a later date.]

his eyes open as statesmen do, what should we say of him? we should pronounce him marching towards bankruptcy, if not to Bedlam. But we see no such merchant. Such blindness is not, such blindness never has been, the property of merchants. It is the property of country gentlemen and their blind guides. While acting for themselves, men are not affected with this blindness. It is only when [they are] acting for others [as statesmen are who regulate foreign trade].

The pitch of blindness and iniquity to which men are [on this occasion] capable of working themselves up by mutual encouragement, is without bounds. They may be as blind to their own interests as unfeeling with regard to the interests of other men.

A complaint with which every man has during his childhood been afflicted, more or less, is that of having, according to the nursery phrase, his eye bigger than his belly. This in the individual is [overcome][1] in a great degree, if not altogether cured, by experience. But in the political, in the national, man it has continued among the wisest and the gravest throughout life.*

A person I know remembers the time when, being an infant, and being pressed for a long time without effect to take some physic that was thought fit to be given him, he yielded at length from no other motive than to prevent its being given to the cow.

What is it that makes our grown children in politics swallow the pill of a losing trade? Only to save themselves the mortification of seeing it taken by the cow.

Every statesman who thinks by regulation to encrease the sum of trade, is the child whose eye is bigger than his belly.

Every statesman who struggles to fix on the hands of his country a losing trade, is the child who took the purging pill that it might not be given to the cow.

[10.] *Exemptions from taxes and other burthens on production*

An exemption from a tax on production, considered as capable of being imposed upon the commodity in the hands of the vender

---

[1][The word is illegible in the MS.]

*Causes of the propensity in statesmen to the meddling or mercantile system: 1. thinking more highly of the export trade than it deserved in comparison with others, from the nominal value of it being brought before their eyes by the tables; 2. self complacency in fancying what they saw to be their own work, the fruit of their own wisdom; 3. self-interest in creating dependents by the encouragements given.

or maker, is a particular modification of a bounty on production; it is a bounty on production granted under particular circumstances.

Correspondent to every sort of tax or other burthen capable of being imposed [1]on any commodity[2] is the negative sort of favour which consists in the not being subjected to it: so many modes of discouragement, so many of encouragement. If of two rival manufactures one has a tax laid on it, the other not: that which is not taxed is, with reference to the other, in the same situation as it would be in if, neither of them being burthened, it were made the object of a bounty.

But there is no sort of manufacture which has not its rivals: if not *special*, *general* at least: since, as every man's capacity of buying is limited by his money and his credit, whatever a man is enabled and induced to buy of one sort of thing, he is prevented from laying out in the purchase of any of the rest.

Considering the nature of this species of encouragement, it is evident that it is only in a relative point of view and not in an absolute one, that it can be an object of blame. The thing to be wished, were it possible, would be that no sort of thing should ever be taxed: that there should be no such thing as taxes. The supposition, and the only one, on which blame can attach on such a forbearance is where an article which, with a view to revenue, would have been subjected to taxation, is on the account in question, or on some other account which would not afford sufficient warrant for this or any other mode of particular encouragement, exempted from such burthen.

It is still so much money thrown away, though in another shape, in pursuit of an object in its own nature unattainable. It is the levying of so much money by the worst of all the modes of taxation in use, instead of doing it in a mode which, by the supposition, is an eligible one: for, since by the introduction of a new and good tax, another tax to the same amount, and therefore the worst of all the subsisting taxes, might be taken off, the difference in point of mischief between such [a] new and good tax, and the worst of all subsisting ones, is always the amount of the detriment sustained by the rejection of the new one. This is the true standard for judging of the mischief resulting from every instance where a tax peculiarly unexceptionable is rejected as well as from every instance where an unnecessary expenditure is incurred.

Whether the tax in question is one that would have been imposed

---

[1] [2][Put into brackets at a later date.]

upon the article itself thus meant to be encouraged, or one that would have been imposed upon some material or instrument necessary to the bringing it to that state, comes in this point of view, it is evident, to the same thing. The advantage ¹gained² is nothing: the detriment ¹sustained² is the difference between that of a tax more or less eligible and the worst existing.

[11.] *Drawbacks on exportation*

What is called giving a *drawback* on exportation, is the restitution of a tax already levied of something in the way of tax[ation]: a man is permitted to *draw back* so much of what he has disbursed.

What a bounty on export is to a bounty on production, a drawback is to a simple exemption from a tax levied on produce. In the first case of each pair, foreigners come in for their share of the boon indiscriminately with our own people: in the other case, they get the whole of it. In all cases, the expected advantage is equally imaginary.

In one point of view, however, the drawback is a more expensive way of throwing away money than the bounty. In the case of the drawback the money is received with one hand, in order to be given back again with the other: and each operation is attended with a separate expence. To this public expence is to be added the private expence which the individual must be at to pay the money and get it back again: an expence of which the trouble and loss of time which in the account of the financier goes for nothing, always forms a very considerable part, often the most considerable: so considerable indeed that instances are by no means wanting where the value of the supposed favour is reduced literally to nothing by the trouble of obtaining it.*

[12.] *Premiums for the immigration of foreign workmen [and for the] importation of foreign arts*

That there are cases in which it would be extremely well worth the while of individuals to pay extraordinary prices to get workmen from abroad, is not to be doubted. Meaning to employ my money to the best account in the way of trade or manufacture, and looking round as far as my reach of thought and faculties and opportunities will carry me, if I observe a branch of manufacture

---

¹ ²[Put into brackets at a later date.]

*Instances: Salt-duty—drawback for fisheries.

for instance, new as yet to this country, and which, if imported from some country abroad, would pay me for example 5 per Cent. interest for my capital more than any other branch I have been able to find, this 5 per Cent. is so much more gained to me and through me to the nation I belong to, than if I had embarked my capital in that one of the old established trades which, of all that have fallen within my cognizance, would be the most advantageous. Extra-expences there doubtless are, and difficulties incident to the task of getting workmen from a foreign country,* supposing even no laws of that country or of our own to add to the amount: but all difficulties and expences of this nature I suppose provided for and surmounted, as in many instances they actually have been provided for and surmounted.

Still then the same argument, and still with undiminished force: the more evidently advantageous for the individual to bestow his money in this way, the more evidently unnecessary for the government to expend that of the nation.

In the first case the burthen is born[e] by him who receives the benefit: in the other case by those who receive no part of it. In the first case, the security against unnecessary expence as well as the probability of success upon the whole, are at their highest pitch: in the other, at the lowest.

[I (b) IMPROPER MEASURES: INDIRECT ENCOURAGEMENTS]

[13.] *Prohibition of rival branches of industry, i.e. of the production of rival manufactures*

Of this species of supposed encouragement to trade thus much may be affirmed, that it can not possibly do good [and] be of service to trade upon the whole, and that it may do harm. Mischief or nothing: such is the alternative.

Unhappily the instances in which it is mischievous are those in which it is most likely to be recurred to: and the more mischievous, the more likely. The more prosperous a branch of trade is, the more likely it is to provoke the envy of its rivals.

All branches of industry, it has been observed, are in some measure rivals to one another: some more, others less perceptibly. It seldom happens that the rivality is comprehended in its whole extent: and

---

*On the part of government in general, the passion for getting arts and hands from abroad does not appear so conspicuous as the dread of losing one's own.

so it happens not unfrequently that of a discouragement which, for the sake of some branch of domestic industry, is thrown in the way of some other branch of domestic industry, some foreign branch shares considerably in the advantage.*

Among that great variety we have seen, or shall see, of measures contrived for the encrease of national wealth, this possesses a peculiar privilege, viz. that of being capable of being applied in some instances without doing any sort of harm. For though it is most likely to be poison, it is equally capable of being a chip in porridge. Such is the case where the branch of industry prohibited in any place is such as, in the nature of things, can not be exercised at all, or at least can not be exercised to any profit, in that place. It was made felony in the reign of Hen. 4 to import *pollards* or *crocards* (coins so called) into this Kingdom: the same prohibition subsists at this present day without any great practical inconvenience. If, under the notion of encouraging the breed of barn door fowls, or with any other such public spirited view, the breeding or importation of phoenixes were prohibited under the same penalty, though neither the farmer's nor the poulterer's trade would be any great gainers by the encouragement, yet neither would they, nor any other, be great losers. Among the trades which Great Britain was so anxious to prevent her colonies from engaging in might be found some perhaps which, in comparison with their proper business, agriculture, it would be as ill worth their while to attempt engaging in as in breeding phoenixes or raising pine apple in the common ground or making calemancos[1] out of cobwebs.

[14.] *Prohibition of rival imports*

In regard to the prohibition of rival imports, simply inefficacious or mischievous is still the alternative.

If the foreign article can not, when imported after payment of the expence of conveyance, be had as cheap [2]in comparison of its goodness[3] as the home article [2]meant to be favoured[3], no importation of it can take place: so long as that is the case, a prohibition is put upon it by nature.

---

*Instance: [The] French prohibition of a set of foreign productions (E. India) favours a set of more obnoxious foreign productions, viz. English.

[1][The MS reads "calemancos" rather than "calamancos" which is the usual spelling.]

[2] [3][Put into brackets at a later date.]

If, had it not been for the prohibition, it could have been sold here cheaper, the prohibition is, in point of burthen, a tax upon us to the amount of the difference in price. I say in point of burthen: for as to that benefit which it is the property of a real tax to produce, viz. a supply for expenditure, or a relief to an equal amount from the burthen of other taxes, it has no existence. It is upon the footing of a tax, the produce of which, as soon as collected, were thrown into the sea.

[15.] *Taxation of rival branches of home manufacture*

The natural and only original object of taxation is *revenue*: but considered merely in as far as it confines itself to that object, it does not belong to our present purpose. Measures, however, are to be considered with regard to their eventual effects of all kinds: such, if any, as were not designed not less, as if they were [*sic*].

A tax upon one of two trades considered as rivals can have no effect in favour of the other but in as far as it operates as a prohibition. If the same quantity of the commodity meant to be discouraged is sold notwithstanding the tax, as would have been sold without the tax, the advantage gained by the commodity meant to be favoured amounts to nothing.

So far as it [operates] as a prohibition, good, we have seen, it can do none: harm it may do, and is likely enough to do: though we have seen, it may also happen not to do any. As a tax it may do good or harm, according to its particular nature: good, if it stands instead of a worse; harm if it stands instead of one less burthensome. I mean always in virtue of its distinctive[1] properties: for in a general way, no law[s] except those by which other laws are repealed, can fail of doing harm, as being so much lumber by the load they add to the system.

[16.] *Taxation of rival imports*

Whether the article thus taxed in the view of favouring another be an article of home production or an article of import, makes in point of advantage no sort of difference. [2]It makes none (for the general reason all along given) with regard to the encrease of trade [or] wealth. The quantity of capital, the efficient cause of wealth,

---

[1][Bowring's text, *Works* III, 65, reads "destructive". A striking example of the superficiality with which he prepared his edition!]

[2][See footnote on page 258.]

R

remaining the same, whatever is added in consequence to the favoured trade, is so much taken from the rest. It makes none with regard to the burthen of taxation: it is the same people, it is our own people, that pay the tax.[3] As far as it prevents the import, it operates as a prohibition: in which capacity, we have seen that with regard to the general encrease of wealth it is of no use.

As far as it fails of preventing the import, it gives no encouragement to the particular trade in question, nor consequently to the particular portion of wealth employed in that trade. What it does is to levy money on the subject in quality of a tax: but the persons on whom the money is levied are our own people: as much as if it were among the articles produced at home. As such it may either be a good tax or a bad tax, as it may happen: though in regard to its temporary consequences, it can not be productive of all the mischief of which a tax on a home manufacture is capable of being productive.

[17.] *Non-importation agreements*

Non-importation agreements, as far as they extend, have the effect of prohibitions: happily they are not so extensive in their action, [so] frequent, so constant, so well executed.

Good they do none: happily wanting the force of prohibitory laws, the mischief they do is seldom so extensive.

[18.] *Treaties obtaining from a foreign nation encouragements in favour of our own exports to that nation*

From what has been said, it will be easy to infer what is to be done, and what is not to be done, by treaties with foreign nations for the benefit of trade.

No encouragements given by any foreign nation to our exports to that nation can contribute any thing to the augmentation of the sum total of our trade. No discouragements can take from it. No measures operating in restriction of the quantity of our exports to any foreign nation, except by their suddenness, in the same way that measures pursued by us in the view of encouraging any rival branch of our own trade, would in the way so often mentioned be productive of a similar effect.

It is only by applying what, in the common language, would be

---

[3] [Crossed out in the MS, whether by Bowring or by Bentham, it is impossible to tell.]

called a discouragement to its own trade, that a foreign nation can lay us under any permanent disadvantage, viz. by imposing a tax on some article of its own export, which we can not do without, and which, notwithstanding the tax, it is out of our power to get cheaper any where else. So circumstanced, a tax upon its own exports, is in effect a tax, not upon its own subjects, but upon us. A treaty prohibitive of such a tax is accordingly a treaty restraining the foreign nation in question from imposing a tax, viz. the particular sort of tax in question, upon us.

[An] example [is afforded by the export of] Russia[n] coarse linnens [to England].

Of certain coarse linnens of Russian manufacture there is, notwithstanding a very heavy duty, no inconsiderable consumption among us. It was in order to prevent that consumption from becoming, to the prejudice of our own manufacture, still more considerable, it was for this reason, I say, and not for the mere [desire] of gain, that this duty was imposed: at least it is for the former reason, and not for the latter that, had it depended upon him, L[or]d Sheffield would have imposed it. Thus far we have discouraged it, because beyond the present pitch we do not choose to see the consumption of it carried: farther we do not carry the discouragement, because to a greater degree we do not wish to see it restrained. We mean that Russia ducks for instance should not sell for less than —— a yard: but we are not desirous to see them sold to us for more. This being the case, what follows? That if the Russians had imposed upon this article of their own exports a duty to half the amount of ours, the duty we should have laid upon them would have been, not a duty equal to the present duty, but a duty equal to but half of it, and no more.

One of the happiest things that could happen to two nations would be to be thoroughly possessed by opposite principles on this head: the one heaping bounties upon bounties on its own exports, the other heaping taxes upon taxes on the same article. If we in England, for example, gave a bounty on the export of our corn to Holland, and the Dutch, when they had got it there, laid a tax upon it. As it happens, this is not a mere supposition: it is the simple fact: so compleatly and happily have we overreached ourselves in our dealings with that prudent people. We give them our money: they accept of it, and every body is content. We are accordingly paying, and have been paying, a tribute for these [exports] I don't know how many years, and all the while, as Monsieur Jourdan talked prose, without knowing any thing about the matter. The Dutch eat our bread and tax our bread, and we are kind enough to pay them for it.

If by this way of proceeding trade is encouraged and encreased in this instance, so would it proportionably in any and every other. To enrich ourselves and empoverish the Dutch, had they a mind to be thus empoverished, of which there can be no great doubt, the matter may be easily settled. A bounty here of 50 per Cent. on all our exports to Holland: a tax there to the same amount upon all imports from this country. Fifty per Cent. then is the exact sum we should lose upon the whole of our exports to that country, and that would be our advantage.

It is in this way and this alone that any trade can be a losing one: a losing one: how? to whom? not to the trader, not in this case more than in any other: if it were, no trader would he be. The loss is to the country at large, who pay the bounty which makes the loss.

[II. PROPER MEASURES]

[19.] *Of patents or exclusive privileges for inventions, and the expediency of granting them*

The utility of exclusive privileges granted for inventions, and the way in which the general stock of wealth receives a clear encrease from the protection thus granted to the offspring of genius and industry, will be placed in an incontestable point of view by a few simple considerations.

Under the general denomination of *labour*, considered as employed in the giving of encrease to wealth in any shape, two particulars may be distinguished: 1. the mere bodily energy employed in the production of the effect in question: 2. the *skill* or mental power displayed in the exercise of the bodily act, in the choice of the bodily operations carried on in that view, and in the mode of carrying them on.

Mere labour, exclusive of skill, can not be copied without equal labour: of mere labour no one therefore can have the benefit but the particular individual at whose expence, or on account of whom, it is exerted.

Of skill, on the other hand, it is the property to be capable of being indefinitely imbibed and diffused and that without any exertion of mental labour comparable to that, at the expence of which it was acquired. Of skill therefore it is the property that the benefit derivable from it, unless effectual measures can be taken and are taken for confining it, may and naturally will be reaped by all persons concerned in any of the businesses to which such skill is capable of being applied: and thereby to the thousands or the millions into whose possession it is come without any expence, as well as to the individual at whose sole expence it has been acquired.

In some instances, skill, being incapable of being exercised without being divulged, is utterly incapable, if once benefitted by, of being confined: in other instances it is capable of being confined, though not without the perpetual hazard of being disclosed.

Skill can not in any instances be acquired without some labour: in some instances it has not been acquired at less expence than the labour of a whole life, including the expence of maintaining the person in the rank of life in which he found himself placed during that whole time.

In most instances also it is not obtained but at the end of a long course of *experiments*: in the conduct of which a great expence has been necessary in materials and hands.

In many instances again, after a great expence [was] incurred as well in a man's own labour as in the purchase of materials and assistance, the species of peculiar skill sought for has not been found, so that the whole expence has been thrown away.

For a man to have acquired adequate satisfaction for the acquisition of new and peculiar skill [three] things are necessary: 1. satisfaction for his own labour at the rate at which he might have got payment for it, if employed in some ordinary and old established branch of industry: 2. satisfaction for the expence he has been at, principal and interest, in the purchase of materials and assistants: 3. compensation for the risk he has been running in the pursuit of an object of which the profit was to such a degree precarious, in preference to some one of the many objects on which it would have been so much less precarious.*

Skill, considered with reference to the period at which it has been recently acquired, is termed *discovery* or *invention*.

An invention will not be brought to light and practised, except in

---

*What is over and above this compensation, if given to the inventor, is not thrown away: who is there that can produce a better title to it? who is there but him that can have fixed his expectations on it? [Later addition to the MS, in Bentham's hand, interpolated at this point.]

as far as it finds a person willing as well as able to bring it to maturity and practise it.

A man will not be at the expence and trouble of bringing to maturity [an][1] invention unless he has a prospect of an adequate satisfaction, that is to say, at least of such a satisfaction as to his eyes appears an adequate one, for such trouble and expence.

It may happen that the measure of reputation which promises to result from an invention, may, in the eyes of one who is capable of bringing it to light, appear an adequate satisfaction.

But for this to happen [two] circumstances must concur: 1. a more than ordinary love of reputation in the breast of the inventor: 2. a fortune sufficient to enable him to bestow on the object in question, without evident imprudence, the measure of labour and expence equal to the greatest which appears beforehand likely to be requisite to the accomplishment of the object.

But the number of instances in which these circumstances concurr with the measure of genius and sort of talent capable of giving birth to invention, are few in comparison of the number of those instances in which the measure of genius [and sort of talent] in question exists without them: and the fewer, the more beneficial and important the nature of the invention: since the more labour and expence an invention requires to bring to light, the less likely it is that the enjoyment expected from the gratification of the love of reputation should rise so high as to afford a satisfaction capable of being an adequate one.

Without reckoning the pleasure of reputation, so long as a man can keep his invention secret without precluding himself from the benefit of exercising it, it may be in his power, upon the supposition of its being of a nature to give encrease to [1]the stock of[2] wealth, to derive from it a satisfaction adequate to the trouble and expence it cost him to bring it into existence, by selling the object in the production of which in the state in question the invention consists, exacting at the same time a price in the requisite degree superior to the measure of recompense ordinarily annexed to labour in that line: in which case the expence of such recompense is borne by him by whom the benefit of the invention is enjoyed, and, since he bestows it voluntarily, can not be more than an adequate satisfaction for [2]that benefit and[3] that expence.

---

[1][The MS reads "and".]
[2][3][Put into brackets at a later date.]

On the other hand, if a man can not keep his invention secret without precluding himself from the benefit of practising it, or can not practise it without disclosing it to those who, in the event of its proving an advantageous one, will be ready to copy it, he not only in many instances can not practise it [and] can not reap any benefit of it, without sharing that benefit with those who have borne no part of the burthen, but in many instances neither will he be able to reap any part of that benefit: some having acquired without any expence that which he did not acquire without considerable expence, it is in their power to prevent his making any profit at all by selling, which they may do with profit, at a price which would afford him none.

But there are many inventions in respect of which such secresy is from the very first impossible: and there are none in which the preservation of it can be absolutely secure.

In as far as the pleasure of reputation fails of affording a sufficient recompense, and the faculty of keeping an invention secret without foregoing the benefit of exercising it fails of being sufficiently secure, it will therefore be in many cases impossible for the author of an invention to derive any profit from it, so long as others remain at liberty to copy it.

On the other hand, were all persons but the author of an invention excluded for a certain time from the liberty of practising it, he would during that time possess the same faculty of deriving a benefit [from][1] it, as if it were remained a secret to every body but himself: since the way in which the concealment of it enables him to derive a benefit from the exercise of it, is only by precluding others from practising it.

But such exclusion can no otherwise be put upon any body but by the hand of law: and hence the necessity and the use of the interposition of law to secure to an inventor the benefit of his invention.

The instrument by which the benefit of an invention is thus secured to the inventor by excluding persons other than the inventor from practising the invention without his license, is in English called a patent.

A patent considered as a recompense for the encrease given to the general stock of wealth by an invention, as a recompense for industry and genius and ingenuity, is proportionate and essentially just. No other mode of recompense can merit either the one or the other epithet.

---

[1][The MS reads "for".]

The only mode of bestowing upon an inventor a recompense for his invention otherwise than by a patent, is by giving him a sum certain, or some favour, the value of which is reducible to a sum certain. Is the reward [given] in this [form] proportionable to the service? It may be so: but against its being so there is infinity to one.

A reward given in any other shape must be given out of the government fund, that is at the expence of the public at large, or in some other way still more remote from justice. In this case, the burthen of the recompense is borne [by many] who reap no share at all of the benefit, and of those who reap a share, the share they have in the burthen is in no proportion with that which they have in the advantage.

If there be any inventions, the nature of which precludes the inventor from reaping an adequate benefit from them in the way of sale or license to practise, in these instances a reward certain at the expence of the publick at large may be just and eligible. Are there any such? That there can be none is more than I will take upon me to say: but none such occurr to me.

Against the utility of the institution of patents objections have been made. A patent, it has been said, is a grant of a monopoly: and as monopolies in general are pernicious institutions, it has been concluded that they are so in this particular instance.

Considered in the legal mode of their creation, they are in truth exactly the same thing: but in their political effects, in the influence they exercise on the sum of wealth in the community, they are as exactly opposite.

In other instances what is the effect of a monopoly [1]as far as it has any[2]? In respect of things probably, it is to cause something not to be produced which, had it not been for the monopoly, would have been produced: in respect of persons at any rate to cause him not to produce a thing who, had it not been for the monopoly, would have produced it.

What is the effect of a patent? In respect of things, to cause that to be produced which, had it not been for this security given to the fruits of industry, would not have been produced: and thence in respect to persons, at the expiration of the term at least, to cause him to produce the thing, who, had it not been for the invention thus brought to light, could never have produced it.

---

[1][2][Put into brackets at a later date.]

So long as men are governed by unexamined prejudices and led away by sounds, it is natural for them to regard patents as unfavourable to the encrease of wealth. So soon as they obtain clear ideas to annex to those sounds, it is impossible for them to do otherwise than recognize them to be favourable to that encrease: and that in so essential a point, that the security given to property can not be said to be compleat without it.*

[20.] *What [is] to be done in respect of security in point of subsistence*

[A] bounty on [the] production [of corn is at once seen to be an ineligible measure: it] could add nothing to the habitual quantity: since whatever part of the adequate consideration, whatever that be, is paid by government, just so much the less is paid by the consumer.

A bounty upon the export of corn, if defensible at all, can only

---

*Property is in fact of two kinds. In the instance of one of them, the creation is effected by interdicting to persons at large in most ways, or perhaps in any way, the use [and the] liberty of occupancy with regard to the thing itself which is deemed the subject of the property in question. In the other instance, the creation is effected by interdicting to persons at large the liberty of occupancy not with regard to any one corporeal object in particular which thereby is constituted the person's *own*, but with regard to all corporeal objects whatsoever, when exercised in such manner as to produce a certain effect: and that not less in the case where the objects in question are to all other purposes the own objects or property of the persons thus interdicted, than in the case of their belonging to any one else, even the person in whose favour this kind of property is thus created.

The end in view in both instances is the securing to a certain individual the enjoyment of a benefit. This benefit he can not enjoy except in the first instance all persons are debarred from acting in certain ways upon a particular thing: in the other instance, except all persons are debarred from acting in certain ways upon all things whatsoever. In the one case, the property has a particular corporeal subject: in the other, it has none. In the one case, an individual corporeal thing can be found of which it can be said that it is the corporeal subject of property: in the other case, no such thing is to be found.

This latter and more confined species of property, not being capable of existing [but][1] among a people who have made a certain progress, and that a very considerable one, in the arts of life, is of course of later date than the other. Literary property is one of the most recent, as well as the most important, species of it.

The case of literary property, so thoroughly agitated not many years ago in Westminster Hall, presented a curious spectacle: multitudes of advocates and all the judges in and out of office talking about property in general, not one of them knowing what it was, nor how it was created: it was an assembly of blind men disputing about colours. But the pleasant thing was to hear on one side contending all the while with great vehemence that it was impossible in the nature of things a certain course of action should ever be observed, viz. the granting the requisite protection to this particular species of property which, according to their own confession, all the while had been ordered by Act of Parliament to be observed, and by virtue thereof, or otherwise, had been observed for ages.

[1][The MS reads "not" rather than "but", but this would mar the sentence.]

be defensible in the character of an establishment for the security
of subsistence.

It is not defensible upon the mere ground of its being a means
of ensuring from losses the persons embarked in this particular
trade: there is no reason why persons embarked in this particular
branch of agriculture should enjoy this benefit at the expence of
the community, any more than the persons embarked in any other
branch of agriculture or in any other branch of industry: graziers,
manufacturers &c.   It is the nature of all trade to be exposed to
losses: and it is the concern of each individual to make provision
against those losses in the best manner he can.

If this be true: 1. it ought not to be extended to any other sort
of corn than bread-corn, i.e. that species of grain which, in the
country in question, is made use of for bread by the bulk of the
people: 2. it ought not to be given at a price so high as that the
exportation in consequence should have the effect of producing a
necessity of re-exportation.

It supposes [1]therefore[2] [two] things: 1. that, without something
done by government, the quantity of bread-corn would be liable in
some years to fall short to such a degree as to amount to a *dearth:*
2. that the effect of such a bounty is to ensure the production, in
years of scarcity, [of] a quantity superior to what would be grown
without it.

The bounty, to be effectual, ought to be regulated by the demand
abroad, not by the price at home.   Suppose [however] a great dearth
abroad—what necessity [is there] for the bounty? Suppose such a
plenty abroad that there is no demand—what will signify your
bounty?—for it is never high enough of itself to create a demand.
The expence then is heavy and certain: the benefit in a variety of
ways uncertain and problematical.

The advantage of the corn-export-bounty, if it has any, is this: it
keeps the quantity more steady: and the farmer's gains more steady.
How? Answer 1. In case of a glut, by preventing the extra-quantity
from hanging so heavy upon the market as it would otherwise, it
prevents people from being deterred, so much as they would otherwise, from sowing corn the next year. 2. By promoting a constant
export of corn, it promotes a general superfluity. By having more
than our own consumption in a moderate year, we may have enough

---

[1] [2][Put into brackets at a later date.]

for our consumption in a dear year. And a superfluity of our own growth is a better dependence than importation.

A glut one year, be it ever so great, will hardly put by many farmers from sowing wheat the next year, since before the glut is known, their arrangements for sowing are taken in consequence of courses of husbandry prearranged.

There seems no reason to apprehend that without the benefit (if any benefit there be) of a bounty, a dearth should ever rise to the degree of a *famine*.

I call it a *famine* when the lowest wages of labour will not produce a family as much bread as it is necessary they should eat, or their healths must suffer by the deficiency.

The great mischief then apprehended from a dearth is discontent, and insurrection, and the various mischiefs of which insurrection may be productive: such as seizing the corn and destroying it, or selling it at under prices; outrages committed against the persons or other property of the dealers; whence encrease of dearth and distress to those who depend upon such dealers for their supply.

But insurrection in case of mere dearth does not take place, unless it be under the notion of some fault on the part of government of a nature to lessen the supply. If, during the continuance of a dearth, exportation were permitted, it is natural that such a measure should be productive of discontent. But it is not in the nature of things that an insurrection should take place for want of a bounty on exportation, i.e. on account of neglect or bad policy imputed to government in not having taken measures, the direct consequence [1]of which[2] is not to encrease the quantity of the commodity in the nation, but to diminish it.

The augmentative tendency of such a measure, [be it] ever so clearly established in the eyes of thinking men, it is not in the nature of things it should ever be so clearly established in the eyes of the vulgar, of the great body of the people, as to make them riotous for the want of it. It is exportation always, not non-exportation, that breeds riots.

The security derived from it [moreover] can never equal the security derivable from county magazines. What you have in your magazine, you are sure you have. You can never be equally sure that the export of one plentiful year will produce a growth in another year to a given amount. What if two very bad years come

[1] [2][Later addition.]

together? The magazines, being always full, [will][1] be a resource: whereas the resource of extra-sowing fails by the supposition.

[Generally speaking, then] regulations relative to import and export cost money and do not produce the [desired] security after all.

Nothing produces absolute security but *magazining*.

Were subsistence assured by magazining, the country might depend upon a foreign country for its supply without inconvenience. Holland which grows no corn, suffers as little from dearths as England which grows so much.

---

[1][The MS reads "with".]

Connection of [the] paper money question with the rest of [the] Manual

Government ought not to give bounties, much [less enforce] prohibitions &c, for [the] encrease of wealth, as they can't encrease wealth because they can't encrease capital.

Is there any thing that it can and ought to do to encrease capital? Does paper money, for instance, encrease capital?

How could it do this: 1. in an insulated state? 2. in an uninsulated state? The paper money stays at home where alone it finds a demand. A quantity (what quantity?) of real money &c, goes abroad for value.

Paper money *strictly* only a promise to deliver so much other money.

Loosely—a promise to deliver money's worth to that amount.

It can add to the wealth [of the country] no further than in as far as such promises are not wanted to be fulfilled.

Unless it be only representative of a money deposited. It then saves wear and tear &c.

Such promises fail of fulfillment: 1. in respect of money, in as far as the real metal is wanted, and money's worth can not be got for it fast enough: 2. in respect of money's worth, in as far as quickly consumables are wanted in a greater proportion than inconsumables or slowly consumables.

The paper money as a promise of money's worth to have its value, it is necessary: 1. that he who issues it has money's worth to the amount in question, or will have by the time of payment: 2. that what he has will answer the purpose of the paper-holder, or be exchangeable for something else that will.

If in Norfolk Island by dint of paper money, [a] man had been induced to accumulate cloaths, flax, [1]&c faster than corn, all the money and wealth of the island would not produce a grain of corn nor prevent a famine.

Therefore the stock of inconsumables and other fixed capital can not furnish a sufficient fund for the support of paper money.

How far paper money circulation can be hurt or favoured by positive agreements or at pleasure.

Every new sale of lands by government in America is a cause of

---

[1][One word illegible.]

drawing labour and money away from other employments to agriculture.

Suppose, according to Hume's supposition,[1] the money in each man's pocket to be doubled instantaneously. It is not true that (as he says) the wealth [of the country] would not be encreased by this.

Real consequences: If doubled by actual coin, the prices of other things would be doubled, saving what corresponds to so much of the coin as was melted and manufactured into plate &c. If the accession was universally known and the principles of economy under this head universally known likewise, the money prices of things would be doubled.

But as this is not the case, the addition would not be so great, for the extra pay which the money-holders would be enabled to give would, by encreasing the quantity of labour, encrease the quantity of saleable commodities, which addition would be another encrease in value to the sum total of wealth in the nation.

The consequence would be the same if, instead of coin, paper money were added (if not in such excess as to destroy its credit). The paper could not serve (it is true) for melting, but there would remain an equal quantity of the coin which would.

Ought the government to emitt paper money of its own?

Ought it to encourage or discourage the emission of it by individuals, or do neither?

Consequence of paper money issued in Norfolk Island:

If all were fully employed, it could not encrease industry.

If any were unemployed, or not fully employed, it might encrease industry *pro tanto*. I will have worked and made such a thing for you by such a time, if you will have worked for me and made such a thing by such a time.

A given individual fails, if by the time of payment he has not to give what he promised to give. So any number of individuals. So the government.

If on Norfolk Island, every individual, being in the habit of producing as much as ever he could produce, had power given him to issue paper money to a certain amount, and issued it accordingly —what would follow? It would be, all of it, bad. *Pro tanto* an universal failure.

Paper money, therefore, in one[?] nation taken together, can add

---

[1][cf. Political Discourses, 1752, Discourse V; cf. also Discourse IV and Discourse III.]

to the quantity of produce only in this[?] way: 1. in as far as it encreases the quantity of labour: 2. in as far as it encreases the productiveness of the given quantity: 3. in Norfolk Island paper money, though bad, might encrease the quantity of wealth by pumping all the real wealth from Rose-hill.

In what events and to what extent will the Assignats of France hold good, i.e. the lands sell for as much as lands would sell for before, and no loss be incurred by any body? 1. If the goodness of the paper money does not require any addition to be made to the quantum or value of the national stock of industry; 2—or, though it does—to the extent of the quantum and value of industry that can and will be added; 3—or to the addition in value that may be made by a more advantageous direction given to the [available] quantity of labour. This is [applicable] in as far as men look upon the possession of such lands as equally secure as [that] of other lands.

Suppose men engage to pay a higher price than before. Actually pay they can not but in proportion to the encrease of circulating capital, which can only be gradual. If they engage to pay at future and distant periods, they may pay the difference in as far as the produce of their frugality is equal to the encrease of price.

Effects of paper money.

1. A tax upon capital, i.e. upon the capital of moneyed men whose money is placed out at interest, in so far as their debtors are able to pay them off.

[2.] In [an]other respect it is a tax on consumption, in as far as it raises the price of all commodities.

Meantime it actually is productive of an addition to the mass of national wealth, in as far as it gets extra hands, or sets them to work at extra hours.

What makes this doubted is that the call for paper money [at present] is [arisen] from past expenditure, from [a] past diminution of the sum of national wealth.

POPULATION

Nothing ought to be done for the particular purpose of promoting population.

Most of the measures that have been or would be pursued in this view are necessarily inefficacious, or otherwise needless. All of them are inexpedient as being coercive.[1]

The quantity of population is not limited by the desire of sexual intercourse, it is limited by the means of subsistence.

The facility of finding subsistence for children is in proportion to the demand for labour: and the demand for labour is in proportion to the relative quantity of capital already in store.

Population has been endeavoured to be promoted:

1. By encouraging marriages in general, in the way of exemption from charges in proportion to the number of children.

2. By encouraging particular marriages by marriage portions.

3. By discouraging marriages promising to be unprolific.

4. By discouraging prolific venery out of marriage.

5. By discouraging venery necessarily unprolific.

6. By prohibiting emigration.

7. By encouraging immigration.

Si venus sit inter voluptates et felicitas constet ex voluptatibus (adeo ut summa felicitatis data summa infelicitatis est ut valor summae voluptatum) summa felicitatis erit caeteris paribus ut summa veneris: quo casu, venus productiva sit nec ne, quid refert?

Qui igitur veneris speciem aliquam proscribere vellet, in eum incumbat probatio casu veneris speciem dolorem gignere, nec solum dolorem, sed ad valorem majorem valore voluptatis.

Sed (abstractione facta doloris) consecutive, quanto gratior voluptatis alicujus species, tanto melior.

Esto centum congressus procreando sufficientes in anno intra annum potentia prolifica media hominis medii.

Sed intra id spatium partus datur non plus quam unicus. Sequitur non plus centesima parte potentiae prolificae qua in mundo est ad generationem posse contribuere. Reliquia nonaginta novem necesse est ut aut supprimantur aut sine effectu prolifico consumantur. Sed pars ista sterilis, supprimatur an consumatur quid ad fecunditatem refert?

---

[1][Here follows a line "1. Needless or inefficacious or both" which is useless in the MS as it stands, as there is no "2." nor any indication what that "2." could possibly be.]

Sequitur dummodo centesima pars tantum potentiae prolificae more prolifico in[sic]*sumeretur, consumptionem non prolificam reliquarum* 99 *populationi officere non posse, quin ea ad maximum offeretur, ut ut iste usus non prolificus in vias antephysicas dictas totus de . . . eret*[?][1]

Sed si desiderii antiphysici dicti quantitas aequalis fuerit quantitati desiderii prolifici, quo sensu ille antiphysici nomen mereri dici poterit?

The quantity of capital dispositive to industry remaining given, population can not be had but at the expence of wealth, nor wealth but at the expence of population: the more people there are, the poorer they will be: the fewer, the richer.

In short, the more children a man has, the poorer he is, at least till they are able to provide altogether for their own maintenance.

---

[1][About four letters indecipherable.]

S

FINANCIAL RESOURCES

ANALYTICAL VIEW [OR] SUMMARY SKETCH OF FINANCIAL RESOURCES, EMPLOYED AND EMPLOYABLE[1]

1794

SOURCES of division:

    I. *Subjection* of the person on whom the tax rests.

    II. Presence or absence of *ability* to bear the tax.

    III. *Fund* from whence the contribution issues.

    IV. *Occasion* on which it is levied.

    V. Presence or absence of an *indemnity*.

    VI. Mode of *collection*[2] in respect of

        1. mode of receiving [?] payment.

        2. form of the official establishment for management.[3]

I. Subjection of the contributor:

1. Subjects of the home dominion. 2. of the co-ordinate out-dominions, viz. Ireland. Exports to Ireland. 3. of the subordinate dominions, [viz.] colonies and E[ast] India dominions. Export to do. 4. of foreign nations. Exports to foreign nations.

II. Ability. Taxes are

1. on ability, keeping pace with ability. Taxes on consumption in some instances. 2. on ability, but not keeping pace with it. Do in other instances. Professional licences payable on entrance. 3. payable, ability or no ability. Poll-taxes, including professional licences. 4. on distress. *1.* Taxes on justice. *2.* on pardons. 2[a]. Taxes on medicinal drugs. *3.* Taxes on sales in individuals instances. *4.* Taxes on certain contracts, viz. borrowers'. Bond. Note of hand.

III. Source or Fund.

1. On income assured. *1.* Land Tax. *2.* Money lent on mortgage.

---

[1][The title continues: ". . . with [a] reflection on the order of preference", but there are no notes on this topic.]

[2] [3][In pencil.]

3. On personal security. *4*. Property in the funds. *5*. Salaries and pensions paid by government.

2. On casual income—the fruit of industry: *1*. Taxes on professional profits, [i.e.] on the profits of trade or profession. 2. Receipt tax in individual instances.

3. On capital. Taxes on *1*. sale 2. succession *3*. on building materials.

IV. Occasion.

1. On liberty in relation to property. *1*. Liberty of consuming. [Sir Matthew] Decker's proposed licences.[1] 2. Of using 1. coach. 2. horse. 3. servant. *3*. Of securing against accident. Insurance tax. *4*. Purchase. 5. Possession. 6. Use. 7. Carriage.

2. [On] liberty in relation to personal conduct. *1*. Of marrying in a certain way. Taxes on marriage licences. 2. Liberty of burying in a certain way.

V. Presence or absence of indemnity.

1. Without indemnity. Taxes on profits of traders and professional men without an exclusive privilege.

2. [With indemnity.] Do if coupled with an exclusive privilege.

---

[1][cf. "Serious Considerations on the Several High Duties which the Nation . . . labour under" 1743, and "An Essay on the Causes of the Decline of the Foreign Trade", 1744.]

SUPPLY WITHOUT BURTHEN
OR
ESCHEAT VICE TAXATION

SUPPLY WITHOUT BURTHEN

OR

ESCHEAT VICE TAXATION:

BEING A PROPOSAL FOR A SAVING OF TAXES
BY AN EXTENSION OF THE LAW OF ESCHEAT:
INCLUDING STRICTURES ON THE TAXES ON COLLATERAL SUCCESSION,
COMPRISED IN THE BUDGET OF 7TH DECEMBER, 1795

1795

[TABLE OF CONTENTS]

§1. General Idea

I N a former Essay,* I pointed out the species of tax which, if the reasoning there given be just, is the *worst* of all taxes existing or possible. The object of the present Essay is, to point out that mode of supply which, for one of so great a magnitude, will, I flatter myself, appear to be absolutely the *best*.

What is that mode of supply, of which the twentieth part is a tax, and that a heavy one, while the whole would be no tax, and would not be felt by any body?

The question has the air of a riddle; but the proposition it involves, paradoxical as it may appear, is not more strikingly paradoxical than strictly true.

The answer is—an extension of the existing Law of *Escheat*; a law coeval with the very first elements of the constitution: to which I would add, as an aid to its operation, a correspondent *limitation*, not an *extinction*, of the power of *bequest*.

Of the extended Law of Escheat, according to the degree of extension here proposed, the effect would be, the appropriating to the use of the public all vacant successions, property of every denomination included, on the failure of *near relations*; will or no will, subject only to the power of bequest as hereinafter limited.

By near relations I mean, for the purpose of the present proposal, such relations as stand within the *degrees* termed *prohibited* with reference to marriage.

As a farther aid to the operation of the law, I would propose, in the instance of such relations *within the pale*,† as are not only childless, but *without prospect of children*,‡ whatever share they would take under the existing law, that, instead of taking that share in *ready money*, they should take only the interest of it, in the shape of an *annuity for life*.

It would be a farther help to the operation of the measure, and (if confined to the cases where from the nature of the relationship

---

*Protest against Law Taxes, printed 1793.

†To save circumlocution, relations whom, under this or any other definition of *near* relations, I should propose to exclude, I shall term relations *without the pale;* those whom I should propose *not* to exclude, relations *within* the pale.

‡Say, in the instance of females, 48; in the instance of males, 60, if no child within five years past; or 55, if married to a wife above 48.

the survivor is not likely to have grounded his plans of life upon the expectation of the succession, or otherwise to have placed any determinate dependence on it) may scarcely if at all be felt, if in such instances, although the relationship be *within* the pale, the public were to come in for a share in the succession, (suppose an *equal* share) though not the whole. This may be applied to the case of the uncle and aunt, to the case of the grandfather and grandmother, and, perhaps, unless under particular circumstances, to the case of the nephew and niece.

With regard to *family settlements,* the persons whose benefit they have in view will be found provided for with few or perhaps no exceptions, by the reservations made in this plan in favour of relations *within the pale.* To make provision for the cases where, in virtue of an old settlement, an estate might devolve to a relation *without the pale,* I would propose to add a proviso, that wherever the deceased, had he been of full age, could, by his single act, have cut off the entail, it shall be as if he had actually done so, for the purpose of excluding the distant relative. This in the instance of settlements already *existing;* as to future ones, there will be still less difficulty about confining *their* operation within the range meant to be allowed them by the spirit of the proposed law.

Regard to the principles of the constitution, not less than to the probability of carrying the measure through the Upper House, would at the same time incline me to exempt the Peerage from its operation, wherever the effect would be, to deprive the title of any property which, under the existing law, would go to the support of it.

As to the latitude to be left to the power of *bequest,* I should propose it to be continued in respect of the *half* of whatever property would be at present subject to that power: the wills of persons in whose succession no interest is hereby given to the public, to be observed in all points as at present; as, likewise, those in whose succession an interest *is* given to the public, saving as to the amount of that interest: the plan consequently not trenching in any degree upon the rights of parents.*

---

*Many writers (Blackstone for one) have treated the right of bequest with very little ceremony: many writers, without having in view any such public benefit as is here in question, have been for abolishing it altogether: (the author of the Code Frederic, for instance; Cocceiji, chancellor to the late King of Prussia: see the Preface to that work.) Without entering into a discussion which is not to the present purpose, it will be sufficient here to observe, that not only the regard due to old

To give the plan its due effect, it will be seen to be indispensably necessary, in the first place, that the whole property, in which the public shall thus have acquired an interest, shall, whatever it consists of, be converted into *ready money:* property in the funds alone excepted, from which the public cannot reap so great a benefit in any other way, as by the sinking of so much of its debt in the first instance: in the next place, that, to prevent collusive undervaluation, and the suspicion of it, the conversion shall, in every instance, be performed in the way of *public auction.* As to the reasons for such conversion, they are tolerably apparent on the face of the proposition; and they will be detailed in their proper place.

What will also be seen to be necessary is, that, wherever the public has any interest at all in any succession under the proposed law, the officer of the public, that is, the officer of the Crown, shall enter into the possession and management of the whole in the first instance, in the same manner as assignees of bankrupts do in respect of the whole property, *real* and *personal,* together, or administrators or executors do in respect of the personalty: not to mention the *real* in some cases, as where, by a clause in the will, it is ordered to be sold.

Of the several extensions above proposed, it may be observed, that, though they operate, all of them, to the augmentation of the produce, and, in so far at least to the *utility* of the measure, yet are they not, any of them, so indispensably *necessary* to its adoption, but that they may be struck out or modified, or even added to, by farther exten-

established privileges and long-existing usages, but the success of the very system here proposed, though established in so great a degree at the expense of the power in question, may depend upon the leaving that power in possession of a very considerable degree of force. If a man were allowed no power at all over what property he left behind him, he would, in many instances, either be indifferent about getting it, or spend it as fast as he got it, or transfer it to some happier clime, where the interests of the community were better understood, and the feelings of individuals treated with more respect; and, in fact, a great part of the value of all property would thus be destroyed.

So much as to the abolishing the power altogether: as to the narrowing it in the manner here proposed, should that be objected to as too great a hardship, let it be considered that the defalcation thereby proposed to be made from the powers of proprietors in general, falls short, by much more than half, of the quantum of restriction imposed, by the terms of marriage settlements, on the description of proprietors whose lot in point of property is most envied, the great body of the nobility and landed gentry. In this plan, there is nothing to preclude a man from *charging* his estate—from *changing the nature* of it as often as he pleases—from *improving* any part by selling or charging another—or from *giving* or *spending* it in his life-time.

sions, and the principle of the plan still adopted—the essence of it still preserved.

It may be a satisfaction to see, at this early stage of the inquiry, the principles by which the *extent* that may with propriety be given to this resource, appears to be marked out and limited. The propositions I would propose in that view are as follows:

I. Whatever power an individual is, according to the received notions of *propriety*, understood to possess in this behalf, with respect to the disposal of his fortune in the way of *bequest*—in other words, whatever degree of power he may exercise, without being thought to have dealt *hardly* by those on whom what he disposes of would otherwise have devolved—that same degree of power the law may, for the benefit of the public, exercise once for all, without being conceived to have dealt *hardly* by any body, without being conceived to have *hurt* any body, and, consequently, without scruple: and even though the money so raised would *not* otherwise have been to be raised in the way of taxes.*

II. Any further power which could be exercised in this way to the profit of the public purse, and of which the exercise, though not altogether clear of the imputation of producing a sense of hardship, would at the same time be productive of *less* hardship than the lightest tax that could be substituted in the room of it, ought, if the public mind can be sufficiently reconciled to it, to be exercised in preference to the establishment of any tax.

III. A power thus exercised in favour of the public purse, would go

---

*If without provocation on the part of my *children*, I were to let in strangers or mere collateral relations for an equal share of my fortune, my children would feel themselves injured, other people would look upon them as injured, my behaviour to them would be universally regarded as cruel and unnatural. A man is considered, indeed, as having his own fortune pretty much in his power, as against one child in comparison of another, but very little so as against his children taken together in comparison with collaterals or strangers. How stands it with regard to *nephews* and *nieces*? Is he considered as lying under the same restraint with regard to *them*? No, nor any thing like it. If it be his pleasure to give them all, so he may, they being his nearest relations, and without being thought to do amiss by any body else: but should it on the other hand be his pleasure to prefer to them a set of individual friends, or a public institution, say with respect to half, yet, so as he does but leave them the other half, they will scarcely be looked upon as ill used. Had he, indeed, exercised no such power at all over his property, had he suffered the law in this behalf to take its own course, they would, it is true, have got the whole. But why?—only because somebody must have it, and as they stand nearest, there is nobody else to take it. I say nothing here of brothers and sisters, fathers and mothers, uncles and aunts, grandfathers and grandmothers; they would lead me too far into details.

beyond the latitude given by the first rule, and would accordingly be productive of a sense of hardship, in as far as it went the length of producing in any degree any of the following effects, viz.

1. If it extended to the prejudice of the joint possession customarily enjoyed by a man's *natural* and necessary *dependents*, such as *children*, and those who stand in the place of children.

2. If it went to the bereaving a man of the faculty of continuing after his death any support he had been in the habit of affording to *relatives* of any other description, whose claims to, and dependence on such support, are, by reason of the nearness of the relationship, too strongly rooted in nature and opinion, to be capable of being dissolved by the dispensations of law.

3. If, by putting it out of the power of a relation of parental age to receive, at the death of a relation of inferior age, an adequate indemnification for requisite assistance given in the way of *nurture*, it threatened, by lessening the inducements, to lessen the prevalence of so useful a branch of natural benevolence.

4. If it went to the bereaving a man of the faculty of affording an adequate *reward for meritorious service*, of whatsoever nature, and by whomsoever rendered, lessening thereby the general disposition among men to the rendering of such service.

5. The effect of such an extension of the proposed power would be purely mischievous, if what were gained thereby on one hand by the augmentation of the share taken into the hands of government, at the expense of the power of bequest, were to be lost on the other hand by a proportionable diminution effected in the whole mass of property in the country, in consequence of the diminution of the inducements to accumulate, and lay up property, instead of spending it.

6. The public mind must in this instance, as in every other, be at any rate treated with due deference. In this instance, as in every other, a law, however good in itself, however good on the supposition of acquiescence, may become bad in any degree by unpopularity: by running too suddenly and directly against opinions and affections that have got possession of mankind.

Thus much for the rules that may serve for our guidance, in adjusting the extent that may be given to this resource. They may be trusted, it should seem, for the present at least, to the strength of their own self-evidence. The application of them to practice, the application of them to the several modes and degrees of relationship and to the several situations and exigencies of families, is matter of detail, that will meet us in its proper place.

§2. ORDER OF THE DETAILS

In continuing the thread of this proposal, the following is the course I propose to take—

1. To give a brief view of the *advantages* or beneficial properties that appear to recommend the measure to the adoption of government—

2. To shew how *distinct* it is in reality from all taxes on *collateral successions*, which have ever been established or proposed, and how much the distinction is to its advantage—

3. To exhibit the best idea I am capable of giving, of the probable amount of the *produce* that may be expected from it—

4. I shall add a few observations, relative to the most eligible *application* to be made of that produce.

Descending further into detail,*

5. I shall give a more particular view of such *regulations* as may seem proper to be inserted for the purpose of applying to practice the principles already exhibited.

6. I shall attempt a sketch of an *official establishment* for the *collection* of the produce.

7. I shall consider the measure with reference to the cases where the interests of individuals belonging to nations altogether *foreign,* or nations *co-ordinate* with or *subordinate* to the British, are concerned.

8. I shall consider it with reference to the cases where the *property* in question happens to be *situated* any where *without* the limits of the laws of Great Britain.

9. I shall attempt a general sketch of a *plan* for the *collection* of the produce: in the course of which attempt I shall have occasion to advert to the differences that may be suggested by the *nature* of the *property* which may come to be collected: to the means of guarding against *concealments,* and other *frauds,* to which the property in its several shapes may be exposed, on the part of such

---

*The matter belonging to the ensuing heads is not all of it included in the present publication. No part of it was sent, the demand for it depending upon the approval or disapproval of the principle of the measure; nor has it ever been thought worth while to work up into form any more than is here subjoined. Note added in Dec. 1795.

individuals whose interest or affections may be at variance, in this behalf, with the interest of the public; as also against any such *abuses of power* and other *mismanagements,* as the servants employed on behalf of the public in this business, stand exposed, by their respective situations, to the temptation of being chargeable with.

In a sort of Appendix, which those who may find themselves already satisfied with the principle of the mode of supply, may spare themselves the trouble of looking into,

10. I shall defend the proposed institution against every *objection,* which my imagination can represent to me, as capable of presenting itself.*

11. I shall shew that a latitude, much beyond what is here proposed to be assumed, stands warranted by the *opinions* of the most respected writers.

12. That it is equally warranted by *precedent,* that is, by the disposition of law in this country from the primitive ages of the constitution down to the present times.

13. Lastly, in the way of supplement to the refutation of the several imaginable objections to the proposed measure, I shall endeavour to give a comprehensive idea of the several *effects,* as well immediate as remote, that appear any way likely to result from it, considered in every imaginable point of view.

§3. ADVANTAGES

The advantageous properties of the proposed resource may be stated under the following heads, viz.

1. Its unburthensomeness—
2. Its tendency to cut off a great source of litigation—
3. Its favourableness to marriage—
4. Its probable popularity on that score.

Its *unburthensomeness,* which is the grand and transcendent advantage, is not matter of surmise: it is testified by experience: it is confirmed, as we shall see, by the most indisputable principles of human nature: by the fundamental constitution of the human feelings.

I. It is testified by *experience.* On the decease of my uncle, who had children before I was born, the law gives every thing to his

---

*Heads of objections, with answers, were sent, in form of a table, and being now printed *verbatim,* form the matter of one of the ensuing sections.—Note added Dec. 1795.

T

children, nothing to me.—What do I suffer from finding myself thus debarred? Just nothing:—no more than at the thoughts of not succeeding to the stranger whose hearse is passing by.

What more should I suffer, if my uncle's property, instead of going to his children, were known before hand to go to the public? In point of personal feeling at least, nothing: sympathy for my cousins, in the case of their being left destitute, is a different concern.

Living under the law of England, I find myself debarred from a succession, in which I should have shared, had I lived under the Law of Spain. What do I suffer at hearing this?—Just nothing: no more than I suffer at the thoughts of not being King of Spain. But if the law of England were to be changed in this behalf in conformity to the measure proposed, what is now the existing law would to me be no more than the law of Spain.

My father gets an office: upon his decease, the office goes to the nominee of the King from whom he got it, not to me. Do I regard the successor as an intruder?—Do I feel his taking possession of the office as a hardship upon me?—No more than I do his Majesty's having succeeded to the crown instead of me.

Under the *existing* Law of Escheat, real property, on the absolute failure of all heirs, lapses to the crown already. Is there any thing of hardship felt by *any* body?—If there were, it would be a cruel hardship, for it would be felt by *every* body.* Give to this branch of the law the extent proposed, confining it always within the bounds above traced out, and it will be even then as unburthensome as it is now.

Thus stands the resource in point of unburthensomeness as demonstrated by experience. What does so singular a property turn upon?— Upon a most simple and indisputable principle in human nature: the feeling of *expectation*. In the case of acquiring or not acquiring, of retaining or not retaining, no hardship without previous expectation. *Disappointment* is expectation thwarted: in the distribution of property no sense of hardship but in proportion to disappointment. But expectation, as far as the law can be kept present to men's minds,

---

*I leave out of the supposition, the case where there is a father left, a grandfather, or a relation of the half blood, and the estate escheats to their prejudice. These are but too real hardships; but they belong to the law in its present state, were ingrafted into it by accident, and would not continue in it in its proposed extended state, if the choice depended upon me. Thus much must be acknowledged: the removal of them is a separate question, bearing no necessary relation to the present measure.

follows with undeviating obsequiousness the finger of the law. Why
should I suffer (bodily distress from want out of the question) why
should I suffer, if the property I call *mine*, and have been used to
regard as mine, were to be taken from me?—For this reason and no
other—because I *expected* it to continue with me. If the law had
predetermined, the property I am now using as mine, should, at the
arrival of the present period cease to be mine, and this determination
of the law had been known to me before I began to treat it as mine,
I should no longer have *expected* to be permitted to treat it as mine:
the ceasing to possess it, the ceasing to treat it as mine, would be no
disappointment, no hardship, no loss to me. Why is it, that I do not
suffer at the reflection that my neighbour enjoys his own property
and not I?—Because I never *expected* to call it mine. In a word:—
In matters of property in general, and succession in particular, thus
then stands the case: *hardship* depends upon *disappointment;
disappointment* upon *expectation; expectation* upon the dispensations, meaning the *known* dispensations of the law.

The riddle begins to solve itself:—a part taken, and a sense of
burthen left; the whole taken and no such effect produced:—the
effect of a part greater than the effect of the whole: the old Greek
paradox verified, a part greater than the whole.*—Suffer a mass of
property in which a man has an interest to *get into his hands*, his
expectation, his imagination, his attention at least, fastens upon the
whole. Take from him afterwards a part, let it be such a part and
no other, as at the time of his beginning to know that the whole was
to come into his hands, he knew that he would have to quit, still,
when the time comes for giving it up, the parting with it cannot
but excite something of the sensation of a *loss:* a sensation, which
will of course be more or less pungent, according to the tenacity of
the individual.—*Ah! why was not this mine too!—Ah why must I
part with it! Is there no possible means of keeping it? Well, I will
keep it as long as I can, however: and perhaps the chapter of acci-
dents may serve me.*—Take from him, now, (I should say, not *take*)
but *keep* from him the whole, so keeping it from him that there shall
never have been a time when he expected to receive it, all hardship,
all suffering, is out of the case; if he *were* a sufferer, he would be a
sufferer indeed; he would be a sufferer for every atom of property

---

*πλεον ημισυ παντος.

in the world possessed by any body else; he would be as miserable as the world is wide.*

Under a tax on successions, a man is led in the first place to look upon the whole in a general view as his own: he is then called upon to give up a part. His share amounts to so much: this share he is to *have;* only out of it, he is to *pay* so much *per cent.* His imagination thus begins with embracing the *whole*: his expectation fastens upon the whole: then comes the law putting in for its *part*, and forcing him to quit his hold. This he cannot do without pain: if he could, no tax at all, not even a tax on property, would be a burthen: neither land-tax nor poor's rate could be too high.†

The utility of that part of the proposal which gives to the public officer possession of the whole, whether the public in conclusion is admitted to the whole, or only to a part, may now be seen in full force. It is a provision not more of *prudence* with a view to the public, than of *tenderness* with a view to the individual. Had he been suffered to *lay his hands* upon the *whole*, being afterwards, or even at the time, called upon to *give* up a *part*, his attention would unavoidably have grasped the whole, the giving up the part would have produced a sensation, fainter perhaps, but similar to that produced by an unexpected *loss:* on the other hand, as according to the proposal, he *takes* nothing that he does not *keep*, no such unpleasant sensation is produced.

The case, where the individual sees a share go from him, for the benefit of the public, in the way of *partition*, stands in this respect, between the case where the public is let into the whole, and that

---

*Better to have nothing than to have a share? (*says an objector.*) *How can that be?—Is not the man himself the best judge?—Ask him then, which is best for him, share or no share?* My answer is—the question does not meet the case. You suppose his attention previously drawn to the subject; you have raised his expectation; you have given him his option between *some* and *none:* that being the case, his answer, it is true, cannot but be as you suppose.—Not to come in for any thing would now be a disappointment: It will even be a disappointment, should the share he gets, prove smaller than what he hoped to get: and the disappointment will be not less but greater, if he gets no share at all. True; but all this depends upon the *option :* accordingly, in the case *you* suppose, there *is* an option given; whereas, in the case *I* suppose, there is *none.* When an estate in England has been limited away from a man altogether, he never looks at it: what should lead him?—he has no more option in it than in the kingdom of Spain.

†Try the experiment upon a hungry child: give him a small cake, telling him after he has got it, or even before, that he is to give back part of it. Another time give him a whole cake, equal to what was left to him of the other and no more, and let him enjoy it undiminished—will there be a doubt which cake afforded him the purest pleasure?

where a part is taken from him in the way of a *tax*. Whether on this plan of partition, the individual shall feel in any degree the sensation of a loss, will depend partly upon the *mode of carving out* the share, partly upon the *proportion* taken by the law, partly after all upon the temper and disposition of the individual. As to the *mode of carving*, the whole secret lies in taking the public officer, and not the individual, for the *carver*, for the reasons that have been seen. As to the *proportion*, to come back to the paradox, the larger the share of the public, the better; even with reference to his feelings: for the larger it is, the more plainly it will shew as a *civil* regulation in matters of succession: the smaller, the more palpably it will have the air of a *fiscal* imposition, the more it will feel in short like a *tax*. The more is taken under the name of a tax, the more burthensome the measure, as every body knows: at the same time the more is taken for the public under the name of *partition*, so long as an equal, or not much more than equal, share is left to the individual, the farther the measure from being burthensome: because the farther from being considered as a tax. The Roman Tax of 5 *per cent.* on collateral successions was considered as a heavy burthen: a tax of 50 *per cent.* imposed under the name of a tax would have been intolerable. At the same time, pass instead of the tax a law of inheritance, giving the public 50 *per cent.* upon certain successions, the burthen may be next to nothing: pass a law of inheritance giving the public the whole, the burthen vanishes altogether. The dominion of the imagination upon the feelings is unbounded: the influence of names upon the imagination is well known. Things are submitted to without observation under one name, that would drive men mad under another. Justice is denied to the great bulk of the people by law taxes, and the blind multitude suffer without a murmur: were the distribution of justice to be prohibited in name, under a penalty to the amount of a tenth part of the tax, Parliament would be blown into the air, or thrown into a mad-house.

Would it be better then, upon the whole, for the public to take *all*, and let no relation in for a share?—Certainly not in every case. The law is powerful here: but even *here* the law is not absolutely omnipotent. It can govern *expectation* absolutely; meaning always in as far as it makes itself present to the mind: it can govern expectation absolutely; but governing expectation is not every thing. It may prevent me from being *disappointed* at not having bread to eat: but if, by preventing my having bread to eat, it starves me, it will not prevent me from suffering by being starved. It can save me in this way from *ideal hardship*, but not from *corporal* sufferance. It can save me from disappointment at not *beginning* to enjoy: but it cannot save me from disappointment at not *continuing* to enjoy, after the habit of enjoyment has grown upon me. Hence the necessity of consulting the rules of precautionary tenderness that have been exhibited above.

Unburthensomeness is a praise that belongs to this mode of supply in another point of view:—with reference to the business of *collection*. In many instances so great is the incidental burthen accruing from this source, as almost to rival in real magnitude, and even eclipse in apparent magnitude, the principal burthen which is the more immediate fruit of the fiscal measure. This is more eminently the case in the instances of the *customs* and the *excise:* of those branches of taxation by which by far the largest portion of the revenue is supplied. The officer of excise goes no where where he is not a guest; and of all guests the most unwelcome. The escheator will have no where to go where he is not *at home:* into no habitation, into no edifice, not so much as upon a foot of land, which is not to this purpose, which is not as against all *individuals*, his *own*. No jealousies; no collision of rights; no partial occupations, extorted at the expense of the comfort and independence of proprietors. The excise is not only the most productive branch of the revenue, but the most capable of extension, and therefore the most liable to be extended. It can surely be no small merit in the proposed supply, in addition to its other merits, that in proportion as it extends, in the same proportion it puts a stop to extensions of the excise.

II. The advantages that follow are of minor importance.

The advantage of *checking litigation* in this way, by the diminution of its aliment, is however not to be despised. The fishing in the troubled waters of litigation, for the whole or a part of the property of a distant relation or supposed relation, is one of the most alluring, and at the same time most dangerous, pursuits, by which adventurers are enticed into the lottery of the law. It is like the search after a gold mine, a search by which the property of the adventurer is too often sunk before the precious ore is raised. Causes of this nature are by no means unfrequent in Westminster Hall; the famous *Selby* cause was a bequest, nominally to relations, really to the profession. This source of litigation would be effectually dried up by the measure here proposed.

An item, which may naturally enough be added to the account of advantage, is the favour shewn to *marriage,* and in particular to *prolific marriages,* the sort of marriages of which the title to legislative favour stands in the most plausible point of view.

That the influence of the system in question would be favourable to marriage, and in particular to prolific marriage, will hardly be disputed. Of fathers and mothers of families it leaves the powers untouched; it places them, in comparison with single persons of both sexes, in a situation of privilege and pre-eminence. Within the threshold of him whose marriage has fulfilled the ends of marriage, the foot of the officer of the revenue has no place. His will is executed in all points; whatever he bequeaths, to whomsoever he bequeaths it, offspring, relation, or stranger, passes without deduction. Whatever restriction it imposes, is all at the expense of the celibatary and unmarried. If with propriety it could be stiled a *tax,* it would be a *tax on celibacy.**

An advantage of a less questionable nature, is the popularity which seems the natural effect of any measure wearing the complexion above-mentioned—for popularity, it must be confessed, popularity, how hollow soever be the ground it stands upon, can never be refused a place among the advantages of a measure. Satisfaction on the part of a people, satisfaction, so long as it subsists, is a real good—so long as it subsists, its title to that appellation is altogether independent of the source from which it flows. If, indeed, the utility of the measure be illusory, then, indeed, when the illusion is dispelled, there is an end of the advantage; but the advantage, so long as it continued, was not the less real. Happily, in the present instance, the advantage is not only *real* but *pure.* Though in the way of affording encouragement to marriage, the proposed measure should in truth be of little service, any farther than as it happened to be thought to be so, the pleasure of seeing it popular on this score may be indulged with the less reserve, as the delusion, if it be one, is not in this instance attended with any pernicious consequences.

---

*In my own estimation, the good that can be done by any encouragements of a *positive* nature given to marriage, shews itself, I must confess, in a very questionable point of view; but the reasons in support of this opinion not being to the present purpose, will be better spared than given. I say *positive;* for as to the negative kind of encouragement that, in the instance where any obstacles of a political nature can be shewn to subsist, may be afforded by the removal of those obstacles, the utility of this species of encouragement stands upon a footing altogether different.

§4. ORIGINALITY

If the proposal relative to this resource be not an *original* one, its want of originality may be seen to afford an objection. If not original it has been *proposed:* and if it has been proposed, it has been *rejected:* for assuredly it has not been adopted any where.

A *tax on successions* might, at first glance, present itself as bearing a resemblance to the resource in question; as being a sort of modification of it, a commencement towards it; as forming, in a manner, a branch of it. But we have already seen how perfectly dissimilar, or rather opposite in effect, the *tax* is to the *regulation,* and how much the difference is to its disadvantage. A tax on successions lies as heavy on the individual, as it falls light into the Exchequer.

Taxes on successions, (not to mention the old Roman tax, the *vicessima hereditatum,* the 5 *per cent.* on collateral successions) exist already in this country; they exist in the form of a stamp duty, in some degree proportional, on probates and letters of administration; they exist in the form of a stamp duty on receipts for legacies and distributive shares. As to the duties on legacies, in what proportion they are *paid* I do not know; but I am sure they are *evaded,* and very frequently evaded. One should be almost sorry if they were *not* evaded; they are evaded in proportion as confidence prevails in families. The whole mass of property goes in the first place, into the hands of individuals; a course which, indeed, it could not but take, so long as the resource is left to stand upon the footing of a tax. The private executor sets out with getting every thing into his hands; the public gets what this most confidential friend of the deceased thinks proper to bestow; of course he will not bestow any thing at the expense of the friend of his testator, so long as he can persuade himself, with any tolerable assurance, that the person he is befriending will not requite his generosity with such a degree of baseness, as to make him pay the legacy over again out of his own pocket.

Another circumstance concurs in diminishing the productive power of a tax upon successions.—When the duty amounts to a sum which appears considerable, the levy being a tax, a tax to be levied on an individual, and levied all at once, it wears so formidable an aspect, that the man of finance himself is startled at it; he accordingly reduces the rate, and the higher the legacy mounts, the more he reduces it; so that all proportionality is destroyed. By this means, the better a man can afford to pay, the less it is he pays, and the tax has the appearance of a conspiracy of the richer against the poorer classes of mankind.—Whence comes this?—only from its being raised by a *tax*, and not by a *regulation*, as above proposed. Under the regulation the public will pay itself; the officer of the public will have the staff in his hands; a partiality as unfriendly to the interests of finance, as it is unseemly in the eyes of justice, will disappear, and wealthy successions will yield in proportion to their opulence.*

§5. PRODUCE

To Mr. ──────

Instead of the matter destined for the present section, I must content myself, for the present, with sending you little more than a blank.—I could not have filled it up, without attempting to lead you into a labyrinth of calculations, which, after all, I could not render complete, for want of *data*, without your assistance, and which, if the *principle* of the measure should not be approved of, would have no claim to notice.

Meantime, as the result of the calculations need not wait for the calculations themselves, and as a supposition of this sort, however imperfectly warranted, may be more satisfactory than a total void, I will beg your indulgence for the following *apperçu*.

Nett annual produce of this resource upwards of £2,000,000 over and above the expense of collection.

EXPENCE OF COLLECTION

Escheators and sub-escheators, at 5 per cent. upon the above produce	£100,000
Judicial establishment for the purpose, at 2½ per cent. which, I apprehend, could not be dispensed with ...	50,000
Total, at 7½ per cent. ...	150,000

It is natural I should be over sanguine; but I must confess, I should expect to find the above sum below the mark rather than

*The freshest and most considerable tax upon legacies and shares in successions (that of 29 Geo. III. chap. 51. ann. 1789) has freed itself so far from this objection; but the duties on probates and letters of administration remain exposed to it; as do the anterior taxes on legacies and shares in successions, imposed by 20 Geo. III. chap. 28. ann. 1780. The reason, in the instance of the duty on probates and letters of administration, seems to be, that in that stage the value of the subject can only be *guessed at;* whereas, in the other cases, it has been *liquidated.*

above it. The calculations, in their present state, point at three millions; but then there are deductions to be made on one hand, as well as additions on the other.*

For my own part, if it depended upon me, I should be very much disposed to turn my back upon calculations; for if the *principle* of the resource be but approved of, £200,000 a year would be as sufficient a warrant for it as £2,000,000 since, whether much or little, it would be all so much clear gain, unfelt by any body in the shape of a loss.

The calculations however, such as they are, can be submitted at any time upon a day or two's notice. They will, at any rate, afford a view of the *data* the subject affords, of the difficulties to be overcome, and of the uncertainties which are not capable of being cleared up without the aid of Parliament.

§6. APPLICATION

A word or two may not be amiss, respecting the application of the produce. In general, this topic may seem foreign enough from the consideration of the supply itself; but that, as we shall see, is not altogether the case here.

In time of full peace, the floating debt provided for, there are but two options with regard to the application of a new supply, reduction of debt, and extinction of taxes: for current service is already provided for by existing funds.

In time of war there are two additional options; pledging for interest of loans, and application to current service.

I will begin with the case of war; for though the measure would be equally fit for establishment at either season, yet war is certainly that which holds out to it the most promising chance for being actually established. *Necessity,* the mother of *invention,* may then be the mother of *adoption* too, which, of the two, is by much the hardest offspring to bring forth.

I should not wish, nor even expect, to see the produce of this resource appropriated to current service: I should not wish, nor even expect, to see it among the mass of pledges given as security for a

---

*The documents resorted to as *data* for calculation, were the instances of *collateral* succession in different degrees, compared with those of *lineal* succession, as indicated by the publications on the peerage. The *data* thus obtained were digested into tables, including Scotch and Irish as well as English and British, existing as well as extinct. Note added Dec. 9, 1795.

loan. The novelty of its complection, the uncertainty of its amount, both seem to preclude it from either destination: it may be prodigious; it may be nothing: there is no saying what it may be *taken* for. Resources more according to the usual model, and, therefore, regarded as more certain, *taxes,* in a word, would be the supplies, naturally destined to such service.

There remain *discharge* of debt and *extinction of taxes.* Between these two employments, I would wish to see it divided, and, perhaps, pretty equally divided.

There is one portion that could not well be refused to the discharge of public debt; even in war time; even under the pressure of any exigency: I mean the portion which exists already in that shape; where the property consists of a debt due from Government to be discharged by an annuity till paid off: in a word, property in Government annuities, or (as it is commonly termed, to the great confusion of ideas) *money in the funds.* The extinction of so much of the debt is here so natural a result that it may be set down as an unavoidable one:—to keep the debt alive, and sell it for the benefit of Government; just as (if it had fallen into individual hands, it might have been sold for the benefit of individuals) will surely not be thought of.*

*Remit taxes? and that in war time?—that would be an extraordinary employment for it indeed!—*Extraordinary indeed: but not on that account the less eligible: Novel blessings shine but the brighter for being new.

An opportunity would by this incident be presented, and, perhaps, this is the only incident by which such an opportunity could be presented, of shaking off the yoke of some of the most oppressive taxes. The whole list would then be to be over-hauled, and the worst chosen picked out and expunged.†

Those which to my conception would stand at the head of the list, are, as I have said already, the taxes upon justice. In relation to

---

*This part, as far as the calculation above given is to be depended upon, may be reckoned at about   th of the year's produce; at about £   [*sic*].

†*Fresh* taxes have, in many instances, been repealed, upon fresh experience of their ineligibility or unpopularity: examples of the repeal of an *old-established* tax are rare, indeed. That of the *tax on coals borne coastwise* is an instance as honourable to those with whom the repeal originated as it is rare. As to the taxes not *taken off,* but *reduced,* on the institution of the Commutation Tax, the reduction was made, not because they were *ill-chosen,* for they were nothing less than ill-chosen, but because they had been strained so high as to become *unproductive :* it was made not for *relief,* but for *revenue.*

these, I can speak with confidence, having sifted them to the bottom, and demonstrated them, or I know not what demonstration is, to be the worst of all taxes, actual or possible.

Further from the precise limits of the subject I will not attempt to stray; unless it be for a fantastic moment in the way of reverie. Pure as we have found the resource to be from *hardship,* and in all human probability from *odium,* how pregnant, may we *imagine* it at least to be, of *relief!* No law taxes:—no prohibition of justice. No tax on medical drugs:—no prohibition of relief from sickness, and from death. No window tax:—no prohibition of air, light, health and cheerfulness. No soap tax:—no prohibition of cleanliness. No salt tax:—no prohibition of the only sustenance of a famished people.* Make the most of this resource, and, if not all these reliefs, at least the most essential of them, might perhaps be afforded, even under the pressure of the war. To do all this, and government never the poorer! To do all this, and have a rich surplus for the sinking fund!—What a feast for humanity! What a harvest of popularity! What a rich reward for wisdom and virtue in a minister!

It is scarce necessary to observe, that neither in any of *those* ways, nor in any other, should specific relief be engaged for, till the means of relief are actually in hand. The produce should be taken for nothing, till it is actually in the Exchequer. When a year of probation is elapsed, the amount will, for any reason that can be alledged to the contrary, be as uniform as that of the steadiest tax.

§7. HEADS OF OBJECTION

WITH

ANSWERS†

OBJECTION I.

Supposed tendency to promote dissipation of the national wealth, by leading men to live upon their capitals, or sell them for annuities *for* their own lives, in consequence of their being restrained from benefiting those that are dear to them after their death.

ANSWER

No such tendency—for

1. A man *will not* bar those that are *dear* to him, from receiving

---

*Fish to the Highlanders of Scotland.

†To Mr. ———. This is but an Index. The Objections and Answers are given at large in the body of the paper.

any part, only because there is *some* part that he *can not* enable them to receive.

2.—Nor *himself,* from disposing in that manner of *any* part, only because there is *some* part that he can *not* so dispose of.

3. The power of benefiting others after death, is not the sole motive to accumulation: another, and a still stronger and more universal one, is the faculty of increasing a man's fund of personal enjoyment during life: a faculty which would be at a stand, if he parted with his capital for an annuity.

4. Such dissipation, were it really to be, in here and there an instance, the result of the measure would only be a *diminution,* and that a most trifling one, from the *benefit* of it, not any *objection* to the *principle* of it.

OBJECTION II.

BREACH of faith, in the instance of property in the funds.

ANSWER

Not unless *confined* to that species of property, which is not proposed—

No more than the *existing* taxes on *distributive shares* and *legacies:* which, in as far as there is nothing else to pay them, must come out of any property a man had in the funds—

No more than any tax on consumption; which must fall upon *stockholders* in common with other people; since, in as far as a man's own income arises out of the funds, every tax he pays, is paid out of what he has in the funds.

Property is not in this way the *more* affected for being in the funds; since in any other shape, it would be equally reached by the proposed regulation.

OBJECTION III.

BREACH of faith, in the instance of foreign stockholders resident abroad, who would not have been affected by the taxes in lieu of which this would come.

ANSWER

NONE: for they may sell out.

REPLY

The sort of obligation they will thereby be laid under to sell out, is still a hardship: the more, as their submitting to it will lower the price—

YES; were many likely to sell out on this account, but that is not the case—

1. Because much of such stock is in the hands of *bodies corporate*—

2.—Among individuals, it is but a small proportion that will be destitute of relations *within the pale.*

3.—Fewer still, who would take to heart to such a degree a restriction from which a man's near relations stand exempted.

4. Feeling it to be in his power to sell out at *any* time, a man would neither sell out at *first,* nor *afterwards.*

OBJECTION IV.

IT is pro tanto *very much exposed at least to evasion.*

ANSWER

1. To none but what may be pretty effectually guarded against by proper *registers,* &c.

2. If it could not, the objection applies—not to the *principle* of the measure, but only to the *quantum* of advantage.

3. It removes *pro tanto* the objection of *breach* of *faith;* so far as a man *evades,* so far he is not *hurt.*

OBJECTION V.

TENDENCY to sink the price of land, by glutting the market with it.

ANSWER

I. No reason for supposing it will tend to *sink* the price in one way, more than it will to *raise* it in another—For

1. Income arising out of *land,* being more generally eligible, will always fetch more than equal income arising out of the *funds:* still more, than income depending upon mere *personal* security—

2. Nothing therefore can sink the price of land, without sinking that and the price of stocks together; nor without sinking the price of stocks more than the price of land: nor raise the price of stocks, without raising the price of land.

3. It will tend to *raise* the price of stocks at any rate, as to that part of the property it attaches upon, which it finds *already* in the shape of stock, and which it will of course extinguish and take out

of the market.—As also in respect of whatever other part is applied to the extinction of the public debt.

Admitted, that a depreciation in the price of property in land, in comparison of that of property in the funds, might take place, if land were as yet at a monopoly price, as Adam Smith seems to think it is. B.3. C.4.

But this does not seem to be the case; since a man can make three *per cent.* by laying out his money in land, when he can make but three and a half *per cent.* by laying it out in the funds; which is no more than an adequate difference, for the difference, in point of general eligibility, between the two sources of income.

II. A fall in the price of land is considered not as an ineligible, but as an eligible event, by Adam Smith (B.3, C.4) though not by me, who referring every thing to the feelings of individuals, regard the sensation of loss thus produced, as an evil outweighing every possible advantage.

OBJECTION VI.

MONEY, thus obtained, will be COLLECTED *at greater* EXPENSE *than if obtained from taxes.*

ANSWER

1. No particular reason for thinking so—

2. Were this clear, it would afford no objection; because none of the *hardship* would be produced here, which is the result of expense when defrayed by taxes.

OBJECTION VII.

INCREASE of the INFLUENCE *of the* CROWN, by the new *places* that would be necessary.

ANSWER

1. Not more from *this* mode of supply, than from any other of equal magnitude.

2. Were the objection any thing determinate, the weight of it would bear—not against a *useful* establishment like this, but against *useless* or *less useful* places.

3. The objection, if it were worth while, might be got rid of in part by giving the appointment of *Escheators* to the *Freeholders*, who now have the appointment of *Coroners*.

OBJECTION VIII.

THE POWERS *that must be given for the purpose of* COLLECTION, *would be* ABUSED.

ANSWER

1. This mode of supply is not more open to abuse of power, to the *prejudice* of the individual, than any other.

2. Abuse of power by undue *indulgence* to the individual, to the prejudice of the revenue, goes only to the *quantum* of the advantage, and forms therefore no objection to the *principle* of the measure: and as to the individual, so far as he is *indulged*, duly or unduly, he is not *hurt*.

3. Abuses of both kinds may be more effectually checked in this instance than in others, viz. by the publicity that, even for other purposes, would require to be given to the proceedings.

The remark, though bad as an *objection*, is good as a *warning*, and as such would be attended to.

OBJECTION IX.

BY the facility it would give to the business of supply, it would be an encouragement to PROFUSION *on the part of government.*

ANSWER

If this were an objection, the most burthensome mode of supply would be the best—

Rendering supply more burthensome than it might be, is a remedy worse than the disease; or rather an aggravation of the disease, to the exclusion of the remedy.

The following are the suppositions which the objection must take for granted—1. that all expenditure is unnecessary; 2. that this mode of supply would be submitted to; 3. that no other would.

It would be a strange inconsistency, if those who could not be brought to adopt other modes of checking profusion, could, in the mere view of checking profusion, be brought to reject this mode of supply.

OBJECTION X.

IT would make a REVOLUTION *in property.*

ANSWER

The tendency of this objection, the force of which consists altogether in the abuse of a word, is to point to a wrong object [—] the just horror conceived against the *French* Revolution. The characteristic of *that* revolution is to trample in every possible way upon the feelings of individuals. The characteristic of *this* measure, is to shew more tenderness to those feelings, than *can* be shewn by the taxes to which it is proposed to substitute it.

OBJECTION XI.

THE property of the nation would thus be SWALLOWED *up in the Exchequer.*

ANSWER

No more than by taxes to the same amount.

OBJECTION XII.

IT would be a SUBVERSION *of the ancient law of inheritance in this country.*

ANSWER

A *quiet* alteration, made by a mere *extension* given to the *old* law, to a branch more ancient than almost any of those at the expense of which it is extended. No *subversion,* except in as far as every *amendment* is a *subversion.*

OBJECTION XIII.

IT would be an INNOVATION.

ANSWER

No more than every *new* law; nor, as we have seen, so *much* as most new laws—No more than a set of taxes to the same amount— Not so much—for all the revenue laws we have, are *innovations* in comparison of the law of *Escheat.*

§8. EXISTING LAW

Can any thing of *harshness* be imputed to the proposed measure? Not when viewed by itself, we have seen already. View it, then, in comparison; turn to existing law. No exclusion of the father *here* as *there*, on pretence of the *ponderosity* of inheritances: no exclusion of the half-blood, as if the son of my father or my mother were a stranger to me: no exclusion of all children but the first-born; as if the first-born only lived upon food, and all others upon air: no exclusion of the better half of the species, as if the tender sex had no need of sustenance. The feelings of

U

individuals, sole elements of public happiness, these, and these only, are the considerations that have *here* been exclusively consulted, and their suggestions undeviatingly adhered to; human feelings, the only true standards of right and wrong in the business of legislation, not lawyers quibbles, nor reasons of other times, that have vanished with the times.

Pursue the comparison yet farther; one the one hand no harshness at all, as we have seen; on the other, a harshness which is incurable. The proposed law, taking nature for its guide, leads expectation by a silken string. The existing law, pursuing the ghosts of departed reasons, thwarts expectation at every step, and can never cease to do so. It does so, because it is in the *speechless* shape of *common* law; and it would do so still, even though *words* were given to it, and it were converted into statute law. Reasons rooted in utility, are so many anchors by which a law fastens itself into the memory; lawyers quibbles are a rope of sand, which neither has tenacity of its own, nor can give stability to any thing else. Rules and quibbles together, the impression they make upon the mind, is that of the wind upon the waves; and when incidents spring up to call them into action, the sensation produced is the sensation of a thunderstroke.

§9. ANTIENT LAW

Shall we dig into antiquity? The result will be still more favourable. Reckoning from the subversion of the Roman empire, property, considered as surviving to the proprietor, is comparatively of modern date. Under the feudal system, in the morning of its days, estates greater than life-estates were unknown: the most fixed of all possessions fell back into the common stock upon the death of the possessor; and before the reign of the Conqueror was at an end, the feudal tree, transplanted from the continent into this our island, had covered almost the whole surface of the kingdom with its gloomy shade. This venerable system had, indeed, before that period, lost a good deal of its vigour, which is the same thing as to say its rigour, and the principle of succession had taken root under it, but not without being loaded with conditions, and weakened by defalcations and distortions, over and above those which have been already glanced at, and which we are plagued with to this day. The relaxation too was an innovation, which, in the vocabulary of antiquarian idolatry, as well as of indiscriminating timidity, means a corruption, of the primæval state of things.

At a much later period, moveable property took, if not exactly the same course with immoveable, a course more opposite to that indicated by utility, and equally repugnant to that which seems prescribed by nature. The more substantial part, the immoveable, had been reserved for the maw of feudal anarchy: the lighter part, the moveable, was carried off by some holy personage for *pious uses;* and of all uses the most pious was his own. Moveable and immoveable together, power without mercy, or imposture without shame, took the whole under their charge; the claims of the widow and the orphan were as little regarded as those of the most distant relative. So late even as the latter part of the reign of Edw. III.* it required an exertion of parliamentary power, to make the man of God disgorge, in favour of the fatherless and the widow.†

The right of bequest, the right of governing property by one who is no longer in existence to enjoy it, is an innovation still more modern. In its relation to moveables, it was conquered from the spiritual power by gradual and undefinable encroachments: the validity of its exercise having, from the conquest to the present time, depended on the decision of that same power, which, till the above-mentioned statute of Edw. III. was interested in denying it: and, after the right was secured, the facility of its exercise must, for a long time, have been confined within narrow bounds, by the scarcity of literary acquirements. In its relation to immoveables, it was not placed on solid ground, till the statute of Henry VIII. and then only by implication: nor (to take the matter in the words of Blackstone) was it "till even after the restoration, that the power of devising real property became so universal as at present."‡

All this while the law of Escheat, coæval with the reign of the Conqueror, dwelt upon as a subject of importance in the reign of Henry the Second,§ touched upon by a numerous series of statutes,

---

*31 Edw. III. p. 1. ch. 11. 9 co. 40. in Burn's Eccl. Law, iv. 197.

†Hume has fallen into a mistake on this subject, in supposing, that in the reign of Henry II. moveables were the prey not of the spiritual power but the temporal. "It appears," (says he [in his "History of England"] vol. i. ann. 1100) "from Glanville, the famous justiciary of Henry II. that in his time, where any man died intestate, an accident which must have been frequent when the art of writing was so little known, the king, or the lord of the fief, pretended to seise all the moveables, and to exclude every heir, even the children of the deceased; a sure mark of a tyrannical and arbitrary government." So far Hume, referring to Glanville, l. vi[i.], c. 16. But what Hume understands of intestates in general, Glanville confines to bastards.

‡II. Comm. ch. 1.

§Glanville, l. vii. c. 17.

reaching down as low as Edward the Sixth, recognised by decisions of so recent a period as the late reign;* exists in indisputable vigour; although the facility of tracing out heirs in these times of universal and instantaneous communication, added to the want of an administrative establishment adapted to the collection of such a branch of revenue, prevent it from being noticed, in its present state, in the account-book of finance.

§10. Blackstone

Is *opinion* worth resorting to? A poor warrant, after the *fiat* of utility, written in characters so legible. In morals, in politics, in legislation, the *table of human feelings,* is, I must confess, to me what the Alcoran was to the good Mussulman: opinions, if unconformable to it, are false; if conformable, useless. Not so to many a worthy mind: for their satisfaction then, even this muddy source of argument shall not remain unexplored. Shall Blackstone then be our oracle? Blackstone, the most revered of oracles though the latest?— From him we have full licence: from him we have a latitude, outstretching, and that even to extravagance, the utmost extent which either humanity or policy would permit us to assume. But let us hear him in his own words.

Blackst. Comm. II. 12. "Wills, therefore" (says he) "and testaments, rights of inheritance and successions, are all of them creatures of the civil or municipal laws, and accordingly are in all respects regulated by them; every distinct country having different ceremonies and requisites to make a testament completely valid: neither does any thing vary more than the right of inheritance under different national establishments. In England particularly, this diversity is carried to such a length, *as if it had been meant to point out the power of the laws in regulating the succession to property, and how futile every claim must be that has not its foundation in the positive rules of the state.* In personal estates the father may succeed to his children; in landed property he can never be their immediate heir, by any the remotest possibility; in general only the eldest son, in some places only the youngest, in others all the sons together, have a right to succeed to the inheritance: in real estates males are preferred to females, and the eldest male will usually exclude the rest: in the division of personal

---

*Atkyns' Reports.

estates, the females of equal degree are admitted together with the males, and no right of primogeniture is allowed."

Thus far our Apollo.—Legatees, we see, are nothing to him: he sacrifices parents to us, and even children: he sees not that children are not only *expectants,* but *co-occupants.* No sympathy for disappointed expectation; no feeling for beggared opulence; no regard for meritorious service; no compassion for repulsive infirmity, obliged to forego assistance, or to borrow it of selfish hope. The law, his idol, has no bowels; why should we? The rights of legatees, the rights of children, are mere creatures of the law: as if the rights of occupants were any thing more. Of wills or even succession, he knows no use, but to prevent a scramble. The business of succession is a theatre which the laws of nations have pitched upon, as it were in concert, for the exhibition of caprice: none with greater felicity than the law of England:—she has her views in this, and they are always wise ones:—to insult the subject, to shew him what arbitrary power is, and to teach him to respect it.

"This one consideration" (continues he) "may help to remove the scruples of many *well-meaning* persons, who set up a *mistaken* conscience in opposition to the rules of law. If a man *disinherits his son,* by a will duly executed, and leaves his estate to a stranger, there are many who consider this proceeding as *contrary to natural justice:* while others so scrupulously adhere to the supposed intention of the dead, that if a will of lands be attested by only *two* witnesses instead of *three,* which the law requires, they are apt to imagine that the heir is bound in conscience to relinquish his title to the devisee. But both of them *certainly proceed upon very erroneous principles:* as if, on the one hand, the son had by *nature* a right to succeed to his father's lands; or as if, on the other hand, the owner was by nature intitled to direct the succession of his property after his decease. Whereas, the *law of nature* suggests, that on the death of the possessor the estate should again become common, and be open to the next occupant, unless otherwise ordered for the sake of civil peace by the positive law of society.

"The right of inheritance," (says he but two pages before) "or descent to the children and relations of the deceased, seems to have been allowed much earlier than the right of devising by testament. We are apt to conceive at first view that it has *nature* on its side*: yet we often *mistake* for *nature* what we find estab-

---

*Quere, What is *"nature"*?

lished by long and inveterate *custom*.* It is certainly a *wise and effectual*, but clearly a *political establishment*;† since the *permanent* right of property,‡ vested in the ancestor himself, was no *natural*, but merely a *civil right*."§

What we learn from all this is, that so long as a man can find a pretence for getting rid of the phrase *contrary to natural "justice"*, there is no harm in his children's being left by him to starve: and that those who would make a *"conscience"* of leaving their children thus to starve, are *"well-meaning"*, but *"mistaken"* people. Quere, who is this same Queen *"Nature"*, who makes such stuff under the name of laws? Quere, in what year of her own, or any body else's reign, did she make it, and in what shop is a copy of it to be bought, that it may be burnt by the hands of the common hangman, and her Majesty well disciplined at the cart's tail?

It being supposed, in point of *fact*, that the children have or have not a right, of the sort in question, given them by the *law*, the only rational question remaining is, whether, in point of *utility*, such a right *ought* to be given them or not?—To talk of a *Law of Nature*, giving them, or not giving them a *natural right*, is so much sheer nonsense, answering neither the one question nor the other.

---

*Quere, The difference between *"nature"* here and *"custom"*?

†Quere, What *"establishments"* there are in the world, besides *"political"* ones? Quere, What signifies whether a *"political establishment"* be a *"natural"* one or no, so long as it is *"a wise and effectual"* one?

‡If an *"impermanent"* right is a *"natural"* one, quere, at what o'clock does it cease to be so?—If it is *natural* a right of property should *commence*, how comes it to be *unnatural* it should *continue*?

§Quere, What signifies whether it was a *"natural right"* or no? Quere, What sort of a thing is a *"natural right"*, and where does the *maker* live, particularly in *Atheist's town*, where they are most rife?

[CALCULATION OF THE PRODUCE]

To what annual sum may the produce of such a mode of supply be expected to amount? This in the case of a tax would be a very material question, and such an one as he who should take upon him to propose the tax, might well be called upon to give an answer: and that not only because upon the amount of the produce would depend the eligibility of the tax, but because it would be hard to find a subject of taxation, which would not afford some *data* from whence a calculation to such a purpose might not with more or less accuracy be made.

In the present instance both grounds fail; neither of these reasons for expecting an answer to such a question hold good. By the probable amount of such a resource the eligibility of it is not at all affected: and this amount of it is scarcely within the reach of calculation or conjecture. The greater it proves, the better: but be it ever so inconsiderable, it is good as far as it goes, for it is all clear gain.

Such grounds for conjecture however as the nature of the case presents to us, it may be a sort of satisfaction to see brought to view, since whatever light they may afford, however faint, may appear preferable to total darkness.*

I. Basis of the calculation—estimate of the total value of the property of the United Kingdom existing at a time.

Rental of land [£]25,000,000: multiply by 28½ years purchase, being the mean between 25, the war price, and 32, the peace price £712,500,000

Rental of houses [£]5,000,000: multiply, say, by 16 years purchase   ...   .   [£]80,000,000

Money out on mortgage, not to be taken into account: since in so far as it exists, in so far is the value of the property in mortgage decreased by it.

Property in the funds—say equivalent to 3 per Cents, to the amount of   ...   .   [£]300,000,000

---

*For Mr. Long. In the present stage of the enquiry it has been impossible for me to produce any thing that would be ripe for the public eye or even for private circulation. Time has been wanting: *data* have been wanting: some absolutely unattainable in the existing state of things: others not attainable but by the assistance of government. All I have been able to do as yet is to throw together a few loose hints respecting the course to be taken for framing a calculation of the produce.

N.B. This is to be taken into the account: since though the total value of the property in the nation is not augmented by it, the receipts on the account of escheat will be augmented as much as by property to equal value in any other form: the loan [?] here being not (as in the case of mortgage) on any specific portion of property actually in existence, but on portions of property not yet brought into existence, the produce of future years as yet to come.

England. Farming stock according to a calculation of Mr. A. Young £4 an acre	[£]184,000,000
Annual produce of manufactures according partly to calculation and partly to conjectures of Mr. A. Young (North. Tour IV. 390) £27,000,000—capital, on a supposition of 10 per Cent. profit	[£]270,000,000
Annual profits of commerce according to a conjecture of Mr. Young £10,000,000—capital at 10 per Cent.	[£]100,000,000
Household furniture of farmers according to the calculation of Mr. A. Young, over and above farming stock (North. Tour IV. 345)	[£]11,200,000
Furniture of houses in the occupation of persons of other descriptions	[£]30,000,000[1]
Scotland. Farming stock[1]	[£]39,000,000[1]
Do other articles as above[1]	[£]100,000,000[1]

[To this sum, the value of the following items would still have to be added:][2] timber; plate; jewels; carriages for pleasure, and other carriages not included in farming stock; horses not included in farming stock; liquors in the possession of individuals not comprized in the foregoing accounts; apparel, trinkets, paintings, books, curiosities natural and artificial, and other miscellaneous articles, in the possession of individuals, as above; money lent upon West-India

---

[1][Filled in at a later date.]

[2][For these items which appear in Bentham's list, no concrete estimates are given in the draft. Yet he obviously considered that their value, taken in the lump, was approximately £173,300,000—the figure inserted in the text—since he based his final calculation on an assumed total of £2,000,000,000.]

mortgages; debts due from foreigners resident abroad, and from the countries co-ordinate with, and those subordinate to, Great Britain; coin over and above what is included in the amount of the capital of husbandry, manufactures, and commerce; paper money over and above what is included as above: this though in itself of no intrinsic value, being nothing more than a pledge for the future possession of a certain portion of the precious metals or other articles of intrinsic value, will however, in as far as it continues to obtain currency, be as valuable, in as far as it falls in by escheat, as coin to the same amount. [All these articles together may roughly be estimated at ... £173,300,000

so that there results a final sum-total of ... ... £2,000,000,000]
The fundamental element of the calculation all this while is the value of the property of all kinds in Great Britain: and for the amount of this value as here assumed no reason, it must be confessed, has here been given. On the other hand, the supposition is grounded on the calculation of a writer of very high repute, Mr. Arthur Young, Secretary to the Board of Agriculture: and if not an exact one, at any rate it can not be charged with being otherwise than an impartial one: on which account it is so much the fitter for the present purpose, from not having been made with any view to the present purpose.

II. Basis of the calculation—population of the United Kingdoms: according to Mr. A. Young 11,000,000
III. Basis of the calculation—proportion of annual deaths in the United Kingdoms to the total of the population.
According to an average of 16 places in France as collected by Mr. A. Young [1 in] 28½: but as these were towns where live [sic] is not so long as in country places, say, in round numbers, 1 in 30.
On this supposition—annual number of deaths in Great Britain 366,666
IV. Basis of the calculation — proportion of persons leaving no relations within the pale to persons having such relations.
Three collections of *data* present themselves which are particularly apposite to the case in hand, and they are of such a nature as promises to add to the certainty of the calculation, while they diminish the

trouble of it. These are 1. the List of Peerages as well extinct as existing: 2. the List of Baronetcies extinct and existing: 3. the admission-rolls of populous manors.

1. Amongst the peerages the few which are descendible to females are those from which the most apposite information is to be obtained. Take the number of the successions of all of them together: divide it into two lists: one containing the instances where the relationship of the successor to his immediate predecessor was within what I have termed the pale: the other containing the instances where the relationship in question was without that mark.

Among documents already public and generally accessible, the List of Peerages descendible in the only mode, in which for some centuries they have been made descendible, viz. to male issue exclusively, may be mentioned in the next place. But as honours so limited are at every step in the order of succession, and that as well in the ascending as in the descending line, exposed to an even chance of failure, from which peerages descendible to females, as well as estates subjected to the regulation here proposed, stand exempted, this source of calculation could not be employed without engaging in such a course of calculation as could not be gone through without a considerable deal of labour, nor exhibited without employing a good deal of paper which for the [sake][1] of those who are to judge, one would wish to save.

These calculations might indeed be saved in each instance where, the honour descending to a relation without the pale, the state of the family stands recorded in any of the publications extant with sufficient minuteness to shew whether there was a failure of all nearer relations of the female sex, as well as of the male.

2.[2] The case of baronetages stands in point of appositeness upon the same footing as that of peerages limited to males: if in other points there be any difference, it will be in respect of the copiousness and accuracy of information, in which articles the inferior species of honour is in proportion to the inferiority of its importance liable to fall short of the superior honour of peerage.

An observation that applies in some measure to both honours, but with particular force to that of the peerage, is that the standard of calculation which they afford is liable, for a reason that will immediately be pointed out, to represent the produce of the mode of supply

---

[1][The MS reads "case".]
[2][The MS reads "3".]

in question less than the truth. Among persons of inferior condition, the difficulty of providing for the encreased expences attendant on the marriage state operates as a powerful restraint to marriage: from this obstacle the elevated situation above mentioned is altogether free. Among persons of ordinary condition marriage, where it is not utterly foregone to the last, is in most instances deferred at least for many years after the time at which nature invites to it. A peer, and the heir apparent to a peer, rich or poor (though where he is poor, it is only in comparison of other peers) is no sooner a man than he is upon the look out for a partner of his honours and his bed. If rich, he can not be too speedy in doing what depends upon him towards the continuance of his titles and his opulence: if poor, he must avail himself of the power which his condition affords him of conquering opulence by marriage: so that in this respect penury, which to an ordinary man [is a powerful restraint], acts in the instance of this elevated rank as an additional incentive.

3.[1] The admission-rolls of manors present a prospect of a body of evidence that would stand pretty clear of the objection above mentioned. Passing over such admissions as are the result of purchase would exhibit an order of succession quadrating with the purpose in question as exactly as the List of Peerages of the class first mentioned. But in the first place, no such admission roll is any where in print in any instance that I ever heard of: in the next place, it may be a matter of some uncertainty whether the degree of relationship between the successor and the predecessor will in every instance be found to be stated with a degree of precision sufficient for the present purpose.*

The fundamental element of the calculation will be the total value of the property of every kind, moveable and immoveable, existing in the United Kingdom: debts due from individual to individual,

---

[1] [The MS reads "4".]

*Some few causes of aberration from the line of exact similarity would be occasioned in this instance by the anomalities [sic] of the law. From the succession of an uncle to his deceased nephew it might be inferred at first sight that [the] father of this nephew was already dead: the inference, if taken for an universal one, would be false; since if the nephew were the purchaser, the estate would go on his death to the uncle, passing by the father: if however he took by descent in the paternal line, the certainty of the inference would be unimpeachable: since in this case the estate could never have come to him, had his father been then alive. How the case stood in those respects would probably be apparent on the face of the rolls. The exclusion of the half blood affords another instance. But the discussion of all these [a]nomalities, and of the allowances to be made for them, would take up a quantity of room which the reader would look upon as ill bestowed.

as well as the debt due from the public to individuals, of course excluded. This, according to Mr. Arthur Young's estimate [outlined above] amounts to £2,000,000,000

The number of deaths is computed in round numbers to amount, town and country taken together, to about 1/30 of the number of inhabitants existing at the same time. By dividing accordingly the above sum of £2,000,000,000 by 30, this gives for the value of all property left vacant by death in every year £66,666,666

From this £66,666,666, for the sake of making even money, deduct (though it be too much) for the value of the property in mortmain, which is only real property, a sum of which the 30th part shall be [£]166,666

Remains	£66,500,000

Deduct for the amount of the property of those not having what is called *bona notabilia*, that is property to such amount as to pay for the trouble and expence of collecting in ... ... [£]500,000*

Remains clear	[£]66,000,000

Among the individuals dying in a year, as the number of those who respectively left a relation within the pale is to the number of those who did not have any such relation, so is the above sum of £66,000,000 to the sum sought, the sum which the proposed measure might be expected annually to produce.

What then in the compass of a year shall be the number of individuals expected to die *relationless quoad hoc*?

---

*The above allowance of £500,000 might at first sight appear too small, but the following calculation will, I imagine, shew it to be quite sufficient:

Total number of inhabitants in Great Britain, say	10,000,000
Number dying in a year (1/30) amounts to	333,333
Number of the above not possessing *bona notabilia* at the time of their death 9/10	300,000
Amount of *bona notabilia* (though a less sum might be collected in to advantage upon the plan proposed) call	£5
Average amount of the property of those whose property does not amount to the above £5, though as the greatest part of them will be infants possessing no property at all, the allowance is considerably too great ...	£2
£2 × 300,000 makes for the whole amount of the property of persons dying in a year who did not possess *bona notabilia*	£600,000
Say, as the allowance was too great, and to make even money	£500,000

If 1 in 20, this will make the annual amount of
this resource ... ... [£]3,300,000
If 1 in 30 ... ... [£]2,200,000
If 1 in 40 ... ... [£]1,650,000
If 1 in 50 ... ... [£]1,220,000
If 1 in 60 ... ... [£]1,100,000

Of the above guesses, which is it that comes nearest to the truth?
A problem this, the investigation [of which] from the stock of statistical *data* ordinarily resorted to would, I should conceive, not be
altogether impracticable: though the process, I should apprehend, is
such as could not be carried [out] without a good deal of trouble.

From the but [insufficient] view I have been able as yet to obtain
of the subject, I should not expect to find the amount of this resource
so much as 3 millions a year, nor so little as 2 millions.*

---

*This view, though it has cost me several weeks to take it, is still very imperfect,
owing partly to the want of *data*, partly to the want of sufficient time to perfect the
employment of such *data* as are within my reach, partly to want of mathematical
science, and of practise in arithmetical operations.

Among the *data* in question there are several items that could not be obtained
without the aid of government. It would be for administration to determine to what
degree of nicety they would wish the calculations to be carried. If the forming any
thing like a correct estimate were an object, I would beg leave to assign over this
part of the business to abler hands. Mr. Pitt could be at no loss for persons eminently
qualified for the task. Mr. *Atwood* in particular occurrs to me in this view: or I should
have little doubt of being able to obtain the assistance of Mr. *Baron Maseres*. In
this case all the use I could hope to be of in this part of the business would be the
conferring with those gentlemen about the choice of the elements to be made use
of in the calculations.

[OBJECTIONS ANSWERED]

[*Objection I. The measure would disrupt the present system of property and legislation.*]

We come now to the head of objections. If the objections are frivolous, it is no fault of mine. They are the strongest I can find. Others, could they have been found, would not have been dissembled. It would have been to no purpose. I confine myself here to radical ones: objections applying to the principle. Objections that apply to the principle on no other supposition than that of its being in such or such a way ill applied, have no place here. Many a remark which might be of excellent use as a caution, is made a bad use of, by being swelled by spleen and prepossession into an objection.

I will begin with the emptiest, as they are those which are but too apt to have most weight. A variety of objections might be urged, all of the same stamp, if variety of language without any distinct meaning were the same thing with variety of objection. That it would make a revolution in property—that it would make the Exchequer a great gulph, by which the whole property of the Kingdom would sooner or later be swallowed up—that it would operate the subversion of the antient Common Law of this country in matter of inheritance —that it would introduce an innovation immeasurable in its extent, and unfathomable in its consequences. All this might be dished up into as great a variety of shapes as there could be found expressions for the alarms and apprehensions which a man might have conceived of himself, or wished to infuse into others.

A revolution in property! it is an idea big with horror, a horror which can not be felt in a stronger degree by any man than it is by me—Why? because, according to the exemplification we are so unhappily and perpetually called upon to make of it, it involves the idea of possessions disturbed, of expectations thwarted: of estates forcibly ravished from the living owners, of opulence reduced to beggary, of the fruits of industry made the prey of rapacity and dissipation—of the levelling of all distinctions, of the confusion of all order and the destruction of all security. Such are the ideas which the words revolution in property are calculated to excite. But with these deplorable effects what have the fruits of the proposed institution in common? What resemblance is born[e] in any instance by the effects of the gradual and unfelt institution here proposed? From a tax to the same amount they would not be apprehended: but from any tax to the same amount they would inevitably be felt in a more or less considerable degree, while from the proposed institution no such effects would be felt at all.

The property of individuals swallowed up by the Exchequer! Yes, so much money exactly as those who should object to this mode of supply would themselves propose to see swallowed up by taxes: for being destined to be applied either to the current service of the year, or towards the payment of the interest of the national debt or towards the extinction of the principal, it will have the very destination and no other [as] the same quantity of property, neither more nor less, were [it] to be raised by taxes.

The antient law of this country subverted in one of its most sacred points, the matter of inheritance! Yes, subvert that the measure would do, it must be confessed, just so far as it alters: it would make one alteration more in that which is in a state as different from what it was in at its origin, as it is from that of any other country that can be named. The law of inheritances has some features in it for which it is valued and justly valued, others for which nobody ever thought of valuing it: some for which it is valued, others in respect of which it is endured, partly from habit, partly from that general ignorance which is the necessary result of the immensity of the mass of which it forms a part, partly from the consciousness men have of being able to defeat it, that is, each man in his own instance to subvert it, by means of the powers which it allows of. What does the measure here proposed? It removes or rather prevents, as far as it goes, those hardships and disappointments of which the law as it stands at present is the perpetual and incorrigible source. It preserves the law unimpaired in respect of every disposition for which it has ever been valued: it alters it in respect of those alone in respect of which it is regarded as indefensible even by the most determined of its admirers and defenders: I say regarded as indefensible: for it is one thing to account for the existence of a law, as Blackstone has for the existence of this part of the law in the cases where needless and fruitless hardship is the perpetual result of it, [and] it is another thing to do what neither Blackstone nor anybody else has attempted to do by it in the instances in question—to defend it.

An innovation? Yes, that it would [be], it must also be confessed. An innovation it would be, for every new law is an innovation. Unhappily so would a tax to the same amount, the tax in the place of which it stands, be also an innovation: for though the practice of taxation taken in the lump has certainly long ago ceased to be an innovation, yet any particular tax is, whenever it falls upon us, an innovation, and that of the most unpleasant kind. An innovation, did I say, in speaking of the mode of supply which it would replace? I should have said a swarm of innovations: for most assuredly it is not by one tax only, but by a multitude of taxes and nothing less, that the occasion for resorting to this new mode of supply could be superseded. Setting innovation then against innovation, which is worst, that from which men suffer much, or that from which they would suffer nothing?

The law of inheritances, it may [still] be said, is a sacred branch of the law: and ought not to be lightly innovated upon, especially in a parenthesis as it were, on the occasion of a measure of finance.

The answer [to this argument] is that with respect to the bulk of the people there would be no innovation in the case. To them the regulation would not present itself in the character of a new one. To them the existing state of the law in these particulars is and ever has been thoroughly unknown: the general prejudices they have imbibed in its favour guard them against all suspicion of the existence of dispositions equally repugnant to untutored feelings and to enlightened reason. Let it present itself to their conception when it will, it presents itself in the garb of novelty: it gives a shock to expectation. It can never present itself to the conception of any rational being without exciting a sentiment of surprize and indignation, which nothing but bigotry and confirmed prejudice can suppress. It is by the existing law then that things are kept out of their natural and expected course*: they are restored to it by the

---

*It is no longer ago than the reign of James 2d that the last hand was put to the law of succession with regard to what is called *personalty*: a denomination which, if confined to the natural class of immoveables, would involve the greatest part of the whole property of the kingdom: and which, when unnaturally extended as it is to estates for years in immoveables, involves again perhaps the greatest part of the remainder. It was so lately as little more than a hundred years ago that I know not what lawyer put the last hand that has been put to this important branch of law: and a bungling job he made of it: no reasons given, no consistency, no precision: though even this is excellence when compared to the wretched patchwork, part feudal part modern, by which the destination of what is called *real property* is determined. Thus it is in comparison of the whole period of the existence of the Common Law that the present state of the most important part of the law of succession is no more than an innovation: and shall it be said that the subjects of George 3d have less experience, less intelligence, less comprehension of their own interests, less knowledge of what is good for them, than those of Charles or James the Second?

proposed new one. The existing law keeps on foot, so to speak, a perpetual innovation: the new law, instead of establishing innovation, wipes it out. Laws which, like those in question, are repugnant to human feelings as well as to human reason, lie under a sort of natural incapacity of being made known to the people: they refuse to take hold of the memory. In vain would instruction force them upon the memory: finding no reason to give them support, they presently drop out, unless where by accident the idea of their singularity and absurdity should give them footing in a susceptible mind. To a lawyer in whose mind reason and common sense have long been in the habit of bending under the yoke of institution, to a practised lawyer, and to him only, a restoration of this sort may present itself in the garb of innovation: he may attribute counter-attachments to the people, but such prejudices, if they manifest themselves, will have been of his own making: among the people, if left to themselves, he will find none. Regulations which build up a wall of separation between those whom nature has drawn together by the closest ties, regulations which refuse to the forlorn parent the only feeble consolation which nature can supply him with under one of the severest of afflictions, are not only palpably absurd but radically immoral: to suppose a nation attached to such deformities, would be a libel upon their national character: as well might they be supposed to be attached to injustice, cruelty, and ingratitude. The continuance of such abominations is a national reproach, nor could it thus long have endured, if these along with the rest of the laws were not kept a perpetual secret from the body of the people, and if in this particular instance the power of bequest had not all along been presenting an obvious though insufficient palliative.

Is a man attached to the present law of succession? Is the conception he entertains of it a favourable one?—It is because to his conception it shews itself under an aspect similar to the one here proposed. If this be true, abstraction made of the mere circumstance of antiquity (a property equally capable of attaching itself to the worst institutions and the best), it is this proposed new one that is the real object of his attachment, not the old established one. If this be doubted of, let the experiment be made. Take any of those anomalous articles which constitute the points of difference, and ask a plain man whether he approves of it. How many men out of a thousand [are there] that will approve of it?—I verily believe not one. Propose it to him, so far from getting him to approve of it, you will scarce

v

persuade him to give credit to its existence: an institution so harsh, so repugnant to human feelings, he will scarce believe can have made a part of a system he has heard so much magnified for [its][1] humanity; an institution so irrational he will scarce believe can have thus long made a part of a system he has heard cried up as the "perfection of reason".

[*Objection II. The measure must have hidden disadvantages, for otherwise it would have been adopted long ago.*]

When a man feels himself favourably inclined towards a proposed institution and disposed to entertain wishes of seeing it brought into existence, a difficulty that naturally presents itself to him, and which he as naturally wishes to see removed, is—how to account for its non-existence. The stronger its title to adoption appears to him, the greater the difficulty of accounting for the fact of its not having been adopted: and this difficulty, though originating in an opinion of the propriety of the measure, is apt, as it were by revulsion, to produce a sort of distrust of that propriety, a sort of latent apprehension, lest the apparent utility should turn out to be secretly over-balanced by some non-apparent inconvenience. For the obviating of this suspicion, nothing [is] so effectual as the indication of such circumstances relative to the proposed institution [2]as[3] afford a mode of accounting for its non-appearance on the list of institutions already established, more natural and to appearance more likely to be true than any want of intrinsic utility on the part of the institution itself. These indications may, it should seem, be afforded by a comparative glance at the law of succession on one hand and the system of finance on the other hand, that is of the two branches of the legal system of the concurrence of which, and the mutual adaptation of them to each other, the proposed institution would be the result.

The law of succession as established by and under the feudal system was at the same time a compleat system of finance. Every landed proprietor was a military officer, a placeman under the king: every portion of landed property was a salary. In this system the limited field assigned to the Law of Escheat by the present proposal was merged and rendered imperceptible. Remote contingencies were eclipsed by the expectation of a speedy reversion, accompanied by the possession [*sic*] of a fund of services regarded as little less than

---

[1][The MS reads "his".]
[2] [3][Interpolated at a later date.]

a present equivalent for the estate on which they were charged. By the time when the feudal system was already sunk into debility, and when, the fund of ways and means which it provided having crumbled away, particular and temporary expedients of finance were called for by the exigencies of the times, the course of private succession on the ground of blood relationship had acquired such force that wherever it pointed, so far as it tended, there was no point at which it could be stopped.

They (Estates in Land holden of the Crown) were at first at will, afterwards for life, afterwards to heirs of the body, at last to heirs at large: the progression was natural and suited to the character of the times. The longer the imagination had brooded over property, the faster the hold it had taken of it. But the same causes which strengthened the ideal connection of the tenant with the land, weakened that of the lord. The longer the tenant had continued in possession of it, the more irksome it would be to him to part with it, the less he could bear to be bereft. The longer the lord on his part had ceased to derive any advantage from it, the less irksome it would be to him to give up the expectation of seeing himself again in possession of it, to part with it altogether. But while the unwillingness to quit was encreasing on the one hand, the power of keeping was fortifying itself on the other. The power of keeping it depended upon the obedience of the vassals: of those whose subsistence was drawn from it and whose existence depended upon the liberty allowed them of making use of [it]. This obedience was the result of habit: the longer the habit, the stronger, and the stronger the habit, the more steady and determinate the obedience in each individual instance.

It was under favour of the difficulty that would often occurr of distinguishing heirs of the body from heirs at large that the latter estate grew out of the former. But if the power of the lord and the vigilance of his agents were unable to prevent the power of the individual family from taking so conspicuous a stride, still less could they find means of stopping the power after it had extended its range from heirs of the body to heirs general [and of arresting its progress] at any of those stages by which one link in the chain of general heirship is distinguished from another. These advances and encroachments were made during the sole reign and under the fostering influence of the Common or Unwritten Law. But it is one of the characteristic properties of this species of law to be incapable of any specific determination with regard to number, weight or measure. It may be influenced more or less in its decisions by the dictates of general utility, but it is incapable of following any such precise and multiplied deflections as are indicated by the numerous considerations of particular utility which come to be suggested from different and distant quarters. It may yield to the sort of instinctive and mute suggestions of general utility which point out the stock of blood relations taken together as possessing a claim which is not to be found on the part of strangers: but it has no eyes for those measured and determinately expressed arguments without which the claims of relations at different degrees can not be distinguished or compared. If children are let in to the succession, so must nephews who so frequently and so naturally stand in the place of children: but a nephew, though unknown to the uncle, or older than the uncle, is still a nephew: and if all nephews are let in, how can brothers, through whom alone nephews are nephews, be excluded? But if nephews must be admitted, so must cousins, such as are of the age of children: and if nearer cousins, so likewise remoter cousins, and so on: and though this or that cousin may, like the nephew, be unknown or of superior age, he is still a cousin, as before. Common Law can not stop at any of these stages: the analogy which has led it thus far urge[s] it on in the same line for ever.

Statute Law on the other hand lends its ear to every suggestion of particular utility and describes in its course the minutest inflection which the dictates of particular utility can indicate. But the Common Law in matters of succession had spun out its thread at a time when Statute Law had scarce crept into existence: at a time when the barons who were absent from the Great Council had scarce settled with themselves whether they were bound by resolutions taken by those who were present: and when the subjects of a succeeding sovereign scarce knew whether they were to be bound by the ordinances of a preceding one.*

The system of finance in its modern shape is of a date posterior to the evolution of [the] legal analogy by which the course of succession was marked out.

It is with finance as with every other branch of legislation, and more so than with most: hasty expedients for pressing exigencies. Money to a certain amount is wanting: money to a certain amount must be found. It is wanted presently: it must be looked for where

---

*See [Daines] Barrington's Observ[ations] on the Statutes, in different places.

it can be laid hold of presently. Taxation, and taxation only, answered the purpose: more needy than the neediest heir, the sovereign could never wait for deaths.

The principle of escheat, it may perhaps be observed, was all this while not only in existence, but in the fullest vigour: how came it to have made no conquests on the ground of succession, not even in its remotest out-skirts? Power so mighty, necessities always so craving on the one hand, on the other claims so weak as the claims of relationship become as the branches encrease in distance from the source! The case is, that if the prerogative possessed itself of every thing beyond the domaine of natural relationship, it was because it found the ulterior space altogether unoccupied: it would have been a very different step and a much wider stride, to attempt to extend its dominion at the expence and in the teeth of a principle co-eval with itself, and so much more strongly rooted in the affections of mankind.

The spirit of the royal prerogative indeed was like the ether of the mechanical philosopher, striving with constant all-pervading pressure to fill up every void that could present itself within the sphere of power: but like the same subtle spirit its dominion ended where it found incompressible matter already in possession and in readiness to resist it.

A centripetal force inherent in the feudal system was continually employed in drawing into the royal focus all the property of the kingdom through a thousand channels: whatsoever was prevented, though but by a momentary cause, from finding its way into other hands, fell regularly into the king's. But the claims of rapacious and sturdy dependents were acting all this while in a centrifugal direction, and throwing the matter back into circulation as fast as it fell in: and while the demands of the spirit of acquisition were thus irresistible, the claims of possession, though in its weakest shape, could not be contemned.

No wonder then that a productive Law of Escheat should not hitherto in any European country have occupied a page of any moment in the account book of finance. From Common Law it was excluded by the antiquity of that branch of law, prior to the exigencies of regular finance, and by the natural progress of it, incapable of stopping at any determinate and regulated stage. From Statute Law is was excluded by the suddenness of the exigencies by which the operations of Statute Law in the field of finance have always been determined. The non-establishment of this resource down to the present period is therefore to be ascribed, not to the inexpediency of it, nor so much as to any opinion of its inexpediency, but to the ¹apparent² remoteness as well as ¹real² magnitude of the resource in question, and to the influence of those causes which have prevented governments from contemplating the field of finance in any comprehensive point of view.

Had this resource happened to have presented itself under a favourable aspect to the Neckers or the Calonnes, and had they succeeded in recommending it to the acquiescence of the nation, the French Revolution, and the flood of miseries with which the earth has been deluged by it, would have been prevented.

[Objection III. The measure must have hidden disadvantages, for otherwise it would never have fallen into disuse.]

Another objection here presents itself.—Being so antient ¹as you represent it, and as it can not be denied to be,² having been so strongly rooted in the constitution, how comes the resource after all to have become antiquated, how comes it to have ever been relinquished? Does not its having for so long a time disappeared out of the constitution afford a strong presumption to its prejudice? a stronger one at least than the fact of its *quondam* existence presents to its advantage?—Does not this antient, this antiquated ingredient in the system of legal polity stand on this account upon a footing not only not more favourable than if it were altogether novel and unexperienced, but even less favourable?

So much more prone are men in general, and political men more especially, to judge from general prejudices than from special and pointed reasons, that even this vague and inconclusive head of objection may appear to claim an answer: an answer accordingly it shall have.

To answer it, it may be requisite to look back for a moment to the original texture of our legal polity, and to state the causes to which the drying up of this resource is, according to appearance, to be attributed. Seeing as we shall do that these causes have nothing to do with the merits of the institution, we shall see that its disappearance in those times affords no argument against its revival now.

In the first place it never was productive enough to be any thing of an object: because the field of its operation was never extensive

---

¹ ²[Put into brackets, apparently at a later date.]

enough to be productive. Reasons of a feudal nature gave it introduction, reasons of the same original limited its extent. Failing relations [1]of the blood[2] of the last tenant, the estate, the fief as it was called, was to fall into the hands of the lord: to fall back into the fund from whence it was originally derived: for there was a fund capable of maintaining, and to be employed in maintaining, a defender of the community: and as the country was continually at war, or in immediate danger of war, defenders for it were always in demand. Failing such relations then, it was necessary the feudal lord should reabsorb this element of defence: but till all such relations utterly failed, the reason did not come into operation. But a total failure of that sort is an event that would rarely be exemplified: rarely in any state of political society, especially [however] in the state then existing, when men clung together in clans, and at a time when the numerous causes of dispersion which are presented nowadays by the goodness and safety of the roads, the encrease of commerce and correspondence, the multiplication of distant colonies and conquests had as yet no existence.

The produce being so inconsiderable and precarious, the more it was so, the more apt it would be not to be adequate to the expence of collection. But the expence of collection which was certain, and such as it was necessary to keep up at all events, could not but be considerable. Officers for the preserving of claims to this purpose required to be kept in constant pay. These officers, to answer the purpose, it was necessary should be numerous: for travelling was rare and difficult, and yet the being apprised of the individual cases in which their interposition was called for required local knowledge. Legal investigation was also more difficult than now in proportion to the barbarousness of the age: and being difficult would be expensive. A legal conclusion would also under the very narrow extent of ground which the institution occupied in its then actual state be beyond measure more difficult to form than under the wide extent which it is here proposed to give it. Whether a man left any near relations, relations so near as to be within the degrees prohibited with reference to marriage, is a point in most instances not only easy to ascertain but generally notorious. Whether a man left any relations at all, near or remote, that could be proved to be so, may be a question of endless intricacy and doubt. Claimants may start up without number and without end. Without the aid of [a] positive

---

[1] [2][Put into brackets at a later date.]

institution, a party whose title should depend upon the non-existence of all such claims would never be safe [and] would never be able to obtain a possession worth contending for. Royal power might give present possession: but nothing but a statute of limitations (a law constituting antiquity of possession itself, when of a certain standing, a bar to claims grounded on all other titles)—nothing but a statute of limitations could give legal security. On such terms grasping at vacant successions would be grasping after moonshine.

The causes then that produced the extinction of this institution considered as a source of revenue in those times, and on the footing it was at those times, afford no argument against the revival of it at the present time, and in the extended form proposed at present to be given to it. Feudal reasons gave birth to the institution: reasons of economy operated to the extinction of it: but reasons of modern complexion and real cogency have succeeded to the feudal reasons in its favour; while the reasons that operated to its extinction in its antient state have no application to it in its proposed form and in the present state of things.

[Objection IV. The measure would destroy the aristocracy and thereby upset the constitution.]

Oh but (says an objector) *the preference to primogeniture is an aristocratical institution: on that ground it is necessary not only as a support to the aristocratical part of the constitution, but to the affections and biases, call them if you will prejudices [connected with it]: to affections that have grown up with the aristocratical part of the system and are necessary to its support.* The utility of the aristocratical part of the constitution I do not dispute*: provision has been made for it in the saving clause on behalf of the privilege of peerage.† The propriety and necessity of bowing down to existing prejudices, were they less salutary than these, shall pass alike uncontroverted.

The ground I proceed upon is that to the upholding of that pillar

---

*Monarchy stands on the shoulders of the peerage. Peers must be high, that the monarch may be the higher. The use of a peer is to command respect, and to command it by his opulence. All currents that bring in wealth to the peerage ought to flow without disturbance that in unquiet times there may not, in any part of the Kingdom, be wanting a man who, by endowments less precarious than personal ones, may be enabled, as well as by interest disposed, to contribute with effect towards the preservation of the peace.

†Proviso in favour of the peerage: estates to descend to peers notwithstanding, or to any one to whom a peer is heir presumptive or apparent.

of the constitution, and to the preserving from concussion those affections and those prejudices, no such article in the law of succession is necessary.

Abstraction made of the support required by the aristocratical part of the constitution, these prejudices will surely be admitted to have no claim to favour: they keep up inequality, and all inequality that has no special utility to justify it is injustice. What is the practical inference? that so far as they are necessary to the support of that branch of the constitution, so far and so far only, they ought to be cultivated and favoured: that as to any thing beyond, it is sufficient to comply with them, without seeking to cultivate and extend them.

To support the aristocracy of the country it is not necessary that every individual should be made a member of it, much less whether he will or not[1]: this would be an odd sort of an aristocracy, a democratical one. It seems sufficient, and one may say amply sufficient, if every individual who chooses to be to this purpose a member of the aristocracy, has power given him to make himself so. A landed proprietor whose income rises to a certain amount, say £10,000, must by every body be considered as forming a portion of this aristocracy: a landed proprietor whose land does not furnish him so much as a subsistence, a mere forty shilling freeholder for instance, can not be considered in that light by any one: and these may perhaps compose the bulk of landholders in the country, in number that is, though certainly not in value. A man of a middling estate, suppose one, two or three hundred a year, may by some be considered as belonging to that body, by others as not belonging to it: by himself he may be considered as belonging to it: or as not belonging to it, as it may happen.

The condition of a body is the situation of the greater part of the individuals who compose it: it is to the condition of the greater part of those whom it applies to [and] whose interests are disposed of by it, that a law should accommodate itself in preference.*

Take it in the lump, the body of landholders can not therefore be said to be an aristocratical body: all that can be said of it is, that it is that body in which the greater part of those who have the best title to be deemed members of that body, are to be found: but

---

[1][May also read "no".]

*[This is] a maxim placed in a light too strong to admitt of denial by universal reason, and recognized even by English lawyers.

it is no such body when taken all together. The mass of property therefore ought not to be taken in the lump and consecrated to the support of aristocracy. The general rule, in as far as particular dispositions are thought fit to be subjected to a general rule, the general rule, were it necessary there should be one, ought to wear a democratical tinge. Were there no medium, were it necessary that all landed estates should take the same course without regard to the wishes of individuals, the aristocratical or the democratical one, it ought rather therefore to be the democratical one. But there is a medium, and that medium is afforded by the inclinations of individuals. Let the general rule then, a rule which applies no further than to the cases where the wishes of the individuals concerned have failed to manifest themselves, let the general rule be accommodated to the condition of the greater number, in a word, let it be of the democratical complexion: leaving it to such of the individuals to become members of the aristocracy as choose to be so. The course will neither be accused of being a harsh one in itself nor such as presents much danger of that exalted body's not being sufficiently filled up. A man can not much complain of being excluded from that body, when without canvass or probation, he can at any time appoint himself a member to it, by the bare expression of his will. There is surely not much danger that a body thus elevated in dignity should find itself understocked, so long as pride, vanity, and ambition are ingredients in the composition of human nature. *Shall my family be a gentleman's family or below a gentleman's? Shall there be a country gentleman in my family or none?* The answer is not likely to be too seldom in the affirmative, though to fit out one member of the family, one child out of half a dozen, for a gentleman, the other five should be left bare.

Another observation, were it wanted for the purpose of the argument, is that the law of primogeniture is not necessary for the support of the aristocracy.

At the time of its institution and for a long time after, the law in favour of primogeniture was a proper one : it might even be termed a wise one, were it not too strongly inculcated by urgent necessity and by unreflecting passion to be entitled to the praise of wisdom. A portion of [property] equal in value to the ordinary quantum of a landed estate would maintain a soldier fit for service :*

*The whole Kingdom, it must be remembered, was by William the Conqueror divided into knight's fees: in number about 60,000.

it would hardly maintain two: it would certainly not maintain a number of males equal to what is not uncommonly found in one man's family. Divided among all the male children, much more if among all the children of both sexes without distinction, it would in many, if not in most, instances have been insufficient to that necessary destination.

[When the Kings of England laid the burden of military service on][1] the proprietors of land, they appropriated to this use the estates of all those who were capable of contributing to it. Capitals in money or money's worth had not as yet been formed: the very little that existed in masses to any such amount was in the hands of jews, a despised and therefore despicable race, equally unable and unwilling to take an active part in the business of national defence.

Individuals who were not proprietors of land had no political existence: such of them as were of the same families as the knights might find subsistence by serving as a sort of upper servants or armour bearers under such knights as could afford to keep them: the rest were either dependents of an inferior order or slaves. What became of them, the bulk of the nation, or of their property, was of no national importance.

Had capitals been ever so considerable, and considerable capitals ever so numerous, the utter insecurity of such possessions would have rendered them a fund of subsistence not to be trusted to for the defenders of the state. Furniture and dead stock of all sorts was liable every moment to be carried off or burnt by some gang of military freebooters together with the hovel that contained it: live stock still more portable, in as much as they served to carry themselves, were equally liable to be driven off: money, concealed in some hole of the ground from every mortal eye but that of the possessor who hid it there, would be lost either to him by his being driven away from the land by superior violence, or to all the world by his decease: land happily for the continuance of the human race could neither be carried away, nor driven away, nor buried and forgotten.

[Such were the circumstances which made the body of landholders, the defenders of the realm, the aristocratical body, and the law of primogeniture which secured their opulence and therewith their power of defence, the law of succession. But the times of feudality have long ago passed by and there is no reason at present why the owners

---

[1][The MS in fact reads: "In taking this care of the estates of the proprietors of land, they . . .". It is hoped that the interpolation in the text righly renders the idea at the back of Bentham's mind.]

of landed estates should be privileged in any way in comparison of the owners of other species of property. An extinction of the aristocratical part of the community by a change in the right of inheritance need not be feared.] Where there is wealth in a country, there will always be a certain portion of it in large masses, that is in few hands: and there will even be a certain portion of it remaining unbroken in the same family: although so long as it remains in large masses, whether it remains in the same family, or changes from family to family, does not seem to be of any material importance. In Russia there is no want of great families: there is no want of an aristocratical body. In Russia all this while the law of primogeniture has no place: yet in point of wealth compared with population, what is Russia to England?

[*Objection V. The measure would be an infringement upon the law of nature.*]

An infringement this, it may be said, of natural rights: of which the right of property is one: a right which it is the business of law not to infringe but to secure. Among the rights of property is the natural right of inheritance. This right has no other limits than the stock of natural heirs.

Succession to kinsmen a natural right? How can that be? when the enjoyment of it, wherever it is enjoyed, depends altogether upon the dispositions and operations of the [positive] law!—Succession a natural, an universal right? How can that be?—when in no two nations it is the same! If natural right had any place in the subject, if the doctrine of natural right had any truth in it at all, or were to the purpose in respect of any branch of the matter of succession, it should surely be in that which respects the succession of children to parents. Yet what becomes of natural right even here? In one and the same nation—not to speak of various nations—in one and the same nation—in our own nation—among men of landed property in most instances the eldest son gets every thing—in a few instances it is the youngest son [who] gets every thing, and here the eldest nothing—and in both cases what becomes of the natural right of the daughters?* Among moneyed men, all the children, sons and daughters, take alike.

---

*If one child may be thus cut off, why not another? if nine children, why not the tenth? If natural law, instead of being a chimera, were a really existing law, and as such capable of being violated, what violations could be more flagrant than those which it has all along sustained, and is now sustaining every day, from the existing law of England?

Whence this astonishing disparity? Whence this invasion upon the very vitals of natural right?—From a reason that existed once—a feudal reason—a reason that for ages has been gone.—To keep one individual member of a family in pay, in expectation of his contributing one soldier upon occasion for the defence of the state, all the other members, to every one of whom nature had given equal necessities and equal claims—all the other members were to be starved: [1]to keep one[3] individual in pay, whether the whole of the succession was wanted for the purpose, or whether a hundredth part would have sufficed[2]. Which then shall meet with greatest deference? a dead and antiquated reason—a reason long time perished, not only in point of use and benefit, but except in a few speculative minds, perished even as a remembrance—or a reason in full vigour—a reason which now is all that the other ever was and infinitely more—a reason as gentle in its operation as that was iniquitous [?] and harsh: a reason that would find the country a hundred defenders where that would have found one?

The[4] infinite diversity [mentioned above] of the footing on which the business of succession stands in different nations is a happy incident for the present purpose. What can be a more demonstrative or a more striking proof how perfectly all these pretended natural rights, or to speak what is at once more material and more intelligible, how perfectly *expectation* in all these instances is at the command of law! Where is the hardship upon me, what do I suffer in England by not having an estate which would have been mine had I belonged to Russia or France?

I know of no natural rights except what are created by general utility: and even in that sense it were much better the word were never heard of. All such language is at any rate false: all such language is either pernicious, or at the best an improper and fallacious way of indicating what is true.

In starting this topic or rather this expression I am full well aware what a deluge of nonsense I am treading up. But as this sort of nonsense is not [only] one of the readiest of arguments, but perhaps the most formidable opponent which a useful and rational proposal can have to struggle with, I know not how to get altogether clear of

---

[1] [2][Possibly a later addition.]
[3] [May also read "an".]
[4] [The MS reads "This".]

mentioning it: but what I do say of it shall be as little and as short
as possible.

Relations have a natural right to succeed to one: and as no one
can say where this right ends, this is as much as to say that it ends
no where. To set bounds to the right of succession any where is
therefore to violate natural rights. But a law by which any natural
right is violated is a grievance and an act of tyranny: and tyran[n]y
ought to be risen up against and resisted: the right of resistance to
oppression is one of these natural rights which are indefeasible and
have not been given up and cannot be, &c. &c. &c.

¹To this head of argument I have two answers. One is that it is
mere nonsense: to say nothing of its being such mischievous nonsense—a topic which is not to the present purpose.

The other is that it is inconsistent nonsense: in as much as, if³
it be intelligible and just, it does not apply with any greater force
against the arrangement here proposed to be made than against every
other arrangement that can be named, actual or possible.²

First then it is stark nonsense: it is a contradiction in terms.

Of a natural right who has any idea? I, for my part, I have none:
a natural right is a round square [or] an incorporeal body. What a
legal right is I know. I know how it was made. I know what it
means when made. To me a right and a legal right are the same
thing, for I know no other. Right and law are correlative terms: as
much so as son and father. Right is with me the child of law:
from different operations of the law result different sorts of rights.
A natural right is a son that never had a father.* By natural right
is meant, a sort of a thing which is to have the effect of law, which

---

¹ ²[Bentham perhaps intended to leave out this passage for, re-reading the draft,
he put across it a large question-mark. The following arguments cover both points
at the same time.]

³[One word illegible.]

*I can conceive indeed another sort of right, distinct from political, and even of
superior force: but still not without the aid of law. From a divine law comes a
divine right just as intelligibly as from a political human law comes a political
human right. Thus from a supposed divine law in favour of monarchy came the
Jus divinum, the divine right, of Kings. This sort of right is certainly as intelligible
as that which every body understands of course who has any understanding about
the matter from the word: this is perfectly intelligible, though, as the existence
of the law for the purpose is always denied and never can be proved, it is as perfectly useless. But the natural rights we hear so much of under that name are of
all things the farthest from being divine rights. For in no mouths are they so
frequent nor so much insisted upon as in the mouths of those by whom the existence
of a divine law and of a divine lawgiver are equally denied.

is to have an effect paramount to that of law, but which subsists not only without law, but against law: and its characteristic property, as well as sole and constant use, is the being the everlasting and irreconciliable enemy of law. As scissors were invented to cut up cloth, so were natural rights invented to cut up law, and legal rights. A natural right is a species of cold heat, a sort of dry moisture, a kind of resplendent darkness.

Name me any right, name me what I mean by a right, the only sort of [right] that with me has either meaning or existence, [in short] name me a legal right either actual or possible, a right existing in this country or in any other, a right past, present, or future, I will shew [?] by what it was made and how it was made. I will point out whatever laws have concurred in its formation. But of these natural rights the boasted property is to exist before laws were made, to exist in the teeth of them [when they] were made, and to exist for ever, though laws should be no more.

If natural rights came not from law, from any sort of law—whence did it [sic] come? I will tell you—It is the spawn of despotism, begot upon incapacity. It is the effusion of a hard heart operating upon a cloudy mind. When a man is bent upon having things his own way and give[s] no reason for it, he says: I have a right to have them so. When a man has a political caprice to gratify, and is determined to gratify it, if possible, at any price, when he feels an ardent desire to see it gratified but can give no reason why it should be gratified, when he finds it necessary to get the multitude to join with him, but either stoops not to enquire whether they would be the better or the happier for so doing, or feels himself at a loss to prove it, he sets up a cry of rights. I have a right to have it so: you have all a right to have it so: none but tyrants can refuse us. Give us then our rights. The dictates of reason and utility are the result of circumstances which require genius to discover, strength of mind to weigh, and patience to investigate: the language of natural rights require[s] nothing but a hard front, a hard heart and an unblushing countenance. It is from the beginning to the end so much flat assertion: it neither has any thing to do with reason nor will endure the mention of it. It lays down as a fundamental and inviolable principle whatever is in dispute: admitt it [and] you are an honest fellow, a true patriot: question it, or so much as ask for a proof of it, you are whatever is most odious, sinning equally against truth and against conscience.

The strength of this argument is in proportion to the strength of lungs in those who use it. The principle of utility, with the united powers of Bacon, Locke, Hume, Smith, [and] Paley to develop it, would be nothing against one Danton bawling out natural rights. The strength of this argument [I say] lies in the strength of lungs: I mean in the first instance: for ultimately it depends upon the sharpness [?] of the daggers which he who uses it has in his pocket. I will speak daggers, says Hamlet, but I will use none: here the distinction has no place. To speak these verbal daggers is to promise upon the first occasion to use real ones, and in that promise consists its force. Weak as it is in the character of an argument, it is proportionably strong as an insult and a menace: and indeed, the plain and simple version of it is a menace and nothing else. List yourself under my banner, join in my howl, swallow my nonsense—or you are a tyrant, or a slave, an accomplice of tyrants: and as to what ought to be done with tyrants and their abettors—who does not know? Remember the ides of March, said one to Caesar to warn him of his fate. Remember the ides of September is a memento I always conceive as given when I hear of natural rights: where this is the imagery displayed in front, I always see in the back ground a cluster of daggers or of pikes introduced in the National Assembly with the applause of the President Condorcet for the avowed purpose of exterminating the King's friends. Of late these pikes and these daggers have been exhibited in broad day, and pointed out to reasonable and reasoning men, as gibbets used to be to murderers and thieves. But though till lately kept behind the curtain, they were always at hand, and but too close to the elbow of many a well-meaning man who hardly suspected how near he was to use them, or how void of all meaning his discourse, his politics, or fancied philosophy was, except in as far as he meant to use them.*

*A book in which the object was to enquire, not what are our natural rights, but what in each instance *ought* to be our legal ones upon the principle of utility, that is, what are the rights which, in each instance, it would be for the happiness of the community that the law should create, and what means it should employ to secure us in the possession of them, a book in which incidentally a few of the inconsistencies which never fail to attend the language of natural rights [were exposed], was once put into the hands of that coldblooded instigator of promiscuous assassination, who now lurks somewhere in a state of well-merited degradation and distress, a fugitive from men superior, if possible, to himself in wickedness. From the passage above mentioned he turned with an instinctive and as it were a prophetic and presaging horror, for without mentioning or thinking of him it unmasked him and was in effect one of the severest satyres on the whole tenor of his language and complexion of his thoughts. No, such enquiries were not to be countenanced—utility was a dangerous

It may be said, and certainly with great truth, that this doctrine, however new in complection and effect, is old enough in point of language: that it has been the language of all sorts of men in all sorts of times—of the quiet as well as of the violent—of the dull as well as the sprightly, of the Grotius's and the Puffendorffs as well as of the Condorcets and Brissots and Robertspierres [*sic*]. True it is that it has been the result not only of the superabundance of zeal, but that, even without a spark of zeal, it has flowed from mere penury of argument: a mere way of speaking and a pretence for talking when a man had nothing to say. Not only quiet and dull men and men who have owed their quietness to their dulness, but many an excellent and many a well-meaning man, who in other points has shewn himself by no means destitute of intelligence: a man who, in other points, has shewn himself not only conspicuous but really useful to mankind.

This, I confess, is not to be disputed, but how close together stand truth and error, littleness and greatness, accuteness and stupidity, clearness and confusion in the minds of the wisest of mankind! In roads infested with epidemic nonsense the traveller has but one alternative, to confute it or to adopt it: to oppose himself to, or to be confounded with, the crowd.

Nonsense it always was from the beginning, but those upon whom it pressed, and who suffered themselves to be imposed upon while its malignity lay concealed, may, now that its malignity has shewn itself in all its full blackness, perhaps suffer themselves to be weaned from it.

[*Objection VI. The measure would unduly encrease the influence of the Crown.*]

Another objection may be grounded on the supposed encrease of the influence of the Crown. To this several observations appear applicable.

1. The objection amounts to nothing, unless the encrease resulting from this mode of supply is greater in proportion than from any other: unless it would be greater than what would result from a

---

and delusive enquiry: it was treachery to the great cause of natural right and natural justice. Natural rights were not to be doubted of or to be made the subject of [investigation]: to engage in any such discussions was to desert the cause. It was endeavouring to open the eyes of the multitudes, and their steadiness depended upon their blindness.

W

new tax to the same amount. Would it be so? that point, were it worth proving, would remain to be proved.

2. It would go not to countervail and annihilate, but only to set-off in quality of a mischief against the benefit of the measure. What is the amount of the mischief? I really do not know. Is it any thing? I really do not know: but of this presently.

3. The objection, were it so strong as to be conclusive, might be got rid of, by striking off sine-cures and useless places to the same amount. To point out such is unhappily as easy as it is difficult to get rid of them.

4. Another way of getting rid of the objection would be to steer clear of the Crown by vesting the appointment [of escheators] in other hands: I mean in the hands of a numerous description of the people: to follow precedent, in the hands of the freeholders, for instance, the same in which the office of which the present was once an appendage is at present.* I state this as a measure that might appear preferable in the eyes of some: it would not, I confess, in mine.[1]

If any man means to urge this effect as an objection to the plan *in toto,* the following are the explanations which he seems called upon to give.

1. To say whether he looks upon that influence to be mischievous *in toto.* If he does, I will consign him for shortness sake [2]to[3] the hands of those who regard such influence as a salutary and essential ingredient in the composition of the constitution.

2. If not mischievous *in toto,* then whether useful or simply indifferent. In either case, where it ceases to be useful or indifferent, and where it begins to be pernicious.

3. Supposing this ascertained, and supposing established that the influence of the Crown ought either to be diminished to a certain point, or at any rate not to be encreased, the objection would then have no application to the measure. The inference would be, not to deprive the country of an establishment of palpable and undeniable utility, but to ease it of places consisting of mere expence without use.

In a word, the consideration of influence, when applied to a proposed establishment of this sort, seems to have no effect upon

---

*Writ *de coronatore eligendo*: the Coroner is Escheator.
[1][This last sentence is possibly a later addition.]
[2] [3][Struck out by mistake.]

the merits. Happily it does not threaten to have much greater effect upon the success. While the arguments against influence do not prevail against useless places, it would be hard were they [to][1] prevail against useful ones. The easing the people of the burthen of those places, at the decease of the respective occupants, would be but a branch as it were of the resource here indicated: it were a pity if the same argument which was found unable to establish the one, should succeed in cutting off the other.

To confess the truth, if an opinion may be given without going to the bottom of the grounds of it in a question of such supposed importance, which comes in here only by a side wind, I never could see reason for attaching so much importance to this question on either side as seems commonly to be attached to it on both sides.

To me it appears not to be of the smallest particle of use in the way of security for the constitution. Two palpable and unanswerable reasons plead against it, the expence and the scandal: they seem as unanswerable as they are obvious. As to the supposed danger to liberty and to the constitution on that side, I have looked for it a good deal and never could spy it out: liberty depends not upon the greater or less influence of the Crown with relation to the servants of the public and the representatives of the people, but on the spirit of the great body of the people itself. I see very well how this spirit should be alarmed and excited by the encrease of such influence, but I do not see how it should in any degree be weakened by it. The moment the great body of the people feel any real grievance, what should hinder their complaining of it: and were the body of the people to complain of a grievance, be it ever so quietly and humbly, what can hinder it from being redressed?

When a common-place upon influence has been confuted by a common place about the venerable fabrick and the wisdom of ages, it has met with its match and received its due.*

The truth is, that the alarm about encrease of influence affords no just argument, against this any more than any other establishment that promises to be in other respects an useful one. Nothing can be more perfectly incommensurable than the danger on one hand and the utility on the other. To do justice to the jealousy of influence,

---

[1][MS reads "should".]

*Did the subject call on me to find out a real source of danger to liberty, I could find one but too readily, in the precarious tenure by which the right of the people to take cognisance in any shape of public measures is held under the subsisting laws: though, it must be confessed, it has never hitherto been held under any better.

set the danger not against the utility of an useful establishment, but against the no-utility of some useless one, if after this addition the body of influence would be too great, retrench it not here, where it has use, but elsewhere where it has none : if it would not be too great, if it draws on no excess, the objection loses its ground.

[*Objection VII. The powers given to the officers of the public for the collection of escheating estates would be abused.*]

A more substantial [and] very different head of objection, though referable to the same word, is the *influence* that may be exercised by the agent of the public in this behalf over several of the descriptions of persons he may have to deal with.

Abuse of power may be figured in various shapes : indulgence, corrupt perhaps, towards some : undue rigour exerted for the purposes of oppression or even of extortion, over others. The danger of indulgence is, however, the less serious, as it operates only in diminution *pro tanto* of the quantum of the supply : it can hardly be urged as an argument against the measure since the effect of it, as far as it goes, is only to lessen the effect of the measure, lessen the mischief of it, if it [is]¹ mischievous : in a word the argument is thus far self-destructive.

Where the indulgence has corruption for its cause, the receipt of the wages of corruption is extortion and falls so far under the other head.

The extortion or other oppression which, in this as in all other instances, may with more or less probability be operated by the abuse of any instrument of power, is a very substantial evil : but does it threaten to subsist in any greater degree of magnitude under this establishment than under a branch equally productive of the existing ones, the Customs or Excise for instance? The contrary I should hope would be found to be the case.

This remark, though not good as an objection, may be very good as a warning, and as such shall meet with due notice. The warning is to introduce as much publicity as possible into the transactions of the officer of the Crown and those whom he has to deal with : and it will be found that a greater measure of publicity by far may be introduced in this instance perhaps than can be introduced, certainly than has hitherto been introduced, in either of those others.

---

¹[The MS reads "if".]

[*Objection VIII. By strongly encreasing the public revenue, the measure would lead to profusion on the part of government.*]

Will it be urged as an objection that the resource by its amplitude will be an encouragement to prodigality on the part of ministers? Objections of no sounder texture have passed current with the best judges.*

It admitts of two answers, either of them decisive.

One is that if it proves any thing, it proves too much. If the sort of resource which is the least burthensome is on that account the least eligible, the most eligible should be that which is the most burthensome.

Rendering or keeping supply burthensome may be one expedient for checking superfluous expenditure, but there are others that are much less uncertain in their effect as well as more immediate.

To render this objection conclusive, the following are the circumstances that must concurr:

1. That all expenditure on the part of government is unnecessary: insomuch that tyranny and taxation are synonymous.

2. That this mode of finding supplies for expenditure would be submitted to.

3. That no other mode more burthensome would be submitted to.

As to the proper modes of checking profusion they have no place here.

Will it be said that, be they what they will, and be they ever so proper, they will not be adopted? still less likely is it then that the rejecting of such a relief should be adopted, a rejection which, considered in the light of a check to profusion, is evidently so feeble and absurd an one. Will those who by the supposition are bent upon profusion, will the majority of the legislature suffer itself to be defeated by a trick after the drift of it has been exposed? If not, of what use is the objection, and to what purpose bring it forward?

The amount of the money proposed to be raised being given, either the quantity of national suffering is diminished by this mode of supply, or it is not: on the first supposition the profusion, however great, being attended with no suffering, affords no argument against the measure: on the other supposition, negativing the measure will

---

*An argument of the same complection and of no stronger texture is among the arguments which have been commonly urged in defence of the restraints laid on the rate of interest, and which passed upon Adam Smith. See *Defence of Usury.*

be of no use, since were the measure to pass, the discontent of the people, which is the incident trusted to as a check to profusion, would remain undiminished.

[*Objection IX. Money thus obtained would be collected at greater expence than money obtained from taxes.*]

An objection that might be urged against this mode of supply at a venture is that money thus collected would be expensive in the collection: more so, it will be said (or else whatever is said amounts to nothing), more so than if the same sum were to be collected in the way of taxes.

Whether the expence of collecting what might without hardship be collected from this source would be greater or less than the expence of collecting an equal sum in the way of taxes, is more than I would take upon me to pronounce. Fortunately it would be useless to enquire. Where the collection of a sum of money is attended with hardship ¹to the contributor,² as it is in a greater or less degree in the instance of every tax whatever [and] of every thing that operates in the shape of a tax, there the question is an essential one: because the greater the expence of collection, the greater the hardship. But here there is nothing of hardship in the case, so that whatever is got, be it little or much, and be there little or much paid out of it for collecting it, so long as more is not paid for collecting it than it amounts to, is all clear again: it is so much got out of the fire.

The expence of collection has been computed in the instance of the Excise at 5 per Cent: the expence of collection in this instance might perhaps be 5: might, for ought I know, amount to 10. But were it 50, it would not [in]³ the present instance amount to an objection to the measure.

[*Objection X. The measure would promote dissipation on the part of individuals and thus diminish national wealth.*]

Another objection may be, that it would have the effect of promoting dissipation on the part of individuals by prompting them to convert their fortunes into annuities for their own lives.

The answer is, that it is only in a very small degree that such an effect can be expected to take place, and that, in as far as it does take

---

¹ ²[Put into brackets at a later date.]
³[Hole in the MS.]

place, it affords no objection to the measure itself: it affords no objection to the principle of the measure, it only affords a diminution *pro tanto* of the benefit that might otherwise be derived from it.

The more narrowly it is looked into, the more inconsiderable will the amount, if any, of this part of its tendency be found. To no case where there is a wife, husband, child, descendant, progenitor, or other near relation *in esse* or in any likelyhood of being *in esse,* does it apply: for here the claims of the Exchequer have no place. Even where there are no such relations nor any prospect of such relations, what motive to such dissipation does it furnish even in that case, in addition to those that subsist already? Because I can not leave my cousin or my friend the whole of my property, is it likely I should not leave him any thing? Half of my fortune the regulation admitts of my leaving him: if my affection for him is so strong that the leaving him the half of my fortune will not content it, shall I content it better by converting it into an annuity for my own life, by buying that annuity of a stranger, and making the stranger altogether, and not my friend in any degree, the better for my death? Is my own personal gratification my sole object? I can equally gratify it as it is, I can contribute to national dissipation under the existing law to as great an extent as under the institution proposed. Is the gratification of my social feelings in that respect the superior gratification in my eye? I can still provide for it under the institution proposed, not quite so well, it is true, as in the existing state of things: but still better by far than were I to take the course apprehended, and deprive him of every benefit he could have derived from me. Were I at liberty as to the whole, I should prefer my friend in this respect to the public: for to him the acquisition would be happiness, and to the public nothing of which my faculties could take account. But because I love him so much better than I do the public, must I therefore hate the public, and that to so intense a degree as for my hatred to over-power and extinguish my affection for my friend? Is a conduct like this at all in nature?

Nor are the social affections the only ones that contribute to disincline a man from the apprehended species of dissipation. If I exchange my money for an annuity, or sell the reversion of my estate, if I augment my present power of expenditure, do I not diminish in proportion that importance which depends on the permanency of property? if I encrease my power of purchasing the objects of consumption, do I not diminish in the same proportion my expectation of those blessings on which imagination sets so high a value, the unbought services and kindnesses of expecting friends?

After all, should a man in any instance, out of spite for not being able to give his friend more than the half of what he leaves, be led to deprive him of the whole, so far, it must be confessed, the provision of the proposed law is evaded and its intention frustrated: but because it may be frustrated by the individual in one instance out of a hundred, is that a reason why it should be given up by the statesman in the other ninety nine? because I can not get a million a year for nothing, is that a reason why I should refuse to get nine hundred and ninety thousand on those terms? At any rate the property thus sunk, if it is not saved, is not thrown away: it is spent in the procurement of gratifications, which is the use of property, and gratifications for which nobody feels himself the poorer, no other individual feels himself the worse: for as to its being spent in mischief, it is no more to be presumed of this parcel of money, than of any other.

[Objection XI. The measure would tend to sink the price of land by glutting the market with it.]

Another objection that may be brought to bear against the measure is, that it will sink the price of land, viz. by bringing land so much oftener into the market, and even under the hammer, than it would come of itself. To this I make two answers: the measure will not sink the price of land: on the contrary, it will contribute more or less to raise it.

[1]The fall that may ensue in the price of land is spoken of by Adam Smith as a desirable one, [3]and measures proposed in the view of their promoting it.[4] My principles do not permitt me to consider it in that light: as far as it takes place I consider it as constituting a drawback, though I do not say a very heavy one, from the benefits of the measure.[2] The price of land, according to Dr. Smith, is at present too high: it is a monopoly price: lower it, and land will more easily find its way into the hands of proprietor-farmers who, farming land that is their own property, will bestow more attention on it than husbandmen who farm the lands of another, and be less sparing of the expence of such improvements as will not answer to an occupier

---

[1] [2][Crossed out in the MS, perhaps at a later date.]
[3] [4][Put into brackets at a later date.]

whose quantity of interest is limited to the duration of an ordinary lease.[1] This consideration seems not to me of any great weight: it sacrifices the certain and immediate feelings of assignable individuals, to a vague and rather problematical interest of the public, that is to an advantage to be reaped by one knows not who, one knows not when, nor how, nor in what proportion.

The mischief, as far as it goes, is this. Those who, having it in contemplation to sell land [and who] have lived in expectation of selling it at a certain price, get less for it. Those who have been living in contemplation of buying land, give less for it, it is true, in the same proportion, but the enjoyment resulting from the gain can not be reckoned equal to the suffering resulting from the loss. I have some land which ere long I shall be obliged to sell: at present [I] get, say, 25 years purchase for it: were the market to be glutted to the degree in which it would be glutted by the operation of the measure, my land would sell for no more, say, than 20 years purchase: this is to me a loss of a fifth part of my fortune, as much as a tax on my capital to the same amount would be.

The gain, on the other hand, to the purchaser is always problematical, and scarcely makes on his sensible faculties the impression made by a known and determinate gain: a man who was hesitating before whether to employ his capital in this way, or in some other, viz., say, the establishment of some species of manufacture, is by this newly constituted cheapness of land determined to give the preference to husbandry. But will husbandry be a more advantageous speculation than the manufacture would have been? This is more than any body can tell. Perhaps it would have been, perhaps not: and whether it would or no, perhaps he thinks so, perhaps not: more will depend upon his temper a great deal, than upon the extra-cheapness of the land.

[It might still be urged in defence of the measure][2] that if it does sink the selling price of land, and thereby take money out of the pockets of those who have to sell land, it takes no more out of their pockets than it puts into the pockets of those who have to buy land. The reply [however, that can rightly be given to this sort of argument] is here as elsewhere, on this occasion as on others, that the advantage, though equal to the inconvenience in pounds, shillings, and pence, is far from being so in respect of human feelings:

[1][cf. Wealth of Nations, bk. III, ch. IV.]
[2][The MS reads "The answer is".]

the purchasers being thereby put into the condition of those who reap a gain, while the sellers are in respect to the same sum put into the condition of those who sustain a loss.

That, as far as this effect obtains, a clear loss of happiness is sustained upon the whole, is not in fair reasoning to be denied: it remains only to ascertain in what cases it really takes place and what may be the amount of it, and to enquire whether, as far as it does obtain, it may not admitt in a certain degree of compensation.

[1]One consideration will be sufficient to put us to a certain degree at our ease. We know the utmost possible amount of the loss, and it is not immoderate. What is at the present or any other given period the difference between the produce of money laid out in the purchase of land, and money laid out in the funds? Somewhere about the difference between 3 per Cent and 3½ per Cent: somewhere about 1/7. Below this pitch we are sure that no possible glut in the quantity of land brought to market, nor any possible scarcity in the quantity of capital brought to market, can ever sink it.

What is more, we are pretty sure that it can never be sunk quite so low: since for a given income landed security, I mean the ownership or condition of landlord in respect to land, will always be preferred by the bulk of mankind to any other. It is a remark that any body may have made, and Adam Smith has put the stamp of his authority upon it.[2]

The price of land may sink and sink to a frightful depth, to such a depth as, if considered by itself, might lead one to suspect the truth of this doctrine. Lands actually did sink under the state of exhaustion produced by the American war to a very frightful depth: to perhaps 20 or 18 years purchase: but then the price of stock and other income fell with it in at least equal proportion. If lands were fallen from 30 to 20 or 18 years purchase, it was when stocks were fallen from 93 or 94 to 53 or 54.

Land, that is income arising out of property in land, has and always hath had a decided preference in comparison of the only other saleable source of secure and perpetual income, government annuities:* annuities payable by government out of the produce of

---

[1] [2][Crossed out in the MS.] [Wealth of Nations, bk. III, ch. I.]

*All other sources of secure and perpetual [income] are either reducible to the two above mentioned, or of too inconsiderable an amount to be worth considering in the present view. Mortgage rights considered in respect of the income [?] are allottments out of landed income: considered in respect of the security, they are

taxes and the other branches of the public income: insomuch that taking men upon an average (particular situations, fancies, and ways of thinking excepted) a man will always be ready to pay a greater price for an income of the former description, than for an equal income of the latter.†

Landed income therefore can not be sunk in price by any cause, but that income in government annuities must sink still more: it can not be sunk by the operation of any cause except of such an one, if such there be, by the operation of which, the prices of both these sources of secure and perpetual income (which for the purpose of the argument at least may be termed the only existing sources of such income) are sunk together.

The commodities in the great property market are on the one hand ready money, with the addition of such paper as has obtained the currency of ready money: on the other hand such sources of perpetual income as are looked upon as secure. These are landed estates, mortgages on landed estates, and public securities.

Sources of perpetual income, all sorts taken together, will sell for more as compared with currency in general, the greater the quantity is of such currency in the country, or, to speak more correctly, the greater the number of the existing masses of currency of such magnitude as to be adequate to the purchase of such sources of perpetual income, taken in like manner together: they will sell for less, the less the quantity of such currency.

The quantity of currency grows relatively scarce, not only by its own diminution, but by any encrease in the quantity of the saleable perpetuities. Of landed estates offered to sale, the quantity can not

contingent rights to the whole. Annuities payable by the E[ast] India Company are annuities charged partly upon the trade, that is upon the personal security of that company, [but] partly and principally upon the revenue raised by them in the exercise of their rights of sovereignty out of their possessions in Hindostan. Incomes arising out of shares in the produce of canals, roads etc., besides being in comparison but trifling objects, are but so many modifications of landed income.

Income derived from these sources I term *secure* and *perpetual*, with reference and in opposition to income derived out of what is called personal security, which is *not perpetual*, and which can not in comparison of either of those other sources be spoken of as *secure*.

†The grounds of this superiority have been in good measure remarked by Adam Smith: the superior security, independent of the solvency of government, the superior importance it conferrs as well by its conspicuousness and publicity, as by the various modifications of power that are attached to it: add to this, in almost all instances, the capacity of encrease, an advantage absolutely denied to property in government annuities.

be encreased by government unless in the way proposed: of estates offered in mortgage, the quantity can not be encreased by government: but of stocks the quantity can be encreased by government, and constantly is in the course of every war encreased by government.

Considered with reference to one another, land at any rate must ever sell for more than either of the other two. For more than stock for the reasons above-mentioned: for more than mortgages of land for the same reasons, though not operating in this instance with altogether equal force. In this point of view landed estates have, in a particular state of things, under the existing laws a particular advantage: and that is, that when the only species of saleable perpetuities that can be suddenly encreased, is encreased accordingly, and that to such an amount as to sink the value of land to such a degree as that 5 per Cent is to be made of money by laying it out in land, money upon mortgages will not be to be had at all: for by the existing restriction, while it subsists, on the rate of interest, more than 5 per Cent can not be given for money to be secured by mortgage.*

There are but two ways in which the price of the whole mass of sources of perpetual income (that is the exchangeable value of such annual income with reference to that of ready money) can be sunk: by an augmentation taking place in the quantum of that mass, or by a diminution in the quantity of ready money.†

But the measure in question neither has, nor will be supposed to have, any tendency to diminish the quantity of ready money in the country: whatever it collects with one hand, it deals out with another.

As little has it any tendency to add any thing to the compound mass just spoken of, with which ready money is contrasted, and of which ready money forms the price.

On the contrary, that natural and, it may be said, unavoidable

---

*At this period it is evident that the fall in the value of the two other species of saleable perpetuities must experience a retardation in comparison of the pitch to which it would arrive otherwise: the money which at present is lent out on mortgage, would by ineligibility of this source of income be thrown back altogether upon the two others, of the benefit of which reflux the price of stocks would of course obtain its share. Government being exempted from the laws against what is called usury, while individuals are bound, this is one reason why in war time especially the removal of those mischievous obstacles to universal convenience and general wealth will be particularly hopeless.

†Under the notion of ready money, paper currency must to this purpose be included.

tendency of the measure is to contribute more or less to the reduction of that mass, viz. by the reduction of such part of it as consists in government annuities.

To this effect it will contribute in a greater or less degree, according to the application made of the produce of the proposed resource. If applied *in toto* to the extinction of the public debt, it will operate in the same proportion to the reduction of the mass of government annuities: it will thereby in a direct way raise the value of the remainder of that mass, and in an indirect way, as we have seen, but by necessary consequence, that of landed income.

This application, it may be said, is not essential to the measure: which must be confessed to be true, though a measure which I recommend as concomitant to the principal one is to apply at least a very considerable part of the produce of the measure in this way.

But in one instance the application thus recommended is so natural a result of the measure it may be considered as constituting a part of it: as in [a] manner included in it: and that is the suffering this course to be taken by such part of the produce as it finds already existing in the shape of government annuities. What it finds in other shapes, and converts accordingly into that of ready money, it may employ either in the current service of the year, or in buying in a proportionable quantum of government annuities. But as to whatever it finds already existing in the shape of government annuities, it would be a violent, an unnatural measure indeed, if, instead of suffering that part to remain extinguished, to the diminution *pro tanto* of the public debt, government were to keep it alive, for the purpose of selling it, and employing in the shape of ready money the produce of the sale.

One thing must all this while be admitted, viz. that if land were in our days, as Adam Smith seems to think it, at a monopoly price, and that price superior to the difference in price resulting from the natural causes of preference above alluded to, an encrease in the frequency of its coming to market might operate to a certain extent a reduction in the price. But when I consider how small the difference is between the interest a man makes of his money by laying it out in the purchase of landed income, and what he makes by laying it out in the purchase of government annuities, I do not see how this difference, to be any thing, can well be less than it is at present.* At

*Enquiring of professional men I was informed that when a man, by laying out his money in government annuities, made no more than 3½ per Cent, he could make as [little as] 3 per Cent clear of Land Tax by laying it out in land [*sic*].

any rate by seeing this difference we see the utmost possible amount of the apprehended depretiation on which the force of the objection I am considering depends:* and I can not but be pretty confident that those who may come to have land to sell, have much more to expect from the tendency the measure has to raise the price of property in land and property in government annuities taken together, than they have to apprehend from its tendency to sink the price of property in land in comparison with property in government annuities.

As to the proposition of Adam Smith, that the event of a fall in the price of land would be a desirable one rather than otherwise, I can state it only as an argument *ad hominem*, calculated to operate on any person with whom the authority of that justly celebrated writer may be conclusive. In his way of viewing the matter, the event appeared a desirable one upon the whole: in my way of viewing the matter, it does not. With me what is called public or national benefit is as nothing, any further than as I see it realized in the bosoms of individuals. Look out for the individuals whose interests will be affected by the measure, and having found them, enquire: is it likely to be attended with an encrease, or with a diminution of satisfaction upon the whole: if it benefits some and prejudices others, does the advantage gained and the enjoyment reaped on the part of those

---

*In conformity to the principles above laid down, it would be easy to shew that the causes which, in the instance of particular commodities, render the depretiation of them a necessary consequence of any encrease in the frequency with which they come to market (the quantity of ready money remaining the same) do not apply to this source of perpetual income. But such a discussion, if given at large, would take up [much] room, and, after what has been said, will, I hope, not be deemed necessary.

The case is that in the affections of mankind, among objects of consumption, every article that comes to market has for its competitor not only every object of similar consumption, but every other object of consumption that a man is acquainted with and has any relish for: not only wearables come into competition with wearables, eatables with eatables, but eatables with wearables, and so on throughout. And the greater [the] number of rival articles each article has, the easier the market is glutted with any one.

On the other hand, in regard to the sources of secure and permanent income there are in a manner but two: property in government annuities and property in land, of which the latter, [as] we have seen, is always the more valuable: whatever depretiation therefore falls upon either, must fall upon both, but in such a manner that the brunt of it will always be born[e] by property in government securities, not by property in land.

As to sources of income on one hand and articles of consumption on the other, it is evident they are altogether incommensurable, and incapable of coming into competition, any otherwise than in as far as the interest of the present comes into competition with the interest of the future.

whom it benefits, appear to exceed or to fall short of the prejudice sustained and suffering undergone by those who will find themselves prejudiced by it? This, and this only, is the scale in which I can ever bring myself to weigh the effects and tendency of a political measure.

[*Objection XII. The measure would be a breach of faith in the instance of property in the funds.*]

Another objection applies only to such part of the property in question as may happen to be invested in the funds. To extend it to property of this sort, it may be said, would be a breach of faith. The proprietors of stock are either persons who have lent their money to government, or purchasers of stock standing in the place of such lenders. Which ever predicament they stand in, what government engaged for was to pay them at least the interest without deduction: to them or their natural representatives, while they thought fit to keep it undisposed of: to those—who soever they may be—to whom they may think fit to dispose of it, whether by transfer or bequest, in the event of their thinking fit to dispose of it. Of this engagement the plan in question is a direct breach: from the natural representative, when removed from the deceased to a certain distance, it takes away interest and principal altogether: from the representative by bequest it takes away in a very considerable measure.

This argument, which I have placed purposely in the strongest point of view, to which I trust I have done no injustice by the manner of stating it, is plausible, but [it] is not conclusive. In engaging to the public creditor to pay him at all events interest at a certain rate in proportion to his capital, what the state engaged for was to continue to him that part of his property in the same state of entirety as the rest of it. A tax falling exclusively upon property in the funds would be a breach of faith of the nature of that which the argument imputes. An eventual defalcation applying to property in the funds in common with every other species of property whatsoever, is no such breach of faith.

If it were, then every tax on consumption, in short with a few or no exceptions every tax whatsoever, is in like manner a breach of faith: for, to instance the plainest case, where is the tax on consumption by which property in the funds is not affected? affected just as much as property of any other kind to equal amount? No sooner does a man make any use of his property, no sooner does it become valuable to him in reality as well as in idea, than the tax attaches on him. He might have forborn to make use of it, it is true, he might have forborn to spend it, and that for ever, he might have kept it in accumulating and that *ad infinitum,* and by that means have preserved himself from being affected by any tax. Yes, to be sure, he might: he might have forborn putting his property to any kind of use: and so long as it was of no use to him, so long as it was his property in name only and not in reality, so long he might have preserved it from ordinary taxation: but the instant he offers to put any part of his property to any kind of use, the tax goes hand in hand with the use.

If he had not invested his property in the funds, if he had not lent it to government, or purchased the debt due to those who had been lenders to government, would it have been untouched, would it have been less exposed to the hand of government than now that it is in the funds? This is the real question to make in order to know whether the plan contains any thing in it incompatible with good faith [or] whether good faith is in any respect violated by the measure.

In no shape does the regulation bear harder upon the proprietor of stock than upon a proprietor of any other denomination: of the burthen, if a burthen it can be called, he has no greater share than every other man: of the relief that results from the employing of this unburthensome mode of supply in lieu of burthensome ones— of the relief he has no less. But (whosoever they apply to) the relief is greater than the burthen: the stockholder then, so far from being a sufferer by the arrangement, is a gainer by it, and that as much as anybody else.

So far as property of this sort is for ever protected from use, it stands protected from the effect of the regulation here proposed: stock in the hands of bodies corporate, which never die, will never be subject to the operation of it.

It has no tendency then to lower the price of stocks [and] to diminish the value of money in the funds. The price of stocks keeps pace with the price of other sources of income in the purchase of which money might equally well be laid out as in the purchase of stock. But all other property is as much subject to the regulation proposed as money in the funds is. A man will save nothing therefore by laying out his money in the purchase of other property rather than laying it out in the purchase of stock. The regulation will therefore afford him no inducement for abstaining to buy into the funds more than he had before. If the regulation were proposed to be confined in its operation to money in the funds, then indeed it would lay property of that description under the disadvantage supposed by the objection: then indeed it would tend, as far as it operated, to lower the price of stocks.

But no such exclusive regulation is proposed.*

[*Objection XIII. The measure would be a breach of faith at least with regard to foreign stockholders.*]

It may be still insisted, that as applied to foreign stockholders, to proprietors of money in our funds resident abroad, the objection will still hold. It is not with respect to them on the footing of a tax on consumption. In a tax on consumption native stockholders would, as well as other proprietors, bear their share. But in a tax on consumption levied in Britain, in a tax on consumables in as far as consumed in Britain, stockholders resident abroad would bear no share. They would however, unless specially exempted, bear their share in the burthen of the proposed regulation. It would therefore be in their instance, notwithstanding any thing that has been said, a breach of faith.

I answer yes, provided they were not at liberty to sell out: but they will remain at liberty to sell out as much as they are at present.

True it is, it may be replied, they are at liberty to sell out. But what is more, they are under a sort of obligation to sell out, or else submitt to a disadvantage of new creation, a disadvantage which formed no part of the conditions under which they bought in. This then is one hardship: and the fall of price which will ensue in proportion as they act under the rod of this obligation and sell out accordingly, is another hardship.

My answer is, that the objection would hold good, [if]¹ the number of persons selling out at a time under a sense of this disadvantage were likely to be considerable enough to effect such a sink [*sic*] in the price of that species of property as would be worth regarding. But

---

*It is equally evident that if money in the funds and no other species of property were to be exempted from this regulation, the tendency of such exemption would be to raise the price of stocks: and would therefore be in so far beneficial, in the eyes of those who look upon the high price of that species of property as a national advantage, [as] an ingredient in the sum of national prosperity, instead of being a symptom only of the existence of other ingredients of real value. But by such an exemption the amount of the resource would *pro tanto* be diminished. And why should it in respect of this article more than another?

¹[The MS reads "were it likely that . . ."]

x

this supposition I can not help looking upon as altogether an improbable one: not a single per Cent should I ever apprehend from it.

1. In the first place, a very large proportion of the money in the British funds held by foreigners resident abroad is said to be held by public bodies:* and to stock in such hands the proposed regulation does not extend.

2. In the next place, the case of a person who has not one such relation as is termed to the present purpose a near relation, is not a very common one.

3. In the next place, neither is it a very common case for a man to bear such an affection for a strange person not connected with him by the ties either of blood or marriage, as that a regulation which, allowing him to bequeath to the stranger the half of his fortune, should restrict him only as to the remaining half, would be [felt]¹ as a very heavy grievance: so heavy as to outweigh the personal advantages, whatever they were, that operate[d] as inducements to prefer this mode of investing his property to every other. And to this point apply the observations, though to be sure not with altogether equal force, which have been already made with relation to the objection grounded on the apprehension that the regulation might operate as an inducement to men to convert their property into annuities for their own lives.

4. In the fourth and last place, were the persons concerned ever so determined at the first appearance of the regulation not to continue their property in our funds upon such terms, neither on this supposition does there seem any sufficient ground to warrant the apprehension of any sudden or very considerable selling out and fall from such a cause. A man may say to himself, *I won't keep my money in;* but the particular day for taking it out will not come. He has his whole life for doing it in: and having such a latitude in point of time, and no wife, no child, no near relation, to urge him to dispatch, what should render him in haste? He will say to himself: *I will wait till I can meet with some way of laying out my money at home or elsewhere that I like better*: he will wait accordingly: and in the meantime the first emotion will be over, the idea will have become familiar to him, and the particular day for executing his former resolution will never come.

A more material observation, though an objection of a contrary

---

*See Smith's Wealth of Nations [bk. V, ch. I, pt. IV and ch. II, pt. I].
¹[The MS reads "left".]

aspect is, that the regulation would, in respect of this part of its subject matter, be peculiarly exposed to evasion: and to this purpose might be quoted the frauds said to be practised by foreigners in the instance of Tontines.

My answer is:

In the first place, that this fraud, like other frauds, will, when pointed out, be of course combated by such checks and guards as [?] the nature of the case shall have been found to suggest.

In the next place, that should those guards prove in here and there an instance ineffectual, the observation in this instance as in others we have seen goes to detract only *pro tanto* from the quantum of the produce and benefit to be expected from the measure, but forms no objection to the principle of it.

In the third and last place, that as far as such frauds prove effectual, they remove the objection grounded on the supposed breach of faith; and as far as the intention of practising them, and the hope of practising them with success, prevails, so far they will operate in diminution of whatever degree of propensity to sell out, the regulation may be looked upon as liable to produce.

OF THE INDIRECT AND REMOTE EFFECTS TO BE
EXPECTED FROM THE PROPOSED MEASURE

A wise minister will never adopt a measure, and in particular a mode of supply, without having before him a picture of its probable effects represented in every point of view. If it be a tax, he will look not only to the effects of it in the way of supply [i.e.] to the quantum of the produce, supposing every thing to be paid that the law shall have ordered to be paid, but to the effects of it in the way of encouragement with relation to rival articles whether of home or foreign produce, to the effects of it in the way of dis[?]couragement with relation to such articles, if any there be, to the production or sale of which it may be necessary or of use: to the frauds [and] evasions to which the collection of the tax may be exposed: to the expedients which the nature of the case may suggest for guarding against such evasions: to the temptations of power to which the execution of those provisions may be in danger of giving birth [or] may expose the probity of those to whom the execution of them is committed.

In the investigation of the effects of the mode of supply here proposed, much remains not to be done. The principal outlines of the picture have already been given [1]for such was the course of this essay marked out.[2] The principal part of this task became requisite to be performed for the purpose of obviating the several objections to which the proposal appeared liable to give birth.

Such part of its effects as have no reference to any particular species of property more than another have already been stated: they need only to be recapitulated: they have been shewn to be as follows:

1. It tends in a certain degree, I do not pretend to say in any very high degree, to promote marriage.

2. It tends thereby to check concubinage: more especially as the share which the concubine and her offspring can receive from the posthumous bounty of the person in question is reduced one half. He is thereby debarred to that amount from doing in their favour what he has it in his power to do in favour of a legitimate object of his affections and her issue.

3. By narrowing in this way the field of posthumous bounty, it affords some incitement to a man to make a partial provision at

---

[1] [2][Put into brackets, perhaps by a later hand.]

least to take effect during his life-time for persons so related to him, and thereby lessens the danger of their being discarded without provision during his life-time, or finding themselves neglected and unprovided for at his death.

4. By the encouragement it affords to marriage it applies in proportion a check to promiscuous fornication.

I proceed now to such part of its effects as result from the quantity of ready money (paper currency included) which it sweeps into the Exchequer: and consequently on the prices of every other species of property which comes to be exchanged for ready money.

The result of this part of its operation will be found to depend upon the application made of the money which it produces: but take any parcel of this money at pleasure, there are but two possible modes in which it can be applied to the public use: 1. to the current service of the year: or 2. in discharge of the public debt.

Taking the whole mass together there are accordingly three different applications which may be conceived to be made of it: 1. the applying the whole to the current service: or 2. the applying the whole to the extinction of debt: or 3. applying part to the current service, and part to the extinction of the public debt. I will begin with the first supposition as the most simple, merely for that reason, since, as we shall see, it is altogether an improbable one.

Applied in the whole to the current service of the year, it will have the same destination as the bulk of that fund which is now collected from taxes: it will come in lieu of, and stand in the place of, so much money as would otherwise be collected by taxes: the measure will *pro tanto* come in lieu of taxes to the same amount.

The ready money which it sweeps into the Exchequer must be distinguished into two parcels: 1. that which it finds already and attaches upon in the shape of ready money, and [2.] that which it obtains from the sale of the several other species of property on which it attaches.

That which it finds in the shape of ready money must also be distinguished into two parcels: that which it finds in small masses destined for the current expenditure of the possessor: and that which it finds in large masses destined for the purchase of landed property, government annuities, farming, manufacturing or mercantile stock or any other of the sources of perpetual income, or to serve in the shape of circulating capital in any one of the branches of industry last mentioned.

That part of it which it finds in the shape of circulating capital was destined to the maintenance of individuals of the productive class, was destined to contribute to the encrease [of] the quantity of wealth in the country: that part of it which was destined for the purchase of a share of the other sources of perpetual income was destined to contribute to the maintenance of individuals of either of the productive or of the unproductive classes, according to the uses which the respective sellers meant to make of the money when received. If to employ it in the production or improvement of other imperishable articles such as land, or slowly perishable articles such as houses and household furniture, [1]or self-reproducing articles such as cattle, fish, and useful vegetables,[2] or to lend it to others who would so employ it, then to the encrease of the quantity of property in the country: if in the production of articles quickly perishable or of quick consumption such as eatables, drinkables, and wearables of a costly nature, that is requiring much more labour to be expended in the production of them than that which might have provided in those ways for an equal number of individuals, then to the diminution of the quantity of wealth in the country, partly by the employment of individuals altogether of the unproductive class,* partly by the employment of individuals of the productive class whose productions, without contributing to the sustenance of man, are of a quickly perishable nature.

In respect of that part of the produce which had been destined for the current expenditure of the possessor, it stands upon a footing not much different from that of an equal sum produced by taxes: but in respect of that part which was destined for the purchase of any of the above mentioned sources of perpetual income, or rather for the contributing in the shape of circulating capital to the encrease of the quantity of property [i.e. wealth] in the country, it stands upon a footing very different.

Of the money which a given individual pays in the course of any year in taxes, either the whole would, had there been no taxes, have been spent by him, or part would have been spent and part saved: as the total expenditure of the nation is to the total of its savings, so is the total of the money paid in taxes to the total of the money

---

[1] [2][Put into brackets, perhaps at a later date.]
*Menial servants, players, singers, dancers.

which would thus have been saved, if it had not been carried off by taxes. But the amount of the national savings in a year bears but a very small proportion to the amount of the national expenditure in a year: the amount of what more would have been saved had it not been for taxes, bears therefore but a very small proportion to the amount of the money paid in taxes.

What is raised by taxes is therefore taken, as to all but a very small part of it, not from national saving, but from national expenditure.

Applied in lieu of taxes, applied to the payment of the interest of the debt, it certainly would act, as to the greatest part of it, in diminution of the national capital: but ought this part of its operation to be placed to the account of disadvantage?—By no means, but rather the contrary.

In the present state of things, in this country of security and property, every year sees an addition made to the quantity of national capital, and this not only to the absolute quantity but to the relative quantity with reference to the number of inhabitants. The effect and proof of this is that unless it be in time of war, every year sees a step made in, or at least towards, a reduction in the rate of interest. But the interest of money constitutes in part or in whole the income of a very large proportion of the people: a reduction in the rate of interest is to this part of the community a proportionable reduction of their income. Of this reduction no particle can ever take place without being proportionably accompanied with the sensation of a loss. The loss thus falling upon one part of the community is attended, it is true, with gain to equal amount accruing to another part. Yes, to equal nominal amount: but in no point of view is the gain equivalent to the loss. It fails of being so even in point of arithmetical effect:* but were it in this sense altogether equal it would want a good deal of being so in point of moral or, to speak more precisely, in point of *pathological* effect: in regard to the effect it has upon the feelings of individuals.

Is the amount of the quantity thus taken away from the national capital in a given year greater than the sum of the savings made in the course of that year? It tends to produce an enhancement of the rate of interest which if it does produce, it produces a sensation of loss upon the whole, it produces a national disadvantage. Is it equal? It keeps the rate of interest steady, it preserves a certain part of the community from the sensation of a decline of fortune, it produces a

*5 taken from 20, takes away ¼: added to 20, it adds only 1/5.

national benefit. Is it inferior? It tends, though with less force, to keep the rate of interest steady and, at any rate as far as it operates, it produces a national advantage.

In two then out of the only three possible cases it is of service, and in the third it is of no disservice. It puts in this case into the hands of the public, masses of capital which otherwise would have been in the hands of individuals. To these individuals the regulation produces no loss, because they neither ever had the money in question, nor ever expected to have it. Were it to be employed all of it in lieu of taxes, were it to be applied none of it to the reduction of the public debt but all of it to the mere payment of interest which would otherwise be paid by taxes, even then it would be of no disservice. Let this resource be carried to its utmost length, let the whole of it be employed in the payment of interest and so in lieu of taxes, the amount of it in a year can never be equal to the sum total of what is saved and laid up all over the nation in the same time. At the utmost therefore it can never effect a diminution of the national capital nor so much as put a stop to its encrease: at the utmost it can only retard the accumulation, and in so doing its effect is rather beneficial, as we have seen, than otherwise.

Of the encrease of the quantity of wealth in a country, any more than of the causes and consequences of that effect, no clear or just idea can be formed, without taking into consideration at the same time the state of the population.

On the relation of wealth to population may be grounded a distinction between an *absolute* and a *relative* encrease of the quantity of wealth in any country. The quantity of wealth in a country may be said to have received an *absolute* encrease during any period, when the sum total of wealth, howsoever it be with the number of inhabitants who share in it, is greater at the end of that period than at the beginning. On the other hand a relative encrease (meaning with reference to population) is what the quantity of wealth can not be said to have received, unless the ratio of the sum total of wealth to the sum total of population be greater at the end of that period than at the beginning: insomuch that supposing at each epoch a perfectly equal division had been made of the whole stock of wealth among the whole number of inhabitants, the shares would have been greater at the second epoch than at the first. The difference being thus explained, it is evident that the connection between an absolute and a relative encrease is, however natural, by no means a necessary one:

the absolute quantity of wealth may have received an encrease when the relative quantity has not received any encrease, or has even received a diminution as [is the case] if population goes on faster than economy: as on the other hand the relative quantity again may have received an encrease when the absolute quantity has not received any encrease or has even received a diminution. Instances [of such a development are] 1. great slaughter with little devastation, 2. pestilence, [and perhaps][1] 3. famine.

Is the nation richer now than it was twenty years ago? To this question different persons may give different answers apparently contradictory and yet both of them true. It is richer: it is not richer: the quantity of wealth has received an absolute encrease; it has not received a relative one. There may be less wealth in the country, and yet the inhabitants may be more at their ease: either because what there remains is more equally divided: or because though the quantity of wealth has suffered a reduction, the number of the inhabitants has suffered a still more considerable one. After an inundation in which, as in those made purposely for national defence as in the Low Countries, the inhabitants have time to take care of themselves, the absolute quantity of wealth and the relative are both reduced. After a plague, the absolute quantity remaining unreduced, the relative is encreased: after a war, the absolute quantity is reduced, the relative may have been either reduced or encreased, or [be] unaffected, as it may happen.

This connection however (the connection between an absolute and the relative encrease in the quantity of wealth in a community) is, though not strictly a necessary, altogether a natural one: and whatever may be the effects produced for the moment by violent and accidental causes, in the ordinary course of things they are perhaps without exception found as constantly connected as if they were inseparable. Where property is tolerably secure, and no worse calamities than now and then a foreign war are experienced, population goes on more or less encreasing, and wealth, the result of economy, at a still greater rate. Children in greater and greater numbers are every year produced, children which for a certain number of years in the earlier part of their lives consume something without producing anything. But wealth in still greater quantities than is necessary for the maintenance of the children during that expensive period of their lives is at the same time every year laid up.

---

[1][The word famine in the MS is followed by a question mark.]

Those who have children lay up money for their children, and more money than their children consume the value of during their non-productive age: those who have no children have still the same reasons for laying up money as long as they can expect to have them: and even they who never possessed such expectation or have lost it, want not reasons to encourage them to thrift.

In aid of this propensity, which is to be found more or less in all men above the rank of savage, comes the further effect of the progress of civilisation and improvements in the arts. At an early period of society land has little expence bestowed on it, buildings are rude and of little value, and in comparison of the articles destined for immediate consumption, such as coarse meats and drinks, articles that are either treasured up for use or are capable of being used for a long while as they are consumed, are proportionably but few. Improved lands, costly buildings, plantations, rich and durable furniture, books, pictures, prints and statues are the accumulating fruits of the encreasing ingenuity and frugality of still riper and riper ages.

All these articles are not only valuable in themselves, but capable of purchasing each other as well directly as by standing as security for the money employed in purchases. All these therefore, in as far as, by standing as security for the money employed as capital in the purchase of income, contribute to diminish the value of money so employed, contribute to diminish the quantity of the income to be had in exchange for such capital, contribute in other words to encrease the value of income to a given amount in comparison of that of the capital which may be had for it.

All these several encreases, the encrease in the absolute quantity of wealth, the encrease of population, and that encrease in the relative quantity of wealth which is the result of the excess in the encrease of the absolute quantity of wealth above the encrease in the population, are capable of being proved and measured by actual enumeration: but if not so accurately measured their existence may be proved at least, with not less certainty and with much greater facility and expedition by observations on the price of land, on the price of funds, and of the current rates of interest. The decrease in the price of any commodity is a certain sign of an encrease in the competition prevailing among those who have it to sell. An encrease in the competition prevailing among those who have a species of commodity to sell is sooner or later a necessary consequence of an encrease in the relative quantity of the article to be sold: that is, of the quantity of it to be sold in comparison of the effectual demand, in comparison of the quantity actually wanted to be disposed of of the article for which the article first mentioned is wanted to be sold.

The sources of *income* furnished in exchange for ready money are landed property, money in the funds, money placed in the way of interest and secured on landed property, income arising out of and secured by the funds, and income guaranteed by more personal security, such as expected profits of trade or profession.

Land itself is not susceptible of encrease but the value of land is, and the quantity of land which has received an improved value is susceptible of encrease and, in a thriving country such as Great Britain, is actually receiving encrease at a very rapid rate every day. When land rises, it is a sign that, of the ready money which has been accumulated, that part which is in hands that are desirous of exchanging it for land, has encreased: and not only encreased, but encreased in a greater degree than the annual value of the whole mass of cultivated land.

When the value of income secured in land rises, that is when the rate of interest of money laid out on mortgage falls, it is a sign that, of the ready money which has been accumulated, that part which is in hands that are desirous of exchanging it for annuities secured on land, has not only encreased, but encreased in a greater degree than the amount of the land which the proprietors are able and willing to pledge for the sake [?] of ready money, as a security for annuities thus granted in exchange for ready money.

When the value of income secured in the funds rises, that is, when the funds rise, in other words, when the sum of money encreases which must be given in order to obtain such a share in the stocks as shall yield a given annual sum in the way of annuity or interest, it is a sign that of the ready money which has been accumulated, that part which is in hands that are desirous of exchanging it for annuities so secured (secured on the money annually paid in the way of taxes or otherwise by individuals to the trustees of the public) has not only encreased, but encreased in a greater degree than the quantity of such annuities which the possessors are able and willing to exchange for ready money: a state of things which may take place, and actually has taken place, notwithstanding many successive encreases in the quantity of the funded national debt, that is in the quantity of the annuities so granted, and thence in that which the possessors are able and willing to dispose of in exchange for ready money.

When income grounded on mere personal security rises in value, that is, when the sum of money encreases which a man must give in order to obtain an annuity so secured to a given amount so secured, in other words, when the annuity so secured which a man can purchase for a given sum of money is diminished, in other words, when the current rate of interest of money so placed out is reduced, it is a sign that of the ready money which has been accumulated that part which is in hands that are desirous of exchanging it for annuities so secured has not only encreased, but encreased in a greater degree than the total demand in the way of ready money on the part of such persons who are not only desirous of borrowing but capable of giving such personal security as is deemed sufficient, that is, capable of presenting such grounds for the expectation of their being able to pay the annuity, for the time it is to last, out of the sale of moveable property or out of the growing profits of trade or profession, as are deemed sufficient.

[1]In the estimate of the effects of so important a system [as that here proposed], of a system of such considerable and extensive influence, its effects upon prices must not be overlooked. From this topic reasons for adoption, but more naturally and more copiously reasons for rejection, well or ill grounded, will be apt to be alledged. The prices in question are that of income in all its shapes compared with ready money, whether the income be secured by the actual ownership of land, or by the eventual possession of land in the way of mortgage, or by an obligation on the part of the public to bestow it annually out of the produce of taxes or other sources of revenue, or by an obligation on the part of an individual to furnish it out of the produce of the sale of moveables or out of the casual profits in the way of profession or trade.[2]

In all these instances, what ought to be the primary object of government? *Steadiness.* This ought to be the first object of its wishes at any rate, if not of its measures.

Why so? since what is lost to one man by a change of price is just so much gained to another, both of them members of the community, the interest of each forming an equal portion of the interest of the community. True: but such is the constitution of human

---

[1] [2][This passage is crossed out in the MS.]

nature, that the enjoyment resulting from a gain is never equal to the suffering resulting from a loss.

Steadiness of price is a branch of that species of security which has property for its object. The one respects property considered in a state of reciprocal migration, as the other respects it when considered in a quiescent state. As property in its quiescent state is affected by robbery, by theft, and fraud, and injustice, and by natural calamity, so is property in its state of migration by fluctuation of prices. What makes the species of insecurity to which its state of migration is exposed the more serious and important, is that it is a state in which almost every kind of article must arrive in order to possess any value [and] to find its value. This is true at least with regard to all individual articles of use and consumption: it is not equally true of the great classes and distinctions of property of which the denomination is taken from its source, viz. landed property, income secured by a share in the funds, income secured by a charge on landed property, and income secured by a personal obligation to furnish it without any specific fund.

The first thing to be wished for is that prices as betwixt all these species of property should remain fixed as much as possible and as long as possible.

The next thing is that in as far as a change must inevitably take place, it be such a change as men are better prepared for rather than any for which they are not so well prepared.

The third and last thing is that the change, if it must take place, should be of that sort which is the result of prosperity, rather than of that sort which is the result of adversity: in other words, that the change which results in the prices of the several species of wealth considered with reference to one another, should be of that sort which is the result of an augmentation of the total mass of wealth in a community, rather than of the sort which is the result of a diminution of that mass.

The effect of an encrease of general prosperity, the effect of an augmentation of the total mass of wealth in a community, is a decrease in the value of capital as compared with income, is a rise of the value of periodical and perpetual income in comparison with an existing mass of moveable property, with a sum of money for instance once paid: or to speak conversely [and] to take the more familiar mode of expression, a decrease in the value of any existing mass of moveable property considered as employed in the purchase of a periodical and perpetual income, a decrease in the value of ready money. Developed and applied to the great divisions of property, the result is that lands sell dearer, that is, for a greater number of years purchase: in other words, ready money laid out in the purchase of landed income fetches less: stocks rise, that is a given annuity secured upon the produce of taxes or other public property fetches more ready money: in other words, a given sum of ready money employed in the purchase of such an annuity fetches less.

[1]Another consideration, if arguments were wanting, might plead with many in favour of this system: the encouragement it affords to marriage.[2] Popularity however is the only merit for which I can take upon me to give it credit on this score. Vain and shallow, I must confess, is to my eyes the policy that seeks to afford encouragement* to the union between the sexes. As soon would I think of giving a bounty on eating or on sleeping as a bounty upon marriage. Keen appetite joins with affections of a more refined and less universal nature in impelling both sexes to an union, in which the female, wheresoever that appetite has left it the capacity of pursuing its acknowledged interest, will not join but upon the terms of marriage. The class of all others which finds least difficulty in marriage is that of the labouring poor. [Hence] the class of all others in which marriages are most abundant, is that which possesses the smallest share of the sort of encouragement which this policy would give.†

To augment the population of a country [by artificial means which would only extend the non-productive part of the community] is [therefore] to diminish its wealth: meaning relative wealth, wealth in proportion to the numbers of those who share it, the only sense in which preeminence in happiness receives any assistance from preeminence in wealth. A bounty upon marriage is a bounty upon poverty. Its tendency is to produce not plenty but scarcity in the political hive: the encrease it produces, if any, is among the drones: on the numbers of the bees it can exert no influence: population

---

[1] [2][This passage is crossed out in the MS.]

*By encouragement I mean here encouragement of a positive nature. Encouragements of the negative cast, consisting merely in the removal of any positive discouragements which have been found in force, stand upon a very different footing. On such an occasion, if to aim at encouragement is weakness, to apply or suffer to subsist any thing of discouragement is cruelty.

†There never was that age or country in which the poor shewed any backwardness to marry: but the poor, that is the great majority of the people, are the class of all others which political speculators are apt not to think of.

among the bees is altogether above its sphere. Such then appears to be the character that may be given of every expedient which aims at encreasing population by affording encouragement to marriage. Needless and ineffective, it is only in virtue of inefficiency that it escapes being pernicious.

In legislation it is not enough that the end in view be a desirable one: the means employed ought to be necessary to the attainment of it. *A great book,* says a Greek proverb, *is a great evil*: a great law-book is so most certainly. As a primary object I should never think of proposing the encouragement of marriage: but where it happens to flow from a law in the character of a collateral result, there is at least no harm in it.

A man or woman who has children or other descendants, has the power of making what disposition he pleases of his fortune: and that not only in favour of one child in preference to another, but in favour of any body he pleases: not only so, but all interference on the part of the public administrator is excluded altogether.

Family pride may on this account recommend marriage to here and there an individual in whose eyes the more general inducements to marriage might not be altogether adequate: to me, as well the continuation of wealth in the same family as the affection by which men are disposed to regard such a continuation as an object of importance, would, it is true, appear of no account: but to others on whom that affection has more sway, the gratification thus administered to it may appear an article entitled to be carried to the account of advantage [1]in an estimate taken of the effects of the system here proposed[2].

---

[1] [2][Put into brackets, perhaps at a later date.]

TAX WITH MONOPOLY

TAX WITH MONOPOLY

OR

HINTS OF CERTAIN CASES

IN WHICH

IN ALLEVIATION OF THE BURDEN OF TAXATION, EXCLUSIVE PRIVILEGES MAY BE GIVEN AS AGAINST FUTURE COMPETITORS, WITHOUT PRODUCING ANY OF THE ILL EFFECTS, WHICH IN MOST CASES ARE INSEPARABLE FROM EVERYTHING THAT SAVOURS OF MONOPOLY

EXEMPLIFIED IN THE INSTANCES OF THE

STOCK-BROKING AND BANKING BUSINESSES

Taxes on the profits of traders would, generally speaking, be impracticable: —

1. The difficulty of ascertaining the profit and loss upon each article would be an endless source of evasion.

2. The measures necessary to be taken against evasion, would be an equally endless source of real or supposed oppression.

3. The disclosure of the secrets of the trade would operate as a prohibition of ingenuity and improvement.

I. Stock-brokers

In the business of a stock-broker, none of these objections have place: —

1. & 2. No difficulty about ascertaining profit and loss: loss, none in any case: rate of profit perfectly fixed: the transactions which gave birth to it are always upon record.

3. No secret, no inventions, no improvement in the case.

II. Bankers

1. 2. & 3. No more difficulty about ascertaining profit and loss, nor anything more of invention than in the case of stock-brokers.

The profit of the banker results from the placing out at interest, in large sums, what he finds to spare, out of the money he receives in large and small sums, on condition of returning it as it is wanted.

If in this case there be any such thing as a *secret*, the disclosure of which might be attended with prejudice to anybody, it lies in the money transactions of the *customers,* who deposit the money and draw for it, and of those who, by getting bills discounted or otherwise, deal with this shop in the character of borrowers. Were the knowledge of these transactions generally spread, or were it easily attainable, it might in some instances be attended with prejudice to the parties, by the information given to *rivals* in business, or other *adversaries.* But, for the purpose in question, the knowledge in question might be confined in each instance to a *single accountant* appointed by the crown, whose attention would be confined to the mere *figures,* having neither time to inquire, nor interest in inquiring, into the *history* of any transaction, in [*sic*] the occasion of which this or that sum was drawn for or deposited.

So much for the *tax*—the *burthen.* Now as to the *exclusive privilege*—the *compensation.* The effects to which this sort of institution, in as far as it is mischievous, stands indebted for its mischievousness, are—

1. Enhancement of the price of the article dealt in.

2. Impairing the quality.

3. Lessening consumption, in the case of consumable goods:—or more generally, diminishing the general mass of benefit depending upon this use of the sort of article, [*sic*] whatever it may be.

4. Enhancement of trouble to the customer, by his having farther to go than if dealers were more numerous.

5. (The exclusion of persons already embarked in the business, a still greater grievance, if it existed, is out of the question here.)

None of these ill effects would take place in any degree, in the instance of either of the above professions. Thus, in the case of

I. *The Stock-broker*

1. The price of the service rendered is a fixed per centage; it is amply sufficient: enhancement might be prevented by law.

2. The quality of the service cannot, from the nature of it, either be improved or impaired: neither skill nor invention, nor so much as any extraordinary degree of exertion, have anything to do with it.

3. The demand for this sort of service cannot in the nature of things, be lessened, or anyways affected, by the limitation of the number of the persons whose profession it is to render it, or by the fixation of the price at which they are to render it.

4. The distance between the agent and his employer cannot receive

any enhancement from the exclusive privilege, or from anything else. The agents, how numerous soever, are confined to a spot by the very nature of their business.

II. *The Banker*

1. The service of receiving and keeping—the service rendered to the *depositor* of money, is rendered *gratis,* and though the number of bankers should ever be lessened, there can be no apprehension of their requiring payment for this service.

The price at which the other sort of customer, the *borrower,* is supplied, is equally incapable of being raised by the operation; the rate of interest will depend upon the quantity of capital accumulated in the whole country, not upon the quantity that happens to be in the hands of bankers. A confederacy, and that a successful one, among all the bankers, town and country, to raise the rate of interest, is in itself scarce possible; besides that the rate is actually limited by law.

2. The *quality* of the service is as little susceptible of being *impaired* by such a cause: it is more likely to be improved: each bank being rendered richer, and thereby safer, in proportion as the number is kept down.

3. As little is the demand for this sort of service capable of being lessened by the restriction of the number of hands allowed to render it: the demand for the service, consisting in the *keeping* of money, will depend upon the quantity of money to be kept: the demand for the service consisting in the *loan* of money, will depend upon the quantity of money wanted for a time by those who have value to give for it when the time is over. In neither of these instances has the demand anything to do with the number of the persons whose business it is to render this sort of service.

4. The distance between the professional man and his customer and employer need not receive any enhancement in that case, any more than in the other. Distance has never been a matter much regarded in this branch of business. As to the *London* bankers, instead of *spreading* themselves equally within the circle of the metropolis, their object seems rather to have been to crowd *into,* or as *near* as possible to, Lombard Street.

In the country, whatever distance the depositor and borrower have been used to go, they might contrive to go, were it necessary, without *much* inconvenience. The inconvenience might be done away entirely by proper reservation, adapted to future demands in places where as yet there is none.

A calculation might easily be made of the progressive value of the indemnity, from a retrospective view of the gradual increase in the number of bankers on the one hand, and in the quantity of circulating cash and paper deposited on the other.

The advantages of monopoly find their way without much difficulty to the eyes of dealers.*

Monopoly would be no innovation in this branch of business; an illustrious example is afforded by the bank of England.

Should the principle be approved of, it might be worth while to look over the list of trades, professions, and other lucrative occupations, for the purpose of ascertaining the instances in which this species of compensation might be given, without any such inconvenience as would outweigh the benefit.

The exclusive privilege being a benefit, ought of course to be coupled with the tax in every instance where it is not attended by a preponderant mass of inconvenience to the public at large.

The stock of these cases being exhausted, then, and not till then, may be the time to look out for the instances, if any, in which the tax might stand alone without the indemnity to lighten it.

---

*Not long ago a great banking-house opened upon the plan of giving 3 per cent. for money on condition of its not being drawn out till after a short notice. This was too much, and so it proved: but an indication seems to be afforded that, even without the benefit of the monopoly, the profits of trade are capable of bearing a deduction in this instance.

PROPOSAL FOR A
MODE OF TAXATION

PROPOSAL FOR A MODE OF TAXATION IN WHICH THE BURTHEN MAY BE ALLEVIATED OR EVEN BALLANCED BY AN INDEMNITY:

SHEWING IN WHAT CASES EXCLUSIVE PRIVILEGES ARE PREJUDICIAL AND HOW THEY MAY BE MADE ALTOGETHER INNOCENT AS ALSO HOW A MODE OF COLLECTION NEWLY INTRODUCED MAY BE EXTENDED AND IN SOME CASES SUBSTITUTED WITH ADVANTAGE TO THE EXCISE APPLIED IN THE FIRST INSTANCE TO THE CASE OF BANKERS

1794

[TABLE OF CONTENTS]

To point out subjects of taxation is but a thankless office: without any other intention but to alleviate, or any motive in prospect but the hope of alleviating, the mass of public burthen, a man [who suggests new sources of public revenue] may be looked upon as the author of it: [yet this would be as reasonable and as just] as if the surgeon were treated as the author of the wound which he steps in to cure [and] the healing of which is the sole object of his endeavours, [or] as if the good Samaritan had been treated as the robber. The robber, in this case, where there is one, is the adviser of unnecessary expences, or, to come to the point at once, of unnecessary wars: for all other profusion is but a drop in the ocean in comparison of the waste of war. The robber is the adviser of wars: I speak always of unnecessary wars: the good Samaritan is the volunteer in finance who employs himself in looking out for public burthens with no other view than that of picking out the lightest. *This is your doing: this is what I may thank you for,* cries the individual who finds himself, or imagines himself, affected by the tax: not considering that, if the burthen were not to fall upon him in this shape, it would perhaps fall on him still heavier in some other. *This we may thank you for!* Such is the return which the good Samaritan may expect: for be his oil and his wine ever so good, they can not be poured into the wound without a momentary smart.

A return of this nature, it must be confessed, is but too well merited by too many of those with whose papers the table of the minister is covered at the approach of the period fixed for the provision of the supplies, whose object is to find out where money is to be had, without vouchsafing or even without thinking to reflect on the feelings of those at whose expence it must be extracted. Such were not the views which gave rise to the present enquiry, whatever may be the success of it. The object of the present paper is to enquire, not what would *go down,* but what ought to go down: what [would] go down, not merely with least disturbance from the outcry of the moment, from the clamour of those who are in a situation to make themselves heard, but with least suffering at the long run, with the slightest wound to the feelings of individuals, and that which promises to be the soonest closed.

[1. OF EQUALITY IN TAXATION]

Equality is equity, says a well-known maxim, long current among English lawyers. Abusive as many of the applications are that have been made of it of late years, its propriety in numerous instances will not be disputed. In the department of finance, equality is *equity* as among taxable individuals in other respects of different descriptions, but of equal ability, considered as objects of taxation: in the same department equality is *good husbandry* too, since whatever may be the highest rate of contribution that can with propriety be imposed on taxable individuals of any one description, the Exchequer will be replenished in proportion as the contributions of individuals of other descriptions can be raised to the same pitch. Equality on this behalf is, in short, not only equity and good husbandry, but propriety in every respect, except in such cases, if any, where the observance of its rules is forbidden by particular and superior considerations. Such exceptions are, it must be confessed, not wanting, derived, as we shall see, from the topics of inflexible justice and humanity. At present let us confine our views to the application that may be made of [the] general rule.

All taxes that are of any continuance, must come some how or other out of income: but in the instance of one class of taxes they are *forced,* and are laid upon the *possession* of income: in the instance of another class they are *voluntary,* and derived from the *expenditure* of it. Taxes on expenditure, to be equal, should be so managed as to be drawn from individuals of all descriptions without distinction: and so they are in the main under the laws of this as well as other countries.

It would naturally be expected at first view that this should equally be the case with regard to taxes *on the possession of income,* or as they may be stiled for shortness, *taxes upon income.* If any exceptions were made, it would as naturally be expected, how little soever it would be to be approved of, that the most opulent and most powerful classes would, if any, be the most spared. How stands it in point of fact? the most opulent and most powerful classes are those who, in this particular, are the most hardly dealt with: most hardly is not strong enough: for the only burthens of this description that are to be found in the catalogue of finance are borne exclusively by them. Upon the income of the owners of landed property, upon the members of the sovereignty, upon all the members, but the King, the members of the Upper House, the members of the Lower House and all their electors a tax of 4s in the pound:* upon the salaries and pensions paid for the maintenance of the servants of the public, another branch of the income of a great part of the members of the same great and governing body and their retainers, a tax to no less amount than 5s 6d in the pound.

Thus fares it with the governing classes—how fares it with the governed? Upon income derived from money lent out at interest, whether on real security or on personal, nothing: upon government annuities, nothing: upon income consisting of annuities resting on personal security, upon income consisting of annuities paid by joint stock companies out of tolls or other profits, nothing: upon income derived from profits in trade or professional earnings on the part of individuals, nothing, or next to nothing.† In this way it is the masters of the country that pay every thing, willing or unwilling: those who are in the country one day and may not belong to it the next, enjoying all the while the protection of its laws as fully as its masters do, contribute nothing to its expences but what they please. Thus different is the lot of these great divisions of the people: and thus hardly are the governors treated in comparison of the governed: at the same time that in respect of their contribution to the other great division of taxes, taxes on consumption, there is not the smallest difference.

As to land-owners, time, coming on the back of other causes, has produced very considerable differences as between individual and individual in different parts of the country: and these inequalities have been the matter of universal and constant observation: while the much wider difference in point of contribution between the lot of these classes of subjects and all others, has scarce ever drawn forth a word.

With regard to proprietors of government annuities, the creditors

---

*The 4s or the 2s are but a part, it is true, and that comparatively a small part, of the burthens resting upon the land: but I reckon as burthens such only as are felt. Tithes according to the computation of Mr. Arthur Young [5]¹s: Poor's tax near 2s. These are burthens on the land indeed: but not on the land-owner. Had they never existed, he might, it is true, have got so much more rent: but they existed before he was born: and no such rent ever came into his hands, or so much as the possibility of it into his view: therefore the not getting it is no loss to him.

¹[Arthur Young, *Annals of Agriculture*, vol. XVI, 1791, p. 278-283.]

†Poll-taxes in the shape of licences for carrying on the business are imposed in a few instances: but as the instances are very few, and the duty bears no proportion to income, and is exacted whether any income be derived from this source or no, individuals of this class can scarcely be considered as subjected to a tax on income.

of the nation, every thing of taxation on that source of income is out of the question. The faith of Parliament is pledged for their[1] perpetual exemption, and that in the most positive terms.* Nor have the rest of the nation been in fact any losers by the seeming partiality here shewn to this description of individuals. Had not those who lent money to the public in the infancy of public credit, had not those who, in the mature and later periods of public credit, parted with their money for perpetual transferable annuities, had not these dealers with the public been protected for ever against every such diminution in the value of the property they purchased, they would not have dealt on such easy terms: either they would not have dealt at all, or they would have been paid over and above for the risk, and, as risk in such cases is more apt to be exaggerated than undervalued, more than according to the value of the risk: so that in reality they are and always have been paying a tax upon their incomes, and that an adequate one, though not so in appearance.

What is more, the very productiveness of [a direct tax on income derived from property in government annuities,][2] in the capacity of a resource, would be more than questionable. It could only operate on the interest of existing loans: applied to future loans it would not produce any thing: since in the terms of such loans, the first stipulation on the part of the lenders would be an indemnity against the tax. On the contrary, it would enhance, it is impossible to say in what degree, the disadvantageousness of such loans: since the practice being once begun, nobody would be able to say where it would stop. Of the moneyed men who now with so much confidence engage in dealings with government, many would relinquish the market altogether: the rest would refuse to engage on any terms which,

---

[1][The MS in fact reads "there".]

*In virtue of [21][3] Geo. 3. ch. [60] in continuation of preceding Acts, the adventurers in the great joint-stock banking company called the Bank of England, who, in virtue of the sums lent by them to government, form a particular class of government annuitants, stand in this respect upon the same footing with government annuitants at large, till the expiration of their Charter, an event which takes place in the year 18[12], at which period they may be either taxed or paid off.

Another joint-stock company called the South-Sea-Company, once a trading company, but now existing in no other capacity than that of proprietor of a certain quantity of government annuities granted in consideration of a sum of money belonging to that company in its corporate capacity, [4]is in the same case.[5]

[2][The MS reads "it".]

[3][The MS reads "25" but there was no Statute concerning these matters in 1785.]

[4] [5][Put into brackets at a later date. A marginal note "Examine how, & state" shows that Bentham wished to express himself more concretely on this point.]

besides making up for the amount of the tax, did not afford them ample compensation for a risk which imagination would not fail to exaggerate. And as the terms of fresh loans are always governed by the price of the existing stock, and the existing stock would have already experienced an exaggerated depretiation, hence another item to the sum of causes contributing to the disadvantageousness of every fresh loan.

Justice then protects against future taxation the income paid by the public to the proprietors of government annuities. The nature of things, still more powerful than justice, affords the like protection to lenders of money deriving income from their loans: humanity concurring with justice in another shape affords it to the borrower, who, so far from deriving income from the bargain, pays income in pursuance of it. In a word, a tax upon the interest of money can not be laid on the lender: for he will either cease to lend, or throw it upon the borrower: upon the borrower it ought not to be thrown: it would be in many instances a tax upon distress: in still more, what is still worse, a prohibition upon borrowing, a denial of relief to those who want to borrow.

The truth of these propositions will presently appear. More than 5 per Cent a man is not permitted to take by law. Five per Cent within a trifle a man may make in the funds at the present price: of its falling, and that soon and very considerably, there is a probability approaching to certainty: of its rising no probability for any period yet assignable. But if income arising from money lent on private security were taxed to any even the smallest amount, so much as five per Cent in that way could no longer be made: every body that had money out upon private security (particular friendship or compassion out of the question), would call it in: nobody would lend any more: there could be no lending without giving. The substantial effect then of such an operation would be, not a tax upon income, but a rise in the price of government annuities: an unnatural rise, effected by cruel means.

Thus it stands with regard even to real security—who then would lend on personal? Thus with regard to future transactions: but between future and existing there is in this case but little difference. Money is seldom lent on any security for any continuance: in the instance of mortgages it is generally revocable at six months notice: in the instance of bonds or notes of hand, at any time.

If stocks were ever so much higher, still no contribution could be levied upon the lender of money placed out on private security. The price of money placed out on private security will always be regulated by the proportion of income derivable from money laid out in government annuities. The difference is that *then* money *would* be lent upon private security upon the terms of the borrower paying the tax, whereas now it would not be lent at all. So long as the law admitted of the raising the rate of interest, it would be raised by mutual consent to the exact amount of the tax: the lender would never lose ½ per Cent or any fraction per Cent (particular friendship out of the question) while he could save it by laying out his money in the funds.

But if it rests on the borrower, it rests on the wrong person, and that in every instance. If the money is borrowed to fill up a gap made by inordinate expence or misfortune, it will be a tax on distress: and then the impropriety of it will be unquestioned. If to pay a charge existing upon an estate coming to a man by descent or purchase, it is still payment upon payment, it is for what he parts with that he pays, not for what he obtains: if (which is the most favourable case) he borrows the money to make a profit by it in the way of trade, it is the profit that would be the proper subject of taxation, not the disbursement: it would be time enough to tax the profit when he reaps it: if in the event instead of a profit he reaps a loss, it will, as before, be a tax upon distress. And, in short, in no case would it be what it purports, and by the supposition is proposed to be, a tax upon income.

Income consisting of life annuities or annuities for terms certain charged on personal or other private security,* is as proper a subject of taxation as income arising out of land.

The same may be said of existing annuities secured on tolls, and on the profits of toll-gathering or other joint-stock companies not protected from taxation by the faith of Parliament.

As to annuities granted in future by individuals, the burthen of the tax as between the buyer and the seller would fall of course upon the neediest of the two. It would fall of course upon persons selling annuities for their own lives. As between persons buying annuities for their own lives and persons charging themselves with annuities for the lives of others, it would operate partly as a tax upon the

---

*Rent charges, that is annuities operating as *specific* loans upon real property, are comprized under the Land Tax. But there are several other ways in which real security may be given for annuities, such as bond or judgment affecting real property in general, vesting the subject in trustees upon trust to secure the payments of the annuity &c.

buyers, partly as a prohibition. The burthen would rest upon the purchasers: for the sellers, rather than make less advantage than they did before, would invest their money in the purchase of permanent income. The prohibition would fall more especially upon the good lives: since the less encrease of interest a man could make by sinking his capital, the less disposed he would be to sink it: and the greater the annuity a man was obliged to grant in consideration of receiving a sum of money to a certain amount, the less ready would he be to consent to an encrease of it.

In respect to annuities not yet granted by joint stock companies, a tax of this sort would, for the present, and no one can see for how much longer, have in general the effect of a prohibition. Five per Cent is, and indeed in general has been, the rate of interest at which annuities thus secured have been granted: less than 5 per Cent then purchasers or lenders have not chosen to take. But impose a tax, be it ever so small, suppose ½ or only ¼ per Cent, a deduction to that amount is what the purchaser or lender must submitt to, the law not permitting the seller or borrower to make it up to him by paying that or any thing in addition to the 5 per Cent.

[2. The Taxation Of Industry]

In respect then of any modifications of assured income that could be subjected to taxation, over and above those on which the hand of the financier has been laid already, the amount of the supply that could be drawn from such sources is but inconsiderable. There remain the several branches of casual income, the fruits of industry in its various shapes, the profits of lucrative occupations: on the occupations of manufacturers, the profits of dealers and shopmen, and the earnings of professional men.

With regard to these, the first idea that occurrs is that while the proprietors of the country and the servants of the public are burthened, and burthened to so heavy an amount, paying at the same time their full proportion to taxes on consumption and all other taxes, individuals of the numerous descriptions above mentioned can not, consistently with the rule of equality, be permitted to go altogether scot-free. Nor can they be saved in the lump by any considerations drawn from the topics of humanity and justice. We have seen the considerations of this nature that plead for the exemption of several classes of proprietors of assured income. None of these considerations are applicable to proprietors of casual income as above distinguished.

z

But though under the auspices of equality they can urge no common plea for a total exemption from contributions of this nature, yet the distinction from which their species of income has been denominated, affords them at first mention an evident ground for abatement in respect of the quantum of their contribution. Let us consider then what shall be the measure of this abatement.

The income of men of property is assured. The income of men of industry is unassured, dependent on a variety of contingencies. How to compare the certain[1] with the uncertain presents, it must be confessed, a variety of difficulties. But in this line as in others of human affairs, certain and uncertain are so but by comparison. The income of proprietors, stock-holders excepted, who are out of the question, is [in fact likewise] exposed to a variety of the contingencies: bad crops, unfaithful agents, losses by fire and other physical calamities, and the like. Besides that under the general denomination of men of property are comprized individuals of very different descriptions in this respect, men whose estate is for ever or for a term of years more valuable than for life, and men whose estate is but for life or for a term less valuable.* The property of individuals of the former description, the income being equal, may be estimated at double the value of that of the latter, at the least. That of the former may be transmitted undiminished to posterity: that of the other where there are children or those that stand in the place of children, must undergo a retrenchment adequate to the present maintenance and future establishment of those objects of necessary care.

On the other hand, neither is the industrious class without its advantages: a manufacture or trade once established, a station in a profession once taken, is in respect of the certainty of its profits but little behind an assured income to that amount. Nor is the man of industry subjected to half the impositions with which, by the law of opinion, the man of property is charged: it is not known how much he gets, and if it were, he would be allowed to spend as little as he chose. He makes his profit of that difference: his mind is turned to thrift, acquiring and saving go together, and the latter requires the least exertion of the two: and accordingly perhaps for twenty

---

[1][The MS in fact reads "uncertain" even here.]

*As to the case of tenant for life with remainder to issue, as in case of settled estates, it is evident, they are to this respect upon a par not with life holders but with tenants in fee.

fortunes made by industry and frugality together, there is not so much as a single one made by frugality alone. Add to this that the natural state of the product of industry is not, like that of unemployed property, stationary, but progressive: nor in respect of continuance are the fruits of industry at so wide a distance from those of property as they might seem to be: for an established trade in most cases, and even a profession in some, is transmissible to children and operates as an inheritance. Incomes may rise indeed in nominal amount, and do in general rise: but when they do rise, it is in general as it were in jerks at distant intervals, which no exertion can lessen, and not always in a degree more than sufficient to counterbalance that fall in the value of money which in a certain degree is an inseparable accompaniment of such rise.

Since absolute equality then in this as in most other instances is impracticable, and since even among men of property the mere life-owner is confounded in point of quantity of burthen with the proprietor in fee, how shall the proportion be established as between the man of property and the man of industry? At a venture, and for a general rule, subject, as we shall see, to a variety of exceptions, it being necessary to name some proportion or other, I would say a *half*: the man of property pays 4s in the pound, a fifth that is of his income: let the man of industry pay as far as a tenth of his.

This share seems not reprobated by reason: and it stands in various instances approved by precedent. The tithe, the old ecclesiastical tax of the tithe, seems to have been meant as a tax to that amount upon the profit of the most important and exclusive division of the sons of industry, though [in reality] it proves to be of treble or quadruple the amount and not borne after all by them: in the same view, the same proportion has been levied upon the profits and earnings of manufacturers, dealers, and professional men in general: and if history is to be believed, times and places have not been wanting when a tithe of the earnings of courtizans composed a part of the revenue of the Church.*

In addition to the above reduction of the rate in comparison of that on proprietors, I would propose the following rules of indulgence [as] proper to be observed.

Dulcis odor lucri ex re qualibet, a maxim avowed by a great temporal sovereign, has been as religiously pursued as if it had been ever so explicitly avowed by many a spiritual potentate. For my part, more indulgent than the holy fountain of indulgences, I would not propose to the financier to lay an oppressive hand upon so meritorious as well as already oppressed a class as the meretricious one.

Rule 1. Insufficient income derived from profits and earnings of any description of individuals ought to be exempted altogether.

Rule 2. Income little more than barely sufficient ought to receive an abatement gradually lessening up to the measure of full sufficiency.

Rule 3. Sufficient and insufficient [are]¹ evidently terms of reference. The reference I make is to the sum which, in the estimation of the world, would enable a man to maintain himself with decency in the station in which he is placed by the occupation from which his income is derived.

Rule 4. To every class of such proposed contributors to which an indemnity can be afforded without prejudice to the interests either of the public in general, or of other individuals, such indemnity ought to be afforded.

Rule 5. A class in the instance of which such indemnity can be brought nearer to a full and compleat one ought, *caeteris paribus*, to be chosen in preference for the tax.

Rule [6].² A class to which such indemnity is not applicable ought not to be subjected to the tax, so long as a proper class can be found to which such indemnity *is* applicable.

[3. OF THE PROPOSED INDEMNITY]

³I shall first speak of the general indemnity: I shall next speak of the selection of the classes to which the burthen may be extended.⁴

As to the indemnity there is one, and but one,* which (speaking of what can be done, not of what ought to be done) the men of industry are capable of receiving. I mean the exclusive privilege derived from a limitation of their number. Nor does the amount of this benefit seem to be in danger of being estimated at a rate at all

---

¹[The MS reads "is".]
²[The MS in fact reads "5".]
³ ⁴[Crossed out in the MS.]

*There is another way in which advantage may be given to men of industry in certain cases, viz. by assisting them in the procurement of capital, I mean no otherwise than [by] removing the obstacles which the law has thrown in the way of their obtaining it, or in some instances by substituting interest payable at a convenient time in the room of capital which is exacted of them not intentionally but by negligence. See a separate proposal, intended to be hereafter submitted, under some such title as that of a *Proposal for obtaining an addition to the Revenue by selling dispensations from diverse impediments thrown by the existing Law in the way of industry, more especially of inventive industry*. But the two species of indemnity are widely different; that which is the subject of the present proposal is applicable only to *classes:* the other only to *individuals*.

below its value by any who would have to share in it. The instances in which it has been possessed are numerous in the history of political economy: and the tenacity with which it has been defended where it has been possessed, is equally well known: to say nothing of the avidity with which it has been grasped at, where it has not been possessed.

In general in the instances in which such privilege has been possessed, it has been attended with considerable disadvantage to the public, [or at any rate] with considerable hardship and oppression to individuals and no advantage to the public whatsoever.

It was prejudicial to the public in general as being an aggregate of the purchaser[s] of the commodities or services in question. It was prejudicial to individuals in their capacity of candidates for the faculty of exercising industry in the line most competent to each: a faculty too often stifled by the privileges in question, for want of a subject on which, in the situation of the candidate, it could, under the prohibition imposed by the privilege, be exerted. It was of no advantage to the state in point of contribution because either no contribution at all, or none worth reckoning, was drawn by the public in return for it.

Sovereigns have even been so weak and their counsellors so wicked as to confine such exclusive privilege in many instances to a single person: who in consequence, being insured against all competitors, has raised the price of the article to the extent of his own conceptions of the demand, thereby imposing to his own profit an enormous tax upon the consumption of the article.

The power of establishing privileges in this their most abusive form was never perhaps in any country so unwarrantably assumed nor so flagrantly abused as it has been in England: in the first instance by a Queen, the general tenor of whose conduct is a much fitter subject of admiration or rather wonder than approbation: and whose example was but too faithfully copied in this as well as the other most reprehensible features of it by her weak and unworthy successor. Had either James or Elizabeth had their way, the greatest part perhaps of the immense revenue now derived from taxes on consumption would have been thrown away, as a great part was in a few years actually thrown away, in the form of monopolies created for, and granted to, favourites.

No wonder then that a strong and general odium should have been attached in this country (not to speak of others) to the term *monopoly*: no wonder that exclusive privileges, even when attended with none of the effects of monopoly, should have been branded by the name and tainted by the odium: no wonder that a general rule should have been laid down that no monopoly should be created: no wonder that such general rule should have extended itself with little or no distinction to exclusive privileges. Understand this of exclusive privileges not yet existing or recently established: for so strong is the power of habit, in matters of government especially, and so weak that of reason, that the self-same institution is defended with as much pertinacity when old as it was reprobated when new, so that the whole fabric of legislation is as yet a heap of contradictions.

The only mischiefs that ever have been or ever can be charged to the account of monopoly or exclusive privilege established in respect to any article, are reducible to the following, viz.

1. Lessening the *quantum* of the *supply*.

2. Enhancement of the *price:* understand the money price.

3. Impairing the *quality* of the article by diminish[ing] the incentive to those *exertions* on the part of the producer by which alone the attainment of the utmost pitch of excellence in his power can be ensured.

4. Impairing the *quality* of the article by diminishing the chance of *extraordinary talent* on the part of the individuals occupied, or who but for the exclusion would have joined themselves to those who are occupied, in producing it.

5. Encreasing the *distance* between the seat of demand and the seat of supply, and thence the real price of it:—a necessary result of any diminution in what was or would have been the number of individuals contributing to the supply, in as far as their residences were or would have been equably distributed among the individuals furnishing the demand.

Under the name of *article*, it is to be observed, may be comprehended not only *goods* belonging to the class of *things*, but *services* rendered in the line of any profession by *persons*: the skill of the physician, the talent of the dancer or musician, the science and eloquence of the advocate.

Such are the evils which result from an exclusive privilege if in any respect it be productive of inconvenience: such are the only evils which ever did or can result from it.*

*The sufferings [are here] excepted which may result from the execution of the law by which the privilege is established and enforced, [because they are] evils which belong to it, not in respect of its being a law creative of an exclusive privilege, but only in as far as it is a penal law.

If, in the instance of any occupation, an exclusive privilege can be established in respect of that occupation, that is in favour of some person or persons exercising it at a certain period, without being attended with any article in the above catalogue of evils, such privilege may be pronounced innocent, and, in as far as the individual is benefitted by the exclusion of competitors, and the public by what is paid for the privilege, not only innocent but beneficial.

[4. Classes To Be Selected]

No tax of this nature ought to be imposed in the instance of an occupation to which the proposed idemnity is inapplicable, while there remains any occupation to which it is applicable. You ought not to impose a heavier burthen upon one man, when you can produce the same good effect by imposing a lighter burthen on another.

The first thing to be done then is to enquire to what kind of occupations the idemnity is applicable with most advantage.

It will be applicable with the more advantage in the first place, the freer it is from the several mischievous consequences that are liable, as we have seen, to result from privileges of this sort when ill applied: in the next place, the more efficacious it is in the instance of any given occupation in the character of an advantage to the sharers in the privilege.

[With regard to the first point, we may lay down the following rules:]

Rule 1. An exclusive privilege ought not to be established in the instance of any business, where it would be attended, at least in any degree worth considering, with any of the evil consequences above reckoned as liable to result from exclusive privileges in certain cases.

Rule 2. A business in respect of which there is little or no danger of lessening the quantum of the supply by the establishment of an exclusive privilege is in so far peculiarly well fitted to the purpose of receiving an idemnity in that shape.

Bankers furnish an example particularly well adapted to the illustration of this rule. The number of banking houses in London is at present 63[1]: exclusive of the immense chartered banking house, the Bank of England. The number of these houses could not be reduced by the amount of a single unit by compulsive law without oppression and injustice. But supposing it reduced by lapse of time or otherwise

---

[1][The figure in the MS looks almost like 68.]

without injustice, there is no imaginable reason for supposing that the market would be supplied with the commodity they deal in with less abundance than it is at present. If instead of 63, there were but 17, there would not be a farthing's worth less money in the country than there is now. The largest dealer of the 17 would not then be placed by the magnitude of his dealings under any greater difficulty of carrying on his dealings [and] of performing his part in the supplying of the market than the smallest dealer of the 63[1] is in at present. The largest dealer in that case would not, in respect of the magnitude of his dealings, approach to what the Bank of England is at present. But in respect to the perfection in which he conducts himself in the contributing of his share in the business of affording the supply, even the smallest dealer can find no cause for boasting in comparison of that gigantic company.

[With regard to the second point, i.e. the capability of a branch of industry of receiving benefit by the establishment of a monopoly, the following rules may be found acceptable in the character of guiding principles:]

Rule 1. The efficiency of an exclusive privilege in the character of an indemnity against the burthen of a tax will depend, not upon the absolute number to which the sharers are reduced by the operation of the privilege, but upon their relative number, upon their number in comparison of the quantity of business to be shared.

Rule 2. If then, in the instance of any occupation, the quantity of business may be expected to encrease, the relative number of the sharers in the privilege may undergo a reduction without any reduction in the absolute number: and if the encrease of business goes on at a certain rate, the absolute number of the sharers may even have received an encrease at the end of a certain period, and yet the relative number may have undergone a diminution.

Rule 3. In the instance of an occupation free from the law of apprenticeship, the operation of the indemnity will be more speedy than in the instance of an occupation subject to that law: since in the former case the influx might, upon any prospect of an opening at any time, but for the privilege, have been sudden and abundant: a suddenness of influx which is not so apt to take place in the latter case: since before a man can hope to benefit from the opening, it may have closed of itself or may have been filled up by others whose apprenticeship is already terminated, or at least considerably in advance.

It would on this account be more speedy, for example, in the instances of bankers, stock-brokers, and notary publics, than in the instance of attorneys. In the three former instances no apprenticeship is necessary: in the other a man can not enter into business till after an apprenticeship of five years.

Rule 4. The operation of the privilege in the character of a benefit will be, if not the more speedy, the more sensible, the more confined the nature of the business is, and the more confined the place which happens to be the scene of it. It would on this account also be more sensible in the several instances of bankers, stock-brokers, and notary publics abovementioned, than in that of attorneys. Of bankers there are in the Metropolis but 63 houses: of notary publics in the Metropolis not so many: of stock-brokers in the only seat of the stockbroking business, the Metropolis, probably not many more. Of attorneys, there were in the year 1788 in all England upwards of 24,000*: without reckoning those in the egg-shel [sic], articled clerks.

The business may in the instance of some occupations be so copious, and the field of it so universal [and] perfectly spread over the whole country that, especially if it happens to [be] loaded with the obligation of apprenticeship, it may be difficult for the supply of candidates for the business to proportion itself with any tolerable accuracy to the demand. It may on this account at almost any given period be so fully stocked or rather over-stocked on the whole, that it may be a long while before a check put by law to the supply of candidates for business, would, in that character, have any sensible effect. This seems to be the case for example with attorneys.

Moreover, when the field of business, as in that case, is spread over the whole country, and from the above causes liable in many instances to be very unequally stocked with candidates, it may

---

*[Sir John] Sinclair on the [History of the Public] Revenue [of the British Empire, 2nd ed., 1790], Part III, p. [133. This page contains the only passage which has any reference to the number of attorneys in the country. Under the heading "Produce of the Stamps from Michaelmas 1787, to Michaelmas 1788" it gives the amount received by the Treasury for "licences on attorneys" as £24,650 17s. 1d. It is obvious that Bentham had this passage in mind when he wrote the above text. Yet his conclusion would only have been correct if the annual stamp duty on attorneys' licences had been £1 0s. 0d. or £1 1s. 0d. In fact, however, it was much higher. According to the statute then in force (Geo. III. c. 80) attorneys in London and Edinburgh paid yearly £5 0s. 0d., those in other parts of the country £3 0s. 0d. Bentham can only have thought of the second edition of Sir John Sinclair's work because the first was not published in three volumes, and the third appeared many years later. Yet in the second edition there is no direct mention of the number of attorneys. Bentham, who obviously quoted from memory, seems to have made a mistake here.]

happen that a very considerable reduction in one place may occasion no sensible effect nor relief in another: for the quitting the place where a man has been already settled, is in every such case an expensive, troublesome, and rather hazardous step, not to mention its being in a certain point of view rather of a discreditable tendency, by affording a sort of confession of disappointment and want of business.

[To these principles for the selection of the classes proposed to be subjected to taxation and indemnified by the establishment of monopoly rights, it seems necessary to annex the following cautions:]

Rule [1]. In framing the texture of the exclusive privilege, all that the law can do without manifest injustice and oppression, is to inhibit or check the accession of future incomers. It can *not* put an exclusion upon any individual already engaged in the way of business in question: the only modes in which any such reduction can take place are by voluntary relinquishment or death.

Rule [2]. The protecting tenderness of the law on this behalf ought to be extended not only, as above, to the possession of such an establishment, but also to the expectation of acquiring it; and that not only in the instance of persons already attached to it by apprenticeship, but also in the instance of children of the persons engaged in it, such children being already in existence at the passing of the law and of a certain age, viz. of such an age as to have been decidedly destined to it, and not past it: suppose between the ages of ten and sixteen where an apprenticeship is required, or ten and twenty two where no apprenticeship is necessary or usual.

The protection of the law in favour of expectants, as above, will be of the more importance, the greater the importance of early introduction in respect of peculiar knowledge, particular connections, or acquired habits, the formation of which is a work of time. Businesses that can be taken up or laid down by any body at any time seem to possess in this respect a weaker claim. In a word, the more the nature of the business approaches to a sort of natural monopoly, the more careful the law ought to be of invading it.

Where the business is susceptible of secrets in respect of the mode of operating to advantage, the faculty of transmitting the advantage to children stands almost upon the footing of an hereditary estate: nor does the claim afforded by the advantage of possessing a local situation peculiarly favourable, or of having formed a system of connections [i.e.] a set of steady customers, fall greatly short of the former in every case.

Rule [3]. Both the above rules, however, seem to admitt of an exception in the case where the business is of the number of those which it is customary for men to carry on incidentally in conjunction with other business, and without making it their principal dependence. Such casual business might be interdicted generally to all who are in the habit of exercising it occasionally or offering themselves to exercise [it], such individuals excepted, if any such there are, who have been used to carry on that business and no other, trusting to it as their sole resource.

This exception has particularly in view the case of undertakers: a class of individuals whose business, rendered lucrative and abundant by the vanity and folly of mankind, seems capable of being turned to considerable account in the way of profit to the revenue. In the Metropolis this business is carried on in some instances perhaps by persons who have no other, but in a great many instances by persons whose dependence is not at all upon this business but upon some other, principally that of an upholsterer or that of a cabinet maker, which afford a much more steady and assured employment. It is a trade which could hardly be hurt by any management: and which, if it could, might be cramped or even demolished without any real prejudice to any body. The business of it could scarcely be ill performed: and it might be ever so ill performed without any body being the worse. 1. It will be easy so to regulate the privilege as that there shall be no want of a sufficient supply of candidates for such service. 2. The price need not be enhanced by the tax or by the privilege: and it would not much signify if it were. 3 & 4. Exertions and talent are altogether out of the question: and as to vicinity of the supply to the market, that is a requisite for which sufficient provision can very easily be made.

The only cautions to be observed are 1. that respecting the tenderness to be shewn to individuals already engaged in the trade: 2. that respecting the tenderness to be shewn to the feelings of customers.

As to the first point, as apprenticeship is out of the question, the first step to be taken, and a step that might be taken without scruple, is the declaring 1. that all persons exercising this profession shall take out a license: 2. to begin with London, the number of the individuals engaged in the business being ascertained by the number of licenses, that no license shall be granted to any other persons till that number shall have been reduced in a certain proportion, say to three fourths or two thirds.

By setting the license high, perhaps the number might be reduced in the first instance without any considerable hardship or inconvenience. Those who did not depend upon this branch of business would quit it and so escape the tax: those who did depend upon it would pay for the license without repining as they would reap the benefit of the vacancy left by the seceders.

These were probably among the considerations which suggested so heavy a license duty as that of £50, imposed upon lottery-office-keepers. Those who approve of so heavy an enhancement as that of the duties on hawkers and pedlars could hardly be restrained by any scruples of the kind in question from imposing a heavy license-duty on undertakers.

[5. OF THE APPOSITE MODE OF COLLECTION]

I come now to speak of the mode of collecting an imposition of this nature: I mean so far as concerns the ensuring the payment of the quota. The farmer sets out his tithe: the man of industry in any other line to which this proposed species of tax shall extend, must in like manner set out his tithe: the public enters itself into partnership with him. He must at the usual periods state an account as one partner does to another, declare the dividend, and hold himself in readiness to pay it. This mode of setting out tithe, it will presently occurr, is not equally convenient in the instance of every branch of industry: in some it will be found so full of difficulties and doubts as to be intolerable: that of the farmer for example who besides is already burthened with a tithe of a more expensive kind: such occupations will accordingly be of the number of those to which it is not applicable with advantage. The account must of course be given in upon oath: and to ensure its veracity, [there is need of] a power lodged somewhere of examining upon occasion *viva voce* and in a summary way the person rendering it, and all other persons capable of throwing light upon it, in the event of its being suspected of being erroneous or defective or obscure.

A tax, a mode of collection, or any provision in a plan for collection, may surely pass muster if in point of hardship it can be justified by comparison, and in point of authority by precedent. The mode here proposed admitts of both justifications.

In point of hardship, what is it in comparison of the Excise? *This* makes known private dealings: true: but so does that infinitely more. For what should a tradesman, if he deal honestly, feel any concern at the thoughts of his dealings being known?—only in the case of their being but small, at the thoughts of its being known that he has less business than his competitors. But under the discipline of the Excise laws it is impossible that the quantity of his dealings, absolute as well as comparative, should not be as fully known as by any other mode of exposure as between partners in the manner here proposed. His whole stock of every kind—every thing that comes in— every thing that goes out. Among the hardships, real or supposed, attendant on the discipline of the Excise, this passes in a manner unnoticed—why?—because in comparison of the others it is so slight [that] the sensation it makes is quite lost in the sensation made by those others. No visits at unseasonable hours—no right of prying into the secrets of manufacture, the fruits of ingenuity matured at great expence by years of experience: no joint possession: no right of stopping business: no right of locking up property from the owner: no *jus noscendi*: no privilege of plaguing. I do not mean this as a sentence of reprobation upon the Excise laws: I do not mean to say that these are other than necessary evils: the only use I mean to make of them is to shew that the utmost inconvenience attendant upon the principle of collection here proposed is in comparison of the inconveniences attendant on that long established mode, no more than a part, and that an almost imperceptible one, in comparison of the whole.

So much for comparative hardship. As to precedent, the auctioneers' tax, without looking out for any further, will afford us one sufficiently in point. In this case the person on whom the duty is imposed is bound to give in the account from which the quantum due results, and that upon oath. As to being examinable *viva voce* then or afterwards for the elucidation of the account, an obligation of that sort is not imposed *in terminis*, but it is in effect.*

The provision respecting the *viva voce* examination of the contributor as well as the persons connected with him for the purpose of

---

*Security is to be given, by bond, for complying with the direction of the Statute. *"The account is to be delivered in in writing"* the person delivering it in is *"to make oath of the truth"* of it: *"if it should appear to the Commissioners"* &c *"that the party giving such Bond hath acted agreeably to the directions of the Act . . .* then they shall cause the Bond to be delivered up: but *if it should appear . . . that any such account was not truly made"* . . . then they may *"cause such Bond to be prosecuted according to law."* (17 Geo. 3. ch. 50 §6).

ensuring the truth of the account is in favour of truth, it must be confessed, in favour of the revenue, but it is at least equally in favour of the contributor himself. It eases him of at least ninety-nine parts out of a hundred of the trouble he would otherwise be subject to: and of the whole of the expence. If he were not to be called to account in this way, in what way would he be?—by a suit in Chancery. He may have to accuse himself.—Yes, verily, if he gives in a false account, knowing it to be a false one: but if he does, who but himself will he have to thank for it? And what can he have to accuse himself of, if the account he gives in contains nothing but what is true: or even though it were full of fals[e]hoods, if the fals[e]hoods were undesigned. To a contributor who has schemes of fraud, this summary mode of accounting can not, it is true, notwithstanding its easiness, but be intolerably irksome—why? because it is utter destruction to all such schemes.

This examination clause is favourable to the proposed contributor by saving him not only from the expence and vexation inseparable from a civil suit according to the regular mode of procedure, but from the still more serious danger of a criminal prosecution such as that for perjury. It may be laid down as a general rule that no statement upon oath ought in any case to be required, without a clause for *viva voce* examination. The former obligation without the latter is but a snare for conscience, and an incentive to perjury. It is owing to the neglect of this necessary association that the inefficiency of a custom house oath, one may say in general a revenue-oath, is become proverbial: and it is to this cause more than to all others put together that we may ascribe those enormous national evils, the abundance of perjuries and the diminution of the revenue.

The reprobation of the summary mode of procedure in revenue cases [and] the elogium of the regular [mode] can come but from one of the [following] three descriptions of men—the man of prejudice without reflection, who suffers himself to be led away by sounds, the man of party out of place who opposes a measure in proportion as it promises to be salutary and efficient, or the smuggler. The summary mode forced upon the Legislature by omnipotent necessity in the teeth of prejudice, the summary mode, though now so fully and so happily established, is an invention comparatively but of yesterday: the regular mode, set aside as regularly as it is applauded, and applauded, for form's sake, in the very act of setting it aside, has the force of prejudice still in its favour. One thing is certain—that, considering the force still maintained by prejudice even now, in spite of generations of experience, the regular mode never could have been set aside if it had not been, not only equally repugnant to the ends of justice and mercy, but totally incapable of answering in these instances the intended purpose of giving execution to the law: nor could any ruin be more compleat or inevitable than that of a nation which should persevere in trusting its revenue [i.e.] the exclusive execution of its revenue laws, to those modes of procedure which, in contradistinction to the summary, are distinguished by the name of regular in the English law.

The next thing to be done then is to enquire what [are the] classes on which a burthen of this nature may, abstractedly from the consideration of its susceptibility of an indemnity, be imposed. As to this point the following rules seem proper to be laid down.

Rule 1. The simpler the mode of dealing in any business is, so much fitter is the business for being subjected to this tax. For the more complicated the nature of the business is, the more exposed it is to doubts in respect of the quantum of the profit: and the effect of these doubts may be not only to occasion vexation in the way of enquiry and litigation, but to subject the contributor to penalties in the event of a decision in his disfavour: though indeed, if the law were properly penned, *bona fides* would find a sufficient shelter under it against every danger of that sort.

Rule 2. A business, in the case of its being in trade, is the more simple, the less the diversity of the articles about which it is conversant, the more bulky they are, the greater the quantity and value of the amount commonly received and issued out at a time, the fewer and less complicated the operations which it requires to be performed in relation to each: and the easier it is to place the profit and loss with precision to the proper account of the respective articles.

Rule 3. A business, in respect of which a man stands already engaged by the nature of the business to keep a full and exact account, is preferable on that score in the present view to a trade which leaves a man altogether or comparatively free in that respect. For the trouble of keeping an account is no small addition to the burthen of contributing to the tax: and persons who are not already established in the habit of keeping regular accounts, would, when thus compelled to begin the practice, be more apt to make omissions and thereby expose themselves without any intention of deceit to the censure of the law in one event, and the public to a loss of its due in the other.

Rule 4. A business is the more suitable to this purpose, the more apt it is from the nature of it, to afford collateral evidence of the truth of any account as may require to be stated in respect of it for the purpose of the proposed tax: the less suitable, the less apt it is to afford such evidence.

The business of a stock-broker is an instance of the highest degree of fitness, as far as depends upon this rule: for scarce any business can be done by a stock-broker the quantum and profit of which is not ascertained by written evidence which it is not in his power either to suppress or falsify, [viz.] the books of the bank, and other similar books according to the nature of the respective funds.

The business of a common carrier in a great road and that of a hackney coachman afford a contrast peculiarly well adapted to the illustration of this rule. Upon a general view, scarce any two businesses can appear more similar. But the receipts of the carrier are in general known to other parties and entered, as it were, of record by the practice of booking: whereas the receipts of the hackney coachman can, taken collectively, be known to nobody but himself. It is this circumstance that in the case of turnpike tolls and duties payable to government on the account of post horses has rendered it in a manner impossible to make the produce turn to account in any other way than that of letting it out to farm.

[6. PRECEDENT]

A few words may not be unsatisfactorily employed in shewing how the mode of taxation [here] proposed stands upon the footing of precedent. Of the ecclesiastical tax of this kind, the *personal* tithe as it was called, I know not that an instance is at present any where to be found. To give it execution, the ecclesiastical power would require to be in fuller vigour than it is now any where in Europe. Nor was it well calculated for full and regular execution even in the barbarous ages which gave it birth. On the part of the contributor it would require the talent of keeping accounts: that is reading, writing, and arithmetic, accomplishments of extreme rarity in those ages. It would require an establishment of officers adapted to the collection of the produce and spread equally and in sufficient numbers over the face of the whole country: an establishment already existing at present in this country, though established for other purposes. I mean that of the Excise.

In modern practice and in this country, I know of no instance of a tax answering in all points to the one here proposed. The one that seems to come nearest to it, is that of the tax on attorneys, imposing a duty of 2s 6d, payable by the attorney and not by the client, in the commencement of a suit. This may be considered as a tax upon profits, though not periodical, nor running in any proportion to profits: and, in comparison to the average total of attorney's profits in a cause, it is minute indeed.

An instance which comes rather nearer in effect, though perhaps not in appearance, is that of the license required to be taken out by the brewers of strong beer. The license is annual, and the price of it is proportioned in some measure to the quantity of barrels brewed. The standard of reference, the *causa solvendi*, is here indeed, not profit, but outgoings: but as the probability is that a man will not brew more beer than he is in the habit of finding custom for, nor in general sell beer without being paid for it, it comes to much the same thing.

[7. Conclusion]

Between [the] three classes of contributions, [viz.] taxes on branches of industry susceptible of an adequate indemnity on the one hand, and taxes on consumption and taxes on branches of industry not susceptible of an adequate indemnity [on the other], the order of preference seems now established, and that as tolerably solid as well as conspicuous: the first demands the preference over both the other two.

But, besides the difficulty resulting from the variable nature of the value of the indemnity, a difficulty which would [make it] necessary to give a separate examination in this view to every species of occupation proposed as a subject for such a tax, the preference due as between taxes on consumption and taxes on industry in cases unsusceptible of indemnity, is not an easy subject for decision.

Were the case such that the whole list of taxes was to be settled for the first time, the answer would be easy enough: no taxes on income, from whence soever derived, while the list of taxes on consumption, existing or not existing, tried or untried, is capable of affording the supply: the best tax on income is attended with inconveniences from which the worst chosen tax on consumption not

AA

amounting to a prohibition is free. But the state of things is far from being so simple. On the one hand, men of property are in the habit of bearing taxes upon their income: on the other hand, men of industry are not in any such habit. Taxes on consumption added at any period to the existing list would *in specie* indeed be new: but *in genere*, to wit in as far as they are taxes on consumption, they are not so. Men of property are in use to bear taxes on consumption in addition to the existing taxes on their income: as also to bear from time to time fresh additions to the list of taxes on consumption, and that in the same degree with the other classes that are not at all taxed in respect of income, and without conceiving themselves to be more aggrieved than those others by any such taxes on consumption antient or new.

PROPOSAL FOR A TAX ON BANKERS

It is not long since a respectable banking house set out with allowing interest at the rate of 3 per Cent to all persons keeping cash there, with no other restriction than that of giving a certain number of days notice before drawing.

As more than 5 per Cent can not be made on personal security, nor could so much by at least 1 per Cent have been made at that time on government security, 2 per Cent was the utmost that, according to that mode of dealing, was to be made: 2 per Cent then, no more than two fifths of the rate of profit made by bankers in general, was the rate of profit which this banking house was content to take.

The observation of this incident gave rise to the following reflection: if the profits of this profession will, in the opinion of the very persons themselves [who pocket them], bear a reduction to so large an amount as three fifths *a fortiori* [they][1] will bear a third part of that reduction:* a reduction precisely equal to that made on the income of men of landed property by the Land Tax at its present rate of 4s in the pound, not to mention offices and pensions.

The mode of collection is a consideration inseparable from that of the nature of the tax. It were in vain to propose a tax unless a mode could be pointed out in which the produce might be collected: a mode either totally free from all objection, or, if that be impossible, free from all objections greater than what stand already over-ruled by established practice.

The mode I would propose is extremely simple. The principle of it is that government should be on the footing of a partner to the amount of its share. All banking-houses keep books: all banking-houses at stated periods make up on the face of those books an account of profit and loss and divide the profits. Let inspectors of bankers' books be appointed by the Treasury. To these inspectors

[1][The MS reads "it".]

*This plan, I understand, was of no long continuance. The quantity of cash poured in upon the house so far exceeded expectation, as to outstrip the faculty of finding employment for it. As by this means they had interest to pay for money for which they could make no greater interest, or perhaps for a time no interest at all, it became necessary to give up [the offer][2] or at least suspend it. But this discontinuance is no proof that a reduction of profit to the proposed amount could not be borne. That it could and would have been borne is evident if influx and employment had kept the same proportion in the business of the banking-house in question as they do in banking-houses in general carrying on business upon the usual terms: that is if either the influx had been diminished to a certain degree, or the employment encreased.

[2][The MS reads "give it up".]

let the periodical statements of profit and loss be exhibited, the truth of the contents being verified by oath, and sworn copies at the same time delivered; let all such books as can serve to prove or disprove the verity of such accounts be accessible to the inspector at seasonable hours with liberty to take copies: and, in case of necessity, upon warrant from the Board of Treasury, let all partners and clerks be at any time examinable *viva voce* upon oath by persons in some respectable judicial office, such as the Commissioners of Public Accounts or any two of them, who, to save trouble and expedite business, should, instead of convening the examinants before them, repair in person to the scene of business, as Committees of the House of Commons have often done on similar occasions.

At the period or periods at which the division of the profits among the partners is made according to the present usage, let the share thus given to the public be paid into the Exchequer.

So much for profits. As to losses, in as far as they are sworn to, they must be deducted from profits. But if at the end of any period they should exceed the profits, the public should not be a sharer in the clear loss. For this is one of those few businesses, if not the only business, in which no clear loss can take place, and indeed scarcely any very considerable loss, without gross negligence or imprudence on the part of the dealer. And there is no reason why the public should suffer for the fault of the individual: and if it did in this way, the inlet to fraud would be unbounded.

By way of indemnity I would propose a restriction of the number of banking-houses to the present number: a sort of relative monopoly, but a most innocent one, as I trust will presently be perceived.

I shall consider first the proposed tax, and then the proposed monopoly: which, though proposed as a concomitant and edulcoration to the tax, is evidently not an inseparable one.

Would there be any hardship in such a tax—any injustice? is it liable to any objection that has not already been decided against and got over in the instance of old-established taxes? Let us imagine ourselves the objects of the tax, and try what objections we can find to make to it.

Objection 1. Bankers are traders, [i.e.] commercial men: the place they carry on their business at is a shop. This is an instance, and the first instance, that was ever proposed of a tax on traders of which it was intended (for the intention will not be denied) that the trader himself should bear the burthen. When a tax was laid on shops in general, it was on the supposition that the burthen would not rest upon them: it turned out that the burthen did rest upon them, and the tax was repealed. The ground, and the sole ground, of the repeal in that case was hardship: here the hardship is beyond comparison greater, for the burthen is. Would the shop-tax have amounted to a fifth of the profit of shop-keepers in general, or any thing like it? would it have amounted to the fiftieth part of the profit of many a shop-keeper? To the hardship which in specie, though not in degree, it shares with the reprobated shop-tax, this imposition adds an injustice which is peculiarly its own. Why single out this branch of trade, this class of traders, when all others are left free?

Answer. A banker a trader? no such thing. He buy[s] nothing: [he] sell[s]¹ nothing. A banker a trader? then so is every individual in the kingdom, who possesses money and lives by lending it and derives income from the interest of it. A banker a trader? Not a peer in the realm then but what either is a trader, or wants nothing but money to become one.

The place a banker does his business in a shop—and the banker who keeps it therefore a shop-keeper? This is not to be denied: though *banking-house* is perhaps the more common expression of the two, and the term *shop* as applied to it is growing a little out of date. A banker then is a shop-keeper, it must be confessed:—but how? just as in London till the 18th [year] of the late King a surgeon was a barber. Goldsmiths were the first bankers: goldsmiths were, till paper money came into circulation, the only bankers. Goldsmiths were the bankers whom Charles the 2d dealt with to their cost. But goldsmiths kept shops: goldsmiths bought and sold. It is thus the appellative of a shop stuck to the counting-house of a banker: it is by keeping this sort of shop that a banker is a trader: it is as if a man were a trader by having apartments over the Exchange.

As to the shop-tax, a tax can scarcely be more unlike it in point of effect than this is. That must equally have been paid, profit or no profit: this attaches only where there is profit, and in exact proportion to that profit. That was sometimes indeed a tax upon affluence; in the instance of thriving shop-keepers certainly so; but too often a tax upon distress. If a shop-keeper got not a farthing, if he sold not a farthingsworth, still the tax was to be paid. The tax on shops was

¹[The MS reads "they sell".]

meant for a tax on consumption: a tax on consumption in general: it turned out to be a tax upon income: that is, sometimes on income, sometimes upon the want of it. Peace then be to the *manes* of the shop-tax which, let us hope, will never again be mentioned, unless in honour of a minister who, having it in his power to look down upon instruction, chose rather to be taught, and taught by adversaries.[1]

Bankers then not being traders, every thing of objection that turns on the supposition of their being traders tumbles to the ground. If not traders, what are they then? Individuals who live upon the interest of money: with this peculiarity about them that the money, upon the interest of which they live, is not their own but other people's. A man whose occupation it is to use other people's money; who, having other people's money given him to keep, uses it as his own (without which doubtless it could never be worth his while to keep it): a man whose business it is to use other people's money as his own, and who is at no more expence about it than if it were his own, unless it be a part of the inconsiderable expence of keeping an account of it: can he afford to give up a portion of the profit in support of that government to whose protection he is indebted for the faculty of keeping it [and] which [therefore] does more towards keeping it than he himself does? The answer, as we have seen, is already given: and it is a banking-house that has given it.

Of a tax upon commodities, the burthen does not fall upon the trader: it is not intended to fall upon him. Of this proposed tax upon bankers the burthen would fall upon bankers: it is indeed intended to fall upon them, and them only: for upon whom else would it fall more lightly, or with better justice?

Objection 2. It would not fall ultimately upon bankers themselves: it would fall ultimately upon government, that is upon the public. The profit would be apparent only, not real. Bankers are the great support of government. In respect of their payments to this tax they would be under compulsion: but in their contracts they are free. Whatever they paid to government in this forced way, they will be enabled, disposed, obliged to get back, and justified in getting back, in their dealings with government.—[Answer.] Yes, if they lent to nobody but government: if nobody but they lent to government: if they all could and all would enter into a conspiracy against govern-

---

[1][Pitt abandoned the shop tax which he had introduced in 1785 (25 Geo. III c. 30) in 1789 (29 Geo. III c. 9) after it had been attacked by Fox.]

ment to save themselves from those burthens which Lords and Commons, which even Kings, Lords and Commons, for themselves as well as others, which all the owners and all the powers of the land, have submitted to with such patience.

Objection 3. The mode of collection proposed is oppressive, and oppressive beyond example: an inquisition into private accounts! an inquisition into the most secret and sacred concerns of individuals! Well might such a mode of collection be proposed: it is essential to the measure: without it the produce would be nothing. Were this class, instead of being proscribed, treated upon a footing as any other of the various descriptions of persons that have been made the subjects of taxation, barristers, attornies, auctioneers, publicans, tea-dealers, or even the heaviest loaded of all, lottery-office keepers, were this innocent and respectable class of subjects treated with even twice the rigour shewn to that scarcely tolerated class which it was the professed object of the Legislature to discountenance, were it £100 a year for a license instead of £50 as in that case, what would it produce?—a pittance scarce worth holding out a hand for. The proposed mode of collection is therefore inseparable from the proposed measure: the objection to the mode is an objection to the measure, and that a peremptory one.

Answer. There are inquisitions which are everlastingly murmured at, and which always will be murmured at: and which are yet continued, and must be continued, and in all probability must be extended. I mean the inquisitions necessitated by the Excise laws: in which, after all, the great grievance, at least the great cause of clamour, is the not being able to smuggle without danger. There are other inquisitions which never have been murmured at: which nobody ever thought of murmuring at. Such [is], for example, the inquisition established by the auction tax: the inquisition here established is precisely of that sort.

Under the Excise laws, the officer of the government is an intruder, present every where: he has every thing under lock and key: he is as much master in the establishment of the manufacturer as the manufacturer himself. Here, what has the officer of the government to look into?—some account books. In the Excise laws, a much talked of grievance, and in some instances really a serious one, is the obligation of exposing to vulgar eyes the secrets of trade, the fruit of years perhaps of great ingenuity and severe application. What secret is there of this sort in the banker's business? He keeps money for some people: he advances money for others: he discounts bills, he lays out his money, sometimes on public security, sometimes on private. The man, not a mean and corruptible Excise officer, but an officer of respectability and rank, looks now and then into these accounts—what is there to fear from him? If the bills that were tendered for discounting and rejected, were to be seen by him, then might be something of delicacy in the business: he would be one person more to whom the rejection would be known in addition to five others, not to insist upon a few clerks. But with these rejected bills he has nothing to do: no traces of them ever appear on the accounts: no traces of them will ever be seen by him.

If antipathy to this class, an innocent one at least, not to say a very useful one, of His Majesty's subjects, if ill-will, and not the necessity of providing for the exigencies of the state, were the fit motive for the common father of all and his advisers to be governed by, the rigour of the tax would be a recommendation of it [and] nothing would be listened to that exhibited a tendency of softening it: an indemnity would neither be looked out for, nor, if discovered and proposed, accepted. The landed interest, it would be said, have no indemnity, why should you have?

Antipathy [however] will not govern the dealings [of] Parliament even towards classes justly obnoxious, still less where there is absolutely nothing to provoke it.

Landholders have no indemnity given them, because, in the nature of things, they can have none. Bankers, if taxed, may have an indemnity, an indemnity by which nobody will be a sufferer; therefore they ought to have [it]. What is this indemnity?—a monopoly. Monopolies in general are pernicious as well as odious institutions. Yet innocent monopolies are not absolutely wanting. But surely of no other monopoly that ever was thought of can the innocence be so pure.

The general idea is, that within the limits of the Metropolis (those limits of course to be properly defined) no new banking house should be opened in future. Existing banking houses need not be debarred from splitting if they choose[1] it: but in that case, the numbers of the partners in the houses so formed should not be capable of being augmented. A prohibition likewise which seems scarcely avoidable is the restricting such houses as have not their full complement: but this would be matter of consideration. Where partners go off by death

---

[1][May also read "chose".]

or otherwise, the liberty of supplying their places to be allowed of course.

The innocence of this monopoly will be shewn presently: at present let us observe the effect of it in the character of an indemnity in the shape of a benefit. The effect of it in this way may be ascertained with the utmost precision. At the rate at which houses of this sort have continued to encrease during the present reign, there is a certain period at which, if not stopped as above proposed, they would have encreased to the amount of a fifth above the present number: at that period, the existing houses will find themselves with regard to future profits, reckoning from that time, neither gainers nor losers by the measure, tax and indemnity taken together: till that period they will have been losers: from and after that period they will be gainers. They will have been losers so long that it will take up nearly an equal period (not quite, on account of the acceleration that may be expected in the rate of encrease) to make up the intermediate loss: but after this second period it will be clear gain.

The encrease in the number of these repositories of wealth has not been greater than in proportion to the encrease of opulence. The table of exports and imports, though not absolutely conclusive evidence of the comparative state of the sum total of national wealth at different periods, is very good and sufficient *prima facie* evidence. In 1767 the exports were £[15,090,001]: the imports £[13,097,153]: number of banking houses 37. In 1793 exports £[20,388,828]: imports £[19,255,116][1]: banking houses 63.

As opulence encreases, so then would the number of banking houses, if it were not to be checked. But even in despite of war, present and future, the non-encrease of opulence need not be apprehended. Spite of all the wars which have afflicted the present reign, accumulation has been checked indeed but never stopped, much less has absolute diminution of national property taken its place. The consumption by war has never equalled the savings of individuals.

So much for the benefit redounding from the monopoly: now as to the innocence of it:

If bankers were traders, and the effect of the monopoly was to lessen to such a degree the number of those traders, that by the

---

[1][The blanks are filled in according to David Macpherson's *Annals of Commerce*, 1805, III, 476, and IV, 288. Bentham could only have secured the figures he needed from the same source on which Macpherson relied, namely, the official Customs House Books.]

lessening of the competition the price of the article they dealt in would be raised, in that case a prejudice would result from the measure: the measure of this prejudice would be the amount of the tax indirectly levied upon the consumer by the difference in point of price, and this would be the disadvantageous effect of the measure to set against whatever advantage might be expected from it. But bankers, we have seen, are not traders. They buy nothing: they sell nothing: all they do is to lend: and in the business of lending they have for competitors not only one another, but every body in the whole country who has ready money, their own customers, as they are called,* not excepted, those whose money the money they have to lend is, and who may lend it themselves or prevent their lending it whenever they please. Under these circumstances an express confederacy, if it were thought of, would have no effect, supposing it practicable. Would it be practicable? there seems not a colour of reason for supposing it. Whatever advantage they could hope to make by such a concert, the same advantage they might at all times have made. But they never did enter into any such confederacy when there were but half the number: what is there that should enable them now the number is doubled?

Even the convenience of customers in so slight an article as the difference of sending from one street to another of the same town would not be affected by the restriction. In setting up new banking houses, local considerations seem scarcely to have been attended to. There are large districts without any house of this kind. The neighbourhood of Cornhill and Lombard Street swarm with them. If of the houses of this kind that are within two hundred yards of the Exchange, all but one were shut up or transferred elsewhere, local convenience to customers would not be at all diminished.

As to impairing quality by lessening exertion or by diminishing the choice of extraordinary perfection, as in the case of artists and professional men of the higher orders, it is out of the question here: one man's money is as good as another's: the best banker is he who takes scrip or discounts notes at the lowest rate.

Country banking houses are not precisely in the same case. The indemnification is not so applicable to their case. These houses,

---

*The real customers of bankers are not those who are called their customers, those who supply them with money, but those to whom they lend [i.e.] those who take from them what they have to dispose of. The customer of the grocer is the housekeeper who buys sugar at his shop, not the merchant who supplies him with it. But in the banking business every thing is out of its name.

numerous as they are, have scarcely yet been set up in every town capable of affording employment for them. But while there are towns as yet unsupplied in this way, a rival house will not be so apt to be set up in a town where a house of that kind exists already. Applied to towns already provided with such houses, the prohibition in question would therefore hold out little appearance of relief: applied to towns not yet provided, it would afford little or no advantage to bankers settled elsewhere, and it would preclude proprietors of cash from a convenience of which the inhabitants of other towns are already in possession.

Another confession must also in this instance be made, viz. that the tax to equal amount on banking houses of this description will bear harder than a tax to equal amount on London banking houses: dealings being so much less extensive, profits can the less easily bear so considerable a defalcation. But though the burthen is greater in this case than in that, it seems hardly to follow that it should be reduced. To form a true judgment of its comparative magnitude, compare it with the burthen of the Land Tax. From this heavy and hitherto unequalled burthen, what individual so poor as to be excused? The individual whose pittance does not exceed 20s a year: for the proprietor of a guinea a year must pay his 4s and 2d¼ out of it. A man will hardly think it worth his while to continue the business of a banker, even of a country banker, whose income from that source does not amount to some hundred times that of many a land-owner, one might almost say the bulk of land-owners. Shall antient property be loaded without mercy and shall growing gains escape? Is it more hardship to pay a fifth out of four hundred pounds than out of forty shillings?

Let even the most opulent receive relief, where relief can be afforded without expence. But where the less opulent can not, without expence to the public, receive a relief which in comparison of so many others is not their due, they must look to the poor landowners around them, and learn to content themselves with their neighbours' fate.

As to the immense banking company stiled the Bank of England, it is protected against the burthen of the proposed tax by an express stipulation ratified by Parliament. At the same time it would enjoy its full share in the benefit of the indemnity.

Might not the company, now that other great companies are coming forward with offers—might not this most flourishing company, by the influence of the same principle, be prevailed upon to waive its privilege in this respect, if not altogether, at least in part?

If not by generosity, might it not in a certain way by apprehension? What, if government were in certain respects to become, or to threaten to become, its own banker? Might not small notes to the amount of the smallest and most numerous class of Bank Notes, might not such notes, if recommended by interest, though at a reduced rate, obtain the preference in circulation over Bank Notes, and even sell at a premium, as India Bonds do, which would, on account of their smallness at least, be preferable to India Bonds? I mention this only as a hasty idea proposed for consideration, as a matter of such delicacy and importance is not immediately to be matured.

GEORGE ALLEN & UNWIN LTD
LONDON: 40 MUSEUM STREET, W.C.1
CAPE TOWN: 58–60 LONG STREET
SYDNEY, N.S.W.: 55 YORK STREET
TORONTO: 91 WELLINGTON STREET WEST
CALCUTTA: 17 CENTRAL AVE., P.O. DHARAMTALA
BOMBAY: 15 GRAHAM ROAD, BALLARD ESTATE
WELLINGTON, N.Z.: 8 KINGS CRESCENT, LOWER HUTT

A Study in the Theory of Inflation

by Dr. Bent Hansen, *Institute of Economics, University of Uppsala*

Demy 8vo. 18s.

This is a study of some of the central economic problems of our post-war world, in particular of suppressed inflation. After his introductory chapters the author develops a monetary theory for suppressed inflation. He deals much more explicitly than is usual in ordinary "Keynesian" theory with the problem of disequilibrium in the labour market, i.e. *overfull employment*. He discusses the market effects of price and wage control, and surveys various measures for abolishing suppressed inflation. The results of changes in productivity are closely considered.

Dr. Hansen also deals with open inflation, with particular regard to scarcities of goods and labour, and an attempt is made to generalize the results obtained in the form of a Walrassian system of equations, without presupposing a static equilibrium. The author thus builds a bridge between ordinary static equilibrium theory and the theory of inflation. Finally he examines the problem of monetary equilibrium, i.e. that of full employment with a stable price-level.

The book may be characterized as a disequilibrium analysis, a "gap-analysis." It borrows its main analytic equipment from the theory of the Stockholm School, and from that school of thought whose leading name is J. R. Hicks. As our adviser wrote : "There has been no comprehensive treatment of this topic, which is one of considerable practical as well as theoretical interest. It is obvious on every page that Hansen is the man to produce such a study." (*Library of Economics.*)

The Commerce of Nations

by J. B. Condliffe   *Illustrated.* 886 *pages. Demy 8vo.* 36s.

Author of *New Zealand in the Making* and for several years editor of the League of Nations annual *World Economic Survey*

In *The Commerce of Nations* the author traces the long and fascinating story of the ebb and flow of world trade from the caravans of the ancient world to the barter agreements and currency blocks of today. Paralleling this account he presents in skilful summary the important contributions to economic thought that have influenced policy and practice. Professor Condliffe then deals with today's international economic problems and devotes the greater part of his book to an examination of modern issues of economic theory and policy.

"A fine summary of its subject, and a brilliant elucidation of its past crises."— *Financial Times.*

"Examines the inter-action of fact, theory and policy from the Mercantilists to the Neutralists, with a wealth of illustration and argument, cleverly marshalled and lucidly set out . . . his book is an indispensable addition to the library."— *The Tribune.*

Ten Great Economists

by Joseph A. Schumpeter   *Demy 8vo. About* 21s.

Author of *Capitalism, Socialism and Democracy,* etc.

In this collection of essays one of the greatest economists of our day has written brilliant evaluations of the men most influential in shaping economic thought during the past century. They are biographical in character but with a penetrating critical approach that makes them classics in their field.

The "ten great economists" are, in chronological order, Karl Marx, Marie Esprit Leon Walras, Carl Menger, Alfred Marshall, Vilfredo Pareto, Eugen von Bohm-Bawerk, Frank William Taussig, Irving Fisher, Wesley Clair Mitchell, and John Maynard Keynes. An Appendix includes George Frederic Knapp, Friedrich von Wieser, and Ladislaus von Bortkiewicz.

Monetary Theory and Public Policy

by Kenneth K. Kurihara   *Demy 8vo.* 30s.

Rurgers University

Monetary Theory and Public Policy treats systematically the important concepts of modern economic theory, particularly as these concepts apply to problems of money and banking and to related public policy, both national and international. The latest developments in monetary theory, Keynesian and non-Keynesian, are discussed. Various theories about the external value of money, the roles of the International Bank and the International Monetary Fund, the international aspects of depression, the problems of a chronic dollar shortage and the related problems of international currency and finance are considered against the background of the changing international setting.

Monetary Theory and Public Policy is a valuable work in a field of first importance. Providing a full examination of monetary theory and of its implications for public policy, it is extremely helpful to an understanding of to-day's major economic problems.

Econometrics

by Dr. Jan Tinbergen   *Illustrated. Demy 8vo.* 35s.

Professor at the Netherlands School of Economics and co-author of *The Dynamics of Business Cycles*

This text-book in applied econometrics has no rivals in English. Requiring very little knowledge of mathematics and statistics, it provides an up-to-date introduction to this young and vital branch of the science. Part I explains the relationship of econometrics to economics and statistics. Part II outlines the process of formulating and testing hypotheses. Part III deals with the component equations of the economic system. Part IV illustrates the use of econometric methods for policy purposes.

The American Economy, 1860-1940

by A. J. Youngson Brown   *Demy 8vo.* 15*s*.

Lecturer in Economic History in the University of Cambridge

The aim of this book is to provide a brief but reasonably comprehensive account of the economic development of the United States from the Civil War to 1940.

To bring out clearly the pattern of development, emphasis is laid on significant details and on major events. Thus attention is concentrated on those factors in American development—the natural resources of the country, the influx of European manpower, the facilities for investment, the influence of world markets, and the general milieu of economic and social ideas in which American business leaders and their employees have operated—which help to explain the phenomenal rate of growth, the rapid changes, and the illusion of remoteness which are so prominent in America's rise to a position of world economic supremacy.

Principles of Private and Public Planning

A STUDY IN ECONOMIC SOCIOLOGY

by Professor Wilhelm Keilhau   *Demy 8vo.* 16*s*.

Despite the swelling amount of literature on the "planned economy," a shorthand phrase for State direction and control of industry and commerce, there is still no adequate scientific exposition of the theory of economic planning. Believing that the laws governing private and public planning are the same, Professor Wilhelm Keilhau, the well-known Norwegian economist, sets out to provide such a theory. The first part examines the fundamental difficulties, caused by the uncertainties of the future and of human behaviour. In the second part of his book he examines public planning in the light of these general principles and discusses the effects of power policies and ideologies.

Studies in the Theory of Money and Capital

LIBRARY OF ECONOMICS

by Erik Lindahl   *2nd Impression. Demy 8vo.* 15*s*.

"It is a classic. Swedish economic theory is well known and in the vogue. Swedish economic policy and practice attract everyone. This book opens to English readers the chapters and verse of Swedish economics. The nature of economic theory, the measurement of values in a dynamic economy, the rate of interest and the nature and function of capital—all are set out in a full and stately way."—DONALD TYERMAN in *Time and Tide*.